Industrial Organization
Theory and Applications

Oz Shy

The MIT Press
Cambridge, Massachusetts
London, England

This book was typeset by the author using the LATEX 2_ε document preparation software developed by Leslie Lamport (a special version of Donald Knuth's TEX program) and modified by the LATEX3 Project Team. All figures are drawn in LATEX using TEXcad by developed by Georg Horn and Jörn Winkelmann. The book was complied using emTEX developed by Eberhard Mattes. Camera-ready copy was produced by Type 2000, Mill Valley, California, and the book was printed and bound by The Maple-Vail Book Manufacturing Group, Binghamton, New York.

Library of Congress Cataloging-in-Publication Data

Shy, Oz.
 Industrial organization: theory and applications / Oz Shy.
  p. cm.
 Includes bibliographical references and index.
 ISBN 0-262-19366-3 (hc : alk. paper). — ISBN 0-262-69179-5 (pb : alk. paper)
  1. Industrial organization (Economic Theory) 2. Industrial organization –Case studies I. title
 HD2326.S565 1996
 338.7–dc20   95-32647
                           CIP

Fourth printing, 1998

For my mother, Hadassa Shy
and in memory of my father, Asher Shy

Contents

Figures

Preface

If we knew what it was we were doing, it would not be called
research, would it?
—A. Einstein

Motivation for Writing This Book

The motivation for writing this book grew from several years of teaching
undergraduate and graduate industrial organization and international
trade courses at SUNY-Albany, Tel Aviv University, and the University
of Michigan. I felt that for both important fields in economics, no theoretical book targeted advanced undergraduate and beginning graduate
students.

Therefore, I was guided by my belief that there should not be any
necessary correlation between mathematical complexity and theoretical
precision. That is, the purpose of this book is to bring to the advanced
student the basic and the latest developments in industrial organization
in a very precise manner, but without resorting to advanced mathematical techniques. By precise I mean that the various market structures and
equilibria—and optimal allocations as well as the rules by which firms
and consumers actually behave—are always carefully defined. I feel that
a student of a theoretical course should be able to make precise definitions of what agents actually do, and that teaching the student how to
precisely define the environment and market structures has nothing to
do with getting more mathematical training. That is, I have attempted
to precisely define the equilibria and the models despite the fact that the
models are solved for specific examples with no mathematical generality.

The Level and Prerequisites

My intention is to make this book readable to undergraduates who have
some training in microeconomics using calculus. However, in some in-

stances, this course can be taught without using calculus (see the list of topics in the next section). Before reading this book, the student should have some experience in maximization techniques for one- and two-variables optimization problems. Occasionally, the student will have to have a very basic knowledge of what probability is and how to calculate the joint probability of two events. Nothing in this book requires methods more advanced than the ones I have described. Students who did not have any training in microeconomics using calculus may not be able to handle several of the market structures. The reader questioning whether this book fits his or her level is advised to look at chapter 3, which reviews the basic microeconomics needed for a comprehensive study of industrial organization.

Industrial Organization without Calculus

Writers of good textbooks should attempt to base most of their arguments on simple logic rather than on long (or short) derivatives. In that respect, I admit that I failed to provide the reader with a completely free of calculus book for a very simple reason: most of our research and publications are based on calculus, and each time I attempted to avoid using calculus, I had to reproduce the theory instead of using an existing one.

The following, however, is a list of topics that are analyzed without the use of calculus:

Basic Concepts in Game Theory: Chapter 2

Durable Goods Monopolies: Subsection 5.5.2

Perfect Competition: Chapter 4

Self-Enforcing Collusion: Section 6.5

Bertrand Price Competition: Section 6.3

Preferential Trade Agreements among Countries: Subsection 6.6.2

Sequential Entry to the Linear City: Subsection 7.3.3

Calculus-free Location Model: Subsection 7.3.4

Concentration Measures: Section 8.1

Entry Barriers: Section 8.3

Investment in Capital Replacement: Subsection 8.4.3

Credible Spatial Preemption: Subsection 8.4.5

Limit Pricing as Entry Deterrence: Subsection 8.4.6

Process Innovation: Section 9.1

Innovation Race: Section 9.2

Licensing an Innovation: Section 9.5

International Subsidies for New Product Development: Subsection 9.6.1

The Economics of Compatibility and Standards: Chapter 10 (excluding subsection 10.1.1)

Advertising: Chapter 11 (excluding section 11.1)

Quality, Durability, and Warranties: Chapter 12 (excluding section 12.2)

Pricing Tactics: Chapter 13 (excluding section 13.4)

Bundling and Tying: Section 14.1 (excluding subsection 14.1.6)

Market Segmentation: Subsection 14.1.5

Killing Off Used Textbook Markets: Section 14.2

Territorial Dealerships: Subsection 14.3.3

The Principal-Agent Problem: Section 15.1

Regulating a Firm under Unknown Cost: Section 15.5

Why Executives Are Paid More than Workers: Section 15.4

Search Theory: Section 16.2

Restaurant Economics: Section 17.1

Multiproduct Firms: Subsection 17.2.1

Price Regulation: Subsection 17.2.3

Law and Economics Appendixes: Most chapters conclude with non-technical appendices discussing the major legal issues and laws concerning the topics analyzed in the body of the chapter.

To the Instructor

Since this book grew out of lecture notes written for upper-division undergraduate and graduate courses, the instructor will (I hope) find this book convenient to use, since almost all derivations are done in the book itself.

If you are constrained to instruct a course without using calculus, then you can teach the list of topics given earlier. If you can use some calculus, then the amount of material that you can cover depends on your preferences and the length of the course.

All the theoretical background the student needs for a comprehensive study of this book is provided in the first part. In fact, not all the material covered in this part is needed to study this book, but it is brought up here for the sake of completeness, or for those readers who have either an insufficient background in economics or none at all. Therefore, the instructor is urged to decide on how much time to devote to this preparation part only after having completed the entire plan for this course. This theoretical preparation is composed of two chapters. Chapter 2 provides all the necessary game theoretic tools needed for the study of this book and for understanding the literature on industrial organization. Background in game theory is not needed for reading this chapter, and no previous knowledge is assumed. The main sections of chapter 2 must be taught before the instructor proceeds with the study of industrial organization. Chapter 3 provides most of the basic microeconomics background needed for the study of industrial organization. The material covered in this chapter is studied in most intermediate microeconomics and in some managerial economics courses and can therefore be skipped.

Two-semester course

A two-semester course can be logically divided into a more technically market-structure-oriented semester, and an application-oriented semester. Thus, the first semester should start with game theory (chapter 2), continued by the sequence of three chapters dealing with market structure: perfect competition (chapter 4), monopoly (chapter 5), homogeneous products (chapter 6), and differentiated products (chapter 7). If time is left, the first semester may include mergers and entry (chapter 8) and research and development (chapter 9).

For the second semester, the instructor is free to select from a wide variety of mostly logically independent topics. A possible starting point could be the theory of network economics and standardization (chapter 10), continuing with selected topics from the remaining chapters:

advertising (chapter 11), durability and quality (chapter 12), pricing tactics (chapter 13), marketing tactics (chapter 14), management and information (chapter 15), price dispersion and search theory (chapter 16), and the special industries (chapter 17).

One-semester course

A common mistake (at least my mistake) in planning a one-semester course would be to treat it as the first semester of a two-semester course. When this happens, the student is left with the wrong impression that industrial organization deals only with the technical formulation of market structures, yet without the knowledge that industrial organization has a lot to say about product design, marketing techniques, and channels (chapters 11, 12, 13, 14, 15, and 17). These chapters have many less technically oriented sections, with direct applications. Some sections rely on the knowledge of Cournot, Bertrand, and sometime Hotelling's market structures, and for this reason, in a one-semester course, I advise the instructor to carefully plan the logical path for this course. Finally, the material on search theory (chapter 16) can be covered with no difficulty.

Let me summarize then: the two-semester course fits the structure and the depth of the coverage of this book. The instructor of a one-semester course using this book should study the list of topics covered in the later chapters, and then, working backwards, should determine what is the minimal knowledge of market structures that students need to acquire in order to be able to understand the later chapters.

New Material

Almost by definition, a textbook is not intended for presenting newly developed material and ongoing research. However, during the course of simplifying I was forced to modify or to develop some new concepts. For example, I felt that it is important to include a location model without using calculus for those courses that do not require the use of calculus. However, as the reader will find, a Nash-Bertrand equilibrium for the discrete location model simply does not exist. For this reason, I was forced to develop the *undercutproof* equilibrium concept described in subsection 7.3.4 on page 158. Three other topics are also new: (a) the concept of ϵ-*foreclosure* developed in subsection 14.1.4 on page 366, (b) *endogenous peak-load pricing* theory (section 13.4 on page 352) that emphasizes the role of the firm in determining which period would be the peak and which would be the off-peak, and (c) *targeted and comparison advertising* theory (sections 11.3 on page 290 and 11.4 on page 294).

Typesetting and Acknowledgments

The book was typeset during the months from June 1993 to July 1994 (Tel Aviv University) and from August 1994 to August 1995 (University of Michigan). The reader will notice that this book does not have any footnotes. Writing a book with no footnotes imposes a significant constraint on the writer, because footnotes enable the integration of quasi-related topics into a text. However, I felt that footnotes impose a great inconvenience to the reader because they tend to disturb the natural flow of reading. For this reason, I decided to eliminate them.

As boring as it may sound, the following cliché is the whole truth and nothing but the truth: Without the help of the people listed below, I would not have been able to complete writing this book! Therefore, I thank: Igal Hendel (Princeton), who was the first person to read the very first draft of several chapters; Val Lambson (Brigham Young), who was the first to test this manuscript in an undergraduate industrial organization class at BYU and was the first to report a success with teaching this material to undergraduates in the United States; Tomer Bloomkin (a doctoral student at Tel Aviv), for reading the manuscript several times and providing many comments and many suggestions throughout that year; Henrik Horn (Stockholm University), for a great many comments and suggestions and for testing the manuscript in a short undergraduate course at Stockholm University; Sougata Poddar (a doctoral student at CORE); Stephen Salant (Michigan) for a great many comments and illuminating discussions; Yossi Spiegel (Tel Aviv), five anonymous reviewers for The MIT Press, and my undergraduate industrial organization and international trade students at Tel Aviv and Michigan. I thank Mike Meurer (SUNY-Buffalo), Christopher Proulx (Michigan), Ennio Stacchetti (Michigan), and Abi Schwartz (Tel Aviv), for providing me with comments on selected topics. Needless to say, I am the only one responsible for all the remaining errors. I also would like to thank Martin Osborne (McMaster) and Hal Varian (Berkeley) for their most helpful advice and Tianlai Shy for all her help.

During the preparation of the manuscript, I was very fortunate in working with Ann Sochi of The MIT Press, to whom I owe many thanks for managing the project in the most efficient way. Finally, I thank the entire MIT Press team for a fast production of this book.

Ann Arbor, Michigan (August 1995)
ozshy@econ.tau.ac.il

Chapter 1

Introduction

The purpose of an economic theory is to analyze, explain, predict, and evaluate.
—Gathered from Joe Bain, *Industrial Organization*

1.1 The Study of Industrial Organization

1.1.1 Major observations

Our approach to analyzing industry behavior is based on four stylized facts:

Concentration: Many industries are composed of few firms.

Product characteristics: Firms in some industries produce homogeneous or almost identical products, whereas firms in others distinguish themselves from the competing firms by selling differentiated brands.

Costly activities: Firms in an industry are engaged in repeated costly activities targeted for the purpose of enhancing the sales of their brands. In some industries, these activities constitute the major cost of the firm and may exceed the cost of producing the product itself. These costly activities may include advertising, quality control, product differentiation costs, marketing and dealership costs.

Research and development: Firms allocate resources for inventing cost reducing production technologies as well as new products. These resource allocations also include large investments in imitations of technologies invented by rival firms (reverse engineering).

It is often thought that these four observations are interrelated. Most of the earlier empirical studies in industrial organization focused on running regressions of variables such as profit margins, firms' size, advertising expenditure, and research and development (R&D) expenditure on concentration (see Goldschmid, Mann, and Weston 1974 for a summary of these works). The purpose of this book is to provide a theoretical linkage of the factors that affect concentration, and how concentration affects the strategic behavior of firms. The reason why we think of concentration as a major issue of industrial organization theory follows from the failure of the competitive market structure to explain why industries are composed of a few large firms instead of many small firms. Thus, the theory of competitive market structure, although easy to solve for if an equilibrium exists, in most cases cannot explain the composition and behavior of firms in the industry.

Given the noncompetitive behavior of firms, markets are also influenced by buyers' reactions to firms' attempts to maximize profits. In this respect, our analysis here will have to fully characterize how consumers determine which brands to buy, how much to buy, and how to search and select the lowest priced brand that fits their specific preferences. For this reason, the approach we take is mostly a strategic one, meaning that both firms and consumers learn the market structure and choose an action that maximizes profit (for the firms) and utility (for the consumers). In addition, given the complexity of decisions made by strategic (noncompetitive) firms, the issue of the internal organization of firms becomes an important factor affecting their behavior. Thus, we briefly address the issue of how management structure under conditions of imperfect information affects the performance of the firm in the market.

Finally, we extensively analyze the role of the regulator. First, from a theoretical point of view we ask whether intervention can increase social welfare under various market structures and firms' activities. Second, we describe and analyze the legal system affecting our industries.

1.1.2 Schools of thought and methodology

The standard approach to the study of industrial organization, as laid out by Joe Bain, decomposes a market into *structure, conduct, and performance* of the market. Structure means how sellers interact with other sellers, with buyers, and with potential entrants. Market structure also defines the product in terms of the potential number of variants in which the product can be produced. Market conduct refers to the behavior of the firms in a given market structure, that is, how firms determine their price policy, sales, and promotion. Finally, performance refers to the welfare aspect of the market interaction. That is, to determine performance we measure whether the interaction in the market leads to a desired outcome, or whether a failure occurs that requires the intervention of the regulator.

Many aspects of performance are discussed in this book. First, is the technology efficient in the sense of whether it is operated on an optimal (cost-minimizing) scale? Second, does the industry produce a socially optimal number of brands corresponding to consumers' preferences and the heterogeneity of the consumers? Third, are the firms dynamically efficient—do they invest a proper amount of resources in developing new technologies for current and future generations? All these efficiency requirements are generally summarized by a particular social welfare function that can combine the trade-off among the different efficiency criteria. For example, the welfare of consumers who have preferences for variety increases with the number of brands produced in an industry. However, if each brand is produced by a different factory where each factory is constructed with a high fixed-cost investment, then it is clear that from a technical point of view, the number of brands produced in an industry should be restricted. Hence, there will always be a trade-off between technical efficiency and consumer welfare that will require defining a welfare function to determine the optimal balance between consumer welfare and efficient production patterns.

In 1939, Edward Mason published a very influential article emphasizing the importance of understanding the market-specific causes of noncompetitive behavior. In that article, Mason discussed the methodology for studying the various markets:

> It goes without saying that a realistic treatment of these questions necessitates the use of analytical tools which are amenable to empirical application. The problem, as I see it, is to reduce the voluminous data concerning industrial organization to some sort of order through a classification of market structures. Differences in market structure are ultimately explicable in terms of technological factors. The economic problem, however, is to explain, through an examination of the structure of markets and the organization of firms, differences in competitive practices including price, production, and investment policies.

Thus, Mason argued that to be able to understand different degrees of competition in different markets, the researcher would have to analyze the different markets using different assumed market structures. The reader will appreciate this methodology after reading this book, where we try to fit an appropriate market structure to the studied specific market, where the variety of market structures are defined and developed in part II.

In his article, Mason emphasized the importance of understanding sources of market power ("market control" in his language) in order to understand how prices are determined in these markets ("price policy" in his language):

> A firm may have a price policy by reason of the existence of rivals of whose action it must take account, of the desirability of considering the effect of present upon future price, of the possibility of competing in other ways than by price, and for many other reasons.

Mason continues and hints at how the degree of industry concentration is correlated with noncompetitive behavior:

> The size of a firm influences its competitive policies in a number of ways....The scale of its purchases and sales relative to the total volume of transactions...the absolute size of a firm, as measured by assets, employees, or volume of sales,...[are] also relevant to price and production policies....Selling practices at the disposal of the large firm may be beyond the reach of its smaller competitors....The size of a firm likewise influences its reaction to given market situations.

Analysts of industrial organization after Mason continued mostly to use a descriptive language, but later ones used price theory (sometimes referred to as the Chicago School). The Chicago price-theory approach conceded that monopoly is possible but contended that its presence is much more often alleged than confirmed. When alleged monopolies are genuine, they are usually transitory, with freedom of entry working to eliminate their influence on price and quantities within a fairly short time period (see Reder 1982). Thus, the so-called Chicago School was not very supportive of the persistent-market-power approach that constituted Bain's major theory of entry barriers.

The fast development of game theory in the 1970s gave a push to the *strategic approach* to industrial organization and later to strategic international trade analysis. Unlike the competitive-markets approach, the strategic approach models the firms on the assumption that they and other firms can affect the market outcome consisting of prices, quantities, and the number of brands. In addition, game theory provided the tools for analyzing dynamic scenarios such as how established firms react to a threat of entry by potential competitors.

Our approach does not attempt to represent any particular school of thought. In fact, the main purpose of this book is to demonstrate that there is no general methodology for solving problems, hence each observation may have to be worked out in a different model. Thus, each time we address a new observation, we generally construct a special ad hoc model, where the term "ad hoc" should not be given a negative connotation. To the contrary, the ad hoc modeling methodology frees the researcher from constraining the theory to temporary "fashions" which are given a priority in the scientific literature and allows the scientist to concentrate on the merit of the model itself, where merit means how well the theory or the model explains the specific observation that the scientist seeks to explain. Nevertheless, the reader will discover that the strategic game-theoretic approach is the dominant one in this book.

1.2   Law and Economics

The legal structure governing the monitoring of the industry is called **antitrust law.** The word "trust" reflects the spirit of the laws aiming at any form of organization, trust, communication, and contract among firms that would impede competition.

In this book we confine the discussion of the legal aspects of the industry mainly to U.S. law. I chose to deal with U.S. law since it is perhaps the most advanced in terms of achieving competition and the restraints of monopoly power. Although not the oldest, the U.S. antitrust system seems to be the most experienced one in terms of famous court cases that put the legal system into effect. For example, the Restrictive Trade Practices Act, which is the British equivalent of the 1890 Sherman Act regarding cartel prohibition, was enacted a very long time after the Sherman Act, in 1956 to be precise. In other words, the U.S. was and remains a leader in antitrust legislation.

It is interesting to note that in the United States real prices of products tend to be the lowest in the world. However, the United States also has the most restrictive antitrust regulation structure in the world. Hence, although it is commonly argued that market intervention in the form of regulation results in higher consumer prices, here we observe that antitrust regulation is probably the cause for low consumer prices in the United States. For this reason, the study of the U.S. antitrust systems is an integral part of the study of industrial organization, especially for those students from countries with less competitive markets.

Several chapters in this book conclude with appendixes discussing the legal matters related to the topics analyzed in the theoretical part of the chapter. In these appendixes, references are always made to the law itself and to its historical origin. Court cases are not discussed in this book, since they are analyzed in a large number of law-and-economics textbooks, for example Asch 1983, Gellhorn 1986, and Posner 1977.

1.2.1   The development of the antitrust legal system

It is not surprising that when the Sherman Antitrust Act was passed in
1890, economists were almost unanimously opposed to it, on the basis
that "trust busting" would involve a loss of the efficiency advantages
of combinations or trusts (West 1987). Interestingly, after a decade of
strict enforcement of the older merger's guidelines issued by the Federal
Trade Commission, the newer 1984 guidelines have brought back the
efficiency argument as an argument for merger in medium concentrated
industries. The reader interested in learning the development of the
antitrust laws should not miss reading Bork 1978. According to Bork,
the major development (and the entire set of disputes and theoretical
conjectures) were all formed during the period from 1890 (Sherman Act)
to 1914 (Clayton Act and the Federal Trade Commission Act).

The Sherman Act of 1890 was intended to strike at cartels, horizontal
mergers of monopolistic nature, and predatory business activities. Section 1 of this act stated that "Every contract, combination in the form
of trust or otherwise,...in restraint of trade or commerce,...is hereby declared to be illegal." Earlier court interpretations followed section 1 of
the act precisely as stated but soon began to adhere to the "rule of reason," in which not every act of merger was considered as a restraint of
trade. The courts began identifying which restraints were reasonable and
which were not. In 1911 a major ruling based on the Sherman Act was
handed down, wherein some of Standard Oil's activities were found to be
illegal, leading to the dissolution of this giant into thirty companies. In
that period, American Tobacco also broke up. A large-scale dissolution
occurred again in 1982, when AT&T responded to pressure to break up
into the seven "baby" Bell companies and AT&T. The AT&T breakup
was effected by consent decree and not by litigation.

The search for which restraints of trade are reasonable led to a more
refined legislation, the Clayton Act of 1914, in which price discrimination, exclusive dealing, and corporate stock acquisition that may lead to
reduced competition were declared illegal. The Federal Trade Commission Act of 1914 mandated the FTC to categorize and identify what
constitute unfair methods of competition.

1.2.2   The "Per Se" versus the "Rule of Reason" approaches

In all the law-and-economics appendixes, we make a use of two methods
of court ruling in antitrust cases: the **per se rule**, and the **rule of
reason**. Bork (1978) defines the rule of reason as a set of general categories that are given content by ideas about the proper goals of the law,
economics, and the requirement of the judicial process. In other words,
court rulings consist of two major categories: (a) business behavior that

is illegal per se, and (b) business behavior that is judged by standards of the party's intent or the effect the behavior is likely to have. For our purposes, we will refer to the rule of reason as category (b).

Bork (1978) regards the per se rule as containing a degree of arbitrariness. The per se rule implies that the judgment is handed down on the basis of the inherent effect of the act committed by the accused party. That is, to have a particular behavior declared illegal per se, the plaintiff needs only to prove that it occurred. The per se rule is justified in cases where the gains associated from the imposition of the rule will far outweigh the losses since significant administrative costs can be saved. That is, the advantage of the per se rule is that the particular case need not be identified, since the act itself is assumed to be illegal.

1.3 Industrial Organization and International Trade

In this book the reader will find a wide variety of international issues, for the simple reason that international markets should not be very different from national markets. Thus, one might expect that concentration would characterize international markets as well as national markets. As a result of this (rather late) recognition that international trade can be characterized by oligopolistic market structures, a tremendous amount of literature emerged during the 1980s (see Krugman 1989).

Once this newer trade theory picked up, a broad new array of issues had to be analyzed. The first was, how can international trade in differentiated products be explained by a monopolistic competition market structure? Then, what are the implications of oligopolistic international market structures for the gains from the imposition of trade barriers? Whereas earlier writers got excited by learning that countries have a lot to gain when imposing trade restrictions or allowing subsidization of industries competing in internationally oligopolistic markets, later writers have managed to calm down this new wave of protectionism by demonstrating that any trade policy recommended under a particular market structure may not be recommended under a different market structure. Thus, since it is hard to estimate what the ongoing market structure is and the form of competition of a particular market, it may be better that governments refrain from intervention at all. These later papers have somewhat mitigated the strong policy actions recommended by the early strategic trade literature.

1.4 References

Asch, P. 1983. *Industrial Organization and Antitrust Policy.* New York: John Wiley & Sons.

Bain, J. 1968. *Industrial Organization.* 2nd ed. New York: John Wiley & Sons.

Bork, R. 1978. *The Antitrust Paradox.* New York: Basic Books.

Gellhorn, E. 1986. *Antitrust Law and Economics in a Nutshell.* St. Paul, Minn.: West Publishing.

Goldschmid, H., H. Mann, and J. Weston. 1974. *Industrial Concentration: The New Learning.* Boston: Little, Brown.

Krugman, P. 1989. "Industrial Organization and International Trade." In *Handbook of Industrial Organization,* edited by R. Schmalensee and R. Willig. Amsterdam: North-Holland.

Mason, E. 1939. "Price and Production Policies of Large-Scale Enterprise." *American Economic Review* 29, pt. 2: 61–74

Posner, R. 1977. *Economic Analysis of Law.* Boston: Little, Brown.

Reder, M. 1982. "Chicago Economics: Performance and Change." *Journal of Economic Literature* 20: 1–38.

West, E. 1987. "Monopoly." In *The New Palgrave Dictionary of Economics,* edited by J. Eatwell, M. Milgate, and P. Newman. New York: The Stockton Press.

PART I

Theoretical Background: Game Theory and Microeconomics

Chapter 2

Basic Concepts in Noncooperative Game Theory

> If you know the enemy and know yourself, you need not fear the result of a hundred battles. If you know yourself but not the enemy, for every victory gained you will also suffer a defeat. If you know neither the enemy nor yourself, you will succumb in every battle.
>
> All men can see these tactics whereby I conquer, but what none can see is the strategy out of which victory is evolved.
> —Sun Tzu, *The Art of War* (490 B.C.)

Game theory (sometimes referred to as "Interactive Decision Theory") is a collection of tools for predicting outcomes for a group of interacting agents, where an action of a single agent directly affects the payoffs (welfare or profits) of other participating agents. The term *game theory* stems from the resemblance these tools to sports games (e.g., football, soccer, ping-pong, and tennis), as well as to "social" games (e.g., chess, cards, checkers, and Diplomacy).

Game theory is especially useful when the number of interactive agents is small, in which case the action of each agent may have a significant effect on the payoff of other players. For this reason, the bag of tools and the reasoning supplied by game theory have been applied to a wide variety of fields, including economics, political science, animal behavior, military studies, psychology, and many more. The goal of a game-theoretic model is to predict the outcomes (a list of actions adopted by each participant), given the assumed incentives of the participating agents. Thus, game theory is extremely helpful in analyzing industries consisting of a small number of competing firms, since any action of each firm, whether price choice, quantity produced, research and development, or marketing techniques, has strong effects on the profit levels of the competing firms.

As the title of this chapter suggests, our analyses focus only on non-cooperative games. We generally distinguish between two types of game representations: *normal form games* (analyzed in section 2.1), and *extensive form games* (analyzed in section 2.2). Roughly speaking, we can say that in normal form games all players choose all their actions simultaneously, whereas in extensive form games agents may choose their actions in different time periods. In addition, we distinguish between two types of actions that players can take: a *pure action*, where a player plays a single action from the player's set of available actions, and a *mixed* action, where a player assigns a probability for playing each action (say by flipping a coin). Our entire analysis in this book is confined to pure actions. However, for the sake of completeness, mixed actions are analyzed in an appendix (section 2.4).

Finally, information plays a key role in game theory (as well as in real life). The most important thing that we assume is that the players that we model are at least as intelligent as economists are. That is, the players that we model have the same knowledge about the structure, the rules, and the payoffs of the game as the economist that models the game does. Also important, our analysis in this chapter is confined to games with *perfect information.* Roughly, this means that in perfect information games, each player has all the information concerning the actions taken by other players earlier in the game that affect the player's decision about which action to choose at a particular time. Games under imperfect information are not used in this book; however, we introduce them in an appendix (section 2.5) for the sake of completeness.

2.1   Normal Form Games

Our first encounter with games will be with normal form games. In normal form games all the players are assumed to make their moves at the same time.

2.1.1   What is a game?

The following definition provides three elements that constitute what we call a game. Each time we model an economic environment in a game-theoretic framework, we should make sure that the following three elements are clearly stipulated:

DEFINITION 2.1 *A* **normal form game** *is described by the following:*

1. *A set of N players whose names are listed in the set $I \equiv \{1, 2, \ldots, N\}$.*

2. *Each player $i, i \in I$, has an* **action set** A^i *which is the set of all actions available to player i. Let $a^i \in A^i$ denote a particular action taken by player i. Thus, player i's action set is a list of all actions available to player i and hence, $A^i = \{a^i_1, a^i_2, \ldots, a^i_{k_i}\}$, where k_i is the number of actions available to player i.*

   Let $a \equiv (a^1, a^2, \ldots, a^i, \ldots, a^N)$ be a list of the actions chosen by each player. We call this list of actions chosen by each player i an **outcome** *of the game.*

3. *Each player i has a payoff function, π^i, which assigns a real number, $\pi^i(a)$, to every outcome of the game. Formally, each payoff function π^i maps an N-dimensional vector, $a = (a^1, \ldots, a^N)$ (the action of chosen by each player), and assigns it a real number, $\pi^i(a)$.*

A few important remarks on the definition of a game follow:

1. It is very important to distinguish between an action set A^i, which is the set of all actions available to a *particular* player i, and an outcome a, which is a list of the particular actions chosen by *all* the players.

2. Part 2 of Definition 2.1 assumes that the each player has a finite number of actions, that is, that player i has k_i actions in the action set A^i. However, infinite action sets are commonly used in industrial organization. For example, often, we will assume that firms choose prices from the set of nonnegative real numbers.

3. We use the notation {*list of elements*} to denote a *set* where a set (e.g., an action set) contains elements in which the order of listing is of no consequence. In contrast, we use the notation (*list*) to denote a vector where the order does matter. For example, an outcome is a list of actions where the first action on the list is the action chosen by player 1, the second by player 2, and so on.

4. The literature uses the term *action profile* to describe the list of actions chosen by all players, which is what we call an *outcome*. For our purposes there is no harm in using the term *outcome* (instead of the term *action profile*) for describing this list of actions. However,

if games involve some uncertainty to some players, these two terms should be distinguished since under uncertainty an action profile may lead to several outcomes (see for example mixed actions games described in the appendix [Section 2.4]).

5. In the literature one often uses the term *strategy* instead of the term *action* (and therefore *strategy set* instead of *action set*), since in a normal form game, there is no distinction between the two terms. However, when we proceed to analyze extensive form games (section 2.2), the term *strategy* is given a different meaning than the term *action*.

The best way to test whether Definition 2.1 is clear to the reader is to apply it to a simple example. A simple way to describe the data that define a particular game is to display them in a matrix form. Consider the following game described in Table 2.1. We now argue that Table 2.1

		Country 2		
		WAR		PEACE
Country 1	WAR	1	1	3	0
	PEACE	0	3	2	2

Table 2.1: Peace-War game

contains all the data needed for properly defining a game according to Definition 2.1. First, we have two players, $N = 2$, called country 1 and 2. Second, the two players happen to have the same action sets: $A^1 = A^2 =$ {WAR, PEACE}. There are exactly four outcomes for this game: (WAR, WAR), (WAR, PEACE), (PEACE, WAR), (PEACE, PEACE). Third, the entries of the matrix (i.e., the four squares) contain the payoffs to player 1 (on the left-hand side) and to player 2 (on the right-hand side), corresponding to the relevant outcome of the game. For example, the outcome $a = $ (WAR, PEACE) specifies that player 1 opens a war while player 2 plays peace. The payoff to player 1 from this outcome is $\pi^1(a) = \pi^1($WAR, PEACE$) = 3$. Similarly, the payoff to player 2 is $\pi^2(a) = \pi^2($WAR, PEACE$) = 0$ since country 2 does not defend itself.

The story behind this game is as follows. If both countries engage in a war, then each country gains a utility of 1. If both countries play PEACE, then each country gains a utility of 2. If one country plays WAR while the other plays PEACE, then the aggressive country reaches the highest possible utility, since it "wins" a war against the nonviolent country with no effort. Under this outcome the utility of the "pacifist country" should be the lowest (equal to zero in our example).

In the literature, the game described in Table 2.1 is commonly referred to as the *Prisoners' Dilemma* game. Instead of having two countries fighting a war, consider two prisoners suspected of having committed a crime, for which the police lack sufficient evidence to convict either
suspect. The two prisoners are put in two different isolated cells and are
offered a lower punishment (or a higher payoff) if they confess of having jointly committed this crime. If we replace WAR with CONFESS,
and PEACE with NOT CONFESS, we obtain the so-called Prisoners'
Dilemma game.

In the present analysis we refrain from raising the question whether
the game described in Table 2.1 is observed in reality or not, or whether
the game is a good description of the world. Instead, we ask a different set of questions, namely, given that countries in the world behave
like those described in Table 2.1, can we (the economists or political
scientists) predict whether the world will end up in countries declaring
war or declaring peace. In order to perform this task, we need to define
equilibrium concepts.

2.1.2   Equilibrium concepts

Once the game is properly defined, we can realize that games may have
many outcomes. Therefore, by simply postulating all the possible outcomes (four outcomes in the game described in Table 2.1), we cannot
make any prediction of how the game is going to end. For example, can
you predict how a game like the one described in Table 2.1 would end
up? Will there be a war, or will peace prevail? Note that formulating
a game without having the ability to predict implies that the game is
of little value to the researcher. In order to make predictions, we need
to develop methods and define algorithms for narrowing down the set
of all outcomes to a smaller set that we call *equilibrium outcomes*. We
also must specify properties that we find desirable for an equilibrium to
fulfill. Ideally, we would like to find a method that would select only
one outcome. If this happens, we say that the equilibrium is *unique*.
However, as we show below, the equilibrium concepts developed here often fail to be unique. Moreover, the opposite extreme may occur where
a particular equilibrium may not exist at all. A game that cannot be
solved for equilibria is of less interest to us since no real-life prediction
can be made.

Before we proceed to defining our first equilibrium concept, we need
to define one additional piece of notation. Recall that an outcome of the
game $a = (a^1, \ldots, a^i, \ldots, a^N)$ is a list of what the N players are doing
(playing). Now, pick a certain player, whom we will call player i, (e.g.,
i can be player 1 or 89 or N, or any player). Remove from the outcome

a the action played by player i himself. Then, we are left with the list of what all players are playing except player i, which we denote by a^{-i}. Formally,

$$a^{-i} \equiv (a^1, \ldots, a^{i-1}, a^{i+1}, \ldots, a^N).$$

Note that after this minor surgical operation is performed, we can still express an outcome as a union of what action player i plays and all the other players' actions. That is, an outcome a can be expressed as $a = (a^i, a^{-i})$.

Equilibrium in dominant actions

Our first equilibrium concept, called equilibrium in dominant strategies, is a highly desirable equilibrium, in the sense that if it exists, it describes the most intuitively plausible prediction of what players would actually do.

The following definition applies for a *single* player in the sense that it classifies actions in a player's action set according to a certain criterion.

DEFINITION 2.2 *A particular action $\tilde{a}^i \in A^i$ is said to be a **dominant action for player** i if no matter what all other players are playing, playing $\tilde{a}^i$ always maximizes player i's payoff. Formally, for every choice of actions by all players except i, a^{-i},*

$$\pi^i(\tilde{a}^i, a^{-i}) \geq \pi^i(a^i, a^{-i}), \text{ for every } a^i \in A^i.$$

For example,

Claim 2.1 *In the game described in Table 2.1, the action $a^1 = WAR$ is a dominant action **for player 1**.*

Proof. It has to be shown that no matter what player 2 does, player 1 is always better off by starting a war. Thus, we have to scan over all the possible actions that can be played by player 2. If player 2 plays $a^2 = $ WAR, then

$$\pi^1(\text{WAR, WAR}) = 1 > 0 = \pi^1(\text{PEACE, WAR}).$$

Also, if player 2 plays $a^2 = $ PEACE, then

$$\pi^1(\text{WAR, PEACE}) = 3 > 2 = \pi^1(\text{PEACE, PEACE}).$$

∎

Similarly, since the game is symmetric (meaning that renaming player 1 as player 2 and vice versa, does not change players' payoffs), the reader can establish that $a^2 = $ WAR is a dominant action for player 2.

We now turn to defining our first equilibrium concept. An equilibrium in dominant actions is simply an outcome where each player plays a dominant action. Formally,

DEFINITION 2.3 *An outcome* $(\tilde{a}^1, \tilde{a}^2, \ldots, \tilde{a}^N)$ *(where* $\tilde{a}^i \in A^i$ *for every* $i = 1, 2, \ldots, N$*) is said to be an* **equilibrium in dominant actions** *if* $\tilde{a}^i$ *is a dominant action for each player* i.

Clearly, since WAR is a dominant action for each player in the game described in Table 2.1, the outcome $(a^1, a^2) = $ (WAR, WAR) is an equilibrium in dominant actions.

Although an equilibrium in dominant actions constitutes a very reasonable prediction of how players may interact in the real world, unfortunately, this equilibrium does not exist for most games of interest to us. To demonstrate this point, let us analyze the following Battle of the Sexes game described in Table 2.2. The intuition behind this (rather

		Rachel			
		OPERA (ω)		FOOTBALL (ϕ)	
Jacob	OPERA (ω)	2	1	0	0
	FOOTBALL (ϕ)	0	0	1	2

Table 2.2: Battle of the Sexes

romantic) Battle of the Sexes game is that it is relatively important for Jacob and Rachel to be together. That is, assuming that the payoffs to the players in Table 2.2 represent utilities to each player under each outcome, each player gains the lowest possible utility when the player goes alone to one of these entertainment events. Both of them gain a higher utility if they go together to one of these events. However, comparing the two outcomes where the players are "together," we can observe that Jacob prefers the OPERA, whereas Rachel prefers FOOTBALL. Thus, the Battle of the Sexes is sometimes referred to as a *coordination game*. The Battle of the Sexes game exhibited in Table 2.2 describes some real-life situations. For example, in chapter 10 we analyze economies in which products operate on different standards (such as different TV systems). The Battle of the Sexes game happens to be an ideal theoretical framework to model two firms with two available actions: choose standard 1, or standard 2. Failure to have both firms choosing the same standard may result in having consumers reject the product, thereby leaving the two firms with zero profits.

After formulating the Battle of the Sexes game, we now seek to find some predictions for this game. However, the reader will probably be disappointed to find out that:

Claim 2.2 *There does* not *exist an equilibrium in dominant actions for the Battle of the Sexes game.*

Proof. It is sufficient to show that one of the players does not have a dominant action. In this case, there cannot be an equilibrium in dominant actions since one player will not have a dominant action to play. Therefore, it is sufficient to look at Jacob: If Rachel chooses $a^R = \omega$, then Jacob would choose ω because

$$\pi^J(\omega, \omega) = 2 > 0 = \pi^J(\phi, \omega).$$

However, when Rachel goes to a football game, $a^R = \phi$, then Jacob would choose ϕ because

$$\pi^J(\phi, \phi) = 1 > 0 = \pi^J(\omega, \phi).$$

So, we have shown that one player does not have a dominant action, and this suffices to conclude that Definition 2.3 cannot be applied; hence, there does not exist an equilibrium in dominant actions for the Battle of the Sexes game.   ∎

Nash equilibrium (NE)

So far we have failed to develop an equilibrium concept that would select an outcome that would be a "reasonable" prediction for this model. In 1951, John Nash provided an existence proof for an equilibrium concept (earlier used by Cournot when studying duopoly) that has become the most commonly used equilibrium concept in analyzing games.

DEFINITION 2.4 *An outcome $\hat{a} = (\hat{a}^1, \hat{a}^2, \ldots, \hat{a}^N)$ (where $\hat{a}^i \in A^i$ for every $i = 1, 2, \ldots, N$) is said to be a* **Nash equilibrium (NE)** *if no player would find it beneficial to deviate provided that all other players do not deviate from their strategies played at the Nash outcome. Formally, for every player i, $i = 1, 2, \ldots, N$,*

$$\pi^i(\hat{a}^i, \hat{a}^{-i}) \geq \pi^i(a^i, \hat{a}^{-i}) \quad \text{for every } a^i \in A^i.$$

The general methodology for searching which outcomes constitute a NE is to check whether players benefit from a unilateral deviation from a certain outcome. That is, to rule out an outcome as a NE we need only demonstrate that one of the players can increase the payoff by deviating to a different action than the one played in this specific outcome, assuming that all other players do not deviate. Once we find an outcome in which no player can benefit from any deviation from the action played in that outcome, we can assert that we found a NE outcome.

We continue our discussion of the NE with the investigation of the relationship between Nash equilibrium and equilibrium in dominant actions. To demonstrate the relationship between the two equilibrium concepts, we first search for the NE outcomes for the game described in Table 2.1. Recall that we have already found that (WAR, WAR) is an equilibrium in dominant actions, but can this fact help us in searching for a NE for this game? Not surprisingly, yes, it can! Since an equilibrium in dominant actions means that each player plays a dominant action, no player would find it beneficial to deviate no matter how the others play. In particular, no player would deviate if the other players stick to their dominant actions. Hence,

Proposition 2.1 *An equilibrium in dominant actions outcome is also a NE. However, a NE outcome need not be an equilibrium in dominant actions.*

Altogether, we have it that (WAR, WAR) is a NE for the game described in Table 2.1. We leave it to the reader to verify that no other outcome in this game is a NE. Therefore, this equilibrium is called unique. The second part of Proposition 2.1 follows from the Battle of the Sexes game, where there exist two NE, but there does not exist an equilibrium in dominant actions.

Multiple Nash equilibria

We now demonstrate that a Nash equilibrium need not be unique. For example, applying Definition 2.4 to the Battle of the Sexes game yields:

Claim 2.3 *The Battle of the Sexes game described in Table 2.2 has two Nash equilibrium outcomes:*
(OPERA, OPERA) and (FOOTBALL, FOOTBALL).

Proof. To prove that (ω, ω) is a NE, we have to show that no player would benefit from deviation, given that the other does not deviate. In this game with two players, we have to show that, given that $a^R = \omega$, player J would play $a^J = \omega$; and that given that $a^J = \omega$, player R would play $a^R = \omega$. These two conditions follow from

$$\pi^J(\omega, \omega) = 2 \quad \geq \quad 0 = \pi^J(\phi, \omega) \qquad (2.1)$$
$$\pi^R(\omega, \omega) = 1 \quad \geq \quad 0 = \pi^R(\omega, \phi).$$

Using the same procedure, it can be easily shown that the outcome (ϕ, ϕ) is also a NE. Finally, we need to show that the other two outcomes, (ω, ϕ) and (ϕ, ω) are not NE. However, this follows immediately from (2.1). ∎

Nonexistence of a Nash equilibrium

So far we have seen examples where there is one or more NE. That is, as in the Battle of the Sexes game displayed in Table 2.2, it is always possible to find games with multiple NE. If the equilibrium is not unique, the model has a low prediction power. In contrast, Table 2.3 demonstrates a game where a Nash equilibrium does not exist. Therefore, consider the variant of the Battle of the Sexes game after thirty years of marriage. The intuition behind the game described in Table 2.3 is that after

		Rachel	
		OPERA (ω)	FOOTBALL (ϕ)
Jacob	OPERA (ω)	2 0	0 2
	FOOTBALL (ϕ)	0 1	1 0

Table 2.3: Nonexistence of a NE (in pure actions)

thirty years of marriage, Rachel's desire for being entertained together with Jacob has faded; however, Jacob's romantic attitude remained as before, and he would always gain a higher utility from being together with Rachel rather than alone.

Proposition 2.2 *The game described in Table 2.3 does not have a NE.*

Proof. We must prove that each outcome is not a NE. That is, in each of the four outcomes, at least one of the player would find it beneficial to deviate.
(1) For the (ω, ω) outcome, $\pi^R(\omega, \phi) = 2 > 0 = \pi^R(\omega, \omega)$. Hence, Rachel would deviate to $a^R = \phi$.
(2) For the (ϕ, ω) outcome, $\pi^J(\omega, \omega) = 2 > 0 = \pi^J(\phi, \omega)$. Hence, Jacob would deviate to $a^J = \omega$.
(3) For the (ϕ, ϕ) outcome, $\pi^R(\phi, \omega) = 1 > 0 = \pi^R(\phi, \phi)$. Hence, Rachel would deviate to $a^R = \omega$.
(4) For the (ω, ϕ) outcome, $\pi^J(\phi, \phi) = 1 > 0 = \pi^J(\omega, \phi)$. Hence, Jacob would deviate to $a^J = \phi$.   ∎

Using "best-response" functions to solve for NE

We now develop a tool called "best-response" functions that facilitates the search for NE.

DEFINITION 2.5

1. *In a two-player game, the* **best-response function** *of player i is the function $R^i(a^j)$, that for every given action a^j of player j assigns an action $a^i = R^i(a^j)$ that maximizes player i's payoff $\pi^i(a^i, a^j)$.*

2. *More generally, in an N-player game, the best-response function of player i is the function $R^i(a^{-i})$, that for given actions a^{-i} of players $1, 2, \ldots, i-1, i+1, \ldots, N$, assigns an action $a^i = R^i(a^{-i})$ that maximizes player i's payoff $\pi^i(a^i, a^{-i})$.*

Let us now construct the best-response functions for Jacob and Rachel described in the Battle of the Sexes game given in Table 2.2. It is straightforward to conclude that

$$R^J(a^R) = \left\{ \begin{array}{ll} \omega & \text{if } a^R = \omega \\ \phi & \text{if } a^R = \phi \end{array} \right. \quad \text{and} \quad R^R(a^J) = \left\{ \begin{array}{ll} \omega & \text{if } a^J = \omega \\ \phi & \text{if } a^J = \phi. \end{array} \right. \quad (2.2)$$

That is, if Rachel plays ω, Jacob's "best response" is to play ω, and if Rachel plays ϕ, Jacob's "best response" is to play ϕ, and so on.

Now, the importance of learning how to construct best-response functions becomes clear in the following proposition:

Proposition 2.3 *If $\hat{a}$ is a Nash equilibrium outcome, then $\hat{a}^i = R^i(\hat{a}^{-i})$ for every player i.*

Proof. By Definition 2.4, in a NE outcome each player does not benefit from deviating from the strategy played in a NE outcome (given that all other players do not deviate). Hence, by Definition 2.5, each player is on her best-response function. ∎

That is, in a NE outcome, each player chooses an action that is a best response to the actions chosen by other players in a NE. Proposition 2.3 is extremely useful in solving for NE in a wide variety of games and will be used extensively.

The procedure for finding a NE is now very simple: First, we calculate the best-response function of each player. Second, we check which outcomes lie on the best-response functions of all players. Those outcomes that we find to be on the best-response functions of all players constitute the NE outcomes. For example, in the Battle of the Sexes game, (2.2) implies that outcomes (ω, ω) and (ϕ, ϕ) each satisfy both players' best-response functions and therefore constitute NE outcomes.

2.1.3   Welfare comparisons among outcomes

So far, our analysis has concentrated on defining equilibrium concepts that enable us to select equilibrium outcomes for predicting how players would end up acting when facing similar games in the real world. However, we have not discussed whether the proposed equilibria yield efficient outcomes. That is, we wish to define an efficiency concept that would enable us to compare outcomes from a welfare point of view. In particular, using the Pareto efficiency criterion, we wish to investigate whether there are outcomes that yield higher payoff levels to some players without reducing the payoffs of all other players. For example, in the Peace-War game of Table 2.1, the outcome (PEACE, PEACE) yields higher payoffs to both players compared with the outcome (WAR, WAR). In this case, we say that the outcome (PEACE, PEACE) Pareto dominates the outcome (WAR, WAR). Formally,

DEFINITION 2.6

1. *The outcome* $\hat{a}$ **Pareto dominates** *the outcome* $\bar{a}$ *(also called* **Pareto superior** *to* $\bar{a}$*) if*

   (a) For every player i, $\pi^i(\hat{a}) \geq \pi^i(\bar{a})$, and

   (b) there exists at least one player j for whom $\pi^j(\hat{a}) > \pi^j(\bar{a})$.

2. *An outcome a^* is called* **Pareto efficient** *(also called* **Pareto optimal***) if there does* **not** *exist any outcome which Pareto dominates the outcome a^*.*

3. *Outcomes $\bar{a}$ and $\tilde{a}$ are called* **Pareto noncomparable** *if for some player i, $\pi^i(\bar{a}) > \pi^i(\tilde{a})$; but for some other player j, $\pi^j(\bar{a}) < \pi^j(\tilde{a})$.*

For example, in the Peace-War game, the outcomes (WAR, PEACE) and (PEACE, WAR) are Pareto noncomparable. In the Battle of the Sexes game of Table 2.2, the outcomes (OPERA, FOOTBALL) and (FOOTBALL, OPERA) are Pareto dominated by each of the other two outcomes. The outcomes (OPERA, OPERA) and (FOOTBALL, FOOTBALL) are Pareto efficient and are also Pareto noncomparable.

2.2   Extensive Form Games

Our analysis so far has concentrated on normal form games where the players are restricted to choosing an action at the same time. In this section we analyze games in which players can move at different times and more than once. Such games are called *extensive form games*. Extensive form games enable us to introduce timing into the model.

Before going to the formal treatment, let us consider the following example. A terrorist boards a flight from Minneapolis to New York. After thirty minutes, after reaching a cruising altitude of thirty thousand feet, the terrorist approaches the pilot and whispers to the pilot that she will explode a bomb if the pilot does not fly to Cuba. Figure 2.1 describes the Pilot-Terrorist game. One player is the pilot and the other is the

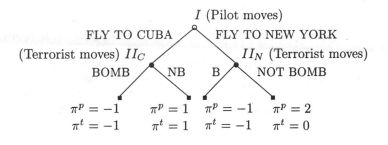

Figure 2.1: The pilot and the terrorist

terrorist. The game is represented by a *tree*, with a starting decision node (point I), other decision nodes (II_N and II_C), and terminal nodes (end points). Note that in some literature, the term *vertex* (vertices) is used in place of the term *node(s)*. The *branches* connecting decision nodes, and decision nodes to terminal nodes describe actions available to the relevant player on a particular decision node.

In this Pilot-Terrorist game, after hearing the terrorist's threat, the pilot gets to be the player to choose an action at the starting node. At the starting node, the pilot's action set is given by $A_I^{\text{pilot}} = \{NY, Cuba\}$. Depending on what action is chosen by the pilot, the terrorist has her turn to move at node II_C or II_N. The terrorist's action set is $A_{II_C}^{\text{terrorist}} = \{B, NB\}$ at the node II_C, and $A_{II_N}^{\text{terrorist}} = \{B, NB\}$ at the node II_N. In this simple game, the terrorist's action sets happen to be the same at both nodes, but this need not always be the case.

We can now give a formal definition to extensive form games with perfect information. Extensive form games with imperfect information are defined in Definition 2.17 on page 38.

DEFINITION 2.7 *An* **extensive form game** *is:*

1. *A game tree containing a starting node, other decision nodes, terminal nodes, and branches linking each decision node to successor nodes.*

2. *A list of $N \geq 1$ players, indexed by i, $i = 1, 2, \ldots, N$.*

3. *For each decision node, the name of the player entitled to choose an action.*

4. *For each player i, a specification of i's action set at each node that player i is entitled to choose an action.*

5. *A specification of the payoff to each player at each terminal node.*

2.2.1   Defining strategies and outcomes in extensive form games

Our preliminary discussion of extensive form games emphasized that a player may be called to choose an action more than once and that each time a player chooses an action, the player has to choose an action from the action set available at that particular node. Therefore, we need to define the following term.

DEFINITION 2.8 *A* **strategy** *for player i (denoted by s^i) is a complete plan (list) of actions, one action for each decision node that the player is entitled to choose an action.*

Thus, it is important to note that a strategy is not what a player does at a single specific node but is a list of what the player does at every node where the player is entitled to choose an action.

What are the strategies available to the terrorist in the Pilot-Terrorist game described in Figure 2.1? Since the terrorist may end up in either node II_C or II_N, a strategy for the terrorist would be a specification of the precise action she will be taking at *each* node. That is, although it is clear that the terrorist will reach either node II_C or II_N but not both, a strategy for this player must specify what she will do at *each* of the two nodes. Therefore, the terrorist has four possible strategies given by (B, B), (B, NB), (NB, B), (NB, NB), where the first component refers to the terrorist's action in node II_C, and the second component refers to her action at node II_N.

Since the pilot is restricted to making a move only at node I, and since his action set has two possible actions, this game has eight outcomes given by (NY, (B, B)), (NY, (B, NB)), (NY, (NB, B)), (NY, (NB, NB)), (C, (B, B)), (C, (B, NB)), (C, (NB, B)), (C, (NB, NB)).

2.2.2   A normal form representation for extensive form games

Now that the game is well defined, we seek to find some predictions. The first step would be to search for a Nash equilibrium. Recalling our definition of Nash equilibrium (Definition 2.4), in extensive form games we look for a Nash equilibrium in strategies, where each player cannot increase the payoff by unilaterally deviating from the strategy played at the NE outcome.

It turns out that in many instances transforming an extensive form game into a normal form makes it easier to find the Nash equilibria. Table 2.4 provides the normal form representation for the Pilot-Terrorist game described in Figure 2.1. Table 2.4 shows that there are three Nash

		Terrorist						
		(B, B)		(B, NB)		(NB, B)		(NB, NB)	
Pilot	NY	−1	−1	2	0	−1	−1	2	0
	CUBA	−1	−1	−1	−1	1	1	1	1

Table 2.4: Normal form representation of the Pilot-Terrorist game

equilibrium outcomes for this game: (NY, (NB, NB)), (NY, (B, NB)) and (CUBA, (NB, B)). Note that here, as in the Battle of the Sexes game, multiple NE greatly reduce our ability to generate predictions from this game. For this reason, we now turn to defining an equilibrium concept that would narrow down the set of NE outcomes into a smaller set of outcomes. In the literature, an equilibrium concept that selects a smaller number of NE outcomes is called a *refinement* of Nash equilibrium, which is the subject of the following subsection.

2.2.3 Subgames and subgame perfect equilibrium

In this subsection we define an equilibrium concept that satisfies all the requirement of NE (see Definition 2.4) and has some additional restrictions. This equilibrium concept may be helpful in selecting a smaller set of outcomes from the set of NE outcomes, by eliminating some undesirable NE outcomes.

Before we proceed to the formal part, let us go back to the Pilot-Terrorist game and look at the three NE outcomes for this game. Comparing the three NE outcomes, do you consider any equilibrium outcomes to be unreasonable? What would you suggest if the pilot were to hire you as her strategic adviser? Well, you would probably tell the pilot to fly to New York. Why? By looking at the terrorist's payoffs at the terminal nodes in Figure 2.1 we can see that if the pilot flies to NEW YORK, the terrorist will NOT BOMB (a payoff of $\pi^t = 0$ compared with $\pi^t = -1$ if she does), and the pilot will gain a payoff of $\pi^p = 2$ compared with a payoff of $\pi^p = 1$ for flying to Cuba. In other words, after the pilot flies to any destination (New York, or Cuba) the terrorist's payoff is maximized by choosing the NOT BOMB action. From this we conclude that the limitation of the NE concept is that it cannot capture the pilot's ability to predict that the terrorist will not have the incentive to explode the bomb once the plane arrives in New York (in to Cuba). More precisely, under the NE outcomes (CUBA, (NB, B)) and (NY, (B, NB)) the terrorist seems to be pulling what game theorists call an *incredible threat*, since the terrorist's payoffs at the terminal nodes indicate that once reaching either node II_C or II_N, the terrorist will not explode the bomb.

We now want to formalize an equilibrium concept that would exclude the unreasonable Nash equilibria. In particular, we look for an equilibrium concept that would exclude outcomes where the terrorist commits herself to the BOMB action, since such an action is incredible. Moreover, we seek to define an equilibrium concept where the player who moves first (the pilot in our case) would calculate and take into account how subsequent players (the terrorist in the present case) would respond to the moves of the players who move earlier in the game. Hence, having computed how subsequent players would respond, the first player can optimize by narrowing down the set of actions yielding higher payoffs. In the Pilot-Terrorist example, we wish to find an equilibrium concept that would generate a unique outcome where the pilot flies to New York.

We first define a subgame of the game.

DEFINITION 2.9 *A* **subgame** *is a decision node from the original game along with the decision nodes and terminal nodes directly following this node. A subgame is called a* **proper subgame** *if it differs from the original game.*

Clearly, the Pilot-Terrorist game has three subgames: One is the game itself whereas the other two are proper subgames with nodes II_C and II_N as starting nodes. The two proper subgames are illustrated in Figure 2.2.

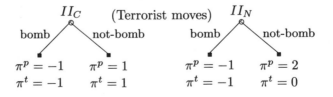

Figure 2.2: Two proper subgames

In 1965, Rheinhard Selten proposed a refinement of the NE concept defined as follows:

DEFINITION 2.10 *An outcome is said to be a* **subgame perfect equilibrium (SPE)** *if it induces a Nash equilibrium in every subgame of the original game.*

Definition 2.10 states that a SPE outcome is a list of strategies, one for each player, consisting of players' actions that constitutes a NE at every subgame. In particular, a SPE outcome must be a NE for the original game since the original game is a subgame of itself. Note that in each subgame, the action NB is a NE.

We now seek to apply Definition 2.10 in order to solve for a SPE of the Pilot-Terrorist game.

Claim 2.4 *The outcome (NY, (NB, NB)) constitutes a unique SPE for the Pilot-Terrorist game.*

Proof. Since a SPE is also a NE for the original game, it is sufficient to look at the three NE outcomes of the original game given by (NY, (B, NB)), (Cuba, (NB, B)) and (NY, (NB, NB)). Next, each proper subgame has only one NE, namely, the terrorist chooses NB. Hence, given that a SPE outcome must be a NE for every subgame, we conclude that the outcomes (NY, (B, NB)), (Cuba, (NB, B)) are not SPE.

Finally, the outcome (NY, (NB, NB)) is a SPE since it is a NE for the original game, and the outcome (action) NB is a unique NE for every proper subgame. ∎

Thus, we have shown that using the SPE refines the NE in the sense of excluding some outcomes which we may consider unreasonable.

We conclude this discussion of the SPE by describing the methodologies commonly used for finding SPE outcomes. The general methodology for finding the SPE outcomes is to use *backward induction,* meaning that we start searching for NE in the subgames leading to the terminal nodes. Then, we look for NE for the subgames leading the subgames leading to the terminal nodes, taking as given the NE actions to be played in the last subgames before the terminal nodes. Then, continuing to solve backwards, we reach the starting node and look for the action that maximizes player 1's payoff, given the NE of all the proper subgames. Note that the backward induction methodology is particularly useful when the game tree is long. Finally, another common methodology is to first find the NE outcomes for the game, say by transforming the extensive form representation into a normal form representation (see subsection 2.2.2). Then, once we have the set of all NE outcomes, we are left to select those outcomes that are also NE for all subgames. This can be done by trial and error, or, as we do in the proof of Claim 2.4, by ruling out the NE outcomes of the original game that are not NE for some proper subgames.

2.3   Repeated Games

Repeated games are used only once in this book, in section 6.5, where we analyze collusion among firms under imperfect competition.

A *repeated game* is a one-shot game that is identically repeated more than once. The importance of analyzing repeated games is that under certain circumstances cooperative outcomes, which are not equilibrium outcomes under a one-shot game, can emerge as equilibrium outcomes in a repeated, noncooperative game.

A repeated game is a special "kind" of an extensive form game in which each period, all players move simultaneously and each player's action set does not vary with time; in a more general extensive form game, actions sets may differ from one time period to another. More precisely, a repeated game is a one-shot game (see Definition 2.1) that is repeated for several periods, where the repeated game is played once in each period. Each period, after the game is played, the players move to the next period. In a subsequent period, the players observe the actions chosen by all players (including their own) in all previous periods, and only then simultaneously choose their actions for the new game. Thus, the important thing to remember is that players can perfectly monitor all the actions chosen in earlier periods prior to choosing an action in a subsequent period. The data collected by perfectly monitoring the actions played in each period is called a history at a period.

To define the players' strategies under a repeated game, we now wish to modify Definition 2.8 to repeated games:

DEFINITION 2.11

1. *A period τ* **history** *of a game, H_τ, is the list of outcomes played in all periods $t = 1, 2, \ldots, \tau - 1$.*

2. *A* **strategy** *of a player in a game repeated T times, is a list of actions that the player takes in each period t, $t = 1, 2, \ldots, T$; where each period t action, $a_t^i \in A^i$, is based on the period t history of the game (i.e., a_t^i maps a history H_t to an action in the set A^i).*

Hence, a strategy of a player in a repeated game is a list of actions to be played in each period τ, where each period τ action of player i is based on the observed list of actions played by all players in all periods $t = 1, 2, \ldots, \tau - 1$ summarized by the history H_τ. Therefore, an outcome of a repeated game would be a list of actions each player is taking in every period, whereas the period τ payoff to each player is a function of the actions played by the players in period τ.

Consider our Peace-War game described in Table 2.1, and suppose that this game is repeated T times, in periods $1, 2, \ldots, T$, where T is an integer number satisfying $1 \leq T \leq +\infty$. We denote by $0 < \rho < 1$ the time discount parameter for each player. That is, the parameter ρ is the present value of one dollar to be received by the player next period. Another way of interpreting ρ is to assume that our players live in a world with perfect capital markets where players can lend or borrow any amount of money at a given (real) interest r, $r > 0$. In this case, we can assume that the economy's real interest r would adjust so that $r = 1/\rho - 1$, or $\rho = 1/(1 + r)$.

We now make the following assumption regarding the players' payoffs in a repeated game:

ASSUMPTION 2.1 *Let a_t^i denote the action taken by player i in period t, $i = 1, 2$, $t = 1, 2, \ldots, T$. Also, let $\pi_t^i(a_t^1, a_t^2)$ be the period t payoff to player i, $i = 1, 2$, where π_t^i is given in Table 2.1. Then, the payoff to player i when the game is repeated T times is defined by*

$$
\begin{aligned}
\Pi^i \;\equiv\; & \sum_{t=1}^{T} \rho^{t-1} \pi_t^i(a_t^1, a_t^2) \\
=\; & \begin{cases} \pi_1^i(a_1^1, a_1^2) + \rho \pi_2^i(a_2^1, a_2^2) + \cdots + \rho^{T-1} \pi_T^i(a_T^1, a_T^2) & \text{if } T < \infty \\[2mm] \pi_1^i(a_1^1, a_1^2) + \rho \pi_2^i(a_2^1, a_2^2) + \rho^2 \pi_3^i(a_3^1, a_3^2) + \cdots & \text{if } T = \infty. \end{cases}
\end{aligned}
$$

If the number of players is greater than two, then replace (a_t^1, a_t^2) with a_t, where $a_t \equiv (a_t^1, a_t^2, a_t^3, \ldots)$.

We distinguish between two types of repeated games: a finitely repeated game $T < +\infty$, and an infinitely repeated game $T = +\infty$.

2.3.1 Finitely repeated game

Suppose that the Peace-War game is repeated T times, in periods $1, 2, \ldots, T$, where T is a finite integer number satisfying $1 \leq T < +\infty$.

In Section 2.1 we have shown that (WAR, WAR) is a unique NE for this one-shot game. Now suppose that the game is played twice in two consecutive periods ($T = 2$). If we apply Definition 2.11, what strategies are available to, say, country 1? More precisely, how many strategies are there in country 1's strategy set?

Claim 2.5 *There are $32 = 2^5$ available strategies to country 1 in this two-action, two-period repeated game.*

Proof. Let us first look at the second period. In the second period there could be four possible histories resulting from the four possible first-period lists of players' actions. That is, period 2 history satisfies $H_2 \in \{(\text{WAR}, \text{WAR}), (\text{WAR}, \text{PEACE}), (\text{PEACE}, \text{WAR}), (\text{PEACE}, \text{PEACE})\}$.

In the second period, there are two possible actions country 1 can take: WAR and PEACE. Now, in order to fully specify a strategy, country 1 has to specify which action will be taken for *every* possible history. Hence, the number of second-period actions is 2^4. On top of this, there are two possible actions available to country 1 in period 1. Hence, the number of strategies available to country 1 in a two-action, two-period repeated game is $2 \times 2^4 = 2^5$. ■

Similarly, if the game is repeated three times $(T = 3)$, the strategy set of country 1 contains

$$2,097,152 = 2^{21} = 2 \times 2^4 \times 2^{16}$$

strategies, since in the third period there are $16 = 4 \times 4$ possible histories (resulting from four possible lists of players' actions in each period).

We now state our main proposition for finitely repeated games:

Proposition 2.4 *For any finite integer T, $1 \leq T < +\infty$, the T-times repeated Peace-War game has a unique SPE where each country plays WAR in each period.*

Thus, Proposition 2.4 states that no matter how many times the Peace-War game is repeated (it could be one, or it could be a billion times), the unique SPE is WAR played by all players in every period.

Proof. Using backward induction, let us suppose that the countries have already played in $T-1$ periods, and that now they are ready to play the final T's period game. Then, since period T is the last period that the game is played, the T's period game is identical to the single one-shot Peace-War game. Hence, a unique NE for the $T's$ period game is WAR played by each country.

Now, consider the game played in period $T-1$. Both players know that after this game is completed, they will have one last game to play in which they both will not cooperate and play WAR. Hence, in $T-1$ each player would play the dominant strategy WAR. Working backwards, in each of the proceeding periods $T-2$, $T-3$ until period 1, we can establish that WAR will be played by every player in each period. ■

2.3.2 Infinitely repeated game

Now, suppose that the game is repeated infinitely many times (i.e., $T = +\infty$). The difference between the infinitely repeated game and the small or large but finitely repeated game is that in an infinitely repeated game, backward induction (used in the proof of Proposition 2.4) cannot be used to arrive at equilibrium outcomes, since there is no final period to "start" the backward induction process.

The trigger strategy

We restrict the discussion of strategy in infinitely repeated games to one type, called *trigger strategies*. In the class of trigger strategies, each player cooperates in period t (playing a_τ^i = PEACE) as long as all players cooperated in period $\tau - 1$. However, if any player did not cooperate and played WAR in period $\tau - 1$, then player i "pulls the trigger" and plays the noncooperative action forever! That is, a_t^i = WAR for every $t = \tau, \tau + 1, \tau + 2, \ldots$. Formally,

DEFINITION 2.12 *Player i is said to be playing a* **trigger strategy** *if for every period τ, $\tau = 1, 2, \ldots$,*

$$a_\tau^i = \begin{cases} \text{PEACE} & \text{as long as } a_t^i = a_t^j = \text{PEACE for all } t = 1, \ldots, \tau - 1 \\ \text{WAR} & \text{otherwise.} \end{cases}$$

That is, country i cooperates by playing PEACE as long as no country (including itself) deviates from the cooperative outcome. However, in the event that a country deviates even once, country i punishes the deviator by engaging in a WAR forever.

Equilibrium in trigger strategies

We now seek to investigate under what conditions the outcome where both countries play their trigger strategies constitutes a SPE.

Proposition 2.5 *If the discount factor is sufficiently large, then the outcome where the players play their trigger strategies is a SPE. Formally, trigger strategies constitute a SPE if $\rho > 1/2$.*

Proof. Let us look at a representative period, call it period τ, and suppose that country 2 has not deviated in periods $1, \ldots, \tau$. Then, if country 1 deviates and plays a_τ^i = WAR, Table 2.1 shows that $\pi_\tau^1 = 3$. However, given that country 1 deviates, country 2 would deviate in all subsequent periods and play a_t^i = WAR for *every* $t \geq \tau + 1$, since country 2 plays a trigger strategy. Hence, from period $\tau + 1$ and on, country 1 earns a payoff of 1 each period. Therefore, the period $\tau+1$ sum of discounted payoffs to country 1 for all periods $t \geq \tau + 1$ is $\frac{1}{1-\rho}$. Note that we used the familiar formula for calculating the present value of an infinite stream of payoffs given by $1 + \rho + \rho^2 + \rho^3 + \ldots = \sum_{t=0}^{\infty} \rho^t = \frac{1}{1-\rho}$. Hence, if country 1 deviates in period τ, its sum of discounted payoffs is the sum period τ's payoff from playing WAR (while country 2 plays PEACE) equal to $\pi_\tau^1(\text{W,P}) = 3$, plus the discounted infinite sum of payoffs when both countries play WAR (sum of discounted payoffs of 1 each period). Thus, if country 1 deviates from PEACE in period τ then

$$\Pi_\tau^1 = \pi_\tau^1(W, P) + \sum_{t=\tau+1}^{\infty} \rho^{t-\tau} \pi_\tau^1(W, W) = 3 + \frac{\rho}{1-\rho}. \qquad (2.3)$$

However, if country 1 does not deviate, then both countries play PEACE indefinitely, since country 2 plays a trigger strategy. Hence, both countries gain a payoff of 2 each period. Thus,

$$\Pi_\tau^1 = \sum_{t=\tau}^{\infty} \rho^{t-\tau} \pi_\tau^1(P, P) = \frac{2}{1-\rho}. \qquad (2.4)$$

Comparing (2.3) with (2.4) yields the conclusion that deviation is *not* beneficial for country 1 if $\rho > 1/2$. Since no unilateral deviation is beneficial to any country at any subgame starting at an arbitrary period τ, we conclude that no unilateral is beneficial to a country at any period t.

So far, we have showed that when both countries play the trigger strategy no country has the incentive to unilaterally deviate from playing PEACE. In the language of game theorists, we showed that deviation from the equilibrium path is not beneficial to any country. However, to prove that the trigger strategies constitute a SPE we need to show that if one country deviates and plays WAR, the other country would adhere to its trigger strategy and would play WAR forever. In the language of game theorists, to prove SPE we need to prove that no player has the incentive to deviate from the played strategy even if the game proceeds *off the equilibrium path*. To prove that, note that if country 1 deviates from PEACE in period τ, then Definition 2.12 implies that country 1 will play WAR forever since Definition 2.12 states that any deviation (by country 1 or country 2) would trigger country 1 to play WAR forever. Hence, country 2 would punish country 1 by playing WAR forever since WAR yields a payoff to country 2 of 1 each period (compared with payoff of 0 if country 2 continues playing PEACE). Altogether, the trigger strategies defined in Definition 2.12 constitute a SPE for the infinitely repeated Peace-War game.   ∎

Proposition 2.5 demonstrates the relationship between the players' time discount factor, given by ρ, and their incentive to deviate from the cooperative action. That is, when players have a low discount factor (say, ρ is close to zero), the players do not care much about future payoffs. Hence, cooperation cannot be a SPE since the players wish to maximize only their first period profit. However, when ρ is large ($\rho > 1/2$ in our case) players do not heavily discount future payoffs, so cooperation becomes more beneficial to the players since the punishment on deviation becomes significant because the discounted flow of payoffs under cooperation (2 per period) is higher than the short-run gain from deviation (a payoff of 3 for one period and 1 thereafter). This discussion leads to the following corollary:

Corollary 2.1 *In an infinitely repeated game cooperation is easier to sustain when players have a higher time discount factor.*

2.3.3 A discussion of repeated games and cooperation

In this section we have shown that a one-shot game with a unique non-cooperative Nash equilibrium can have a cooperative SPE when it is repeated infinitely. However, note that in the repeated game, this SPE is not unique. For example, it is easy to show that the noncooperative outcome where each country plays WAR in every period constitutes a SPE also. Moreover, the *Folk Theorem* (Folk, because it was well known to game theorists long before it was formalized) states that for a sufficiently high time discount factor, a large number of outcomes in the repeated game can be supported as a SPE. Thus, the fact that we merely show that cooperation is a SPE is insufficient to conclude that a game of this type will always end up with cooperation. All that we managed to show is that cooperation is a possible SPE in an infinitely repeated game.

Finally, let us look at an experiment Robert Axelrod conducted in which he invited people to write computer programs that play the Prisoners' Dilemma game against other computer programs a large number of times. The winner was the programmer who managed to score the largest sum over all the games played against all other programs. The important result of this tournament was that the program that used a strategy called Tit-for-Tat won the highest score. The Tit-for-Tat strategy is different from the trigger strategy defined in Definition 2.12 because it contains a less severe punishment in case of deviation. In the Tit-for-Tat strategy, a player would play in period t what the opponent played in period $t-1$. Thus, even if deviation occurred, once the opponent resumes cooperation, the players would switch to cooperation in a subsequent period. Under the trigger strategy, once one of the players deviates, the game enters a noncooperative phase forever.

2.4 Appendix: Games with Mixed Actions

The tools developed in this appendix are not implemented in this book, and are brought up here only for the sake of completeness. Thus, this appendix is not necessary to study this book successfully, and the beginning readers are urged to skip this appendix.

Games with mixed actions are those in which the players randomize over the actions available in their action sets. Often, it is hard to motivate games with mixed actions in economics modeling. This is not because we think that players do not choose actions randomly in real life. On the contrary, the reader can probably recall many instances in which he or she decided to randomize actions. The major reason why games with mixed actions are hard to interpret is that it is not always clear why the players benefit from randomizing among their pure actions.

The attractive feature of games with mixed actions is that a Nash equilibrium (in mixed actions) always exists. Recall that Proposition 2.2 demonstrates that a Nash equilibrium in pure actions need not always exist.

In what follows, our analysis will concentrate on the Top-Bottom-Left-Right given in Table 2.5. The reason for focusing on the game in

		Ms. β			
		L(left)		R(right)	
Ms. α	T(top)	0	0	0	-1
	B(bottom)	1	0	-1	3

Table 2.5: NE in mixed actions

Table 2.5 is that we show that a Nash equilibrium in mixed actions exists despite the fact that a Nash equilibrium in pure actions does not (the reader is urged to verify that indeed a Nash equilibrium in pure actions does not exist).

We now wish to modify a game with pure strategies to a game where the players choose probabilities of taking actions from their action sets. Recall that by Definition 2.1, we need to specify three elements: (a) the list of players (already defined), (b) the action set available to each player, and (c) the payoff to each player at each possible outcome (the payoff function for each player).

DEFINITION 2.13

1. A **mixed action** of player α is a probability distribution over playing $a^\alpha = T$ and playing $a^\alpha = B$. Formally, a mixed action of player α is a probability τ, $(0 \leq \tau \leq 1)$ such that player α plays T with probability τ and plays B with probability $1 - \tau$.

2. A mixed action of player β is a probability λ, $(0 \leq \lambda \leq 1)$ such that player β plays L with probability λ and plays R with probability $1 - \lambda$.

3. An **action profile** of a mixed actions game is a list (τ, λ) (i.e., the list of the mixed action chosen by each player).

4. An **outcome** of a game with mixed actions is the list of the realization of the actions played by each player.

Definition 2.13 implies that the mixed-action set of each player is the interval $[0,1]$ where player α picks a $\tau \in [0,1]$ and player β picks a $\lambda \in [0,1]$. The reader has probably noticed that Definition 2.13 introduces a new term, *action profile,* which replaces the term *outcome* used in normal form games, Definition 2.1. The reason for introducing this term is that in a game with mixed actions, the players choose only probabilities for playing their strategies, so the outcome itself is random. In games with pure actions, the term *action profile* and the term *outcome* mean the same thing since there is no uncertainty. However, in games with mixed actions, the term *action profile* is used to describe the list of probability distributions over actions chosen by each player, whereas the term *outcome* specifies the list of actions played by each player after the uncertainty is resolved.

Our definition of the "mixed extension" of the game is incomplete unless we specify the payoff to each player under all possible action profiles.

DEFINITION 2.14 *A payoff function of a player in the mixed-action game is the expected value of the payoffs of the player in the game with the pure actions. Formally, for any given action profile (λ, τ), the expected payoff to player i, $i = \alpha, \beta$, is given by*

$$
\begin{aligned}
E\pi^i(\tau, \lambda) \;\equiv\;\; & \tau\lambda\pi^i(T,L) + \tau(1-\lambda)\pi^i(T,R) \\
+\;\; & (1-\tau)\lambda\pi^i(B,L) + (1-\tau)(1-\lambda)\pi^i(B,R).
\end{aligned}
$$

According to Definition 2.1 our game is now well defined, since we specified the action sets and the payoff functions defined over all possible action profiles of the mixed actions game.

Applying the NE concept, defined in Definition 2.4, to our mixed-actions game, we can state the following definition:

DEFINITION 2.15 *An action profile $(\hat{\tau}, \hat{\lambda})$ (where $\hat{\tau}, \hat{\lambda} \in [0,1]$), is said to be a* **Nash equilibrium in mixed actions** *if no player would find it beneficial to deviate from her or his mixed action, given that the other player does not deviate from her or his mixed action. Formally,*

$$
\begin{aligned}
E\pi^\alpha(\hat{\tau}, \hat{\lambda}) \;&\geq\; E\pi^\alpha(\tau, \hat{\lambda}) \quad \text{for every } \tau \in [0,1] \qquad (2.5) \\
E\pi^\beta(\hat{\tau}, \hat{\lambda}) \;&\geq\; E\pi^\beta(\hat{\tau}, \lambda) \quad \text{for every } \lambda \in [0,1] \; .
\end{aligned}
$$

We now turn to solving for the Nash equilibrium of the mixed-actions extension game of the game described in Table 2.5. Substituting the payoffs associated with the "pure" outcomes of the game in Table 2.5 into the "mixed" payoff functions given in Definition 2.14 yields

$$\mathrm{E}\pi^{\alpha}(\tau,\lambda) \quad = \quad \tau\lambda \times 0 + \tau(1-\lambda) \times 0 \qquad\qquad\qquad (2.6)$$
$$+ \quad (1-\tau)\lambda \times 1 + (1-\tau)(1-\lambda) \times (-1) = (1-\tau)(2\lambda - 1)$$

and

$$\mathrm{E}\pi^{\beta}(\tau,\lambda) \quad = \quad \tau\lambda \times 0 + \tau(1-\lambda) \times (-1) \qquad\qquad\qquad (2.7)$$
$$+ \quad (1-\tau)\lambda \times 0 + (1-\tau)(1-\lambda) \times 3 = (1-\lambda)(3-4\tau).$$

Restating Definition 2.15, we look for a pair of probabilities $(\hat{\tau}, \hat{\lambda})$ that satisfy two conditions: (a) for a given $\hat{\lambda}$, $\hat{\tau}$ maximizes $\mathrm{E}\pi^{\alpha}(\tau, \hat{\lambda})$ given in (2.6), and (b) for a given $\hat{\tau}$, $\hat{\lambda}$ maximizes $\mathrm{E}\pi^{\beta}(\hat{\tau}, \lambda)$ given in (2.7).

It is easy to check that the players' payoffs (2.6) and (2.7) yield best-response functions (see Definition 2.5) given by

$$R^{\alpha}(\lambda) = \begin{cases} 1 & \text{if } \lambda < 1/2 \\ [0,1] & \text{if } \lambda = 1/2 \\ 0 & \text{if } \lambda > 1/2 \end{cases} \quad \text{and} \quad R^{\beta}(\tau) = \begin{cases} 0 & \text{if } \tau < 3/4 \\ [0,1] & \text{if } \tau = 3/4 \\ 1 & \text{if } \tau > 3/4. \end{cases}$$
$$(2.8)$$

That is, when player β plays R with a high probability $(1-\lambda > 1/2)$, player α's best response is to play T with probability 1 $(\tau = 1)$ in order to minimize the probability of getting a payoff of -1. However, when player β plays L with a high probability $(\lambda > 1/2)$, player α's best response is to play B with probability 1 $(\tau = 0)$ in order to maximize the probability of getting a payoff of $+1$. Similar explanation applies to the best-response function of player β.

The best-response functions of each player are drawn in Figure 2.3. Equations (2.8) and Figure 2.3 show that when β plays $\lambda = 1/2$, player α is indifferent to the choice among all her actions. That is, when $\lambda = 1/2$, the payoff of player α is the same (zero) for every mixed action $\tau \in [0,1]$. In particular, player α is indifferent to the choice between playing a pure strategy (meaning that $\tau = 0$ or $\tau = 1$) and playing any other mixed actions $(0 < \tau < 1)$. Similarly, player β is indifferent to the choice among all her mixed actions $\lambda \in [0,1]$, when player α plays $\tau = 3/4$.

Although a NE in pure actions does not exist for the game described in Table 2.5, the following proposition shows:

Proposition 2.6 *There exists a unique NE in mixed actions for the game described in Table 2.5. In this equilibrium, $\tau = 3/4$ and $\lambda = 1/2$.*

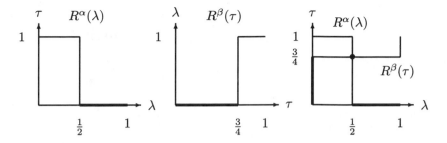

Figure 2.3: Best-response functions for the mixed-action extended game

The proposition follows directly from the right-hand side of Figure 2.3 that shows that the two best-response functions given in (2.8) have a unique intersection.

Finally, the best-response functions given in (2.8) have a property of being composed of horizontal or vertical line segments. Since the equilibrium occurs when the two curves intersect in their "middle" sections, we have it that under the NE mixed outcome, each player is indifferent to the choice among all other probabilities that can be played, assuming that the other player does not deviate from the mixed action. This result makes the intuitive interpretation of a mixed-action game rather difficult, because there is no particular reason why each player would stick to the mixed action played under the NE.

2.5   Appendix: Games with Imperfect Information

Games with imperfect information are brought up here only for the sake of completion, and the beginning readers are urged to skip this appendix. Games with imperfect information describe situations where some players do not always observe the action taken by another player earlier in the game, thereby making the player unsure which node has been reached. For example, Figure 2.4 describes a variant of the Pilot-Terrorist game given in Figure 2.1. In Figure 2.4 we suppose that the terrorist cannot monitor the direction in which the pilot is flying, say because the terrorist cannot read a compass or because the pilot disables some of the navigation equipment. The broken line connecting nodes II_C and II_N describes an *information set* for the terrorist. The information set tells us that in this game, the terrorist cannot distinguish whether node II_C or II_N has been reached. Thus, when the terrorist has her turn to make a move, she has to choose an action without knowing the precise node she is on. Formally,

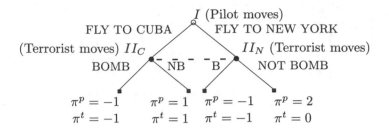

Figure 2.4: A game with imperfect information: Information sets

DEFINITION 2.16 *An* **information set** *for a player is a collection of nodes in which the player has to choose an action. When a player reaches an information set, the player knows that the particular information set has been reached, but if the information set contains more than one node, the player does not know which particular node in this collection has been reached.*

We now have the tools to define a game with imperfect information:

DEFINITION 2.17 *An extensive form game is called*

1. *A game with* **imperfect information** *if one of the information sets contains more than one node;*

2. *A game with* **perfect information** *if each information set contains a single node.*

Thus, all the extensive form games analyzed in Section 2.2 are games with perfect information since each information set coincides with a single node.

We now slightly extend our definition of a strategy (Definition 2.8) to incorporate games with imperfect information:

DEFINITION 2.18 *In a game with imperfect information, a* **strategy** *for a player is a list of actions that a player chooses at any information set where the player is entitled to take an action.*

Thus, Definition 2.18 provides a more general definition of a strategy (compared with Definition 2.8) since a strategy is a list of actions a player chooses in each information set rather than in each node where the player is entitled to take an action. Under perfect information, of course, Definitions 2.8 and 2.18 coincide, since under perfect information each information set is a singleton.

Finally, we need to extend our definition of subgames (Definition 2.9) to incorporate games with imperfect information.

DEFINITION 2.19 *A subgame is an information set that contains a single node, and all the subsequent decision and terminal nodes, provided that all subsequent nodes are not contained in information sets containing nodes that cannot be reached from the subgame.*

Figure 2.5 illustrates a game with imperfect information. In Figure 2.5, the nodes labeled A, D, and G are starting nodes for a subgame. However, the nodes labeled B, C, E, and F are not starting nodes for a subgame since some subsequent nodes are contained in information sets containing nodes that cannot be reached from these nodes.

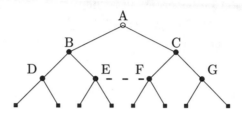

Figure 2.5: Game with imperfect information: Subgames

For example, the modified Pilot-Terrorist game described in Figure 2.4 has only one subgame, which is the original game itself, because all subsequent nodes are contained in information sets containing more than one node.

We conclude our discussion of games with imperfect information with solving for NE and SPE for the modified Pilot-Terrorist game described in Figure 2.4. First, all the possible outcomes for this game are given by (NY, B), (NY, NB), (Cuba, B), and (Cuba, NB). Thus, in the Pilot-Terrorist game under imperfect information, the number of outcomes has been reduced from eight to four since the terrorist now takes a decision at one information set (compared with two nodes, under perfect information). Second, since this game does not have any proper subgames, any NE is also a SPE. Hence, in this case, the set of NE outcomes coincides with the SPE outcomes. Thus, we can easily conclude that (NY, NB) constitutes both NE and SPE outcomes.

2.6 Exercises

1. Using Definition 2.5,

    (a) Write down the best-response functions for country 1 and country 2 for the Peace-War game described in Table 2.1, and decide which outcomes constitute NE.

    (b) Write down the best-response functions for Jacob and Rachel for the game described in Table 2.3, and decide which outcomes constitute a NE (if there are any).

    (c) Write down the best-response functions for player 1 and player 2 for the game described in Table 2.5, and decide which outcomes constitute a NE (if there are any).

2. Consider the normal form game described in Table 2.6. Find the conditions on the parameters a, b, c, d, e, f, g, and h that will ensure that

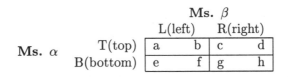

Table 2.6: Normal form game: Fill in the conditions on payoffs

    (a) the outcome (T, L) is a NE;

    (b) the outcome (T, L) is an equilibrium in dominant actions;

    (c) the outcome (T, L) Pareto dominates all other outcomes;

    (d) the outcome (T, L) is Pareto noncomparable to the outcome (B, R).

3. Consider the Traveler's Dilemma, where two travelers returning home from a remote island where they bought identical rare antiques find out that the airline has managed to smash these rare antiques. The airline manager assures the passengers of adequate compensation. Since the airline manager does not know the actual cost of the antiques, he offers the two travelers the opportunity to write down separately on a piece of paper the true cost of the antiques, which is restricted to be any number between 2 and 100.

    Let n_i denote that value stated by traveler i, $i = 1, 2$, and assume that the travelers cannot communicate with each other during this game. The airline manager states the following compensation rules: (a) If traveler i writes down a larger number than traveler j, (i.e., $n_i > n_j$), then he assumes that j is honest and i is lying. Hence, in this case, the airline manager will pay $n_i - 2$ to traveler i, and $n_j + 2$ to traveler j. Thus, the manager penalizes the traveler assumed to be lying and rewards the one assumed to be honest. (b) If $n_i = n_j$, then the manager assumes that both travelers are honest and pays them the declared value of the antiques. Letting n_1 and n_2 be the actions of the players, answer the following questions:

(a) Under Definition 2.6, which outcomes are Pareto Optimal?

(b) Under Definition 2.4, which outcomes constitute a Nash equilibrium for this game.

4. Consider a normal form game between three major car producers, C, F, and G. Each producer can produce either large cars, or small cars but not both. That is, the action set of each producer i, $i = C, F, G$ is $A^i \equiv \{SM, LG\}$. We denote by a^i the action chosen by player i, $a^i \in A^i$, and by $\pi^i(a^C, a^F, a^G)$ the profit to firm i. Assume that the profit function of each player i is defined by

$$
\pi^i \equiv
\begin{cases}
\gamma & \text{if } a^j = LG, \text{ for all } j = C, F, G \\
\gamma & \text{if } a^j = SM, \text{ for all } j = C, F, G \\
\alpha & \text{if } a^i = LG, \text{ and } a^j = SM \text{ for all } j \neq i \\
\alpha & \text{if } a^i = SM, \text{ and } a^j = LG \text{ for all } j \neq i \\
\beta & \text{if } a^i = a^j = LG, \text{ and } a^k = SM, \ j \neq k \neq i \\
\beta & \text{if } a^i = a^j = SM, \text{ and } a^k = LG, \ j \neq k \neq i.
\end{cases}
$$

Answer the following questions.

(a) Does there exist a Nash equilibrium when $\alpha > \beta > \gamma > 0$? Prove your answer!

(b) Does there exist a Nash equilibrium when $\alpha > \gamma > \beta > 0$? Prove your answer!

5. Figure 2.6 describes an extensive form version of the Battle of the Sexes game given initially in Table 2.2. Work through the following problems.

(a) How many subgames are there in this game? Describe and plot all the subgames.

(b) Find all the Nash equilibria in each subgame. Prove your answer!

(c) Find all the subgame perfect equilibria for this game.

(d) Before Rachel makes her move, she hears Jacob shouting that he intends to go to the opera (i.e., play ω). Would such a statement change the subgame perfect equilibrium outcomes? Prove and explain!

6. (This problem refers to mixed actions games studied in the appendix, section 2.4.) Consider the Battle of the Sexes game described in Table 2.2.

(a) Denote by θ the probability that Jacob goes to the OPERA, and by ρ the probability that Rachel goes to the OPERA. Formulate the expected payoff of each player.

(b) Draw the best-response function for each player $[R^J(\rho)$ and $R^R(\theta)]$.

(c) What is the NE in mixed actions for this game?

(d) Calculate the expected payoff to each player in this NE.

(e) How many times do the two best-response functions intersect? Explain the difference in the number of intersections between this game and the best-response functions illustrated in Figure 2.3.

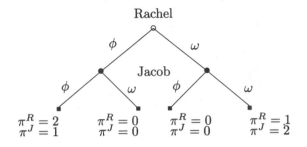

Figure 2.6: Battle of the Sexes in extensive form

2.7   References

Aumann, R. 1987. "Game Theory." In *The New Palgrave Dictionary of Economics,* edited by J. Eatwell, M. Milgate, and P. Newman. New York: The Stockton Press.

Axelrod, R. 1984. *The Evolution of Cooperation.* New York: Basic Books.

Binmore, K. 1992. *Fun and Games.* Lexington, Mass.: D.C. Heath.

Friedman, J. 1986. *Game Theory with Applications to Economics.* New York: Oxford University Press.

Fudenberg, D., and J. Tirole. 1991. *Game Theory.* Cambridge Mass.: MIT Press.

Gibbons, R. 1992. *Game Theory for Applied Economists.* Princeton, N.J.: Princeton University Press.

McMillan, J. 1992. *Games, Strategies, and Managers.* New York: Oxford University Press.

Moulin, H. 1982. *Game Theory for the Social Sciences.* New York: New York University Press.

Osborne, M., and A. Rubinstein. 1994. *A Course in Game Theory.* Cambridge, Mass.: MIT Press.

Rasmusen, E. 1989. *Games and Information: An Introduction to Game Theory.* Oxford: Blackwell.

Chapter 3

Technology, Production Cost, and Demand

Large increases in cost with questionable increase in performance can be tolerated only for race horses and fancy [spouses].
—Lord Kelvin 1824–1907 (President of the Royal Society)

This chapter reviews basic concepts of microeconomic theory. Section 3.1 (Technology and Cost) introduces the single-product production function and the cost function. Section 3.2 analyzes the basic properties of demand functions. The reader who is familiar with these concepts and properties can skip this chapter and proceed with the study of industrial organization. The student reader should note that this chapter reflects the maximum degree of technicality needed to grasp the material in this book. Thus, if the reader finds the material in this chapter to be comprehensible, then the student should feel technically well prepared for this course.

3.1 Technology and Cost

The production function reflects the know-how of a certain entity that we refer to as the firm. This know-how enables the firm to transform factors of production into what we call final goods. In general, we refrain from addressing the philosophical question of where technological know-how comes from. However, in chapter 9 (Research and Development) we do analyze some factors that affect the advance of technological know-how.

3.1.1   The production function

We assume that two inputs are needed to produce the single final good. We call these inputs *labor* and *capital*. Note that we restrict our discussion to production technologies for producing one and only one type of output. In reality, many production processes yield more than one type of output. For example, an oil refinery yields a variety of oil and plastic products from the same input of crude oil. We postpone the discussion of multiproduct production activities to our analysis of the airline industry given in section 17.2.

The production function represents a mapping from the amount of labor (denoted by l) and the amount of capital (denoted by k) employed in the production process to the number of units of output produced. We represent this relationship by a function f, where the number of units of output is given by $Q = f(l, k)$.

Assuming that the function f is twice continuously differentiable (with respect to both arguments), we define the *marginal product* of labor function $(MP_L(l, k))$ as the amount of output increase associated with a small increase in the amount of labor. Formally, we define the marginal product of labor and capital functions by

$$MP_L(l, k) \equiv \frac{\partial f(l, k)}{\partial l} \quad \text{and} \quad MP_K(l, k) \equiv \frac{\partial f(l, k)}{\partial k}. \tag{3.1}$$

For example, the marginal-product functions associated with the class of production functions $Q = (l^\alpha + k^\alpha)^\beta$, where $\alpha, \beta > 0$ are given by

$$MP_L(l, k) = \beta\alpha(l^\alpha + k^\alpha)^{\beta-1} l^{\alpha-1} \text{ and } MP_K(l, k) = \beta\alpha(l^\alpha + k^\alpha)^{\beta-1} k^{\alpha-1}.$$

It is important to note that the marginal product of a factor is a function (not necessarily a constant) of the amount of labor and capital used in the production process. In our example, $\lim_{l \to 0} MP_L(l, k) = +\infty$, meaning that in this production process, the marginal product of labor gets larger and larger as the amount of labor becomes scarce.

So far, we have not discussed the relationship between the two factors. We therefore make the following definition.

DEFINITION 3.1

1. *Labor and capital are called* **supporting factors** *in a particular production process if the increase in the employment of one factor raises the marginal product of the other factor. Formally, if*

$$\frac{\partial MP_L(l, k)}{\partial k} = \frac{\partial MP_K(l, k)}{\partial l} > 0.$$

2. *Labor and capital are called* **substitute factors** *in a particular production process, if the increase in the employment of one factor decreases the marginal product of the other factor. Formally, if*

$$\frac{\partial MP_L(l,k)}{\partial k} = \frac{\partial MP_K(l,k)}{\partial l} < 0.$$

In our example, the reader can verify that labor and capital are supporting factors if $\beta > 1$, and substitute factors if $\beta < 1$.

    We conclude the discussion of the production function by looking at the effect of input expansion on the amount of production. Formally,

DEFINITION 3.2 *Let λ be any number greater than 1. Then, a production technology $Q = f(l,k)$ is said to exhibit*

1. **Increasing returns to scale (IRS)** *if $f(\lambda l, \lambda k) > \lambda f(l,k)$. That is, if expanding the employment of labor and capital by the factor of λ will increase the output by more than a factor of λ.*

2. **Decreasing returns to scale (DRS)** *if $f(\lambda l, \lambda k) < \lambda f(l,k)$. That is, if expanding the employment of labor and capital by the factor of λ will increase the output by less than a factor of λ.*

3. **Constant returns to scale (CRS)** *if $f(\lambda l, \lambda k) = \lambda f(l,k)$. That is, if expanding the employment of labor and capital by the factor of λ will increase the output by exactly a factor of λ.*

In our example, the production technology $Q = f(l,k) = (l^\alpha + k^\alpha)^\beta$ exhibits IRS if

$$[(\lambda l)^\alpha + (\lambda k)^\alpha)]^\beta > \lambda (l^\alpha + k^\alpha)^\beta \text{ if and only if } \alpha\beta > 1.$$

3.1.2   The cost function

The cost function is a mapping from the rental prices of the factors of production and the production level to the total production cost. The cost function is a technological relationship that can be derived from the production function.

    Let W denote wage rate, and R the rental price for one unit of capital. The cost function is denoted by the function $TC(W, R; Q)$ measures the total production cost of producing Q units of output, when factor prices are W (for labor) and R (for capital).

    We define the average cost function by the ratio of the total production cost to output level. Formally, the *average cost function* (the cost per unit of output) at an output level Q is defined by $AC(Q) \equiv TC(Q)/Q$.

We define the *marginal cost function* as the change in total cost resulting from a 'small' increase in output level. Formally, the marginal cost function at an output level Q is defined by $MC(Q) \equiv \frac{\partial TC(Q)}{\partial Q}$.

As an example, consider the total cost function given by $TC(Q) = F + cQ^2$, $F, c \geq 0$. This cost function is illustrated on the left part of Figure 3.1. We refer to F as the *fixed cost* parameter, since the fixed

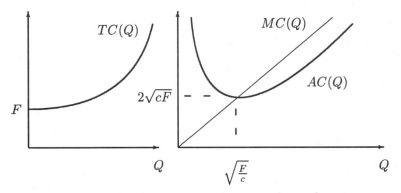

Figure 3.1: Total, average, and marginal cost functions

cost is independent of the output level.

It is straightforward to calculate that $AC(Q) = F/Q + cQ$ and that $MC(Q) = 2cQ$. The average and marginal cost functions are drawn on the right part of Figure 3.1. The $MC(Q)$ curve is linear and rising with Q, and has a slope of $2c$. The $AC(Q)$ curve is falling with Q as long as the output level is sufficiently small ($Q < \sqrt{F/c}$), and is rising with Q for higher output levels ($Q > \sqrt{F/c}$). Thus, in this example the cost per unit of output reaches a minimum at an output level $Q = \sqrt{F/c}$.

We now demonstrate an "easy" method for finding the output level that minimizes the average cost.

Proposition 3.1 *If the average cost function reaches a minimum at a strictly positive output level, then at that particular output level the average cost equals the marginal cost. Formally, if $Q^{\min} > 0$ minimizes $AC(Q)$, then $AC(Q^{\min}) = MC(Q^{\min})$.*

Proof. At the output level $Q^{\min}$, the slope of the $AC(Q)$ function must be zero. Hence,

$$0 = \frac{\partial AC(Q^{\min})}{\partial Q} = \frac{\partial \left(\frac{TC(Q^{\min})}{Q^{\min}} \right)}{\partial Q} = \frac{MC(Q^{\min})Q^{\min} - TC(Q^{\min})}{(Q^{\min})^2}.$$

Hence,

$$MC(Q^{\min}) = \frac{TC(Q^{\min})}{Q^{\min}} = AC(Q^{\min}).$$

∎

To demonstrate how useful Proposition 3.1 could be, we now return to our example illustrated in Figure 3.1, where $TC(Q) = F + cQ^2$. Proposition 3.1 states that in order to find the output level that minimizes the cost per unit, all that we need to do is extract $Q^{\min}$ from the equation $AC(Q^{\min}) = MC(Q^{\min})$. In our example,

$$AC(Q^{\min}) = \frac{F}{Q^{\min}} + cQ^{\min} = 2cQ^{\min} = MC(Q^{\min}).$$

Hence, $Q^{\min} = \sqrt{F/c}$, and $AC(Q^{\min}) = MC(Q^{\min}) = 2\sqrt{cF}$.

3.1.3 Duality between production and cost functions

We now provide a simple illustration of the relationship between production and cost functions, for the case of a single-input production function. Suppose that only labor is required for producing the final good, and let the production technology be given by $Q = f(l) = l^{\gamma}$, $\gamma > 0$. This production function is illustrated in the upper part of Figure 3.2, for three parameter cases where $0 < \gamma < 1$, $\gamma = 1$, and $\gamma > 1$.

In what follows, we show how the cost function can be derived from the production function. Let w denote the wage rate. Now, by inverting the production function we obtain $l = Q^{1/\gamma}$. The total cost is the wage rate multiplied by the amount of labor employed in the production process. Hence, $TC = wl = wQ^{1/\gamma}$, which is illustrated in the middle part of Figure 3.2, again for the three parameter cases where $0 < \gamma < 1$, $\gamma = 1$, and $\gamma > 1$.

We conclude this discussion by looking at the relationship between the production and cost function regarding the expansion of the production activity. More precisely, applying Definition 3.2 to the production function $Q = l^{\gamma}$, we have it that

$$(\lambda l)^{\gamma} > \lambda l^{\gamma} \quad \text{if and only if} \quad \gamma > 1.$$

Hence, this production exhibits IRS when $\gamma > 1$, CRS when $\gamma = 1$, and DRS when $\gamma < 1$.

It is important to realize that since the total cost function is derived from the production function, we should be able to infer from the shape of the average cost function whether the production process exhibits IRS, CRS, or DRS. When $\gamma > 1$, there are IRS. The case of IRS is

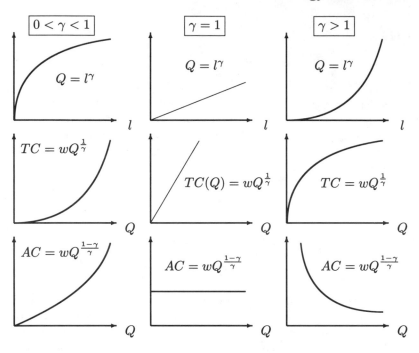

Figure 3.2: Duality between the production and cost functions

illustrated on the right side of Figure 3.2. Under IRS, the average cost declines with the output level, reflecting the fact that under IRS the cost per unit declines with a larger scale of production, say, because of the adoption of assembly line technology. Under CRS, the cost per unit is constant, reflecting a technology where an increase in the output level does not alter the per unit production cost. The left side of Figure 3.2 reflects a DRS technology, where an increase in the output level raises the per unit production cost.

Finally, recall our two-input example where $Q = (l^\alpha + k^\alpha)^\beta$. We showed that this production technology exhibits IRS if $\alpha\beta > 1$ and DRS if $\alpha\beta < 1$. Deriving the cost function of this production technology would take us beyond the level of this book. However, for the sake of illustration we state that the cost function associated with this technology is given by

$$TC(W, R; Q) = \phi Q^{\frac{1}{\alpha\beta}} \quad \text{where } \phi \text{ is a nonnegative function of } W \text{ and } R.$$

Now, in this case $AC(Q) = \phi Q^{1/(\alpha\beta)-1}$. Then, $AC(Q)$ is declining with Q if $1/(\alpha\beta) - 1 < 0$, or $\alpha\beta > 1$, which is the condition under which the technology exhibits IRS. In contrast, $AC(Q)$ is rising with Q

if $1/(\alpha\beta) - 1 > 0$, or $\alpha\beta < 1$, which is the condition under which the technology exhibits DRS.

3.2 The Demand Function

We denote by $Q(p)$ the (aggregate) demand function for a single product, where Q denotes the quantity demanded and p denotes the unit price. Formally, a demand function shows the maximum amount consumers are willing and able to purchase at a given market price. For example, we take the *linear* demand function given by $Q(p) = \frac{a}{b} - \frac{1}{b}p$ where a and b are strictly positive constants to be estimated by the econometrician. Alternatively, we often use the *inverse* demand function $p(Q)$, which expresses the maximum price consumers are willing and able to pay for a given quantity purchased. Inverting the linear demand function yields $p(Q) = a - bQ$, which is drawn in Figure 3.3. Note that part of the

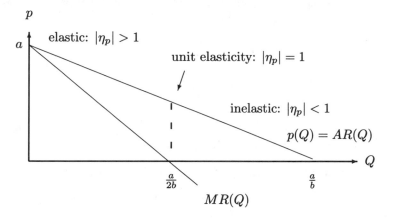

Figure 3.3: Inverse linear demand

demand is not drawn in the figure. That is, for $p > a$ the (inverse) demand becomes vertical at $Q = 0$, so the demand coincides with the vertical axis, and for $Q > a/b$, it coincides with the horizontal axis.

An example of nonlinear demand function is the constant elasticity demand function given by $Q(p) = ap^{-\epsilon}$ or $p(Q) = a^{1/\epsilon}Q^{-1/\epsilon}$, which is drawn in Figure 3.4. This class of functions has some nice features, which we discuss below.

3.2.1 The elasticity function

The elasticity function is derived from the demand function and maps the quantity purchased to a certain very useful number which we call

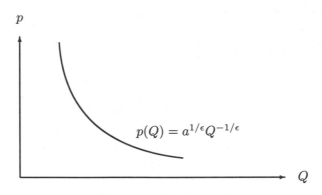

$$p(Q) = a^{1/\epsilon}Q^{-1/\epsilon}$$

Figure 3.4: Inverse constant-elasticity demand

the *elasticity at a point* on the demand. The elasticity measures how fast quantity demanded adjusts to a small change in price. Formally, we define the demand price elasticity by

$$\eta_p(Q) \equiv \frac{\partial Q(p)}{\partial p}\frac{p}{Q}. \tag{3.2}$$

DEFINITION 3.3 *At a given quantity level Q, the demand is called*

1. **elastic** *if $\eta_p(Q) < -1$ (or, $|\eta_p(Q)| > 1$),*

2. **inelastic** *if $-1 < \eta_p(Q) < 0$, (or, $|\eta_p(Q)| < 1$),*

3. *and has a* **unit elasticity** *if $\eta_p(Q) = -1$ (or, $|\eta_p(Q)| = 1$).*

For example, in the linear case, $\eta_p(Q) = 1 - a/(bQ)$. Hence, the demand has a unit elasticity when $Q = a/(2b)$. Therefore, the demand is elastic when $Q < a/(2b)$ and is inelastic when $Q > a/(2b)$. Figure 3.3 illustrates the elasticity regions for the linear demand case.

For the constant-elasticity demand function $Q(p) = ap^{-\epsilon}$ we have it that $\eta_p = a(-\epsilon)p^{-\epsilon-1}p/(ap^{-\epsilon}) = -\epsilon$. Hence, the elasticity is constant given by the power of the price variable in demand function. If $\epsilon = 1$, this demand function has a unit elasticity at all output levels.

3.2.2   The marginal revenue function

The inverse demand function shows the maximum amount a consumer is willing to pay per unit of consumption at a given quantity of purchase. The *total-revenue function* shows the amount of revenue collected by sellers, associated with each price-quantity combination. Formally, we define the total-revenue function as the product of the price and quantity: $TR(Q) \equiv p(Q)Q$. For the linear case, $TR(Q) = aQ - bQ^2$, and for the constant elasticity demand, $TR(Q) = a^{1/\epsilon}Q^{1-1/\epsilon}$. Note that a more suitable name for the revenue function would be to call it the total expenditure function since we actually refer to consumer expenditure rather than producers' revenue. That is, consumers' expenditure need not equal producers' revenue, for example, when taxes are levied on consumption. Thus, the total revenue function measures how much consumers spend at every given market price, and not necessarily the revenue collected by producers.

The *marginal-revenue* function (again, more appropriately termed the "marginal expenditure") shows the amount by which total revenue increases when the consumers slightly increase the amount they buy. Formally we define the marginal-revenue function by $MR(Q) \equiv \frac{dTR(Q)}{dQ}$.

For the linear demand case we can state the following:

Proposition 3.2 *If the demand function is linear, then the marginal-revenue function is also linear, has the same intercept as the demand, but has twice the (negative) slope. Formally, $MR(Q) = a - 2bQ$.*

Proof.

$$MR(Q) = \frac{dTR(Q)}{dQ} = \frac{d(aQ - bQ^2)}{dQ} = a - 2bQ.$$

∎

The marginal-revenue function for the linear case is drawn in Figure 3.3. The marginal-revenue curve hits zero at an output level of $Q = a/(2b)$. Note that a monopoly, studied in chapter 5, will never produce an output level larger than $Q = a/(2b)$ where the marginal revenue is negative, since in this case, revenue could be raised with a decrease in output sold to consumers.

For the constant-elasticity demand we do not draw the corresponding marginal-revenue function. However, we consider one special case where $\epsilon = 1$. In this case, $p = aQ^{-1}$, and $TR(Q) = a$, which is a constant. Hence, $MR(Q) = 0$.

You have probably already noticed that the demand elasticity and the marginal-revenue functions are related. That is, Figure 3.3 shows that $MR(Q) = 0$ when $\eta_p(Q) = 1$, and $MR(Q) > 0$ when $|\eta_p(Q)| > 1$. The complete relationship is given in the following proposition.

Proposition 3.3

$$MR(Q) = p(Q)\left[1 + \frac{1}{\eta_p(Q)}\right].$$

Proof.

$$MR(Q) \equiv \frac{\mathrm{d}\,TR(Q)}{\mathrm{d}Q} = \frac{\mathrm{d}[p(Q)Q]}{\mathrm{d}Q} = p + Q\frac{\mathrm{d}p(Q)}{\mathrm{d}Q}$$

$$= p\left[1 + \frac{Q}{p}\frac{1}{\frac{\mathrm{d}Q(p)}{\mathrm{d}p}}\right] = p\left[1 + \frac{1}{\eta_p(Q)}\right].$$

■

3.2.3   Consumer surplus

We conclude our discussion of the demand structure by a gross approximation of consumers' welfare associated with trade. We define a measure that approximates the utility gained by consumers when they are allowed to buy a product at the ongoing market price. That is, suppose that initially, consumers are prohibited from buying a certain product. Suppose next that the consumers are allowed to buy the product at the ongoing market price. The welfare measure that approximates the welfare gain associated with the opening of this market is what we call *consumer surplus* and we denote it by *CS*.

In what follows we discuss a common procedure used to approximate consumers' gain from buying by focusing the analysis on linear demand functions. Additional motivation for the concept developed in this section is given in the appendix (section 3.3). Figure 3.5 illustrates how to calculate the consumer surplus, assuming that the market price is p.

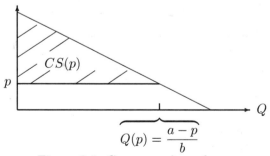

Figure 3.5: Consumers' surplus

For a given market price p, the consumer surplus is defined by the area beneath the demand curve above the market price. Formally, denoting by $CS(p)$ the consumers' surplus when the market price is p, we define

$$CS(p) \equiv \frac{(a-p)Q(p)}{2} = \frac{(a-p)^2}{2b}. \tag{3.3}$$

Note that $CS(p)$ must always increase when the market price is reduced, reflecting the fact that consumers' welfare increases when the market price falls.

In industrial organization theory, and in most partial equilibrium analyses in economics, it is common to use the consumers' surplus as a measure for the consumers' gain from trade, that is, to measure the gains from buying the quantity demanded at a given market price compared with not buying at all. However, the reader should bear in mind that this measure is only an approximation and holds true only if consumers have the so-called quasi-linear utility function analyzed in the appendix (section 3.3).

3.3 Appendix: Consumer Surplus: The Quasi-Linear Utility Case

The analysis performed in this appendix is brought up here only for the sake of completeness; quasi-linear utility is used only once in this book, in section 13.1, where we analyze two-part tariffs. We therefore advise the beginning student to skip this appendix.

In this appendix, we demonstrate that when consumer preferences are characterized by a class of utility functions called *quasi-linear utility function*, the measure of consumer surplus defined in subsection 3.2.3 equals exactly the total utility consumers gain from buying in the market.

Consider a consumer who has preferences for two items: money (m) and the consumption level (Q) of a certain product, which he can buy at a price of p per unit. Specifically, let the consumer's utility function be given by

$$U(Q, m) \equiv \sqrt{Q} + m. \tag{3.4}$$

Now, suppose that the consumer is endowed with a fixed income of I to be spent on the product or to be kept by the consumer. Then, if the consumer buys Q units of this product, he spends pQ on the product and retains an amount of money equals to $m = I - pQ$. Substituting into (3.4), our consumer wishes to choose a product-consumption level Q to maximize

$$\max_Q U(Q, I - pQ) = \sqrt{Q} + I - pQ. \tag{3.5}$$

The first-order condition is given by $0 = \partial U/\partial Q = 1/(2\sqrt{Q}) - p$, and the second order by $\partial^2 U/\partial Q^2 = -1/(4Q^{-3/2}) < 0$, which constitutes a sufficient condition for a maximum.

The first-order condition for a quasi-linear utility maximization yields the inverse demand function derived from this utility function, which is given by

$$p(Q) = \frac{1}{2\sqrt{Q}} = \frac{Q^{-1/2}}{2}. \tag{3.6}$$

Thus, the demand derived from a quasi-linear utility function is a constant elasticity demand function, illustrated earlier in Figure 3.4, and is also drawn in Figure 3.6.

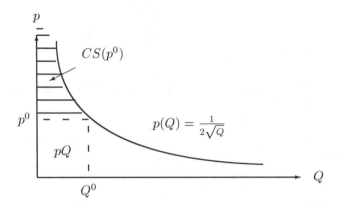

Figure 3.6: Inverse demand generated from a quasi-linear utility function

The shaded area in Figure 3.6 corresponds to what we call consumer surplus in subsection 3.2.3. The purpose of this appendix is to demonstrate the following proposition.

Proposition 3.4 *If a demand function is generated from a quasi-linear utility function, then the area marked by $CS(p)$ in Figure 3.6 measures exactly the utility the consumer gains from consuming Q^0 units of the product at a market price p^0.*

Proof. The area $CS(p)$ in Figure 3.6 is calculated by

$$\begin{aligned} CS(p) \quad &\equiv \quad \int_0^{Q^0} \left(\frac{1}{2\sqrt{Q}}\right) dQ - p^0 Q^0 \tag{3.7}\\ &= \quad \sqrt{Q^0} - p^0 Q^0 = U(Q^0, I - p^0) - I. \end{aligned}$$

$\blacksquare$

3.4   Exercises

1. Consider the Cobb-Douglas production function given by $Q = l^\alpha k^\beta$, where $\alpha, \beta > 0$.

(a) For which values of the parameters α and β does this production technology exhibit IRS, CRS, and DRS?

(b) Using Definition 3.1, infer whether labor and capital are supporting or substitute factors of production.

2. Consider the production function given by $Q = l^{\alpha} + k^{\alpha}$, where $\alpha > 0$.

   (a) For which values of α does this production technology exhibit IRS, CRS, and DRS?

   (b) Using Definition 3.1, infer whether labor and capital are supporting or substitute factors of production.

3. Does the production function given by $Q = l + \sqrt{k}$ exhibit IRS, CRS, or DRS? Prove your answer!

4. Consider the cost function $TC(Q) \equiv F + cQ$, where $F, c > 0$.

   (a) Calculate and plot the $TC(Q)$, $AC(Q)$ and $MC(Q)$.

   (b) At what output level is the average cost minimized?

   (c) Infer whether this technology exhibits IRS, CRS, or DRS. Explain!

5. Consider the demand function $Q = 99 - p$.

   (a) At what output level does the elasticity equal -2 ?

   (b) At what output level does the elasticity equal -1 ?

   (c) Calculate and draw the marginal-revenue function associated with this demand.

   (d) At what output level does the marginal revenue equal zero?

   (e) Calculate the consumers' surplus when $p = 33$ and $p = 66$.

6. Consider the constant-elasticity demand function $Q = Ap^{-\epsilon}$, where $A, \epsilon > 0$.

   (a) Solve for the inverse demand function $p(Q)$.

   (b) Using (3.2), calculate the demand price elasticity.

   (c) For what values of ϵ is the demand elastic? For what values is the demand inelastic?

   (d) Using Proposition 3.3, show that the ratio of the marginal-revenue function to the inverse demand function, $p(Q)/MR(Q)$, is independent of the output level Q.

PART II

Market Structures and Organization

We define *market structure* as a description of the firms' behavior in a given industry or market. The list of items defining firms' behavior include precise specifications of (1) The actions available to each firm, (e.g., choosing a price, setting quantity produced, setting production capacity or location, etc.). (2) The number of firms in the industry, and whether this number is fixed or whether free entry of new firms is allowed. (3) Firms' expectation about the actions available to competing firms, and how the competing firms will respond to each firm's action. (4) Firms' expectation about the number of firms and potential entry. Thus, specifying a market structure is similar to specifying the *rules of the game* or *rules for interaction* among existing or potentially entering new firms. In many cases, specifying a market structure is similar to defining a game according to Definition 2.1 on page 13.

Figure II.1 on page 61 lists most of the market structures used in this book. The top of the tree in Figure II.1 shows that market structures are classified into two categories: competitive and imperfectly competitive. The competitive market structure studied in chapter 4 (and which you have probably studied in your intermediate microeconomic class) assumes that each firm's action set is its production quantity, while each firm takes the market price as given, where the market price is determined by the intersection of the market demand curve and the industry's aggregate supply curve. Competitive market structures can be solved for by assuming either a fixed number of firms (sometimes referred to as *short-run equilibrium*) or free entry (sometimes referred to as a *long-run equilibrium*).

Among the imperfectly competitive market structures, the reader is probably most familiar with the monopoly market structure, which is studied in chapter 5. Under this market structure, there is only one seller, who can choose any price-output combination on the consumers' aggregate demand curve. Given the one-to-one relationship between price and quantity implied by the market demand curve, the monopoly is restricted to choosing a price or a quantity produced but not both. Monopoly market structures can be classified as static, where the monopoly sells its product only once, or dynamic, where the monopoly sells (durable or nondurable goods) over more than one period. Monopoly market structures are then classified into discriminating and nondiscriminating monopolies. A discriminating monopoly can earn a higher profit than a nondiscriminating one by selling the product to different consumers at different prices.

The duopoly (two sellers) and the oligopoly (more than two sellers) market structures are classified as cooperative and noncooperative. Cooperative behavior is defined by firms' colluding by agreeing to produce in total the monopoly's profit-maximizing output level, or to charge the monopoly's price. A noncooperative behavior can be modeled either using one-shot games where all firms choose their strategic variables (quantity produced or price) once and at the same time, or dynamically, where the firms move in sequence. Whether firms move simultaneously, or whether they move in sequence, firms choose either prices (Bertrand) or quantity produced (Cournot).

Finally, one market structure that economists tend to focus on assume that firms are engaged in a repeated interaction of a simultaneous-move oligopoly game. That is, in each period, each firm chooses its action from the same action set after observing what actions have been chosen in earlier periods. The upward arrow in Figure II.1 hints that a fascinating possible outcome of an infinitely repeated oligopoly game is where firms choose to play their collusive (cooperative) actions (output level or price).

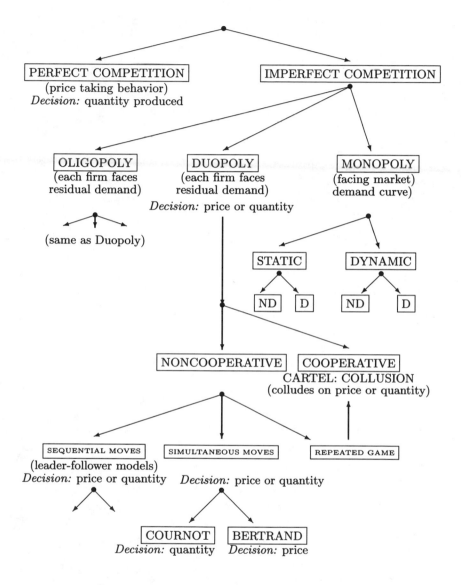

Figure II.1: Commonly assumed and used market structures.
(*Note:* D=discriminating, ND=nondiscriminating)

Chapter 4

Perfect Competition

> In perfect markets, whether monopolistic or competitive, price is hardly a matter of judgment and where there is no judgment there is no policy.
> —Edward S. Mason, "Price and Production Policies of Large-Scale Enterprise"

This chapter describes perfectly competitive markets. We first need to define what do we mean by the term *competitive market,* or equivalently, a *perfectly competitive market.* We define a competitive market (or perfect competition) as a market where agents (buyers and sellers) behave competitively. But, what do we mean by competitive behavior? In economics, the following definition is commonly used for competitive behavior.

DEFINITION 4.1 *A buyer or a seller (agent in what follows) is said to be* **competitive** *(or alternatively, to behave competitively) if the agent assumes or believes that the market price is given and that the agent's actions do not influence the market price.*

Thus, the assumption of competitive behavior relates only to what agents believe about the consequences of their actions. That is, competitive behavior implies that agents think that their actions (say, quantity-produced) will not have any effect on the market price.

It is important to note that the assumption of competitive behavior is independent of how many firms or consumers there are in the market; it relates only to beliefs. More precisely, assuming competitive behavior does not imply that the number of sellers is large. In fact, one of the exercises accompanying this discussion asks you to define and solve for the competitive equilibrium price when there is only one seller in the market. Thus, as long as the agents behave competitively, the competitive equilibrium price can be solved for any number of buyers and sellers.

The common mix-up between the assumption of competitive behavior and the assumption that the number of sellers must be large stems from two reasons: First, the assumption of price-taking behavior seems more reasonable when the number of firms is large, and each firm sells a small amount relative to the aggregate industry sales. Second, the equilibrium price solutions for some imperfectly competitive market structures converge on (get closer to) the competitive price when the number of firms increases. Therefore, when there is a large number of sellers, equilibrium price under various market structures gets closer to the price solved by competitive behavior; nevertheless, the definition of competitive behavior is completely independent of the number of firms.

Suppose that our consumers demand a homogeneous product. Denoting the price of the product by p and the (aggregate) quantity demanded by Q, we assume that consumers' aggregate inverse demand function is linear and is given by

$$p(Q) = a - bQ, \quad \text{where } a, b > 0. \tag{4.1}$$

4.1   Non-Increasing Returns to Scale

Suppose that there are two firms (named firm 1 and firm 2) producing this homogeneous product. We denote by q_i the quantity produced by firm i, and by $TC_i(q_i)$ the total cost function of firm i, $i = 1, 2$. To be more specific, let us assume that the firms have constant returns to scale technologies summarized by linear cost functions given by

$$TC_i(q_i) = c_i q_i, \quad i = 1, 2, \quad \text{where } c_2 \geq c_1 \geq 0. \tag{4.2}$$

The linear cost functions have the property that the marginal cost (the increment in cost due to a small increase in the production level) equals the average cost (cost per unit of production). Formally, c_1 and c_2 are called *constant unit* costs of production if c_i satisfies

$$MC_i(q_i) = \frac{\partial TC_i(q_i)}{\partial q_i} = c_i = \frac{TC_i(q_i)}{q_i} = AC_i(q_i), \quad \text{for every } q_i, \ i = 1, 2. \tag{4.3}$$

In general, constant unit costs are associated with constant-returns-to-scale (CRS) production functions since CRS production functions represent technologies where doubling the inputs would double the output; constant unit costs mean that doubling the output will exactly double the total cost of production.

Observe that in equation (4.2) we assumed with no loss of generality that firm 2 has a higher unit production cost than firm 1 (or an equal one). Figure 4.1 illustrates the demand and the unit costs in the price-output space.

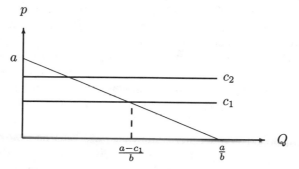

Figure 4.1: Competitive equilibrium under constant returns to scale

Now that the economy is well defined, we define a competitive equilibrium as a vector of quantities produced and a price such that (1) each firm chooses its profit-maximizing output at the given equilibrium price, and (2) at the equilibrium price, aggregate quantity demanded equals aggregate quantity supplied. Formally,

DEFINITION 4.2 *The triplet $\{p^e, q_1^e, q_2^e\}$ is called a* **competitive equilibrium** *if*

1. *given p^e; q_i^e solves*

$$\max_{q_i} \pi_i(q_i) = p^e q_i - TC_i(q_i), \quad i = 1, 2$$

2. *$p^e = a - b(q_1^e + q_2^e);$ $p^e, q_1^e, q_2^e \geq 0.$*

Now that we have defined competitive equilibrium, we seek to solve for this equilibrium for the industry described in (4.1) and (4.2). The first step would be to calculate the supply functions of the two firms, which are found from the profit-maximization procedure defined in part 1 of Definition 4.2.

Lemma 4.1 *The supply functions are given by*

$$q_i = \begin{cases} \infty & \text{if } p > c_i \\ [0, \infty) & \text{if } p = c_i \\ 0 & \text{if } p < c_i \end{cases} \quad i = 1, 2. \tag{4.4}$$

Proof. Since each firm i treats p as a constant, the firm's profit margin defined by $p - c_i$ is constant. Hence, $p - c_i$ is treated by the firm as the constant per-unit profit (loss if negative). Therefore, if $p - c_i > 0$, the firm would produce $q_i = \infty$, and if $p - c_i < 0$, the firm would produce $q_i = 0$, whereas if $p - c_i = 0$, the firm makes a zero profit at every level of production implying that the output level is indeterminate.   ∎

We search for the equilibrium price that would satisfy Definition 4.2. However, observing (4.4) can tell us which prices cannot constitute an equilibrium. More specifically, any price above the unit cost of firm 1 ($p > c_1$) cannot be an equilibrium price, since (4.4) tells us that if $p > c_1$, $q_1 = \infty$; however, the demand function (4.1) tells us that the quantity demanded (at any price) is always finite. Hence, for $p > c_1$ the quantity supplied exceeds the quantity demanded, thereby violating part 2 of Definition 4.2.

Thus, if a competitive equilibrium exists, it must be that $p^e \leq c_1$. However, if $p < c_1 \leq c_2$, the supply functions (4.4) imply that $q_1 = q_2 = 0$; and since the quantity demanded is greater than zero, it exceeds the quantity supplied, thereby violating part 2 of Definition 4.2. Hence,

Proposition 4.1 *If $a > c_2 \geq c_1$, the unique competitive equilibrium price is $p^e = c_1$, and*

1. *if $c_2 > c_1$, $q_2^e = 0$ (firm 2 is not producing) and $q_1^e = \frac{a - c_1}{b}$*

2. *if $c_2 = c_1$, then $Q^e = q_1^e + q_2^e = \frac{a - c_1}{b}$ and $q_1, q_2 \geq 0$. That is, the aggregate industry output level is determined, but the division of the industry output between the firms is indeterminate.*

Finally, let us make three remarks: (a) Observe that if $a < c_1$, (meaning that the demand is low), then neither firm would produce. (b) This model can be easily extended to any number of firms. Clearly in equilibrium, only the firm(s) with the lowest unit cost would produce. (c) Definition 4.2 allows us to impose the competitive market structure even if there is only one firm. For example, if there is only one firm with a unit cost $c \geq 0$, then $p^e = c$ and $q^e = Q^e = \frac{a - c}{b}$ constitute a unique competitive equilibrium.

4.2   Increasing Returns to Scale

The analysis in subsection 4.1 is valid only if firms' technologies exhibit decreasing or constant returns to scale technologies. Suppose now that firms have increasing-returns-to-scale (IRS) technologies. To simplify, we assume that there is only one firm whose total cost of production is composed of a fixed cost (independent of the production level) and a constant marginal cost. Formally, the total cost of producing q units of output is given by

$$TC(q) = \begin{cases} F + cq & \text{if } q > 0 \\ 0 & \text{if } q = 0. \end{cases} \qquad (4.5)$$

Figure 4.2 illustrates the marginal and average-total-cost functions associated with this technology, showing that the average cost decreases and approaches the (constant) marginal cost as the output level increases (since the average fixed cost approaches zero).

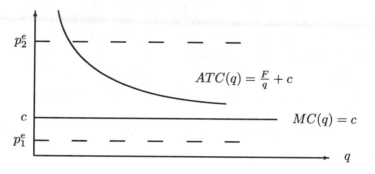

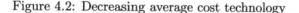

Figure 4.2: Decreasing average cost technology

Our main result is given in the following proposition:

Proposition 4.2 *Let $a > c$. If firms' technologies exhibit increasing returns to scale (decreasing average cost), a competitive equilibrium does not exist.*

Proof. By a way of contradiction, suppose that a competitive equilibrium exists. Then, from Figure 4.2, the equilibrium price has to satisfy one of the following: $p^e \leq c$, or $p^e > c$.

(a) Suppose that $p^e = p_1^e \leq c$. Then, $p_1^e < F/q + c = ATC(q)$ for every $q > 0$. That is, the equilibrium price is below that average cost for all strictly positive output levels. Hence, the firm would produce $q^e = 0$. But, $q^e = 0$ cannot be an equilibrium, since at this price range, the quantity demanded is strictly positive, and excess demand violates part 2 of Definition 4.2.

(b) Now, suppose that $p^e = p_2^e > c$. Then, $p_2^e > F/q + c = ATC(q)$ for q exceeding a certain level. That is, the equilibrium price is above the average cost for sufficiently large output levels. Moreover, the per-unit profit measured by $p_2^e - ATC(q)$ increases with q, implying that the competitive firm produces $q^e = +\infty$. But $q^e = +\infty$ cannot be an equilibrium; the quantity demanded is always finite, and excess supply violates part 2 of Definition 4.2. ∎

4.3   Marginal-Cost Pricing and Social Welfare

In this section we demonstrate a very important feature of the competitive-equilibrium outcome. More precisely, in this section we demonstrate that the perfectly competitive market structure yields a market outcome that maximizes social welfare, to be defined below.

We first wish to define a social welfare function for our economy. In subsection 3.2.3 on page 52 we defined the concept of consumer surplus, denoted by $CS(p)$, and showed that this measure approximates consumers' utility level at a given market price. In order to fully capture the economy's welfare, we also need to take into consideration the fact that firms are owned by our consumers, and therefore we defined social welfare by the sum of consumer surplus and firms' profits. Formally,

DEFINITION 4.3 *Let the market price be given by p, and suppose that there are $N \geq 1$ firms in the industry. We define social welfare by*

$$W(p) \equiv CS(p) + \sum_{i=1}^{N} \pi_i(p).$$

In what follows we show that the perfectly competitive market structure yields a market price that maximizes social welfare as defined in Definition 4.3. Indeed, we are going to prove something more general than that. We will show that when the market price equals the marginal cost of producing firms, then the quantity produced and consumed maximizes social welfare. Now, given that competitive equilibrium results in marginal-cost pricing, it is clear the competitive outcome maximizes welfare. Figure 4.3 illustrates the welfare level for every given market price.

Figure 4.3 illustrates three important areas under the inverse demand curve, if we assume that the market price is $p_0 > 0$. The consumer surplus, defined in subsection 3.2.3, is given by $CS(p_0) = \alpha$. The industry profit is the distance between price and unit cost multiplied by the quantity sold, and is therefore given by $\sum \pi(p_0) = \beta$. By definition, the total welfare is given by $W = \alpha + \beta$.

Figure 4.3 shows that the area marked by γ is not part of measuring welfare. Indeed, the area measured by γ is considered to be the *deadweight loss* associated with higher-than-marginal-cost pricing. The intuition behind the definition of the deadweight loss area is that since the demand function slopes downward, a higher-than-marginal-cost price would reduce the quantity demanded. The consumer surplus loss associated with a lower consumption level cannot be fully captured by a higher profit level (if any) associated with a higher price.

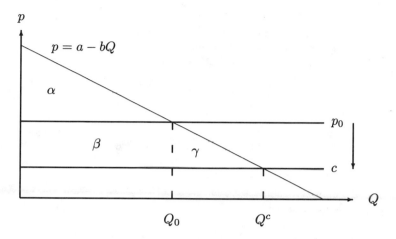

Figure 4.3: Marginal-cost pricing and social welfare: $CS(p) = \alpha$, $\sum \pi_i(p) = \beta$, $W(p) = \alpha + \beta$

Figure 4.3 shows that when the market price is reduced from p_0 to $p = c$, the deadweight-loss area merges into the consumer surplus. In addition, the reduction in industry profit is offset by the increase in consumer surplus. Altogether, social welfare increases with a price reduction as long as price exceeds marginal costs. Finally, notice that we do not discuss cases where market prices are below unit costs $(p < c)$ since when the price is reduced below marginal cost, the increase in firms' loss exceeds the increase in consumer surplus.

4.4 Exercises

The market demand curve for a certain product is given by $Q(p) = 120 - p$, where p is the market price and Q denotes the quantity purchased by the consumers. Suppose that the product is produced with a single factor of production called labor, denoted by L. Assume that each firm i can hire any amount of labor at a fixed given wage rate, denoted by $w > 0$. The production function of each firm i is given by $q_i \equiv \sqrt{L_i}$, where L_i is the amount of labor employed by firm i.

1. Suppose that there is only one firm producing this product; call it firm 1. Solve the firm's profit maximization problem and prove that the firm's supply curve is given by

$$q_1 = \frac{p}{2w}.$$

2. Suppose now that $w = 1$. Using Definition 4.2, solve for the competitive equilibrium price and quantity for this single-firm industry.

3. Calculate the profit of this firm in a competitive equilibrium.

4. Now, suppose that there are two firms, whose output levels are denoted by q_1 and q_2. Solve for the competitive equilibrium price and quantities produced by each firm.

5. Compare the market price and aggregate production when the competitive equilibrium is solved for a single firm and when it is solved for a two-firm industry.

6. Draw the supply curve of each firm, and then plot the aggregate industry-supply curve. Label production on the horizontal axis and price on the vertical axis. Then, draw the industry's demand curve, and graphically solve for the competitive-equilibrium price.

4.5   References

Mason, E. 1939. "Price and Production Policies of Large-Scale Enterprise." *American Economic Review* 29, pt. 2: 61–74.

Chapter 5

The Monopoly

Every person who shall monopolize, or attempt to monopolize, or combine and conspire with any other person or persons, to monopolize any part of the trade or commerce ..., shall be deemed guilty of a felony.
—Sherman Antitrust Act of 1890.

In this chapter we develop a theory of a *single seller* facing competitive (price-taking) consumers in one or several markets, over one or several periods. It is important to fully understand the extreme monopoly case since when few firms compete, the firms can always exercise some monopoly power. In addition, for the sake of simplicity several arguments in this book are demonstrated only for the monopoly case rather than for some other forms of market structures.

A single seller is facing a downward sloping demand curve. Thus, since consumers are always on their demand curve, the monopoly can determine either the price for the product or the quantity supplied. That is, a decision about price implies a decision about quantity produced and vice versa, since quantity and price are related via the demand curve. For this reason, the monopoly needs to devote resources to the careful study of the demand curve facing its product, that is, the monopoly has to familiarize itself with all the demand properties discussed in section 3.2. After estimating the demand curve, the monopoly has to study the market demand to determine its profit-maximizing output.

Section 5.1 presents the familiar monopoly profit-maximization problem for a single market. Section 5.2 (Monopoly and Welfare) reviews the "standard" welfare argument demonstrating the welfare loss associated with a lower-than-optimal production level. Section 5.3 (Discriminating Monopoly) departs from the single-market assumption and analyzes a profit-maximizing monopoly that can charge different prices in different

markets. Section 5.4 (The Cartel and the Multiplant Monopoly) analyzes two forms of collusive contractual arrangements among all the firms
producing in the industry that, together, behave as a monopoly profit-
maximizing entity. Section 5.5 (Durable Good Monopolies) analyzes the
monopoly's behavior over a period of time, where the monopoly sells a
good that provides services for more than one period. The appendix
(section 5.6) discusses the legal antitrust approach to the monopoly and
to price discrimination.

5.1   The Monopoly's Profit-Maximization Problem

The technology of the firm is summarized by its cost function, which
relates the quantity produced to the cost of producing this quantity.
Let $TC(Q)$ denote the total cost function of the monopoly. Denoting by
$\pi(Q)$ the monopoly's profit level when producing Q units of output, the
monopoly chooses Q^m to

$$\max_Q \pi(Q) = TR(Q) - TC(Q).$$

A necessary (but not sufficient) condition for $Q^m > 0$ to be the monopoly's
profit-maximizing output is

$$0 = \frac{d\pi(Q^m)}{dQ} = \frac{dTR(Q^m)}{dQ} - \frac{dTC(Q^m)}{dQ} = MR(Q^m) - MC(Q^m). \quad (5.1)$$

Notice that (5.1) is only a necessary condition, meaning that if the profit-
maximizing output is strictly positive, then it has to satisfy (5.1). However, especially if the monopoly has to pay high fixed costs, it is possible
that the monopoly's profit-maximizing output level is $Q^m = 0$. Altogether, (5.1) implies that if a profit-maximizing monopoly produces
a strictly positive output level Q^m, then the profit output level must
satisfy the condition $MR(Q^m) = MC(Q^m)$.

Thus, the easiest method for finding the monopoly's profit-maximizing
output level is first to solve for Q^m from (5.1), and then to substitute
it into the total profit function to check whether $\pi(Q^m)$ is greater than
or equal to zero. If it is not, then the monopoly sets $Q^m = 0$, and
if profit is nonnegative, then the output level solved from (5.1) is the
profit-maximizing output level.

After finding the monopoly's profit-maximizing output, the price
charged by the monopoly can be found by substituting Q^m into the
demand function. Figure 5.1 illustrates the monopoly solution for the
case where $TC(Q) = F + cQ^2$, and a linear demand function given by
$p(Q) = a - bQ$. Figure 5.1 (left) shows the case where the demand
is high enough (or the fixed cost is low enough) so that the monopoly

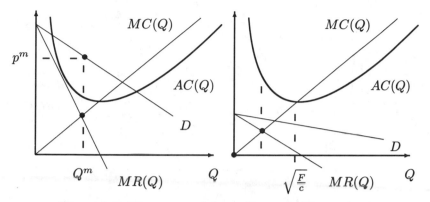

Figure 5.1: The monopoly's profit maximizing output

would produce $Q^m > 0$, and hence would charge a price of p^m. Figure 5.1 (right) illustrates a case where the demand is so low that the monopoly's price cannot cover the average cost. Hence, $Q^m = 0$.

To solve it explicitly, note that by Proposition 3.2 we have it that $MR(Q) = a - 2bQ$. Hence, if $Q^m > 0$, then by (5.1) Q^m solves $a - 2bQ^m = 2cQ^m$, implying that

$$Q^m = \frac{a}{2(b+c)} \text{ and hence } p^m = a - bQ^m = \frac{a(b+2c)}{2(b+c)}.$$

Consequently,

$$\begin{aligned} \pi(Q^m) &\equiv TR(Q^m) - TC(Q^m) \\ &= \frac{a^2(b+2c)}{4(b+c)^2} - F - c\left(\frac{a}{2(b+c)}\right)^2 = \frac{a^2}{4(b+c)} - F. \end{aligned}$$

Altogether, the monopoly's profit-maximizing output is given by

$$Q^m = \begin{cases} \dfrac{a}{2(b+c)} & \text{if } F \le \dfrac{a^2}{4(b+c)} \\ 0 & \text{otherwise .} \end{cases}$$

5.2 Monopoly and Social Welfare

The U.S. legal system discourages monopolies (see the appendix, subsection 5.6.1). In what follows, we provide two arguments for why monopolies are discouraged.

5.2.1 The conventional argument against a monopoly

Figure 5.2 illustrates the conventional argument against monopolies. The monopoly equilibrium (p^m, Q^m) is illustrated in the left side of

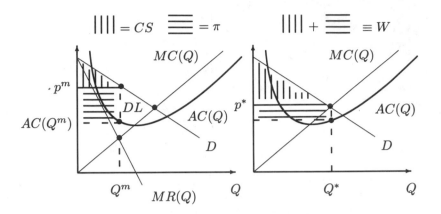

Figure 5.2: Monopoly and social welfare

Figure 5.2, where the area CS measures the consumers' surplus (see subsection 3.2.3). We define the total welfare, W, as the sum of industry profit and consumers' surplus. Formally, $W \equiv \pi + CS$, which is measured by the entire shaded area of the left side of Figure 5.2.

The right side of Figure 5.2 illustrates a welfare-improving case involving marginal-cost pricing associated with perfectly competitive markets (see section 4.3 on page 68). Comparing the monopoly outcome with the marginal-cost pricing outcome reveals that whereas the industry's profit is lower under marginal-cost pricing (possibly zero), the CS is clearly much larger under marginal-cost pricing. That is, the gain to total welfare when the market outcome changes from monopoly to perfect competition is precisely the deadweight-loss area (marked by DL) associated with the monopoly market structure.

5.2.2   The social cost of a monopoly

Posner (1975) argued that the cost to the society associated with the existence of a monopoly is much higher than the deadweight-loss area marked by DL in Figure 5.2. That is, following Tullock (1967), he argued that the pursuit of monopoly rents is itself a competitive activity, and one that consumes resources. This activity was given the term *rent seeking* by Krueger (1974). More precisely, Tullock and Posner argued that the social cost of having a monopoly should also include the costs of deterring competition that are analyzed in section 8.3 and in Section 8.4. The point is that firms, wishing to obtain a monopoly status or wishing to maintaining a monopoly position, must allocate resources for that goal. These resources may or may not be counted as a waste to the economy. Resources allocated to establishing or maintaining monopoly power that should *not* be considered as reducing welfare include:

1. R&D leading to a patent monopoly right for seventeen years (see section 9.4) since the R&D improves technologies and results in new products

2. Bribes to politicians or civil servants for the purpose of getting exclusive business rights (since this constitutes only a transfer of wealth)

Now, resources allocated to the establishment of monopoly power that may count as social waste include:

1. Persuasive advertising (see section 11.1), needed to convince consumers that alternative brands are inferior

2. Resources needed to preempt potential entrants from entering the industry. Also, excessive production or investment in capital for the purpose of making entry unprofitable for potential competitors (see section 8.3)

3. Lobbying costs, needed to convince the legislators that a particular monopoly is not harmful (provided that these costs divert resources from productive activities)

4. Excessive R&D resulting from a patent race

5.3 Discriminating Monopoly

Our analysis so far has focused on monopolies charging a single, uniform price to all customers. A firm can, however, increase its profit by charging different prices to consumers with different characteristics. That is, a firm may be able to differentiate among consumers according to tastes, income, age, and location in order to charge consumers with different characteristics different prices. Note, however, that in order to be able to charge consumers different prices, a firm must possess the means for making arbitrage (buying low for the purpose of reselling at a high price) impossible. In other words, price discrimination is impossible when those consumers who are able to purchase at a low price can make a profit by reselling the product to the consumers who buy at high prices. Thus, firms resort to various marketing techniques to prevent arbitrage from taking place. For example,

1. Firms can charge different prices at different locations. In this case, in order for price discrimination to be sustained, the markets

should be isolated by geography, by prohibitive taxes (such as tariffs), or by prohibitive transportation costs such as those resulting
from product spoilage while being transported from one location
to another.

2. Firms that provide services (such as transportation companies,
restaurants, and places of entertainment) charge senior citizens
lower prices than they charge younger consumers. In this case, for
the price discrimination to be sustained, the firm must demand
that senior citizens present their ID cards.

3. Firms can sell discount tickets to students. In this case, the seller
will ask for a student ID card from those consumers seeking to
purchase at a discount.

4. Book publishers manage to charge institutions higher prices than
they charge individuals by selling hardcovers to institutions and
softcovers to individuals.

In what follows, we do not analyze how the monopoly manages to
segment the markets so that no arbitrage can take place between two
markets with different market prices. The examples given above provide some explanations of how a firm can prevent arbitrage between
two markets. In addition, subsection 14.1.5 demonstrates that a firm
can prevent arbitrage by tying the basic product to some service for
service-demanding consumers while selling it without service to other
consumers. Here, we merely assume that arbitrage cannot take place.

Consider a monopoly selling in two different markets. We assume
that the two markets are isolated in the sense that the monopoly can
charge different prices, and the consumers cannot perform arbitrage by
buying in the low-price market and selling in the high-price market. We
now seek to investigate how a monopoly determines the output level
(hence, the price) in each market. Figure 5.3 illustrates the demand
schedules in the two markets (market 1 and market 2). The left side
of Figure 5.3 illustrates the demand function and the derived-marginal-
revenue function in market 1. The middle figure illustrates the demand
and marginal-revenue functions in market 2. The right side of Figure 5.3
illustrates the aggregate demand facing the monopoly $(D_1 + D_2)$, and
the *horizontal sum* of the marginal-revenue functions $(\sum MR)$.

The monopoly chooses the output levels sold in each market, q_1^m and
q_2^m, that solve

$$\max_{q_1, q_2} \pi(q_1, q_2) = TR_1(q_1) + TR_2(q_2) - TC(q_1 + q_2). \qquad (5.2)$$

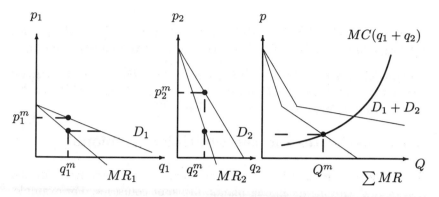

Figure 5.3: Monopoly discriminating between two markets

If the monopoly sells a strictly positive amount in each market, then the following two first-order conditions are satisfied:

$$0 = \frac{\partial \pi(q_1^m, q_2^m)}{\partial q_i} = MR_i(q_i^m) - MC(q_1^m + q_2^m) \quad \text{for each } i = 1, 2. \quad (5.3)$$

Hence, the discriminating monopoly equates $MR_1(q_1^m) = MR_2(q_2^m) = MC(q_1^m + q_2^m)$, when it sells the profit-maximizing output levels in each market.

The intuition behind this condition is as follows: If the monopoly chooses q_1^m and q_2^m such that $MR_1(q_1^m) > MR_2(q_2^m)$, then it is clear that the monopoly should transfer one unit from market 2 to market 1. In this case the reduction in revenue in market 2 is smaller than the increase in revenue in market 1.

To solve for the profit-maximizing output levels q_1^m and q_2^m, we need to solve two equations with the two variables given in (5.3). Instead, we provide a three-step graphical illustration for how to solve this problem. First, note that Figure 5.3 illustrates how the total production level is determined by the intersection of $\sum MR$ with the $MC(q_1^m + q_2^m)$ to determine the aggregate production level $Q^m = q_1^m + q_2^m$. Second, to geometrically find the output level sold in each market, draw a horizontal line from the intersection of $\sum MR_i = MC(Q^m)$ to the MR_1 and MR_2 functions. This determines the amount of output sold in each market (q_1^m and q_2^m). Third, to find the price charged in each market, note that consumers are "always on their demand curves," hence, extend vertical lines from q_1^m and q_2^m to the corresponding demand curves to locate p_1^m and p_2^m.

Finally, to find the relationship between the price charged in each market and the demand elasticities, Proposition 3.3 and equation (5.3) imply that $p_1^m(1 + 1/\eta_1) = p_2^m(1 + 1/\eta_2)$. Hence, $p_2^m > p_1^m$ if $\eta_2 > \eta_1$, (or $|\eta_2| < |\eta_1|$, recalling that elasticity is a negative number). Hence,

Proposition 5.1 *A discriminating monopoly selling a strictly positive amount in each market will charge a higher price at the market with the less elastic demand.*

5.4   The Cartel and the Multiplant Monopoly

The cartel and the multiplant monopoly are forms of organizations and *contractual agreements* among plants, firms, or countries. For example, if we view the oil-producing countries as plants, the cartel is an organization that contracts with the countries on how much each would produce and hence on what would be the world price. Other examples of cartels include the IATA (International Air Transport Association), which regulates airfares, and bar associations, which regulate attorneys.

The *multiplant monopoly* is very similar to the cartel, except that all the plants are put under a single ownership. Multiplant monopoly occurs when several firms in the industry merge together into a single firm (horizontal merger), or when a monopoly firm opens several plants producing the same product.

Thus, unlike the cartel, the multiplant monopoly has the power to decide whether to shut down some of its plants (or whether to open several more). A cartel generally does not shut down plants or countries for the simple legal reason that the cartel does not own the plants, and no plant would join the cartel knowing that it could be shut down.

We assume a linear aggregate demand given by $p = a - bQ$. We now define the technology of each plant. We assume that there are N plants, indexed by i, $(i = 1, 2, \ldots, N)$. Let q_i denote the output level of plant i, and assume that each plant has the technology summarized by the total cost function given by

$$TC_i(q_i) \equiv F + c(q_i)^2, \quad F, c > 0. \tag{5.4}$$

Thus, we assume that all plants have identical cost functions, and that each plant has a fixed (output independent) cost of F. The plant's average and marginal-cost functions are given by $ATC_i(q_i) = F/q_i + cq_i$ and $MC_i(q_i) = 2cq_i$. Figure 5.1 on page 73 illustrates this cost structure, which is common to all plants.

5.4.1   The cartel

The cartel organizes all the N plants by directing each plant to produce a certain amount. The objective is to maximize the sum of the profits of all the N plants. Let $\pi_i(q_i)$ denote the profit of plant i, and let the aggregate cartel output be denoted by Q, $Q \equiv \sum_{i=1}^{N} q_i$. The objective of the cartel is to choose $q_1, q_2, \ldots, q_N$ to

$$\max_{q_1, q_2, \ldots, q_N} \Pi(q_1, q_2, \ldots, q_N) \equiv \sum_{i=1}^{N} \pi_i(q_i) \tag{5.5}$$

$$= \left[a - b \sum_{i=1}^{N} q_i \right] \left(\sum_{i=1}^{N} q_i \right) - \sum_{i=1}^{N} TC_i(q_i).$$

The cartel has to solve for N quantities, so, after some manipulations, the N first-order conditions are given by

$$0 = \frac{\partial \Pi}{\partial q_j} = a - 2b \sum_{i=1}^{N} q_i - MC_j(q_j) = MR(Q) - MC_j(q_j), \quad j = 1, 2, \ldots, N. \tag{5.6}$$

Thus,

Proposition 5.2 *The cartel's profit-maximizing output produced by each plant is found by equating the marginal-revenue function (derived from the market demand curve, evaluated at the aggregate cartel-output level) to the marginal-cost function of each plant.*

Since all plants have identical cost functions, we search for a symmetric equilibrium where the cartel directs each plant to produce the same output level. That is, $q_1 = q_2 = \ldots = q_N \equiv q$. Hence,

$$a - 2bNq = 2cq \quad \text{implying that} \quad q = \frac{a}{2(bN + c)}. \tag{5.7}$$

The total cartel's output and the market price are given by

$$Q = Nq = \frac{Na}{2(bN + c)} \quad \text{and} \quad p = a - bQ = \frac{a(bN + 2c)}{2(bN + c)}. \tag{5.8}$$

Notice that when $N = 1$, the cartel's output and price coincide with the pure monopoly levels. It can be easily verified that as the number of firms in the cartel increases (N increases), both the output level of each firm and the market price fall (q and p decrease). Hence, the total revenue and profit of each firm must fall with an increase in the number of cartel members. For this reason, many professional organizations, such as those of lawyers and accountants, impose restrictions on new candidates who wish to practice in their profession.

5.4.2   The multiplant monopoly

The multiplant monopoly is very similar to the cartel, except that it has the authority (ownership) to shut down some plants, thereby "saving" variable and fixed costs associated with maintaining the plant. Thus, if we suppose that the multiplant monopoly can choose the number of plants, that is, N is a choice variable by the multiplant monopoly owner, then the question is: What is the profit-maximizing number of plants operated by the multiplant monopoly?

The answer is very simple: given that the multiplant monopoly can add or discard plants, the monopoly would seek to adjust the number of plants to minimize the cost per unit of production. In other words, the multiplant monopoly will adjust the number of plants to minimize $ATC(q_i)$ for every plant in operation.

In order to demonstrate how the number of plants is determined, we approximate the number of firms by a real (continuous) number rather than by an integer number. Like the cartel, the multiplant monopoly would equate $MR(Q) = MC_i(q_i)$ for every operating plant (yielding output levels given in (5.7) equal to $q_i = \frac{a}{2(bN+c)}$), and in addition, will adjust N so that each operating plant would operate at minimum $ATC_i(q_i)$, given by $q_i = \sqrt{F/c}$. Hence, equating $\sqrt{F/c} = \frac{a}{2(bN+c)}$ and solving for N yields that the profit-maximizing number of plants is

$$N^m = \frac{a\sqrt{c}}{2b\sqrt{F}} - \frac{c}{b}.$$

Thus, the multiplant monopoly's profit-maximizing number of plants increases with an increase in the demand parameter a, and decreases with the fixed cost parameter of each plant F.

5.5   Durable-Goods Monopolies

Our analysis so far has focused on one type of goods called *flow goods*. By flow goods we mean goods that are purchased repeatedly and that perish after usage, for example, food products such as apples and bananas, and many plastic and paper single-use products. In contrast, *durable goods* are bought only once in a long time and can be used for long time, for example, cars, houses, and land. Clearly, with the exception of land, all goods eventually perish, so these two concepts are relative to a certain time horizon that is relevant to consumers.

Coase (1972) first pointed out that a monopoly selling a durable good will behave differently from the (familiar) monopoly selling a perishable good analyzed earlier in this chapter. Coase considered the extreme case of a person who owns all the land in the world, and wants to sell it at the largest discounted profit. Clearly, Coase chose to analyze land because it is definitely a good example of a durable good. If land were perishable, then our analysis implies that the monopoly would not sell all the land. That is, the monopoly would restrict output (land) and raise the price high enough so that not all the land would be sold.

Now, suppose that the monopoly charges the monopoly price and sells half of its land by the end of this year. Let us try to predict what will happen next year. Well, the monopoly still owns the remainder of the world's land, and there is no reason why the monopoly will not offer that land for sale next year. However, it is clear that next year (if population is not growing very fast) the demand for land will be lower than the demand for land this year. Thus, the monopoly land price next year will be lower than the monopoly price this year.

Given that the monopoly's next-year price will be (substantially) lower than the monopoly land price this year, it is clear that those consumers who do not discount time too heavily would postpone buying land until next year. Hence, the current demand facing the monopoly falls, implying that the monopoly will charge a lower price than what a monopoly selling a perishable would charge.

Coase's discussion of durable goods monopolies was formalized in Bagnoli, Salant, and Swierzbinski 1989; Bulow 1982, 1986; Gul, Sonnenschein, and Wilson 1986; and Stokey 1981. In what follows, we provide two simple but rigorous analyses of durable-goods monopolies. Subsection 5.5.1 demonstrates Coase's conjecture in an example for a downward sloping demand curve. Subsection 5.5.2 provides an example for a discrete demand in which there is a finite number of consumers, each buys, at most, one unit of a durable good, and demonstrates that Coase's analysis is false under this demand structure.

5.5.1 Durable-good monopoly facing a downward sloping demand

Suppose there is a continuum of consumers having different valuations for the annual services of a car that are summarized by the familiar downward sloping demand curve. Suppose that consumers live for two periods denoted by t, $t = 1, 2$, and that a monopoly sells a durable product that lasts for two periods. Thus, if a consumer purchases the product, she will have it for her entire life, and she will not have to replace it ever again. The consumers have different valuations for the product summarized by the aggregate period $t = 1$ inverse demand function for one period of service given by $p = 100 - Q$ and illustrated in Figure 5.4 (left). Figure 5.4 assumes that in period 1 there is a continuum of consumers, each having a different valuation for purchasing

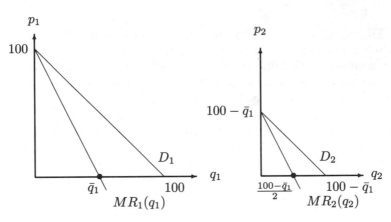

Figure 5.4: Durable-good monopoly: the case of downward sloping demand

one unit of the product. Altogether, they form a downward sloping demand illustrated in Figure 5.4 (left).

In the following two subsubsections, we compare the monopoly's profit under two types of commercial transactions: selling and renting. To formally distinguish between selling and renting we state the following definition.

DEFINITION 5.1

1. *By* **selling** *a product to a consumer, for a price of p^S, the firm transfers all rights of ownership for using the product and getting the product back from the consumer, from the time of purchase extended indefinitely.*

2. *By* **renting** *a product to a consumer, for a price of p^R, the renter maintains ownership of the product, but contracts with the consumer to allow the consumer to derive services from the product for a given period specified in the renting contract.*

Thus, selling means charging a single price for an indefinite period, whereas renting means charging a price for using the product for a specific, limited time period. It should be emphasized that Definition 5.1 does not imply that by selling, the manufacturer always transfers all rights on the product sold. For example, even when a product is sold (rather than rented) the new owner does not have the rights to produce identical or similar products if the product is under patent protection.

A renting monopoly

Assume that each period the monopoly rents a durable product for one period only. For example, a common practice of firms in several industries, in particular in the car industry, is to lease a car for a given time period rather than sell the car. Although there could be several explanations (taxes, etc.) why such a trade benefits firms and consumers, in this subsection we prove that leasing would yield a higher profit than selling. Suppose that in each of the two periods the monopoly faces the demand drawn in Figure 5.4 (left).

Assuming zero production cost, we recall from section 5.1 that the monopoly would rent an amount determined by the condition $MR(Q_t) = 100 - 2Q_t = 0 = MC(Q_t)$, implying that $Q_t^R = 50$ and $p_t^R = 50$, and $\pi_t^R = 2,500$ for $t = 1, 2$. Hence, the life-time sum of profits of the renting monopoly is given by $\pi^R = 5,000$.

A seller monopoly

A seller monopoly knows that those consumers who purchase the durable good in $t = 1$ will not repurchase in period $t = 2$. That is, in $t = 2$ the monopoly will face a demand for its product that is lower than the period 1 demand by exactly the amount it sold in $t = 1$. Therefore, in period 2 the monopoly will have to sell at a lower price resulting from a lower demand, caused by its own earlier sales.

Formally, we define this two-period game as follows: The payoff to the monopoly is the total revenue generated by period 1 and period 2 sales. The strategies of the seller are the prices set in period 1, p_1, and the price set in period 2 as a function of the amount purchased in period 1, $p_2(\bar{q}_1)$. The strategies of the buyers are to buy or not to buy as a function of first period price, and to buy or not to buy as a function of second period price. We look for a SPE for this simple game (see Definition 2.9 on page 26). The methodology for solving this finite horizon game is to solve it backwards—to determine how the monopolist would behave in period 2 for each possible set of buyers remaining then.

The second period

Figure 5.4 (right) shows the (residual) demand facing the monopoly in period 2 after it has sold $\bar{q}_1$ units in period 1, given by $q_2 = 100 - \bar{q}_1 - p_2$ or $p_2 = 100 - \bar{q}_1 - q_2$. Since production was assumed to be costless, in the second-period the monopoly sets $MR_2(q_2) = 100 - \bar{q}_1 - 2q_2 = 0$ implying that $q_2 = 50 - \bar{q}_1/2$. Hence, the second period price and profit levels are given by $p_2 = 100 - \bar{q}_1 - (50 - \bar{q}_1/2) = 50 - \bar{q}_1/2$, and $\pi_2 = p_2 q_2 = (50 - \bar{q}_1/2)^2$.

The first period

Suppose that the monopolist sells in the first period to $\bar{q}_1$ buyers with the highest reservation prices. Then, the marginal buyer, with a reservation price $100 - \bar{q}_1$, will be indifferent between purchasing in the first period (gaining utility of $2(100 - \bar{q}_1) - p_1$) and buying in the second period (gaining utility of $(100 - \bar{q}_1) - p_2 = (100 - \bar{q}_1) - (50 - \bar{q}_1/2)$. Thus,

$$2(100 - \bar{q}_1) - p_1 = (100 - \bar{q}_1) - (50 - \bar{q}_1/2). \tag{5.9}$$

Solving (5.9) for p_1 yields

$$p_1 = 150 - \frac{3\bar{q}_1}{2}. \tag{5.10}$$

Let us note that equation (5.10) can also be derived by observing that the first-period price should include the second-period price in addition to pricing the first-period services because buying in the first period yields services for the two periods, hence, the product can be resold in the second period for a price of p_2. Therefore,

$$p_1 = 100 - \bar{q}_1 + p_2 = 100 - \bar{q}_1 + 50 - \frac{\bar{q}_1}{2} = 150 - \frac{3\bar{q}_1}{2},$$

which is identical to (5.10).

In a SPE the selling monopoly chooses a first-period output level $\bar{q}_1$ that solves

$$\max_{q_1}(\pi_1 + \pi_2) = \left(150 - \frac{3q_1}{2}\right) q_1 + \left(50 - \frac{q_1}{2}\right)^2 \tag{5.11}$$

yielding a first-order condition given by

$$0 = \frac{\partial(\pi_1 + \pi_2)}{\partial q_1} = 150 - 3q_1 - \frac{100 - q_1}{2} = 100 - \frac{5q_1}{2}.$$

Denoting the solution values by a superscript S, we have that $q_1^S = 40$, $q_2^S = 50 - 40/2 = 30$, $p_2^S = 50 - 40/2 = 30$ and $p_1^S = 100 - 40 + 30 = 90$. Hence,

$$\Pi^S = p_1^S q_1^S + p_2^S q_2^S = 4,500 < 5,000 = \Pi^{pm}.$$

Therefore,

Proposition 5.3 *A monopoly selling a durable goods earns a lower profit than a renting monopoly.*

The intuition behind Proposition 5.3 is that rational consumers are able to calculate that a selling-durable-good monopoly would lower future

prices due to future fall in the demand resulting from having some consumers purchasing the durable product in earlier periods. This calculation reduces the willingness of consumers to pay high prices in the
first period the monopoly offers the product for sale. In other words,
since the monopoly cannot commit itself not to reduce future prices, the
monopoly is induced to lower its first-period price.

An argument such as Proposition 5.3 led some economists to claim
that monopolies have the incentives to produce less than an optimal
level of durability (e.g., light bulbs that burn very fast). We discuss the
(in)validity of this argument in section 12.3.

5.5.2   Durable-good monopoly facing a discrete demand

The analysis of subsection 5.5.1 has confined itself to a demand curve
with a continuum of nonatomic buyers. Following Bagnoli, Salant, and
Swierzbinski (1989), we now provide an example which demonstrates
that Coase's Conjecture is false when the number of consumers is finite.

Let us consider an economy with two consumers living only for two
periods. Both consumers desire car services for the two periods of their
lives, however, the consumers differ in their willingness to pay for car
services. The maximum amount a consumer denoted by H is willing to
pay for one period of car service is V^H, and the maximum amount a
consumer denoted by L is willing to pay for one period of car service
is V^L. We assume that the consumers' willingness to pay per period of
car service are substantially different.

ASSUMPTION 5.1 *Type H consumers are willing to pay more than twice
as much for a period of car service as type L consumers. Formally,
$V^H > 2V^L > 0$.*

Figure 5.5 (left) illustrates the aggregate inverse demand function for
one period of service facing the monopoly each period.

Because the product is durable, consumers buy it once in their life
either at $t = 1$ or $t = 2$. The utility functions for consumers type
$i = H, L$ that yield the demand structure illustrated in Figure 5.5 are
given by

$$U^i \equiv \begin{cases} 2V^i - p_1 & \text{if he buys a car in period 1} \\ V^i - p_2 & \text{if he buys a car in period 2} \\ 0 & \text{if he does not buy a car in any period.} \end{cases} \quad (5.12)$$

Thus, if consumer i, $i = H, L$, buys a car in the first period, he gains a
benefit of $2V^i$ since the car provides services for two periods, and he pays
whatever the monopoly charges in $t = 1$. In contrast, if the consumer

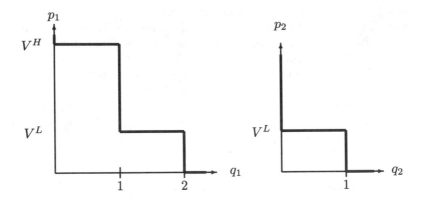

Figure 5.5: Durable-good monopoly: the case of discrete demand

waits and purchases the car in $t = 2$, he gains only one period of utility of V^i minus the price charged in period 2.

On the production side, we assume that there is only one firm producing cars, at zero cost. Like the consumers, the monopoly firm lives for two periods and maximizes the sum of profits from the sales during the two periods. We denote by q_t the amount produced and sold by the monopoly, and by p_t the period t price of a car set by the monopoly in period t, $t = 1, 2$.

The monopoly chooses p_1 and p_2 to maximize the sum of revenue from two periods worth of sales given by $\pi \equiv p_1 q_1 + p_2 q_2$. Note that we have implicitly assumed that buyers and the monopoly do not discount future utility and profit, since assuming otherwise would not have a qualitative effect on the results.

A renting monopoly

Suppose now that the monopoly firm does not sell cars, but instead rents cars for one period only. Thus, each consumer who rents a car in $t = 1$, has to return the car at the end of the first period and rent it again in the second period. We denote by p_t^R the rental price for one period of renting in period t.

Since car rentals last for one period only, it is sufficient to calculate the price for each period separately. Since the renting firm is a monopoly, it has two options: (1) setting $p_t^R = V^H$, which by (5.12) induces only consumer H to rent a car each period, while consumer L will not rent; (2) setting $p_t^R = V^L$, which induces both consumers to rent a car each period. In the first case, the two-period profit is $\pi^R = 2V^H$, and in the second case, $\pi^R = 4V^L$. However, by Assumption 5.1, $V^H > 2V^L$. Hence,

Proposition 5.4 *A renting monopoly would rent cars only to the high-valuation consumer by setting a rental price equal to $p_t^R = V^H$, $t = 1, 2$; and it will earn a two-period profit of $\pi^R = 2V^H$.*

A seller monopoly

Now, suppose that the monopoly sells the cars to consumers. We denote the selling prices by p_t^S, $t = 1, 2$. By Definition 5.1, the period 1 selling price, p_1^S, means that the consumer pays for two periods of using the car (compared with the renting price p_1^R that entitles the consumer to use the car for period 1 only).

The second period

The effect of selling in the first period on the second period demand is illustrated in Figure 5.5 (right). If consumer H purchases in period 1, only consumer L demands a car in the second period. If consumer H does not purchase in the first period, then the second period demand is the given rental demand curve (Figure 5.5 (left)). The lower part of Figure 5.6 illustrates the subgames associated with consumer H's decision whether to purchase in the first period.

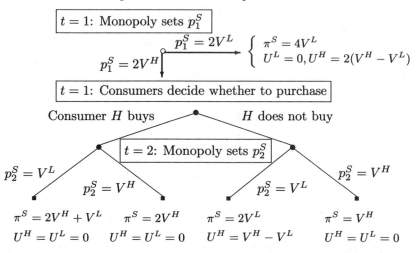

Figure 5.6: Two-period game of a durable-good monopoly facing discrete demand.

Figure 5.6 illustrates that when consumer H buys in the first period, the monopoly will maximize second period profit by setting $p_2^S = V^L$

and will earn a second period profit of $\pi_2 = V^L$ (the monopoly will extract all surplus from consumer L).

If consumer H does not buy in period 1, then in the second period the monopoly faces the entire demand, hence, by Assumption 5.1, the monopoly charges $p_2^S = V^H$ (selling only to consumer H) yielding a second period profit of $\pi_2 = V^H$.

The first period

In the first period, the monopoly sets p_1^S, and consumers decide whether to purchase or not. Figure 5.6 illustrates the sequence of moves in the two periods.

Since consumer L knows that the price in the last period will never fall below V^L, consumer L will buy in the first period at any price below $2V^L$. Hence, if the seller sets $p_1^S = 2V^L$ both consumers would purchase initially. To simplify the game tree, we report in Figure 5.6 the payoffs to the three players if the monopoly sets this low price.

Clearly, the monopoly will not set $p_1^S > 2V^H$ because this price exceeds the two period sum of consumer H's valuation. Therefore, we now check whether $p_1^S = 2V^H$ is the profit maximizing first period price for the seller monopoly. From the second period analysis we conclude that consumer H earns a utility of zero ($U^H = 0$) whether or not he buys the product in the first period. Hence, buying the product is an optimal response for consumer H to the first period price $p_1^S = 2V^H$. Thus, in a SPE (see Definition 2.10 on page 27), $p_1^S = 2V^H$, consumer H buys in period 1, $p_2^S = V^L$, and consumer L buys in period 2, constitute a SPE equilibrium path for this game. Hence, in contrast to Proposition 5.3, we now state our main proposition, which demonstrates that Coase's conjecture is false under discrete demand.

Proposition 5.5 *A durable-good selling monopoly facing a discrete demand will*

1. *charge a first period selling price that is equal to the sum of the per-period rental prices, $p_1^S = 2p_t^R$;*

2. *earn a higher profit than the renting monopoly;*
   that is, $\pi^S = 2V^H + V^L > 2V^H = \pi^R$.

Thus, in the case of discrete demand, a selling monopoly can extract a higher surplus from consumers than the renting monopoly. Coase conjectured that the ability of a durable-good monopoly to extract consumer surplus is reduced when the monopoly is forced to sell rather than rent. Here, we demonstrated the opposite case, where selling enables the monopoly to price discriminate among different consumers by setting prices which would induce different consumers to purchase at different time periods.

5.6 Appendix: The Legal Approach to Monopoly and Price Discrimination

5.6.1 Antitrust law and the monopoly

Section 2 of the Sherman Act of 1890 states that

> Every person who shall monopolize, or attempt to monopolize, or combine and conspire with any other person or persons, to monopolize any part of the trade or commerce among several States, or with foreign nations, shall be deemed guilty of a felony.

At first glance, it seems that section 2 makes it clear that a monopoly is illegal, but a closer look reveals that the act does not provide the court with any guidelines that define what degree of market power or market concentration constitutes a monopoly. Therefore, in practice, courts tend to focus on abuses of monopoly power in a concentrated market and on the intent of the monopoly to keep its position; monopoly status alone is not illegal.

Anticompetitive activities such as predatory pricing have to be established to turn a monopoly into an illegal practice. To establish illegal activities, the court first defines the product and the geographic market. Second, the court considers the market share of the accused firm. Third, the court considers the ease of entry, availability of secondhand and new substitutes, and whether the accused has the ability to raise prices. Defining the product is basically deciding which products should be considered as close substitutes. Defining the geographic market should consider the magnitude of transportation costs, which in many cases are insignificant, thereby leading the court to define the entire nation as the geographic market. When these tests are unclear, the court resorts to a hypothetical question: In a particular geographic market, can the accused firm raise the price without attracting competition? If the answer is positive, then the market is well defined. During the years courts have added a *refusal to deal,* when a manufacturer refuses to sell to dealers for the purpose of establishing a monopoly power on all distribution channels, as an abuse of monopoly power.

5.6.2 Antitrust law and cartels

Cartels may involve price fixing, output controls, bid rigging, allocation of consumers, allocation of sales by product or territory, establishment of trade practices, or common sales agencies (Weiss 1987). Cartels have existed as guilds in the Europe of the Middle Ages, and were common in most European countries throughout the nineteen century and the first third of the present century. The Sherman Act of 1890 made cartel illegal. Exceptions were made during the Great Depression, and for some special quasi-public industries such as agriculture, coal, civil aviation, and oil refining.

Section 1 of the Sherman Act 1890 states that

> Every contract, combination in the form of a trust or otherwise, or conspiracy, in restraint of trade or commerce among the several States, or with foreign nations, is declared to be illegal.

Clearly, the most severe and most common cartel contract is a price-fixing contract. Firms that are found guilty of price fixing are subject to treble-damage penalties. Recently, several authors raised the question of whether treble-damage penalty would result in market-price reduction or market-price increase. Salant (1987) showed that treble-damage penalty can increase the market price above the price that would be charged by a cartel without the enforcement of this antitrust law.

Earlier court cases interpreted section 1 to mean that every contract constituted a restraint of trade, thereby leading courts to rule on a per se basis, defined in subsection 1.2.2 on page 6 of this book. That is, every price fixing was illegal. In some later cases, courts considered some price-fixing arrangements under the rule of reason. However, courts began learning that any judgment under the rule of reason involves tremendous administrative costs, since it is not clear what a reasonable price is, and it is hard to measure marginal-cost functions to determine whether the price is fixed with a high markup. It was also clear that prices should often fluctuate with cost variations, something that may not occur in the presence of price fixing. Hence, courts began judging price fixing under the per se rule. The logic was that if price-fixing agreements do not have an effect on prices, then these agreements would not be formed. Thus, price-fixing agreements should be illegal per se. The per se rule was also applied to other forms of contracts, such as market allocations.

Finally, one advantage of the per se rule is that it warns the firms in advance about the consequences (generally, treble damages) associated with price-fixing agreements, whereas the rule of reason may leave some doubts whether, with a good defense, a cartel can survive section 1 in a lawsuit.

To summarize, we can say that the major effect of section 1 of the Sherman Act is rather noticeable: The act indeed eliminated major cartels from American markets. Most noticeable cartels nowadays for example, OPEC and IATA, are international, and cannot be challenged for rather visible price-fixing agreements.

5.6.3 Antitrust law and price discrimination

Section 2 of the Clayton Act of 1914 amended by the Robinson-Patman Act of 1936, states that

> It shall be unlawful for any person engaged in commerce, in the course of such commerce, either directly or indirectly, to discriminate in price between different purchasers of commodities of like grade and quality, ... where the effect of such discrimination may be substantially to lessen competition or tend to create a monopoly in any line of commerce, or to injure, destroy, or prevent competition with any person who either grants or knowingly receives the benefit of such discrimination, or with the consumers of either of them: Provided, That nothing herein contained shall prevent differentials who make only due allowance for differences in the cost of manufacture, sale, or delivery.

Thus, section 2 explicitly states that price discrimination should not be considered illegal (a) unless price discrimination substantially decreases competition, and (b) if price differences result from differences in production or delivery costs. Thus, the coupons appearing in the Sunday newspapers offering a price reduction upon the presentation of a piece of paper is a good example of price discrimination between people with a high value on time and a low value on time; however, there is nothing illegal in using coupons for providing discounts.

The Robinson-Patman Act of 1936 came during the Great Depression and was intended to strike against large, chain grocery stores that engaged in local price cutting to deter competition. Note that at that time the legislators were not concerned whether price discrimination and price cutting are efficient. In fact, Varian (1989) shows conditions under which the act of price discrimination is welfare improving, compared with a uniform price mechanism. Also, note that the GATT (General Agreement on Tariff and Trade) enacted a rule similar to the one enacted in Robinson-Patman stating that dumping (selling below cost in a foreign country) is illegal. However, it has never been theoretically established that dumping reduces welfare, and it is possible to demonstrate that dumping can actually improve social welfare.

Altogether, it is not clear whether price discrimination has anything to do with anticompetitive behavior, and in fact, price discrimination can actually be procompetitive. Bork (1978) warns against possible damages inflicted by this act by conjecturing that there may be hundreds of thousands of pricing decisions every year that are altered through fear of the Robinson-Patman Act, meaning that hundreds of thousands of quantity discounts and promotional discounts are foregone at the expense of having consumers paying higher prices. However, during the years following this act, the FTC rarely enforced this law, thereby making price differences more observable.

5.7   Exercises

1. Consider a monopoly selling at a single market where the demand is given by $Q(p) \equiv ap^{-\epsilon}$, $\epsilon > 1$. Suppose that the cost function of this monopoly is given by $TC(Q) \equiv cQ$, $c > 0$.

   (a) Calculate the demand elasticity, and, using Proposition 3.3, write down the marginal-revenue function as a function of price.

   (b) Using your above calculation, find the price charged by the monopoly as a function of ϵ.

   (c) What happens to the monopoly's price when ϵ increases. Interpret your result.

   (d) What happens to the monopoly's price as $\epsilon \to 1$? Explain!

   (e) Calculate the total-revenue function $TR(Q)$ and the marginal-revenue function $MR(Q)$.

   (f) What is the monopoly's profit-maximizing output?

2. Consider the market for the G-Jeans (the latest fashion among people in their late thirties). G-Jeans are sold by a single firm that carries the patent for the design. On the demand side, there are $n^H > 0$ high-income consumers who are willing to pay a maximum amount of V^H for a pair of G-Jeans, and $n^L > 0$ low-income consumers who are willing to pay a maximum amount of V^L for a pair of G-Jeans. Assume that $V^H > V^L > 0$, and that each consumer buys only one pair of jeans.

   Suppose that the G-Jeans monopoly cannot price discriminate and is therefore constrained to set a uniform market price.

   (a) Draw the market aggregate-demand curve facing the monopoly.

   (b) Find the profit-maximizing price set by G-Jeans, considering all possible parameter values of n^H, n^L, V^H, and V^L. Assume that production is costless.

3. Suppose that a monopoly can price discriminate between two markets: market 1, where the demand curve is given by $q_1 \equiv 2 - p_1$, and market ,2 where the demand curve is given by $q_2 = 4 - p_2$. Suppose that once the product is sold, it cannot be resold in the other market. That is, assume that arbitrage is impossible, say, due to strict custom inspections on the border between the two markets. Assume that the monopoly produces each unit at a cost of $c = 1$.

(a) Calculate the profit-maximizing output level that the monopoly sells in each market. Calculate the price charged in each market.

(b) Calculate the monopoly's profit level.

(c) Suppose that markets 1 and 2 are now open, and all consumers are free to trade and to transfer the good costlessly between the markets. Thus, the monopoly can no longer price discriminate and has to charge a uniform price denoted by p, $p = p_1 = p_2$. Find the profit-maximizing value of p.

4. A discriminating monopoly sells in two markets. Assume that no arbitrage is possible. The demand curve in market 1 is given by $p_1 = 100 - q_1/2$. The demand curve in market 2 is given by $p_2 = 100 - q_2$. We denote the monopoly's aggregate production by Q where $Q \equiv q_1 + q_2$. The monopoly's cost function depends on total production and is given by $TC(Q) = Q^2$. Answer the following questions:

(a) Formulate the monopoly's profit function as a function of q_1 and q_2.

(b) Calculate the monopoly's profit-maximizing quantity sold in market 1 and market 2.

(c) Calculate the profit level of the discriminating monopoly.

(d) Suppose now that a new management assumed control of this firm. The young CEO decides to decompose the monopoly plant into two plants, where plant 1 sells in market 1 only and plant 2 sells in market 2 only. Calculate the profit-maximizing output level sold by each plant.

(e) Calculate the sum of profits of the two plants.

(f) Conclude whether this plant decomposition increases or decreases profit. Explain your answer by investigating whether the above technology exhibits increasing or decreasing returns to scale (Consult Definition 3.2 on page 45).

5. The demand elasticity in market 1 is measured to be $\eta_1 = -2$. The demand elasticity in market 2 is measured to be $\eta_2 = -4$. Suppose that a monopoly that can price discriminate between the markets sets the price p_1 in market 1, and p_2 in market 2. Prove whether the following statement is right or wrong: "The price in market 1, p_1, will be 150% the price in market 2, p_2 (i.e., 50% higher)."

6. In a two-period lived economy, one consumer wishes to buy a TV set in period 1. The consumer lives for two periods, and is willing to pay a maximum price of $100 per period of TV usage. In period 2, two consumers (who live in period 2 only) are born. Each of the newly born consumers is willing to pay a maximum of fifty dollars for using a TV in period 2. Suppose that in this market there is only one firm producing TV sets, that TV sets are durable, and that production is costless.

(a) Calculate the prices the monopoly charges for TV sets in periods 1 and 2.

(b) Answer the previous question assuming that in the first period, a consumer who lives two periods is willing to pay no more than twenty dollars per period for TV usage.

7. A monopoly is facing a downward sloping linear demand curve given by $p = a - Q$. The monopoly's unit production cost is given by $c > 0$. Now, suppose that the government imposes a specific tax of t dollars per unit on each unit of output sold to consumers.

(a) Show that this tax imposition would raise the price paid by consumers by less than t. *Hint:* One way to find the monopoly's profit-maximizing output level is to solve the equation $MR(Q) = c + t$, and then to solve for consumer and producer prices.

(b) Would your answer change if the market demand curve has a constant elasticity and is given by $p = Q^{-\frac{1}{2}}$?

5.8   References

Bagnoli, M., S. Salant, and J. Swierzbinski. 1989. "Durable-Goods Monopoly with Discrete Demand." *Journal of Political Economy* 97: 1459–1478.

Bork, R. 1978. *The Antitrust Paradox.* New York: Basic Books.

Bulow, J. 1982. "Durable Goods Monopolists." *Journal of Political Economy* 15: 314–32.

Bulow, J. 1986. "An Economic Theory of Planned Obsolescence." *Quarterly Journal of Economics* 51: 729–748.

Coase, R. 1972. "Durable Goods Monopolists." *Journal of Law and Economics* 15: 143–150.

Gellhorn, E. 1986. *Antitrust Law and Economics in a Nutshell.* St. Paul, Minn.: West Publishing.

Gul, F., H. Sonnenschein, and R. Wilson. 1986. "Foundations of Dynamic Monopoly and the Coase Conjecture." *Journal of Economic Theory* 39: 155–190.

Krueger, A. 1974. "The Political Economy of the Rent-Seeking Society." *American Economic Review* 64: 291–303.

Posner, R. 1975. "The Social Costs of Monopoly and Regulation." *Journal of Political Economy* 83: 807–827.

Salant, S. 1987. "Treble Damage Awards in Private Lawsuits for Price Fixing." *Journal of Political Economy* 95: 1326–1336.

Stokey, N. 1981. "Rational Expectations and Durable Goods Pricing." *Bell Journal of Economics* 12: 112–128.

Tullock, G. 1967. "The Welfare Costs of Tariffs, Monopolies, and Theft." *Western Economic Journal* 5: 224–232.

Varian, H. 1989. "Price Discrimination." In *Handbook of Industrial Organization,* edited by R. Schmalensee, and R. Willig. Amsterdam: North-Holland.

Weiss, L. 1987. "Cartel." In *The New Palgrave Dictionary of Economics,* edited by J. Eatwell, M. Milgate, and P. Newman. New York: The Stockton Press.

Chapter 6

Markets for Homogeneous Products

> Only theory can separate the competitive from the anticompetitive.
> —Robert Bork, *The Antitrust Paradox*

In this chapter we analyze the behavior of firms and consumer welfare under several oligopolistic market structures. The main assumption in this chapter is that the products are *homogeneous,* meaning that consumers cannot differentiate among brands or distinguish among the producers when purchasing a specific product. More precisely, consumers cannot (or just do not bother) to read the label with the producer's name on the product they buy. For example, non-brand-name products sold in most supermarkets—bulk fruit, vegetables, containers of grain—are generally purchased without having consumers learning the producer's name.

In what follows, we assume that consumers are always price takers (henceforth, competitive) and have a well-defined aggregate-demand function. However, firms behave according to the assumed market structures analyzed below.

Our oligopoly analysis starts with section 6.1 (Cournot), which assumes that firms set their output levels simultaneously, believing that the output levels of their rival firms remain unchanged. Historically, as we discuss below, Cournot was the first to provide this modern treatment of oligopoly equilibrium. Section 6.2 (Sequential Moves) modifies the static Cournot setup, by assuming that firms move in sequence, and analyzes whether a firm benefits by setting its output level before any other one does. Following Bertrand's criticism of the use of quantity produced as the actions chosen by firms, section 6.3 (Bertrand) analyzes a market structure where firms set their prices by assuming that the prices of their rival firms remain unchanged. We then discuss how the extreme result of price games leading to competitive prices obtained under the Bertrand competition can be mitigated by introducing capacity constraints. Section 6.4 (Cournot Versus Bertrand) analyzes the relationship between the Cournot and the Bertrand market structures. Section 6.5 (Self-Enforcing Collusion) analyzes the conditions under which firms can maintain higher prices and lower output levels compared with the Cournot levels, assuming that the firms interact infinitely many times. Section 6.6 (International Trade) analyzes international markets in homogeneous products.

6.1   Cournot Market Structure

Noncooperative oligopoly theory started with Antoine Augustin Cournot's book, *Researches into the Mathematical Principles of the Theory of Wealth,* published in France in 1838. In that book, Cournot proposed an oligopoly-analysis method that we today view as identical to finding a Nash equilibrium in a game where firms use their production levels as strategies. Cournot earned his doctorate in science in 1821, with a main thesis in mechanics and astronomy. Cournot's writings extended beyond economics to mathematics and philosophy of science and philosophy of history (see Shubik 1987).

Cournot was central to the founding of modern mathematical economics. For the case of monopoly, the familiar condition where marginal revenue equals marginal cost come directly from Cournot's work (Shubik 1987). In chapter 7 of his book, Cournot employs the inverse-demand function to construct a system of firms' marginal-revenue functions, which could be then solved for what we will call the Cournot output levels. Then, he introduced firms' cost functions and the system of first-order conditions to be solved. Cournot did not consider the possibility that firms with sufficiently high cost may not be producing in this equilibrium.

In what follows, we develop the Cournot oligopoly model where firms sell identical products. In this model, firms are not price takers. Instead, each firm is fully aware that changing its output level will affect the market price.

6.1.1   Two-seller game

Let us consider a two-firm industry summarized by the cost function of each firm i (producing q_i units) given by

$$TC_i(q_i) = c_i q_i, \quad i = 1, 2, \quad \text{where } c_2, c_1 \geq 0, \tag{6.1}$$

and the market-demand function given by

$$p(Q) = a - bQ, \quad a, b > 0, \quad a > c_i, \quad \text{where } Q = q_1 + q_2. \qquad (6.2)$$

In contrast to chapter 4, where we solved for a competitive equilibrium for this industry, here we solve for a Cournot oligopoly equilibrium. We first have to define a two-firm game that corresponds to a definition of a game given in Definition 2.1. Let each firm's action be defined as choosing its production level, and assume that both firms choose their actions simultaneously. Thus, each firm i chooses $q_i \in A_i \equiv [0, \infty)$, $i = 1, 2$. Also, let the payoff function of each firm i be its profit function defined by $\pi_i(q_1, q_2) = p(q_1 + q_2)q_i - TC_i(q_i)$. Now, the game is properly defined since the players, their action sets, and their payoff functions are explicitly defined. All that is left to do now is to define the equilibrium concept.

DEFINITION 6.1 *The triplet $\{p^c, q_1^c, q_2^c\}$ is a **Cournot-Nash equilibrium** if*

1. (a) *given $q_2 = q_2^c$; q_1^c solves* $\max_{q_1} \pi_1(q_1, q_2^c)$
   $= p(q_1 + q_2^c)q_1 - TC_1(q_1) = [a - b(q_1 + q_2^c)]q_1 - c_1 q_1$
   (b) *given $q_1 = q_1^c$; q_2^c solves* $\max_{q_2} \pi_2(q_1^c, q_2)$
   $= p(q_1^c + q_2)q_2 - TC_2(q_2) = [a - b(q_1^c + q_2)]q_2 - c_2 q_2$

2. $p^c = a - b(q_1^c + q_2^c), \quad p^c, q_1^c, q_2^c \geq 0.$

That is, according to Definition 6.1, a Cournot equilibrium is a list of output levels produced by each firm and the resulting market price so that no firm could increase its profit by changing its output level, given that other firms produced the Cournot output levels. Thus, Cournot equilibrium output levels constitute a Nash equilibrium in a game where firms choose output levels.

Now that the equilibrium concept is well defined, we are left to calculate the Cournot equilibrium for this industry. Firm 1's profit-maximization problem yields the first-order condition given by

$$0 = \frac{\partial \pi_1(q_1, q_2)}{\partial q_1} = a - 2bq_1 - bq_2 - c_1$$

which yields the familiar profit-maximizing condition in which each firm (firm 1 in this equation) sets its marginal revenue ($MR(q_1) = a - 2bq_1 - bq_2$) equal to marginal cost (c_1). The second-order condition guaranteeing a global maximum is satisfied since $\frac{\partial^2 \pi_1}{\partial (q_1)^2} = -2b < 0$ for every q_1 and q_2. Solving for q_1 as a function of q_2 yields the *best-response function* (also commonly known as *reaction function*) of firm 1, which we denote by $R_1(q_2)$. Hence,

$$q_1 = R_1(q_2) = \frac{a - c_1}{2b} - \frac{1}{2}q_2. \tag{6.3}$$

Similarly, we can guess that firm 2's best-response function is given by

$$q_2 = R_2(q_1) = \frac{a - c_2}{2b} - \frac{1}{2}q_1. \tag{6.4}$$

The best-response functions of the two firms are drawn in Figure 6.1 in the (q_1, q_2) space.

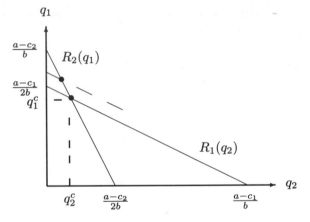

Figure 6.1: Cournot best-response functions (the case for $c_2 > c_1$)

The two best-response functions are downward sloping, implying that for each firm, if the rival's output level increases, the firm would lower its output level. The intuition is that if one firm raises its output level, the price would drop, and hence in order to maintain a high price the other firm would find it profitable to decrease its output level. A perhaps more intuitive explanation for why a firm's best-response function is downward sloping is that an increase in a rival's output shifts the residual demand facing a firm inward. Hence, when a firm faces a lower demand it would produce a smaller amount.

Now, the Cournot equilibrium output levels can be calculated by solving the two best-response functions (6.3) and (6.4), which correspond to the intersection of the curves illustrated in Figure 6.1. Thus,

$$q_1^c = \frac{a - 2c_1 + c_2}{3b} \quad \text{and} \quad q_2^c = \frac{a - 2c_2 + c_1}{3b}. \tag{6.5}$$

Hence, the aggregate industry-output level is $Q^c = q_1^c + q_2^c = \frac{2a - c_1 - c_2}{3b}$, and the Cournot equilibrium price is

$$p^c = a - bQ^c = \frac{a + c_1 + c_2}{3}. \tag{6.6}$$

It is easy to confirm from (6.5) that the output of the high-cost firm is lower than the output level of the low-cost firm. That is, $c_2 \geq c_1$ implies that $q_1 \geq q_2$.

Altogether, the Cournot profit (payoff) level of firm i, as a function of the unit costs for firms i and j, $i \neq j$, is given by

$$
\begin{aligned}
\pi_i^c &= (p^c - c_i)(q_i^c) = \left(\frac{a + c_i + c_j}{3} - c_i \right) \left(\frac{a - 2c_i + c_j}{3b} \right) \\
&= \frac{(a - 2c_i + c_j)^2}{9b} = b \left(q_i^c \right)^2.
\end{aligned} \tag{6.7}
$$

We conclude this section with some comparative static analysis. Suppose that firm 1 invents a new production process that reduces its unit production cost from c_1 to $\bar{c}_1$, where $\bar{c}_1 < c_1$. The type of R&D leading to cost reduction is called "process innovation," to which we will return in Chapter 9. Equation (6.5) implies that q_1^c increases while q_2^c decreases. This is also shown in Figure 6.1, where a decrease in c_1 shifts $R_1(q_2)$ to the right, thereby increasing the equilibrium q_1^c while decreasing q_2^c. Also, (6.6) implies that a decrease in c_1 (or c_2) would decrease the equilibrium price p^e, and (6.7) implies that a decrease in c_1 would increase the profit of firm 1 while lowering the profit of firm 2.

6.1.2 *N*-seller game

Suppose now the industry consists of N firms, $N \geq 1$. We analyze two types of such industries: (a) N identical firms, all having the same cost function, or (b) heterogeneous firms, where some firms have cost functions different from others. Since solving the general case of firms with different cost functions would require solving N first-order conditions (intersecting N best-response functions), we first solve the model by assuming that all firms have identical technologies. That is, $c_i = c$ for every $i = 1, 2, \ldots, N$. In the appendix (section 6.7) we introduce a procedure that makes solving the heterogeneous-firms case easy.

Since all firms have the same cost structure, the first step would be to pick up one firm and calculate its output level as a function of the output levels of all other firms. In other words, we would like to calculate the best-response function of a representative firm. With no loss of generality, we derive the best-response function of firm 1. Thus, firm 1 chooses q_1 to

$$\max_{q_1} \pi_1 = p(Q)q_1 - cq_1 = \left[a - b \left(\sum_{i=1}^{N} q_i \right) \right] q_1 - cq_1.$$

The first-order condition is given by

$$0 = \frac{\partial \pi_1}{\partial q_1} = a - 2bq_1 - b \sum_{i=2}^{N} q_i - c.$$

Hence, the best-response function of firm 1 as a function of the output levels of firms $q_2, q_3, \ldots, q_N$ is given by

$$R_1(q_2, q_3, \ldots, q_N) = \frac{a - c}{2b} - \frac{1}{2} \sum_{i=2}^{N} q_i. \tag{6.8}$$

In the general case, where firms have different cost functions, we would have to derive the best-response function for each of the N firms. However, since all firms are identical, we can guess that in a Cournot equilibrium, the firms would produce the same output levels: we guess (and later verify) that $q_1^c = q_2^c = \ldots = q_N^c$. Thus, we denote the common output level by q, where $q = q_i$ for every i. Note that a common mistake among students is to substitute q for q_i before the best-response functions are derived. This procedure is obviously leading to the wrong solution, since it implies that each firm "controls" the output level of all firms. Therefore, here we substitute the common q only into the already derived best-response functions. The use of symmetry here is purely technical and is done to facilitate solving N equations with N unknowns. From (6.8), we have it that $q = \frac{a-c}{2b} - \frac{1}{2}(N-1)q$. Hence,

$$q^c = \frac{a - c}{(N + 1)b} \quad Q^c = Nq^c = \left(\frac{a - c}{b} \right) \left(\frac{N}{N + 1} \right). \tag{6.9}$$

The equilibrium price and the profit level of each firm are given by

$$p^c = a - bQ^c = \frac{a + Nc}{N + 1} \quad \text{and} \quad \pi_i^c = \frac{(a - c)^2}{(N + 1)^2 b} = b(q^c)^2. \tag{6.10}$$

Varying the number of firms

We now ask how would the Cournot price, quantity produced, and profit levels change when we change the number of firms in the industry? First, note that substituting $N = 1$ into (6.9) and (6.10) yields the monopoly solution described in section 5.1. Second, substituting $N = 2$ yields the duopoly solution described in (6.5), (6.6), and (6.7).

Now, we let the number of firms grow with no bounds, $(N \to \infty)$. Then, we have it that

$$\lim_{N\to\infty} q^c = 0, \quad \text{and} \quad \lim_{N\to\infty} Q^c = \lim_{N\to\infty} \left(\frac{a-c}{b}\right)\left(\frac{N}{N+1}\right) = \left(\frac{a-c}{b}\right).$$
(6.11)

That is, in a Cournot equilibrium, as the number of firms grows indefinitely, the output level of each firm approaches zero whereas the industry's aggregate output level approaches the competitive output level given in Proposition 4.1. Also,

$$\lim_{N\to\infty} p^c = \lim_{N\to\infty} \frac{a}{N+1} + \frac{Nc}{N+1} = c = p^e.$$
(6.12)

Hence, the Cournot equilibrium price approaches the competitive price that equals the unit production cost of a firm (see Proposition 4.1). These results often cause some confusion among students, leading them to believe that competitive behavior occurs only when there are many (or infinitely many) firms. However, as we pointed out in chapter 4, we can assume a competitive market structure for any given number of firms, and even solve for a competitive equilibrium for the case where $N = 1$. What equations (6.11) and (6.12) say is that the Cournot market structure yields approximately the same price and industry output as the competitive market structure when the number of firms is large.

6.1.3 Cournot equilibrium and welfare

Since our analysis starts with given demand functions (rather than the consumers' utility functions), we cannot measure the social welfare by calculating consumers' equilibrium-utility levels. Instead, we approximate social welfare by adding consumers' surplus and firms' profits (see subsection 3.2.3 on page 52 for a justification of this procedure of welfare approximation). Note that profit should be part of the economy's welfare because the firms are owned by the consumers, who collect the profits via firms' distributions of dividends.

Substituting the Cournot equilibrium price (6.10) into (3.3) on page 52, we obtain the consumers' surplus as a function of the number of firms, N. Hence, $CS^c(N) = \frac{N^2(a-c)^2}{2b(N+1)^2}$. Clearly, $\frac{\partial CS(N)}{\partial N} > 0$, meaning that consumers' surplus rises with the entry of more firms, due to the reduction in price and the increase in the quantity consumed.

We define social welfare as the sum of consumers' surplus plus the industry aggregate profit (see section 4.3 on page 68 for a definition). Thus, if we recall (6.10),

$$W^c(N) \equiv CS^c(N) + N\pi^c(N)$$
(6.13)

$$= \left(\frac{(a-c)^2}{2b} \right) \left(\frac{N^2 + 2N}{N^2 + 2N + 1} \right) = \frac{(a-c)^2}{2b} \Bigg|_{N \to \infty}.$$

Also, note that $\frac{\partial W^c(N)}{\partial N} > 0$. Hence, although the industry profit declines with an increase in the number of firms, the increase in consumers' surplus dominates the reduction in the industry profit. Thus, in this economy, free entry is welfare improving!

6.2 Sequential Moves

In the previous section, we analyzed industries where firms strategically choose their output levels. All those games were static in the sense that players simultaneously choose their quantity produced. In this section, we assume that the firms move in sequence. For example, in a two-firm, sequential-moves game, firm 1 will choose its output level before firm 2 does. Then, firm 2, after observing the output level chosen by firm 1, will choose its output level, and only then will output be sold and profits collected by the two firms. This type of market structure is often referred to as *Leader-Follower* on the basis of von Stackelberg's work (1934) (see Konow 1994 for von Stackelberg's biography). This type of behavior defines an extensive form game studied in section 2.2.

In this section we do not raise the important question of what determines the order of moves, that is, why one firm gets to choose its output level before another. We return to this question in chapter 8, where we distinguish among established firms (called incumbent firms) and potential entrants. Here, we assume that the order of moves is given, and we develop the tools for solving an industry equilibrium under a predetermined order of moves.

We analyze a two-stage game, where firm 1 (the leader) chooses the quantity produced in the first stage. The quantity chosen in the first stage is irreversible and cannot be adjusted in the second stage. In the second stage, only firm 2 (the follower) chooses how much to produce after observing the output level chosen by firm 1 in the first stage. Here, the game ends after the second stage, and each firm collects its profit. Our main questions are (a) Is there any advantage for moving in the first stage rather than the second? and (b) How would the equilibrium market price and production levels compare to the static Cournot equilibrium price and output levels?

Following Definition 2.9 on page 26, this game has a continuum of subgames indexed by the output level chosen by firm 1 in the first stage. A finite-horizon dynamic game is generally solved backwards. We look for a subgame perfect equilibrium (Definition 2.10 on page 27) for this game. Hence, we first analyze the players' (firm 2 in our case) action in the last period, assuming that the actions played in previous period are given. Then, we go one period backwards, and analyze firm 1's action given the *strategy* (see Definition 2.8 on page 24) of how firm 2 chooses its output level based on the first-period action. To simplify the exposition, let all firms have identical unit cost, $c_1 = c_2 = c$.

The second-period subgames

In the second period, only firm 2 moves and chooses q_2 to maximize its profit, taking firm 1's quantity produced, q_1, as given. As you probably noticed, we have already solved this problem before, since the second-period problem of firm 2 is identical to the problem firm 2 solves in a Cournot market structure. This maximization results in the best-response function of firm 2 given in (6.4). Hence, $R_2(q_1) = \frac{a-c}{2b} - \frac{1}{2}q_1$. Note that the function $R_2(q_1)$ constitutes firm 2's strategy for this game, since it specifies its action for every possible action chosen by firm 1.

The first-period game

In period 1, firm 1 calculates $R_2(q_1)$ in the same way as firm 2. Thus, firm 1 is able to calculate how firm 2 will best reply to its choice of output level. Knowing that, firm 1 chooses q_1^s to

$$\max_{q_1} \pi_1^s = p(q_1 + R_2(q_1))q_1 - cq_1 = \left[a - b\left(q_1 + \frac{a-c}{2b} - \frac{q_1}{2}\right)\right]q_1 - cq_1.$$

(6.14)

We leave it to the reader to derive the first- and second-order conditions. Thus, the quantity produced by the leader is

$$q_1^s = \frac{a-c}{2b} = \frac{3}{2}q_1^c > q_1^c.$$

(6.15)

Hence, under the sequential-moves market structure, the leader produces a higher level of output than the Cournot market structure. Substituting (6.15) into $R_2(q_1)$ yields the followers' equilibrium-output level:

$$q_2^s = \frac{a-c}{4b} = \frac{3}{4}q_2^c < q_2^c$$

(6.16)

implying that the follower's output level falls compared with the Cournot output level. Thus, the leader's gain in output expansion comes partly from the reduction in the follower's output level. The equilibrium price and aggregate output levels are given by

$$p^s = \frac{a+3c}{4} < \frac{a+2c}{3} = p^c \quad \text{and} \quad Q^s = \frac{3(a-c)}{4b} > \frac{2(a-c)}{3b} = Q^c.$$

(6.17)

Therefore,

Proposition 6.1 *A sequential-moves quantity game yields a higher aggregate industry-output level and a lower market price than the static Cournot market structure.*

Thus, the equilibrium market outcome under a sequential-moves game is more competitive than the Cournot equilibrium outcome in the sense that this outcome is somewhere in between the competitive equilibrium outcome derived in chapter 4 and the Cournot outcome derived in section 6.1. The intuition behind Proposition 6.1 is as follow: Under the Cournot market structure, firm 1 perceives the output produced by firm 2 as given. However, under sequential-moves market structure, firm 1 knows firm 2's best-response function and therefore calculates that firm 2 will reduce its output level in response to its increase in output level. Hence, when firm 1 expands output, it expects the price to fall faster under Cournot than under sequential-moves market structure. Therefore, in order maintain a high price, firm 1 will produce more under the sequential game than it will under Cournot. Now, (6.15) and (6.16) demonstrate that the increase in aggregate output stems from the fact that the follower does not find it profitable to cut its output level by the same amount as the increase in the leader's output level. This happens because the reaction functions are sloped relatively flat (slope is negative but exceeds -1), implying that a firm reduces its output level by less than the increase in the output level of the rival firm.

We now compare firms' profit levels under sequential moves to the Cournot profit levels. We leave it to the reader to verify that the leader's profit increases while the follower's declines. That is,

$$\pi_1^s = \frac{(a-c)^2}{8b} > \pi_1^c \quad \text{and} \quad \pi_2^s = \frac{(a-c)^2}{16b} < \pi_2^c, \qquad (6.18)$$

where π_1^c and π_2^c are given in (6.7). Note that we could have concluded even without going into the precise calculations that the leader's profit under the sequential-game equilibrium will be higher than under the Cournot. How? It is very simple! Since firm 2 reacts in a "Nash fashion," firm 1 could just choose to produce the Cournot output level q_1^c. In this case, firm 1 would earn exactly the Cournot profit. However, since in the sequential game firm 1 chooses to produce a different output level, it must be increasing its profit compared with the Cournot profit level. The kind of reasoning we just described is called a *revealed profitability* argument, and the reader is urged to learn to use this kind of reasoning whenever possible because performing calculations to investigate economic effects does not generate an intuitive explanation for these effects. In contrast, logical deduction often provides the necessary intuition for understanding economic phenomena.

Finally, we can logically deduce how industry profit under sequential moves compare with industry profit under Cournot. Equations (6.17) show that the market price under sequential moves is lower than it is under Cournot. Since the Cournot market price is lower than the monopoly's price, and since monopoly makes the highest possible profit, it is clear that industry profit must drop when we further reduce the price below the monopoly's price. Hence, whenever $c_1 = c_2$, industry profit must be lower under sequential moves. In a more general environment, this argument may not holds when the industry profit is not a concave function of p.

6.3   Bertrand Market Structure

In a Cournot market structure firms were assumed to choose their output levels, where the market price adjusted to clear the market and was found by substituting the quantity produced into consumers' demand function. In contrast, in a Bertrand market structure firms set prices rather than output levels. The attractive feature of the Bertrand setup, compared with the Cournot market structure, stems from the fact that firms are able to change prices faster and at less cost than to set quantities, because changing quantities will require an adjustment of inventories, which may necessitate a change in firms' capacity to produce. Thus, in the short run, quantity changes may not be feasible, or may be too costly to the seller. However, changing prices is a relatively low-cost action that may require only a change in the labels displayed on the shelves in the store. Let us turn to the Bertrand market structure.

In 1883 Joseph Bertrand published a review of Cournot's book (1838) harshly critical of Cournot's modeling. It seems, however, that Bertrand was dissatisfied with the general modeling of oligopoly rather than with the specific model derived by Cournot. Today, most economists believe that quantity and price oligopoly games are both needed to understand a variety of markets. That is, for some markets, an assumption that firms set quantities may yield the observed market price and quantity produced, whereas for others, a price-setting game may yield the observed market outcomes. Our job as economists would then be to decide which market structure yields a better approximation of the observed price and quantity sold in each specific market.

We now analyze the two-firm industry defined in (6.1) and (6.2) and look for a Nash equilibrium (see Definition 2.4) in a game where the two firms use their prices as their actions. First, note that so far, our analysis has concentrated on a single market price determined by our assumption that consumers are always on their demand curve. However, in a Bertrand game we have to consider outcomes where each firm

sets a different price for its product. Therefore, we now make two explicit assumptions about consumers' behavior under all possible prices
announced by both firms:

1. Consumers always purchase from the cheapest seller.

2. If two sellers charge the same price, half of the consumers purchase
   from firm 1 and the other half purchase from firm 2.

Formally, we modify the demand given in (6.2) to capture the quantity
demand faced by each firm i, $i = 1, 2$. Therefore, we assume that

$$q_i = \begin{cases} 0 & \text{if } p_i > a \\ 0 & \text{if } p_i > p_j \\ \frac{a-p}{2b} & \text{if } p_i = p_j \equiv p < a \\ \frac{a-p_i}{b} & \text{if } p_i < \min\{a, p_j\} \end{cases} \qquad i = 1, 2, \ i \neq j. \qquad (6.19)$$

Equation (6.19) is the quantity demand facing firm i at any given p_1
and p_2 and incorporates what is commonly called a *rationing rule*, which
tells us how the market demand is divided between two firms selling a
homogeneous product. Thus, if firm i charges a higher price than firm j,
then no consumer would purchase the product from firm i. In contrast,
if $p_i < p_j$, then all the consumers will purchase only from firm i, and
none will purchase from firm j. In this case, the quantity demanded from
firm i is calculated directly from (6.2). Finally, if both firms charge the
same prices, then the quantity demand determined in (6.2) is equally
split between the two firms.

DEFINITION 6.2 *The quadruple* $\{p_1^b, p_2^b, q_1^b, q_2^b\}$ *is a* **Bertrand-Nash
equilibrium** *if*

1. *given* $p_2 = p_2^b$, p_1^b *maximizes* $\max_{p_1} \pi_1(p_1, p_2^b) = (p_1 - c_1)q_1$

2. *given* $p_1 = p_1^b$, p_2^b *maximizes* $\max_{p_2} \pi_2(p_1^b, p_2) = (p_2 - c_2)q_2$

3. q_1 *and* q_2 *are determined in* (6.19).

Definition 6.2 states that in a Bertrand-Nash equilibrium, no firm can
increase its profit by unilaterally changing its price.

In the next two subsections we apply Definition 6.2 to two types of
markets: the first, where firms do not have capacity constraints and
can produce any amount they wish under the assumed cost structure;
and the second, where we assume that firms' capacities are limited and
therefore, in the short run, they are unable to expand production.

6.3.1   Solving for Bertrand equilibrium

Before we characterize the Bertrand equilibria, it is important to understand the discontinuity feature of this game. In the Cournot game, the payoff (profit) functions are continuous with respect to the strategic variables (quantities); in the Bertrand price game, by contrast, equation (6.19) exhibits a discontinuity of the payoff functions at all the outcomes where $p_1 = p_2$. That is, if one firm sells at a price that is one cent higher than the other firm, it would have a zero market share. However, a two-cent price reduction by this firm would give this firm a one 100 percent market share. The action of a firm to slightly reduce the price below that of its competitor is called *undercutting*. Since undercutting involves setting a price slightly lower than the competitor's, we need to examine the types of currencies used in order to determine the smallest possible undercutting actions available to firms. Therefore, we make the following definition:

DEFINITION 6.3 *Let ϵ be the smallest possible monetary denomination (smallest legal tender). The medium of exchange (money) is said to be* **continuous** *if $\epsilon = 0$, and* **discrete** *if $\epsilon > 0$.*

Examples of discrete smallest legal tenders are: in China, $\epsilon = 1$ Fen; in Finland, $\epsilon = 10$ Penniä; in Israel, $\epsilon = 5$ Agorot; and in the US, $\epsilon = 1$ cent.

The following proposition characterizes Bertrand equilibria.

Proposition 6.2

1. *If the medium of exchange is continuous and if the firms have the same cost structure, $(c_2 = c_1 \equiv c)$, then a Bertrand equilibrium is $p_1^b = p_2^b = c$, and $q_1^b = q_2^b = (a - c)/(2b)$.*

2. *Let the medium of exchange be discrete, and assume that c_2 is denominated in the medium of exchange. That is, $c_2 = \lambda\epsilon$, where $\lambda \geq 1$ is an integer. Also let ϵ be sufficiently small, that is, satisfying $(c_2 - \epsilon - c_1)\left(\frac{a - c_2 + \epsilon}{b}\right) > (c_2 - c_1)\left(\frac{a - c_2}{2b}\right)$. Then, if $c_2 - c_1 > \epsilon$, the unique Bertrand equilibrium is $p_2 = c_2$, $p_1 = c_2 - \epsilon$, $q_2^b = 0$, and $q_1^b = (a - c_2 + \epsilon)/b$.*

Thus, if firms have equal unit costs, the Bertrand equilibrium price and aggregate output are the same as for the competitive equilibrium. In other words, undercutting reduces the prices to marginal cost. In cases where firm 1 has a lower unit cost than firm 2, firm 1 undercuts firm 2 by charging the highest possible price that is lower than c_2, which is given by $p_1 = c_2 - \epsilon$.

Proof. Part 1: In equilibrium, each firm must make nonnegative profit. Hence, $p_i^b \geq c_i$, $i = 1, 2$.

We first establish that in a Bertrand equilibrium both firms charge the same prices. By way of contradiction suppose that $p_1^b > p_2^b > c$. Then, by (6.19), firm 1 makes zero profit. However, since the medium of exchange is continuous, firm 1 can increase its profit by reducing its price to $p_2^b > \tilde{p}_1 > c$ and grab the entire market, thereby making strictly positive profit, a contradiction.

By way of contradiction suppose that $p_1^b > p_2^b = c$. Then, since the medium of exchange in continuous, firm 2 can raise its price slightly while still maintaining a lower price than firm 1. Hence, firm 2 will deviate, a contradiction.

Now that we have established that $p_1^b = p_2^b$, by way of contradiction assume that $p_1^b = p_2^b > c$. Clearly, this cannot constitute a Nash equilibrium in prices since firm 1, say, would have an incentive unilaterally to reduce its price to $\tilde{p}_1 = p_1^b - \epsilon$, where ϵ can be as small as one wants, thereby grabbing the entire market. For ϵ sufficiently small, this deviation is profitable for firm 1.

Part 2: To briefly sketch the proof of part 2, observe that firm 2 makes a zero profit and cannot increase its profit by unilaterally raising its price above $p_2^b = c_2$. Hence, firm 2 does not deviate. Now, for firm 1 to be able to sell a positive amount, it must set $p_1^b \leq c_2$. If $p_1^b = c_2 = p_2^b$, then (6.19) implies that the firms split the market by selling each $q_i = \frac{a - c_2}{2b}$. In this case, the profit of firm 1 is

$$\pi_1 = (c_2 - c_1)q_1 = (c_2 - c_1)\frac{a - c_2}{2b}. \tag{6.20}$$

However, if firm 1 undercuts by the smallest legal tender, then it becomes the sole seller and sells $q_1 = \frac{a - (c_2 - \epsilon)}{b}$. In this case,

$$\pi_1 = (c_2 - \epsilon - c_1)q_1 = (c_2 - \epsilon - c_1)\frac{a - (c_2 - \epsilon)}{b}. \tag{6.21}$$

Comparing (6.20) with (6.21) yields the condition stated in part 2. ∎

6.3.2 Bertrand under capacity constraints

The previous section demonstrated that when the firms have the same cost structure, price competition reduces prices to unit costs, thereby making firms earn zero profits. Economists often feel uncomfortable with this result, especially since it makes the number of firms in the industry irrelevant, in the sense that under symmetric Bertrand competition, price drops to unit cost even when there are only two firms. Now, if most industries are indeed engaged in a Bertrand competition as described in this section, then we should observe unit-cost prices for those industries with two or more firms. If this case is realistic, then the antitrust authority should not have to worry about industries' concentration levels and should devote all its effort to fighting monopolies. Clearly, we rarely observe intense price competition among industries with a small number of firms, and therefore the antitrust authority challenges mergers of firms that lead to highly concentrated industries (see Section 8.6).

One way to overcome this problem is to follow Edgeworth (1925) and to assume that in the short run, firms are constrained by given capacity that limits their production levels. The Irish economist Francis Ysidro Edgeworth, who made enormous contributions to economic theory and other disciplines, identified some discontinuity properties of the firms' profit functions when firms produce under increasing marginal cost (decreasing returns to scale) technologies. In Edgeworth's words (Edgeworth 1925, 118):

> In the last case there will be an intermediate tract through which the index of value will oscillate, or rather vibrate irregularly for an indefinite length of time. There will never be reached that determinate position of equilibrium which is characteristic of perfect competition.

We demonstrate Edgeworth's argument by assuming an extreme version of increasing marginal cost, which is letting the cost of expanding production beyond a certain output level (which we call capacity) be infinite. Figure 6.2 illustrates a market-demand curve composed of four consumers, each buying, at most, one unit.

Figure 6.2 assumes that consumer 1 is willing to pay a maximum of $3 for one unit, consumer 2 a maximum of $2, consumer 3 a maximum of $1, and consumer 4 will not pay at all. Such prices are commonly termed as consumers' *reservation prices.*

Suppose now that there are two firms and that each is capable of producing at zero cost, $c_1 = c_2 = 0$. Then, Proposition 6.2, proved in the previous subsection, shows that if firms are not subject to capacity constraints, then Bertrand competition would lead to prices of zero, $p_1^b = p_2^b = 0$.

To demonstrate Edgeworth's argument, suppose now that in the short run each firm is limited to producing, at most, two units. Then, it is easy to show that the prices $p_1 = p_2 = 0$ no longer constitute a Nash equilibrium. To see this, observe that firm 1 can increase its profit from $\pi_1 = 0$ to $\pi_1 = 3$ by increasing its price to $p_1 = 3$, and selling its unit to the consumer with the highest reservation price. In this outcome, firm 1 sells one unit to the consumer with a reservation price of 3, whereas firm 2 sells a unit to one of the other consumers for the price of $p_2 = 0$. Since one firm would always want to deviate from the unit cost pricing, we conclude that the Bertrand equilibrium prices under no capacity constraints need not be Nash equilibrium prices under capacity constraints.

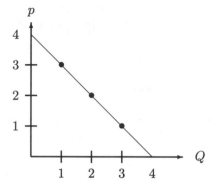

Figure 6.2: Edgeworth Cycles: Bertrand competition under capacity constraints

We are left to show that in the present example there does not exist a Nash equilibrium in prices. This result is sometimes referred to as *Edgeworth Cycles* since under any pair of firms' prices, one firm would always find it profitable to deviate. To see this, let us look at the outcome $p_1 = 3$ and $p_2 = 0$. Clearly, firm 2 would deviate and undercut firm 1 by setting $p_2 = 3 - \epsilon$, where ϵ is a small number. In this case firm 1 sells nothing, whereas firm 2 sells its unit to the consumer with the highest reservation price, and earns a profit of $\pi_2 = 3 - \epsilon \approx 3$. Clearly, firms continue undercutting each other's prices and a Nash equilibrium in prices is never reached. Hence, we showed that marginal-cost pricing is not an equilibrium under capacity constraint, and that firms will keep changing prices without reaching any Nash equilibrium in prices.

Finally, it should be pointed out that introducing capacity constraints on the firms is not the only way to generate above-marginal-cost equilibrium prices. Above-marginal-cost pricing can be an equilibrium outcome (a) when products are differentiated (see next chapter), (b) when demand randomly fluctuates, and (c) when firms are engaged in an infinitely pricing repeated game.

6.4   Cournot versus Bertrand

In sections 6.1 and 6.3 we analyzed the same industry where in the Cournot-market-structure firms use quantity produced as actions, whereas in the Bertrand-market-structure firms use prices as actions. The analyses of these sections show that in general, the two types of market structures yield different market outcomes (prices and quantity produced). Thus, when we change the firms' actions from choosing quantities to choosing prices, the Nash equilibrium yields a completely different outcome because under Cournot, firms make positive profit, since the resulting market price exceeds unit cost, whereas under Bertrand, prices drop to unit cost. Moreover, in a Bertrand game, only the low-cost firm produces, which is generally not the case for the Cournot game. Therefore, we can state that in a one-shot (static) game there is no correspondence between the Cournot solution and the Bertrand solution.

However, Kreps and Scheinkman (1983) constructed a particular environment (a particular two-period dynamic game) where, in the first period, firms choose quantity produced (accumulate inventories) and in the second period, the quantities are fixed (cannot be changed) and firms choose prices. They showed that the quantities chosen by firms in the first period and the price chosen in the second period are exactly the Cournot outcome given in (6.5) and (6.6). That is, they show that for some market games where two firms choose how much to produce in period 1, and then set prices in period 2, a subgame perfect equilibrium (see Definition 2.10 on page 27) yields the exact quantity produced and price as those in a one-shot Cournot-market-structure game, where firms choose only how much to produce.

We will not bring a complete proof of their proposition; however, we illustrate the idea in our simple two-firm industry for the case where $p = 10 - Q$, and both firms have a unit cost of $c = 1$.

As we discussed earlier, the easiest way of solving for a subgame perfect equilibrium for a dynamic finite game is to solve it backwards. Therefore, we begin with the second period and ask what prices will be chosen by firms in a Nash-equilibrium one-shot price game, where the quantity produced is taken as given by first-period choices. Then, we analyze the first period looking for a subgame perfect equilibrium in first-period production levels, where firms can calculate and take into account the second-period equilibrium market prices, which depend on first-period production levels.

The second-period subgame

Assume that for some reason, the firms choose to produce the Cournot capacity levels $q_1^c = q_2^c = 3$. Hence, total industry output is $Q^c = 6$. We now show that in a Nash equilibrium for the second-period subgame both firms will choose to set prices that clear the market under the Cournot outcome. That is, each firm will set $p_i = 4 = p^c$. Figure 6.3

illustrates the Cournot outcome.

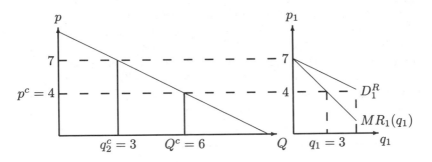

Figure 6.3: Residual demand when firms have fixed inventories

Note that in the second period, firms are free to choose any price they wish so that the Nash equilibrium prices may differ from $p^c = 4$. To demonstrate that this is not the case, we now show that given $p_2 = 4$, firm 1 will not deviate and will also choose $p_1 = 4$. First, note that firm 1 will not lower its price below $p_1 = 4$ because a price reduction will not be followed by an increase in sales (the capacity is limited to $q_1 = 3$.) Thus, lowering the price will only lower its revenue.

Second, we must show that firm 1 cannot increase its profit by raising its price and selling less than $q_1^c = 3$. The right side of Figure 6.3 exhibits the *residual* demand facing firm 1 when it raises its price above $p_1^c = 4$. Residual demand is the demand facing firm 1 after the quantity supplied by firm 2 is subtracted from the aggregate industry demand. In the present case, we subtract $q_2^c = 3$ from the aggregate demand curve to obtain the residual demand curve facing firm 1, given by $q_1 = 10 - p - 3 = 7 - p$ or its inverse $p = 7 - q_1$. The most important observation to be made about Figure 6.3 is that the marginal-revenue curve derived from this residual-demand function $(MR_1(q_1) = 7 - 2q_1)$ is strictly positive for all output levels satisfying $(q_1 \leq 3.5)$, implying that the residual demand is elastic at this interval. Therefore, increasing p_1 will only reduce the revenue of firm 1. This establishes the following claim.

Lemma 6.1 *If the output (capacity) levels chosen in period 1 satisfy $q_1 + q_2 \leq 6$, then the Nash equilibrium exhibits both firms choosing the market-clearing price in the second period.*

Lemma 6.1 shows that, given firms' choices of output levels, in the second-period price game firms will strategically choose to play the market price that clears the market at the given aggregate output level.

The first-period game

In the first period, firms observe that the second-period price would be the market-clearing price (Lemma 6.1). Therefore, for each firm, the first-period-capacity-choice problem is precisely the Cournot-quantity-choice problem as formulated in Definition 2.4. Hence, in the first period, firms would choose the Cournot quantity levels $p_1^c = p_2^c = 3$. Intuitively, in the first period both firms know that the second-period price choices by both firms would be the price that clears the market for the first-period production levels. This knowledge makes the firms' first-period-output-choice problem identical to firms' output choices in a Cournot market structure as defined in Definition 6.1.

Finally, note that this illustration does not provide a complete proof for this statement, since in Lemma 6.1 we assumed that the firms did not choose "very high" capacity levels in the first period. In that respect, Lemma 6.1 is not proven for output levels exceeding $q_1 + q_2 > 6$. We refrain from proving that in order to avoid using mixed strategies in this book. Also, from time to time this result causes some confusion among students and researchers, leading them to state that there is no reason for using Bertrand price competition anymore since the two-period, capacity-price game would yield the same outcome as the Cournot market structure. Note that this statement is too strong, since it holds only for the particular two-period game analyzed in the present section.

6.5   Self-Enforcing Collusion

In this section we extend the basic static Cournot game to an infinitely repeated game in which firms produce output and collect profits in each period. Although the analysis in this section is self-contained, the reader is urged to obtain some background on repeated games by reading section 2.3.

One very important result will emerge from analyzing an infinitely repeated Cournot game, namely, that the outcome in which all firms produce the collusive output levels (see the cartel analysis in subsection 5.4.1) constitutes a subgame perfect equilibrium for the noncooperative repeated Cournot game. More precisely, in subsection 6.1.2 we proved that under the Cournot market structure with two or more firms, aggregate industry output exceeds the monopoly output level (which equals the cartel's total output level). Moreover, we showed that as the number of firms increases, the output level increases and converges to the competitive output level. Altogether, firms have a lot to gain by colluding rather than competing under any market structure. In this section we show that if the Cournot game is repeated infinitely, then the collusive output level can emerge as a noncooperative equilibrium. The importance of this result is that it implies that observing an industry where production levels are limited and firms make strictly positive profits does not imply that the firms are engaged in any cooperative activities. In fact, what we show in this section is that the cooperative collusive output levels can be sustained as a noncooperative equilibrium.

In the subsection 6.5.1 we develop a simple Cournot duopoly model and analyze the incentives to collude among firms and the incentive for each firm to unilaterally deviate from collusion when the game is played only once. Subsection 6.5.2 analyzes equilibrium outcome when the one-shot game is repeated infinitely.

6.5.1 The one-shot game

Consider the following basic one-shot Cournot game: There are two firms denoted by $i = 1, 2$. We denote by q_i the output level of firm i. The demand facing the industry is $p = 1 - q_1 - q_2$. Let $Q \equiv q_1 + q_2$ denote the aggregate industry-output level, and assume that production is costless.

In the following subsubsections we quickly derive the already familiar Cournot duopoly equilibrium, the collusion (cooperative) monopoly equilibrium, and then the incentives to deviate from the cooperative outcome.

Duopoly: Non-cooperative behavior

In view of Definition 6.1, in a Cournot market structure firm 1 maximizes $\pi_1 = (1-q_1-q_2)q_1$, yielding a best-response function: $q_1(q_2) = (1-q_2)/2$ and the equilibrium output levels $q_1 = q_2 = 1/3 \equiv M$, where M stands for medium production level. Hence, $Q = 2/3$, and $p = 1/3$, implying that $\pi_i = 1/9$. The profits of the firms under duopoly are displayed in the second column and second row of Table 6.1.

		Firm 2				
		$q_2 = L = \frac{1}{4}$		$q_2 = M = \frac{1}{3}$		$q_2 = H = \frac{3}{8}$
	$q_1 = L = \frac{1}{4}$	$\frac{1}{8}$	$\frac{1}{8}$	$\frac{5}{48}$	$\frac{5}{36}$	$\frac{3}{32}$ $\frac{9}{64}$
Firm 1	$q_1 = M = \frac{1}{3}$	$\frac{5}{36}$	$\frac{5}{48}$	$\frac{1}{9}$	$\frac{1}{9}$	$\frac{7}{72}$ $\frac{7}{64}$
	$q_1 = H = \frac{3}{8}$	$\frac{9}{64}$	$\frac{3}{32}$	$\frac{7}{64}$	$\frac{7}{72}$	$\frac{3}{32}$ $\frac{3}{32}$

Table 6.1: Cooperation L; Noncooperative Cournot duopoly M; Defection from cooperation H.

Collusion: Cooperative behavior

We assume that when the two firms collude, they act as a cartel, analyzed in subsection 5.4.1. Since the firms have identical technologies that exhibit constant returns to scale, the present case is easy to analyze because under CRS there is no difference whether under collusion they operate one or two plants. In any case, the cartel's profit-maximizing output is found by equating $MR(Q) = 1 - 2Q = 0 = MC_i$, implying that $Q = 1/2$, $p = 1/2$. Hence, equal division of output between the two colluding firms imply that $q_i = L = 1/4$, where L stands for "low" output levels. Thus, as expected, collusion implies that both firms restrict their output levels below the Cournot output levels. The two firms equally divide the profit, so $\pi_i = pQ/2 = 1/8$, which is displayed in the first column and row in Table 6.1.

Deviation from collusion

Suppose that firm 2 plays the naive collusive output level $q_2 = L$. We now show that in this one-shot game, firm 1 can increase its profit by unilaterally increasing its output level. To see that, for given $q_2 = 1/4$, firm 1 chooses q_1 to max $\pi_1 = (1 - q_1 - 1/4)q_1$, yielding $0 = 3/4 - 2q_1$. Hence, $q_1 = 3/8 \equiv H$. Thus, if firm 2 does not deviate from $q_2 = L$, firm 1 has the incentive to increase its output to a high level. In this case, $Q = 3/8 + 1/4 = 5/8$, $p = 3/8$, $\pi_1 = 9/64$ and $\pi_2 = 3/32$; both are displayed in the first column, third row in Table 6.1.

Equilibrium in the one-shot game

The first part of the next proposition follows directly from equation (6.5) and also from Table 6.1. The second part follows from Definition 2.6 and Table 6.1.

Proposition 6.3 *In the one-shot game:*

1. *there exists a unique Cournot-Nash equilibrium, given by*
   $q_1 = q_2 = M = 1/3;$

2. *the equilibrium outcome is Pareto dominated by the "cooperative outcome" $q_1 = q_2 = L = 1/4$.*

Note that we use the Pareto criterion to refer only to the profit of firms, thereby disregarding consumers' welfare.

6.5.2   The infinitely repeated game

Suppose now that the two firms live forever. The game proceeds as follows: In each period t both firms observe what both firms played in *all* earlier periods (observe period t history as defined in Definition 2.11) and then play the one-shot game described in Table 6.1. That is, in each period t, each firm i chooses $q_i(t)$, where $q_i(t) \in \{L, M, H\}$, $i = 1, 2$ and $t = 0, 1, 2, \ldots$. A strategy of firm i is a list of output levels chosen each period by firm i after the firm observed all the output levels chosen by each firm in all earlier periods (see Definition 2.11 for a precise definition of a strategy in repeated games).

Let $0 < \rho < 1$ be the discount factor. Note that in perfect capital markets, the discount factor is inversely related to the interest rate. Let r denote the interest rate. Then, $\rho = \frac{1}{1+r}$. As r rises, ρ falls, meaning that future profits are less valuable today. Following Assumption 2.1, we assume that the objective of each firm is to maximize the sum of present and discounted future profits given by

$$\Pi_i \equiv \sum_{t=1}^{\infty} \rho^{t-1} \pi_i(t) \tag{6.22}$$

where the values of $\pi_i(t)$ are given in Table 6.1.

The trigger strategy

We restrict the discussion here to one type of strategies called *trigger strategies*, meaning that in every period τ each player cooperates (playing $q_i(\tau) = L$) as long as all players (including himself) cooperated in all periods $t = 1, \ldots, \tau - 1$ (see Definition 2.11 for a precise definition). However, if any player deviated in some period $t \in \{1, \ldots, \tau - 1\}$, then player i plays the noncooperative (duopoly) strategy forever! That is, $q_i(t) = M$ for every $t = \tau, \tau + 1, \tau + 2, \ldots$. Formally, let us restate Definition 2.12 for the present game.

DEFINITION 6.4 *Player i is said to be playing a* **trigger strategy** *if for every period τ, $\tau = 1, 2, \ldots$,*

$$q_i(\tau) = \begin{cases} L & \text{as long as } q_1(t) = q_2(t) = L \text{ for all } t = 1, \ldots, \tau - 1 \\ M & \text{Otherwise.} \end{cases}$$

In other words, firm i cooperates by restricting its output as long as all firms restrict their output levels in earlier periods. However, if any firm deviates even once, then firm i produces the static Cournot-Nash duopoly output level forever.

Equilibrium in trigger strategies

We now seek to investigate under what conditions playing trigger strategies constitutes a subgame perfect equilibrium (see Definition 2.10). It turns out that for a small discount factor, a firm may benefit by deviating from the cooperative output level, thereby collecting a temporary high profit by sacrificing the extra future profits generated by cooperation. However, for a sufficiently large discount factor we can state the following proposition:

Proposition 6.4 *If the discount factor is sufficiently large, then the outcome where both firms play their trigger strategies is a SPE. Formally, trigger strategies defined in Definition 6.4 constitute a SPE if $\rho > 9/17$.*

Proof. We look at a representative period, call it period τ, and suppose that neither firm has deviated in periods $t = 1, \ldots, \tau - 1$. Then, if firm 1 deviates and plays $q_1(\tau) = H$ (the best response to $q_2(\tau) = L$), Table 6.1 shows that $\pi_1(\tau) = 9/64 > 1/8$. However, given that firm 1 deviates, firm 2's equilibrium strategy calls for playing $q_2(t) = M$ for every $t \geq \tau + 1$. Hence the period $\tau + 1$ sum of discounted profits of firm 1 for all periods $t \geq \tau + 1$ is $\frac{1}{1-\rho}\frac{1}{9}$. Note that we used the familiar formula for calculating the present value of an infinite stream of profits given by $1 + \rho + \rho^2 + \rho^3 + \ldots = \sum_{t=0}^{\infty} \rho^t = \frac{1}{1-\rho}$. Hence, if firm 1 deviates in period τ, its sum of discounted profits is

$$\Pi_1 = \frac{9}{64} + \frac{\rho}{1-\rho}\frac{1}{9}. \tag{6.23}$$

However, if firm 1 does not deviate in period τ, then both firms continue producing the collusive output yielding

$$\Pi_1 = \frac{1}{1-\rho}\frac{1}{8}. \tag{6.24}$$

Comparing (6.23) with (6.24) yields the conclusion that deviation is *not* profitable for firm 1 if $\rho > 9/17$.

As we noted in the proof of Proposition 2.5, to prove subgame perfection we need to show that each firm would find it profitable to respond with deviation when it realizes that deviation occurred in an earlier period, as stated in the definition of the trigger strategy described in Definition 6.4. That is, we still need to show that a firm would produce a level of M forever once either firm deviated in an earlier period. In the language of game theorists, we need to show that the trigger strategy is the best response even if the game "drifts" off the equilibrium path. However, Definition 6.4 implies that if firm j deviates, then firm j would produce M in all future periods. Then, Table 6.1 shows that firm i's best response to firm j's playing M is to play M. Hence, the trigger strategies defined in Definition 6.4 constitute a SPE. ∎

Discussion of trigger strategies and extensions

The purpose of section 6.5 was to demonstrate that in an infinitely repeated game, the set of oligopoly equilibria is larger than that of a one-shot game and includes cooperative outcomes in addition to the familiar noncooperative outcome. Readers who wish to learn more about cooperation in oligopolistic market structures are referred to Abreu 1986, Friedman 1971, 1977, Green and Porter 1984, Segerstrom 1988, Tirole 1988, chap. 5, and more recent books on game theory noted in the references to chapter 2.

We conclude our analysis of dynamic collusion with two remarks: (a) We have not discussed what would happen to our cooperative equilibrium when we increase the number of firms in the industry. Lambson (1984) has shown that under general demand conditions the cooperation continues to hold as long as the demand for the product increases at the same rate as the number of firms. The intuition behind this result is as follows: If the number of firms grows over time but the demand stays constant, then the future profit of each firm would drop, implying that firms would have a stronger incentive to deviate from the collusive output level. Hence, in such a case, collusion is less likely to be sustained. (b) Another natural question to be asked is how booms and recessions affect the possibility of collusion among firms. Rotemberg and Saloner (1986) analyze collusion under stochastic demand. The problem they investigate is whether collusion is more sustainable during booms (a high realization of the demand) than during recessions (a low demand realization).

6.6   International Trade in Homogeneous Products

In this section we analyze two issues related to international trade in homogeneous products. Subsection 6.6.1 demonstrates the possibility that countries sell homogeneous products below cost in other countries. Subsection 6.6.2 evaluates how the formation of customs unions and free trade agreements affect international trade in homogeneous products.

6.6.1   Reciprocal dumping in international trade

An application of the Cournot equilibrium for international trade is given in Brander and Krugman 1983. Suppose that there are two identical trading countries indexed by k, $k = 1, 2$. The demand schedule in each country is given by $p_k(Q_k) = a - bQ_k$, where Q is the sum of local production and import. In each country there is one firm producing a homogeneous product that is sold both at home and abroad. To keep this example simple, assume that production is costless, that is, $c = 0$.

The two countries are separated by an ocean, and therefore, shipping the good across the continents is costly. Also, assume that the transportation cost is paid by the exporting firm.

Let τ denote the per-unit international transportation cost, and let q_k denote the production level of the firm located in country k, $k = 1, 2$. Since each firm sells both at home and abroad, the output of firm k is decomposed into home (local) sales (denoted by q_k^h) and foreign (export) sales (denoted by q_k^f). Therefore, the total output sold in country 1 is $Q_1 = q_1^h + q_2^f$, and the total output sold in country 2 is $Q_2 = q_2^h + q_1^f$.

The profit of each firm is the revenue collected in each country minus the cost of production (assumed to be zero) minus export transportation cost. Formally, the profit of the firm located in country 1 is

$$\pi_1 = p_1(q_1^h + q_2^f)q_1^h + p_2(q_1^f + q_2^h)q_1^f - \tau q_1^f. \qquad (6.25)$$

The profit of the firm located in country 2 is

$$\pi_2 = p_2(q_2^h + q_1^f)q_2^h + p_1(q_2^f + q_1^h)q_2^f - \tau q_2^f. \qquad (6.26)$$

The first-order conditions for (6.25) are

$$0 = \frac{\partial \pi_1}{\partial q_1^h} = a - 2bq_1^h - bq_2^f \quad \text{and} \quad 0 = \frac{\partial \pi_1}{\partial q_1^f} = a - 2bq_1^f - bq_2^h - \tau.$$

Notice that the two first-order conditions are independent in the sense that q_1^f (foreign sales) does not appear in the first condition and q_1^h (home sales) does not appear in the second. This follows from our particular use of the linear cost structure. In general, when the cost function is nonlinear, the two conditions would not be independent. The first-order conditions for (6.26)

$$0 = \frac{\partial \pi_2}{\partial q_2^h} = a - 2bq_2^h - bq_1^f \quad \text{and} \quad 0 = \frac{\partial \pi_2}{\partial q_2^f} = a - 2bq_2^f - bq_1^h - \tau.$$

Using this special case, we can solve for the Cournot equilibrium output levels for each country separately. In this case (6.5) implies that for firm k, $k = 1, 2$,

$$q_k^h = \frac{a + \tau}{3b}, \quad q_k^f = \frac{a - 2\tau}{3b}, \quad Q_k = \frac{2a - \tau}{3b}, \quad \text{and} \quad p_k = \frac{a + \tau}{3}. \qquad (6.27)$$

Note that as transportation becomes more costly (τ increases), the share of domestic sales increases in each country, whereas the level of export declines. Also, as τ increases, p_k increases.

Dumping

One of the major rules of GATT (General Agreement on Tariffs and Trade) is that dumping is prohibited. Before we define dumping we need to distinguish between two types of prices used in international transactions: (a) FOB price (free-on-board), meaning the price received by the producer when the product leaves the plant. This price does not include the payments for transportation and insurance. (b) CIF price (cost-insurance-freight), which includes all transportation as well as insurance costs. If we assume away dealers, which would make the CIF price even higher, the consumer pays the CIF price, whereas the exporter receives the FOB price per unit of export.

Brander and Krugman (1983) use the term *dumping* to describe a situation where the FOB export price is lower than the price charged for domestic sales. Formally, in the present model,

$$p_k^{CIF} = p_k = \frac{a + \tau}{3} \quad \text{and} \quad p_k^{FOB} = p_k^{CIF} - \tau = \frac{a - 2\tau}{3}. \qquad (6.28)$$

Thus, each firm in each country "dumps" the product in the other country by "subsidizing" the transportation cost. Another commonly used definition of dumping is when a firm sells abroad at a price below cost. This does not happen in the present model.

Finally, note that for this problem, the Cournot market structure generates inefficient trade since the world could save the transportation cost if each firm sells only in its home country. However, in general, making each firm a monopoly in its own country would generate the other familiar inefficiencies.

6.6.2 Homogeneous products and preferential trade agreements among countries

There are three general types of trade agreements among countries: (1) the free-trade agreement (FTA), which is an agreement among countries to eliminate trade barriers among the member countries, but under which each country is free to set its own trade restrictions against trade with nonmember countries; (2) the customs union (CU), which is an agreement among countries to eliminate tariffs on goods imported from other member countries of the union and to set a uniform trade policy regarding nonmember countries; and (3) the common market (CM), where, in addition to the elimination of tariffs among member countries and in addition to the common tariff policy toward nonmembers, there is a free movement of factors of production among member countries.

Formal analyses of these agreements were first given by Viner, Meade and Vanek, and the interested reader is referred to surveys of literature given in Corden 1984 and Vousden 1990, or in almost any elementary book on international trade.

Consider the following world. There are three countries: the European Community (EC), the Far East (FE) and Israel (IL). Assume that IL is a small country, thus it cannot affect the world prices. Only FE and EC produce carpets that are imported by IL. Assume that carpets cannot be produced in IL. We further assume that IL's demand for imported carpets is given by $p^{IL} = a - Q$, where Q denotes the quantity demanded and p^{IL} is the domestic tariff-inclusive price.

Assume that initially (period 0), IL sets a uniform tariff of $\$t$ per carpet irrespective of where the carpets are imported from. Then, in period 1 assume that IL signs a free-trade agreement (FTA) with EC.

Period 0: IL levies a uniform tariff on carpets

We denote by p_{EC} the price of a carpet charged by EC's producers, and by p_{FE} the price charged by FE's producers. Hence, with a uniform tariff of t, the price paid by IL's consumers for carpets imported from EC is $p_{EC}^{IL} = p_{EC} + t$, and the price paid for carpets imported from FE is $p_{FE}^{IL} = p_{FE} + t$. We make the following assumption:

ASSUMPTION 6.1 *The export price of carpets in EC exceeds the export price in FE. Formally, $p_{EC} > p_{FE}$.*

Figure 6.4 illustrates IL's demand for imported carpets and the prices (with and without the tariff) on carpets imported from EC and FE. Figure 6.4 shows that IL will import from the cheapest supplier, which is

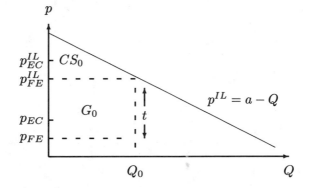

Figure 6.4: IL's import level under a uniform tariff

FE, so that the import level would be Q^0. In this case, the government's revenue from import-tariff collection would be $G^0 = tQ^0$. The IL's consumer surplus (see subsection 3.2.3 for a definition) is given by $CS^0 = (a - p_{FE}^{IL})Q^0/2$. Also, note that $Q^0 = a - p_{FE}^{IL} = a - p_{FE} - t$.

We define IL's social welfare as the sum of consumer surplus plus IL's government revenue from tariff collection. Note that in modeling international trade it is very important not to forget the existence of government's revenue and to assume that the government returns the tariff revenue to consumers in a lump-sum fashion or by other services. Hence,

$$W_{IS}^0 \equiv CS^0 + G^0 = (a - p_{FE}^{IL} + 2t)Q^0/2 = (a - p_{FE} + t)Q^0/2$$

implying that

$$W_{IS}^0 = \frac{(a - p_{FE} + t)(a - p_{FE} - t)}{2} = \frac{(a - p_{FE})^2 - t^2}{2}. \qquad (6.29)$$

Note that the last step in (6.29) uses the mathematical identity that $(\alpha + \beta)(\alpha - \beta) \equiv \alpha^2 - \beta^2$. Equation (6.29) shows that the welfare of country IL decreases with the tariff rate t and with FE's price of carpets.

Period 1: IL signs a free-trade agreement with the EC

Now suppose that IL signs a FTA with EC, so that the tariff on carpets imported from EC is now set to zero, whereas the tariff on imports from FE remains the same at the level of t per unit. Figure 6.5 illustrates that IL switches from importing from FE to importing from only EC for a price of $p_{EC}^{IL} = p_{EC}$. Given that the price of carpets drops in IL, the

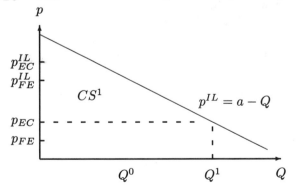

Figure 6.5: IL's import under the FTA

quantity of imported carpets increases to $Q^1 = a - p_{EC} > Q^0$. Notice that although IL's consumer price of carpets has decreased, IL now buys carpets from the more expensive source.

Under the FTA, since all the imports are from EC, the government collects zero revenue, that is $G^1 = 0$. Hence, IL's social welfare equals IL's consumer surplus. That is, $W^1 = CS^1$. The consumers' surplus is illustrated in Figure 6.5 and is calculated to be

$$W_{IL}^1 = CS^1 = (a - p_{EC})Q^1/2 = (a - p_{EC})^2/2. \qquad (6.30)$$

Welfare analysis of the free-trade agreement

We now analyze whether IL gains from the FTA with EC. Comparing (6.29) and (6.30), we see that the FTA improves IL's welfare if $W^1 > W^0$. That is,

$$(a - p_{EC})^2 > (a - p_{FE})^2 - t^2$$

or,

$$t > \sqrt{(a - p_{FE})^2 - (a - p_{EC})^2}. \qquad (6.31)$$

Therefore,

Proposition 6.5 *A free-trade agreement between IL and EC is more likely to be welfare improving for IL when (a) the initial uniform tariff is high, and (b) when the difference in prices between the two foreign exporters is small; that is, when p_{EC} is close to p_{FE}.*

We conclude this analysis with a graphic illustration of the gains and loss from the FTA. Figure 6.6 illustrates the welfare implication of IL's signing the FTA with EC. In Figure 6.6, the area denoted by ϕ

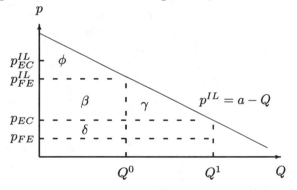

Figure 6.6: The welfare effects of the free-trade agreement

measures IL's consumer surplus prior to signing the FTA. The sum of the areas $\beta + \delta$ measures IL's government tariff revenue prior to signing the agreement. Hence, IL's welfare prior to signing the agreement is $W^0 = \phi + \beta + \delta$.

In Figure 6.6, the sum of the areas $\phi + \beta + \gamma$ measures IL's consumer surplus after the FTA is signed. Since there are no tariff revenues after the FTA (all carpets are imported from the EC), the welfare of IL after the FTA is $W^1 = \phi + \beta + \gamma$.

Altogether, the welfare change resulting from signing the FTA is given by $\Delta W \equiv W^1 - W^0 = \gamma - \delta$.

DEFINITION 6.5 *The change in consumer surplus due to the increase in the consumption of the imported good (area γ in Figure 6.6) is called the* **trade-creation effect** *of the FTA. The change in the importing country's expenditure due to the switch to importing from the more expensive country (area δ in Figure 6.6) is called the* **trade-diversion effect** *of the FTA.*

Thus, the importing country gains from the FTA if the (positive) trade-creation effect associated with the increase in the import level dominates the (negative) trade-diversion effect associated to switching to importing from the more expensive source.

6.7   Appendix: Cournot Market Structure with Heterogeneous Firms

In this appendix we extend the analysis conducted in Subsection 6.1.2, and solve for the Cournot-market-structure equilibrium when there is a large number of firms with different cost functions. Following Bergstrom and Varian (1985), we introduce a method for calculating a Cournot-Nash equilibrium output level without resorting to solving N first-order conditions for the equilibrium N output levels.

In a Cournot market structure with N firms, each with a unit cost of $c_i \geq 0$, $i = 1, \ldots, N$, each firm i chooses its output q_i that solves

$$\max_{q_i} \pi_i(q_i, q_{-i}^c) = \left[a - bq_i - b \left(\sum_{j \neq i} q_j^c \right) \right] q_i - c_i q_i$$

yielding, assuming $q_i^c > 0$ for all i, a first-order condition

$$a - 2bq_i^c - b \left(\sum_{j \neq i} q_j^c \right) = c_i, \quad i = 1, \ldots, N.$$

Now, instead of solving N equations (N first-order conditions) for N output levels, we solve for the aggregate production level by rewriting the first-order conditions in the form of:

$$a - bq_i^c - bQ^c = c_i, \quad i = 1, \ldots, N.$$

Summing over all q_i, $i = 1, \ldots, N$ yields

$$Na - bQ^c - bNQ^c = \sum_{i=1}^{N} c_i.$$

Hence, the Cournot equilibrium aggregate industry output and market price are given by

$$Q^c = \frac{Na}{(N+1)b} - \frac{\sum_{i=1}^{N} c_i}{(N+1)b} \quad \text{and} \quad p^c = \frac{a}{N+1} + \frac{\sum_{i=1}^{N} c_i}{N+1}. \quad (6.32)$$

Hence,

Proposition 6.6 *In an industry where firms have constant unit costs, if in a Cournot equilibrium all firms produce strictly positive output levels, then the Cournot aggregate industry equilibrium output and price levels depend only on the sum of the firms' unit costs and not on the distribution of unit costs among the firms.*

The result stated in Proposition 6.6 is important, since it implies that under constant unit costs, industry output, price, and hence, total welfare can be calculated by using the sum of firms' unit costs, without investigating the precise cost distribution among firms. Moreover, the proof of Proposition 6.6 does not rely on linear demand and therefore also applies to nonlinear demand functions.

We conclude this appendix by illustrating a simple application of Proposition 6.6. Consider an industry consisting of two type of firms: high-cost and low-cost firms. Suppose that there are $H \geq 1$ high-cost firms with a unit production cost given by c_H, and $L \geq 1$ low-cost firms with a unit production cost given by c_L, where $c_H \geq c_L \geq 0$. Substituting into (6.32) yields

$$Q^c = \frac{(H+L)a}{(H+L+1)b} - \frac{Hc_H + Lc_L}{(H+L+1)b} \quad \text{and} \quad p^c = \frac{a}{H+L+1} + \frac{Hc_H + Lc_L}{H+L+1}. \quad (6.33)$$

Hence, the Cournot output and price equilibrium levels depend only on $Hc_H + Lc_L$. The advantage of learning this method for calculating Cournot equilibrium outcomes becomes clear in the case where there is an entry (or exit) of some firms. For example, suppose we observe that three additional low-cost firms have joined the industry. Then, the new Cournot equilibrium industry output and price can be immediately calculated by replacing $Hc_H + Lc_L$ with $Hc_H + (L+3)c_L$ in (6.33).

6.8   Exercises

1. Two firms produce a homogeneous product. Let p denote the product's price. The output level of firm 1 is denoted by q_1, and the output level of firm 2 by q_2. The aggregate industry output is denoted by Q, $Q \equiv q_1 + q_2$. The aggregate industry demand curve for this product is given by $p = \alpha - Q$.

    Assume that the unit cost of firm 1 is c_1 and the unit cost of firm 2 is c_2, where $\alpha > c_2 > c_1 > 0$. Perform the following:

    (a) Solve for a competitive equilibrium (see Definition 4.2 on page 65). Make sure that you solve for the output level of each firm and the market price.

    (b) Solve for a Cournot equilibrium (see Definition 6.1 on page 99). Make sure that you solve for the output level of each firm and the market price.

    (c) Solve for a sequential-moves equilibrium (see Section 6.2 on page 104) assuming that firm 1 sets its output level before firm 2 does.

    (d) Solve for a sequential-moves equilibrium, assuming that firm 2 sets its output level before firm 1 does. Is there any difference in market shares and the price level between the present case and the case where firm 1 moves first? Explain!

    (e) Solve for a Bertrand equilibrium (see Definition 6.2 on page 108). Make sure that you solve for the output level of each firm and the market price.

2. In an industry there are N firms producing a homogeneous product. Let q_i denote the output level of firm i, $i = 1, 2, \ldots, N$, and let Q denote the aggregate industry production level. That is, $Q \equiv \sum_{i=1}^{N} q_i$. Assume that the demand curve facing the industry is $p = 100 - Q$. Suppose that the cost function of each firm i is given by

$$TC_i(q_i) \equiv \begin{cases} F + (q_i)^2 & \text{if } q_i > 0 \\ 0 & \text{if } q_i = 0. \end{cases}$$

    Solve the following problems:

    (a) Suppose that the number of firms in the industry N is sufficiently small so that all the N firms make above-normal profits. Calculate the output and profit levels of each firm in a Cournot equilibrium.

    (b) Now, assume that firms are allowed to enter or the exit from the industry. Find the equilibrium number of firms in the industry as a function of F. *Hint:* Equate a firm's profit level that you found earlier to zero and solve for N.

3. Consider a three-period version of the sequential-moves equilibrium analyzed in section 6.2. Assume that the market inverse demand curve is

given by $p = 120 - Q$, and suppose that there are three firms that set their output levels sequentially: firm 1 sets q_1 in period 1, firm 2 sets q_2 in period 2, and firm 3 sets q_3 in period 3. Then, firms sell their output and collect their profits. Solve for the sequential-moves equilibrium (assuming that production is costless). Make sure that you solve for the output level of each firm, and the market price.

4. Two firms compete in prices in a market for a homogeneous product. In this market there are $N > 0$ consumers; each buys one unit if the price of the product does not exceed \$10, and nothing otherwise. Consumers buy from the firm selling at a lower price. In case both firms charge the same price, assume that $N/2$ consumers buy from each firm. Assume zero production cost for both firms.

   (a) Find the Bertrand equilibrium prices for a single-shot game, assuming that the firms choose their prices simultaneously.

   (b) Now suppose that the game is repeated infinitely. Let ρ denote the time-discount parameter. Propose trigger price strategies for both firms yielding the collusive prices of (10, 10) each period. Calculate the minimal value of ρ that would enforce the trigger price strategies you proposed.

   (c) Now suppose that the unit production cost of firm 2 is \$4, but the unit cost of firm 1 remained zero. Find the Bertrand equilibrium prices for the single-shot game.

   (d) Assuming the new cost structure, propose trigger price strategies for both firms yielding the collusive prices of (10, 10) each period, and calculate the minimal value of ρ that would enforce the trigger price strategies you propose.

   (e) Conclude whether it is easier for firms to enforce the collusive prices when there is symmetric industry cost structure, or when the firms have different cost structures. Explain!

5. Consider the free-trade agreement model analyzed in subsection 6.6.2. Suppose that the world consists of three countries denoted by A, B, and C. Country A imports shoes from countries B and C and does not have local production of shoes. Let the export shoe prices of countries B and C be given by $p_B = \$60$ and $p_C = \$40$. Also, suppose that initially, country A levies a uniform import tariff of $t = \$10$ per each pair of imported shoes. Answer the following questions:

   (a) Suppose that country A signs a FTA with country B. Does country A gain or lose from this agreement? Explain!

   (b) Suppose now that initially, the export price of shoes in country C is $p_C = \$50.01$. Under this condition, will country A gain or lose from the FTA? Explain!

6. In a market for luxury cars there are two firms competing in prices. Each firm can choose to set a high price given by p_H, or a low price

given by p_L, where $p_H > p_L \geq 0$. The profit levels of the two firms as a function of the prices chosen by both firms is given in Table 6.2. The rules of this two-stage market game are as follows: In the first

Firm 2

		p_H		p_L	
Firm 1	p_H	100	100	0	120
	p_L	120	0	70	70

Table 6.2: Meet the competition clause

stage firm 1 sets its price $p_1 \in \{p_H, p_L\}$. In the second stage firm 1 cannot reverse its decision, whereas firm 2 observes p_1 and then chooses $p_2 \in \{p_H, p_L\}$. Then, the game ends and each firm collects its profit according to Table 6.2.

(a) Formulate the game in extensive form (Definition 2.7 on page 24) by drawing the game tree, and solve for the subgame perfect equilibrium (Definition 2.10 on page 27) for this game.

(b) Suppose now that firm 1 offers its consumers to match its price with the lowest price in the market (the so-called meet the competition clause). Solve for the subgame perfect equilibrium for the modified game. *Hint:* Modify the game to three stages, allowing firm 1 to make a move in the third stage only in the case where it chose p_H in the first stage and firm 2 chose p_L in the second stage.

7. This problem is directed to highly advanced students only: Suppose there are $N > 2$ firms that set their output sequentially, as described in section 6.2. Suppose that all firms have identical unit costs given by c, and suppose that the market inverse demand curve facing this industry is given by $p = a - Q$, where $a > c \geq 0$ and $Q \equiv \sum_{i=1}^{N} q_i$.

(a) Solve for the sequential-moves equilibrium by showing that the output level of the firm that moves in period i, $i = 1, \ldots, N$ is given by

$$q_i^s = \frac{a - c}{2^i}.$$

(b) Show that the aggregate equilibrium-output level is given by

$$Q^s \equiv \sum_{i=1}^{N} q_i = \left[1 - \frac{1}{2^N}\right](a - c).$$

(c) Conclude what happens to the aggregate industry-output level when the number of firms (and periods) increases with no bounds, (i.e., when $N \to \infty$).

6.9 References

Abreu, D. 1986. "Extremal Equilibria of Oligopolistic Supergames." *Journal of Economic Theory* 39: 191–225.

Bergstrom, T., and H. Varian. 1985. "When Are Nash Equilibria Independent of the Distribution of Agents' Characteristics?" *Review of Economics Studies* 52: 715–718.

Bertrand, J. 1883. Reviews of *Théories Mathematique de la Richesse Sociale,* by Léon Walras; and of *Recherches sur les Principles Mathematiques de la Théorie des Richesses,* by Augustin Cournot. *Journal des Savants* 67: 499–508.

Bork, R. 1978. *The Antitrust Paradox.* New York: Basic Books.

Brander, J., and P. Krugman. 1983. "A 'Reciprocal Dumping' Model of International Trade." *Journal of International Economics* 15: 313–321.

Corden, M. 1984. "The Normative Theory of International Trade." In *Handbook of International Economics,* edited by R. Jones and P. Kenen. Amsterdam: North-Holland.

Cournot, A. 1929 [1838]. *Researches into the Mathematical Principles of the Theory of Wealth.* Translated by Nathaniel Bacon. New York: Macmillan.

Edgeworth, F. 1925 [1897]. "The Pure Theory of Monopoly." In *Papers Relating to Political Economy,* edited by F. Edgeworth. London: Macmillan.

Friedman, J. 1971. "A Noncooperative Equilibrium for Supergames." *Review of Economic Studies* 38: 1–12.

Friedman, J. 1977. *Oligopoly and the Theory of Games.* Amsterdam: North-Holland.

Green, E., and R. Porter. 1984. "Non-cooperative Collusion Under Imperfect Price Information." *Econometrica,* 52: 87–100

Konow, J. 1994. "The Political Economy of Heinrich von Stackelberg." *Economic Inquiry* 32: 146–165.

Kreps, D., and J. Scheinkman. 1983. "Quantity Precommitment and Bertrand Competition Yield Cournot Outcomes." *Bell Journal of Economics* 14: 326–337.

Lambson, V. 1984. "Self-Enforcing Collusion in Large Dynamic Markets." *Journal of Economic Theory* 34: 282–291.

Rotemberg, J., and G. Saloner. 1986. "Supergame-Theoretic Model of Business Cycles and Price Wars During Booms." *American Economic Review* 76: 390–407.

Segerstrom, P. 1988. "Demons and Repentance." *Journal of Economic Theory* 45: 32–52.

Shubik. M. 1987. "Cournot, Antoine Augustin." In *The New Palgrave Dictionary of Economics,* edited by J. Eatwell, M. Milgate, and P. Newman. New York: The Stockton Press.

von Stackelberg, H. 1934. *Marktform und Gleichgewicht (Market structure and equilibrium)*. Vienna: Springer-Verlag.

Tirole, J. 1988. *The Theory of Industrial Organization*. Cambridge, Mass.: MIT Press.

Vousden, N. 1990. *The Economics of Trade Protection*. Cambridge: Cambridge University Press.

Chapter 7

Markets for
Differentiated Products

> You can have it any color you want as long as it's black.
> —Attributed to Henry Ford

In this chapter we analyze oligopolies producing differentiated products. Where in chapter 6 consumers could not recognize or did not bother to learn the producers' names or logos of homogeneous products, here, consumers are able to distinguish among the different producers and to treat the products (brands) as close but imperfect substitutes.

Several important observations make the analysis of differentiated products highly important.

1. Most industries produce a large number of similar but not identical products.

2. Only a small subset of all possible varieties of differentiated products are actually produced. For example, most products are not available in all colors.

3. Most industries producing differentiated products are concentrated, in the sense that it is typical to have two to five firms in an industry.

4. Consumers purchase a small subset of the available product varieties.

This chapter introduces the reader to several approaches to modeling industries producing differentiated products to explain one or more of these observations.

Product differentiation models are divided into two groups: non-address models, and address (location) models. Figure 7.1 illustrates the logical connections among the various approaches. The non-address

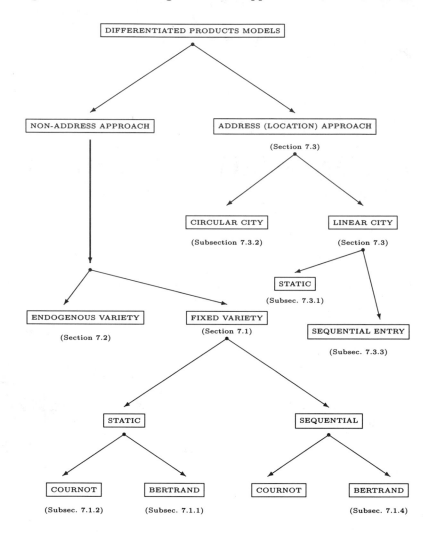

Figure 7.1: Approaches to modeling differentiated-products industries

approach, displayed on the left main branch of Figure 7.1, is divided into two categories: a fixed number of differentiated brands models, and endogenously determined variety models. The fixed number of brands approach is analyzed in section 7.1 (Simple Models for Differentiated

Products), where we analyze and compare quantity and price competition between the two differentiated-brands producers. Basic definitions for the degrees of product differentiation are provided and utilized in the two types of market structures. Section 7.2 (Monopolistic Competition) analyzes a general equilibrium environment where free entry is allowed, so the number of brands in an industry is determined in the model itself. We assume that the economy is represented by a single consumer whose preferences exhibit love for variety of differentiated brands, and that firms' technologies exhibit returns to scale together with fixed cost of production. Assuming free entry of firms enables us to compute the equilibrium variety of differentiated brands. The monopolistic competition approach proves to be extremely useful in analyzing international markets, which is discussed in subsection 7.2.2.

The address (location) approach, displayed on the right main branch of Figure 7.1, is analyzed in section 7.3 (Location Models). This approach provides an alternative method for modeling product differentiation by introducing location, or addresses, into consumers' preferences that measure how close the brands actually produced are to the consumers' ideal brands. This approach is useful to model heterogeneous consumers who have different tastes for the different brands.

Together, sections 7.2 and 7.3 discuss the two major approaches to product differentiation: the non-address approach and the address approach, respectively (see a discussion in Eaton and Lipsey 1989). The major difference between the approaches is that in the non-address approach all consumers gain utility from consuming a variety of products and therefore buy a variety of brands (such as a variety of music records, of movies, of software, of food, etc.). In contrast, the address (location) approach, each consumer buys only one brand (such as one computer, one car, or one house), but consumers have different preferences for their most preferred brand. A third approach to product differentiation, not discussed in this chapter, is found in Lancaster 1971. Lancaster's "characteristics" approach assumes that each product consists of many characteristics (such as color, durability, safety, strength); in choosing a specific brand, the consumer looks for the brand that would yield the most suitable combinations of the product's characteristics. Finally, a reader interested in applications of product differentiation to the ready-to-eat cereals industry is referred to Scherer 1979 and Schmalensee 1978.

7.1 Simple Models for Two Differentiated Products

Consider a two-firm industry producing two differentiated products indexed by $i = 1, 2$. To simplify the exposition, we assume that production is costless. Following Dixit (1979) and Singh and Vives (1984), we assume the following (inverse) demand structure for the two products:

$$p_1 = \alpha - \beta q_1 - \gamma q_2 \quad \text{and} \quad p_2 = \alpha - \gamma q_1 - \beta q_2, \quad \text{where} \quad \beta > 0, \ \beta^2 > \gamma^2.$$
$$(7.1)$$

Thus, we assume that that there is a fixed number of two brands and that each is produced by a different firm facing an inverse demand curve given in (7.1). The assumption of $\beta^2 > \gamma^2$ is very important since it implies that the effect of increasing q_1 on p_1 is larger than the effect of the same increase in q_2. That is, the price of a brand is more sensitive to a change in the quantity of this brand than to a change in the quantity of the competing brand. A common terminology used to describe this assumption is to say that the *own-price effect* dominates the *cross-price effect*.

The demand structure exhibited in (7.1) is formulated as a system of inverse demand functions where prices are functions of quantity purchased. In order to find the direct demand functions, (quantity demanded as functions of brands' prices) we need to invert the system given in (7.1). The appendix (section 7.4) shows that

$$q_1 = a - bp_1 + cp_2 \quad \text{and} \quad q_2 = a + cp_1 - bp_2, \quad \text{where} \qquad (7.2)$$

$$a \equiv \frac{\alpha(\beta - \gamma)}{\beta^2 - \gamma^2}, \quad b \equiv \frac{\beta}{\beta^2 - \gamma^2} > 0, \quad c \equiv \frac{\gamma}{\beta^2 - \gamma^2} > 0.$$

How to measure the degree of brand differentiation

We would now like to define a measure for the degree of product differentiation.

DEFINITION 7.1 *The brands'* **measure of differentiation**, *denoted by* δ, *is*

$$\delta \equiv \frac{\gamma^2}{\beta^2}.$$

1. *The brands are said to be* **highly differentiated** *if consumers find the products to be very different, so a change in the price of brand j will have a small or negligible effect on the demand for brand i. Formally, brands are highly differentiated if δ is close to 0. That is, when $\gamma^2 \to 0$, (hence $c \to 0$).*

2. *The brands are said to be* **almost homogeneous** *if the cross-price effect is close or equal to the own-price effect. In this case, prices of all brands will have strong effects on the demand for each brand, more precisely, if an increase in the price brand j will increase the*

demand for brand i by the same magnitude as a decrease in the price of brand i, that is, when δ is close to 1, or equivalently when $\gamma^2 \to \beta^2$, (hence $c \to b$).

Figure 7.2 illustrates the relationships between the the demand parameters β and γ as described in Definition 7.1. In Figure 7.2 a hori-

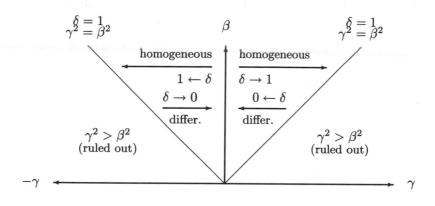

Figure 7.2: Measuring the degree of product differentiation

zontal movement toward the diagonals implies that the products are becoming more homogeneous, $(\gamma^2 \to \beta^2)$. In contrast, a movement toward the center is associated with the products becoming more differentiated, $(\gamma \to 0)$.

7.1.1 Quantity game with differentiated products

We now solve for the prices and quantity produced under the Cournot market structure, where firms choose quantity produced as actions. Just as we did in solving a Cournot equilibrium for the homogeneous products case, we look for a Nash equilibrium in firms' output levels, as defined in Definition 6.1 on page 99.

Assuming zero production cost, using the inverse demand functions given in (7.1), we note that each firm i takes q_j as given and chooses q_i to

$$\max_{q_i} \pi_i(q_1, q_2) = (\alpha - \beta q_i - \gamma q_j)q_i \quad i,j = 1,2, \ i \neq j. \qquad (7.3)$$

The first-order conditions are given by $0 = \frac{\partial \pi_i}{\partial q_i} = \alpha - 2\beta q_i - \gamma q_j$, yielding best response functions given by

$$q_i = R_i(q_j) = \frac{\alpha - \gamma q_j}{2\beta} \quad i, j = 1, 2, \ i \neq j. \qquad (7.4)$$

Figure 7.3 illustrates the best-response functions in the $(q_1 - q_2)$ space. Notice that these functions are similar to the ones obtained for the Cournot game with homogeneous products illustrated in Figure 6.1. Notice that as $\gamma \nearrow \beta$ (the products are more homogeneous), the best-

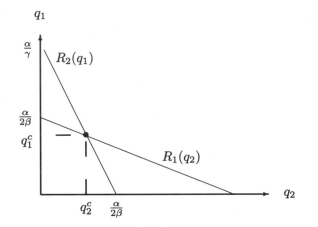

Figure 7.3: Best-response functions for quantity competition in differentiated products

response function becomes steeper, thereby making the profit-maximizing output level of firm i more sensitive to changes in the output level of firm j (due to stiffer competition). In contrast, as $\gamma \searrow 0$, the best-response function becomes constant (zero sloped), since the products become completely differentiated.

Solving the best-response functions (7.4), using symmetry, we have that

$$q_i^c = \frac{\alpha}{2\beta + \gamma}, \quad p_i^c = \frac{\alpha\beta}{2\beta + \gamma}, \quad \pi_i^c = \frac{\alpha^2\beta}{(2\beta + \gamma)^2} \quad i = 1, 2. \qquad (7.5)$$

Clearly, as γ increases (the products are less differentiated), the individual and aggregate quantity produced, the prices, and the profits all decline. Hence,

Proposition 7.1 *In a Cournot game with differentiated products, the profits of firms increase when the products become more differentiated.*

The importance of Proposition 7.1 is that it can explain why firms tend to spend large sums of money to advertise their brands: because firms would like the consumers to believe that the brands are highly differentiated from the competing brands for the purpose of increasing their profits. In other words, differentiation increases the monopoly power of brand-producing firms.

7.1.2   Price game with differentiated products

We now solve for the prices and quantity produced under the Bertrand market structure, where firms choose prices as their actions. Just as we did in solving for a Bertrand equilibrium for the homogeneous products case, we look for a Nash equilibrium in firms' prices, as defined in Definition 6.2 on page 108 for the homogeneous product case.

Using the direct demand functions given in (7.2), each firm i takes p_j as given and chooses p_i to

$$\max_{p_i} \pi_i(p_1, p_2) = (a - bp_i + cp_j)p_i \quad i, j = 1, 2, \ i \neq j. \qquad (7.6)$$

The first-order conditions are given by $0 = \frac{\partial \pi_i}{\partial p_i} = a - 2bp_i + cp_j$, yielding best-response functions given by

$$p_i = R_i(p_j) = \frac{a + cp_j}{2b} \quad i, j = 1, 2, \ i \neq j. \qquad (7.7)$$

The best-response functions are drawn in Figure 7.4. You have probably

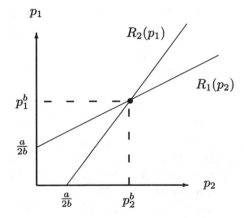

Figure 7.4: Best-response functions for price competition in differentiated products

noticed that there is something different in Figure 7.4 compared with
what is in Figure 7.3: In price games, the best-response functions are
upward sloping, meaning that if one firm raises its price, the other would
respond by raising its price as well. Well, this "discovery" deserves a
definition (Bulow, Geanakoplos, and Klemperer 1985):

DEFINITION 7.2

1. *Players' strategies are said to be* **strategic substitutes** *if the best-response functions are downward sloping.*

2. *Players' strategies are said to be* **strategic complements** *if the best-response functions are upward sloping.*

Note that this terminology may be misleading, since there is no relationship between this definition and whether goods are substitutes or
complements in consumption. Definition 7.2 implies that in a quantity
game the quantities are strategic substitutes, whereas in a price game
prices are strategic complements.

   Solving (7.7) yields for $i = 1, 2$,

$$p_i^b = \frac{a}{2b - c} = \frac{\alpha(\beta - \gamma)}{2\beta - \gamma}, q_i^b = \frac{ab}{2b - c}, \pi_i^b = \frac{a^2 b}{(2b - c)^2} = \frac{\alpha^2 \beta(\beta - \gamma)}{(2\beta - \gamma)^2(\beta + \gamma)}$$
$$(7.8)$$

The profit levels decline when the products become less differentiated
(γ increases). In the limit, when $\gamma = \beta$, the products become homogeneous, and the profits drop to zero as in the Bertrand equilibrium for
homogeneous products analyzed in section 6.2. Hence,

Proposition 7.2 *In a Bertrand game with differentiated products, the
profits of firms increase when the products become more differentiated.*

As with the Cournot case, product differentiation increases the monopoly
power of brand-producing firms by loosening up price competition among
the brand-producing firms.

7.1.3   Cournot versus Bertrand in differentiated products

Which market structure, a Cournot or a Bertrand, would yield a higher
market price? How would changing the degree of product differentiation affect the relative difference between the two market-structure
outcomes? As you may expect, the price under Bertrand is indeed
lower than it is under the Cournot market structure. Formally, comparing (7.5) with (7.8) yields

$$p_i^c - p_i^b = \frac{\alpha\beta}{2\beta + \gamma} - \frac{a}{2b - c} = \frac{\alpha\beta}{2\beta + \gamma} - \frac{\alpha(\beta - \gamma)}{2\beta - \gamma} = \frac{\alpha}{4\frac{\beta^2}{\gamma^2} - 1}. \quad (7.9)$$

Thus,

Proposition 7.3 *In a differentiated products industry:*

1. *The market price under Cournot is higher than it is under Bertrand. Formally $p_i^c > p_i^b$.*

2. *The more differentiated the products are, the smaller the difference between the Cournot and Bertrand prices. Formally, $\frac{\partial[p_i^c - p_i^b]}{\partial \gamma} > 0$.*

3. *This difference in prices is zero when the products become independent. Formally, $\lim_{\gamma \to 0}[p_i^c - p_i^b] = 0$.*

The intuition behind Proposition 7.3, given in Vives 1985, is as follows: Under Cournot market structure each firm expects the other firm to hold its output level constant. Hence, each firm would maintain a low output level since it is aware that a unilateral output expansion would result in a drop in the market price. In contrast, under the Bertrand market structure each firm assumes that the rival firm holds its price constant, hence output expansion will not result in a price reduction. Therefore, more output is produced under the Bertrand market structure than under the Cournot market structure. Cheng 1985 provides some additional graphical intuition for the differences between the market outcomes obtained under the two market structures.

7.1.4 Sequential-moves price game

Consider a two-period, price-setting sequential game that is similar to the sequential-moves quantity game described in section 6.2; but here, we let firms set prices rather than quantity produced. In order to have some fun, let us take a specific numerical example for the demand system given in (7.2):

$$q_1 = 168 - 2p_1 + p_2 \quad \text{and} \quad q_2 = 168 + p_1 - 2p_2. \qquad (7.10)$$

For this particular example, (7.8) implies that the single-period game Bertrand prices and profit levels are $p_i^b = 56$ and $\pi_i^b = 6272$.

Following the same logical steps as those in section 6.2, we look for a SPE in prices where firm 1 sets its price before firm 2. Thus, in the first period, firm 1 takes firm 2's best-response function (7.7) as given, and chooses p_1 that solves

$$\max_{p_1} \pi_1(p_1, R_2(p_1)) = \left(168 - 2p_1 + \frac{168 + p_1}{4}\right) p_1. \qquad (7.11)$$

The first-order condition is $0 = \frac{\partial \pi_1}{\partial p_1} = 210 - \frac{7}{2}p_1$. Therefore, $p_1^s = 60$, hence, $p_2^s = 57$. Substituting into (7.10) yields that $q_1^s = 105$ and $q_2 = 114$. Hence, $\pi_1^s = 60 \times 105 = 6300 > \pi_1^b$, and $\pi_2^s = 57 \times 114 = 6498 > \pi_2^b$.

Why do we bother to go over this exercise under a price game? Well, the following proposition yields a rather surprising result concerning the relationship between firms' profit levels and the order of moves.

Proposition 7.4 *Under a sequential-moves price game (or more generally, under any game where actions are strategically complements):*

1. *Both firms collect a higher profit under a sequential-moves game than under the single-period Bertrand game. Formally, $\pi_i^s > \pi_i^b$ for $i = 1, 2$.*

2. *The firm that sets its price first (the leader) makes a lower profit than the firm that sets its price second (the follower).*

3. *Compared to the Bertrand profit levels, the increase in profit to the first mover (the leader) is smaller than the increase in profit to the second mover (the follower). Formally, $\pi_1^s - \pi_1^b < \pi_2^s - \pi_2^b$.*

It this amazing? What we have learned from this example is that being the first to move is not always an advantage. Here, each firm would want the other firm to make the first move. The intuition behind this result is as follows. When firm 1 sets its price in period 1, it calculates that firm 2 will slightly undercut p_1 in order to obtain a larger market share than firm 1. This calculation puts pressure on firm 1 to maintain a high price to avoid having firm 2 set a very low market price. Hence, both firms set prices above the static Bertrand price levels. Now, firm 1 always makes a lower profit than firm 2, since firm 2 slightly undercuts firm 1 and captures a larger market share.

Finally, note that we could have predicted that the profit of firm 1 will increase beyond the static Bertrand profit level even without resorting to the precise calculations. Using a *revealed profitability* argument, we can see clearly that firm 1 can always set $p_1 = p_1^b$ and make the same profit as under the static Bertrand game. However, given that firm 1 chooses a different price, its profit can only increase.

Finally, part 1 of Proposition 7.4 reveals the major difference between the price sequential-moves game and the quantity sequential-moves game analyzed in section 6.2. Here, the profit of firm 2 (the follower's) is higher under the sequential-moves price game than its profit under the static Bertrand game. In contrast, under the sequential-moves quantity game the followers' profit is lower than it is under the static Cournot game.

7.2 Monopolistic Competition in Differentiated Products

In this section, we analyze a monopolistic-competition environment (Chamberlin 1933). Our major goal is to calculate the equilibrium number of differentiated brands produced by the industry.

The main features of this environment are that: (1) consumers are homogeneous (have identical preferences) or can be represented by a single consumer who loves to consume a variety of brands. Thus, this model better describes markets in which consumers like to consume a large variety of brands—such as a variety of music records, of video, of clothes, and of movies—rather than markets for cars where most individuals consume, at most, one unit; (2) there is an unlimited number of potentially produced brands; and (3) free entry of new brand-producing firms.

It should be pointed out that this model is a general equilibrium one. Unlike the partial equilibrium models, the general equilibrium model is one where consumers' demand is derived from a utility maximization where the consumers' income is generated from selling labor to firms and from owning the firms. Subsection 7.2.1 analyzes a single-economy monopolistic competition, and subsection 7.2.2 extends the model to two open economies.

7.2.1 The basic model

We analyze here a simplified version of Dixit and Stiglitz 1977. Consider an industry producing differentiated brands indexed by $i = 1, 2, 3, \ldots, N$, where N is an endogenously determined number of produced brands. We denote by $q_i \geq 0$ the quantity produced/consumed of brand i, and by p_i the price of one unit of brand i.

Consumers

In this economy, there is a single (representative) consumer whose preferences exhibit the love-for-variety property. Formally, the utility function of the representative consumer is given by a constant-elasticity-of-substitution (CES) utility function:

$$u(q_1, q_2, \ldots) \equiv \sum_{i=1}^{\infty} \sqrt{q_i}. \qquad (7.12)$$

This type of utility function exhibits love for variety since the marginal utility of each brand at a zero consumption level is infinite. That is, $\lim_{q_i \to 0} \frac{\partial u}{\partial q_i} = \lim_{q_i \to 0} \frac{1}{2\sqrt{q_i}} = +\infty$.

In addition, Figure 7.5 illustrates that the indifference curves are convex to the origin, indicating that the consumers like to mix the brands in their consumption bundle. Also, note that the indifference curves touch

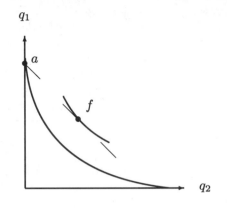

Figure 7.5: CES indifference curves for $N = 2$

the axes, therefore making it possible for the consumers to gain utility even when some brands are not produced (hence not consumed). We use the word *representative* consumer for this utility function since, in reality, individual consumers do not purchase the entire variety of products. Sattinger (1984) proposed a method for aggregating individuals who purchase a single brand into aggregate market demand facing all the brand-producing firms.

Finally, the consumer's income (denoted by I) is composed of the total wages paid by the producing firms plus the sum of their profits (if any). We denote by $\pi_i(q_i)$ the profit of the firm producing brand i. We also normalize the wage rate to equal 1, so all "monetary" values (p_i, I, and π_i) are all denominated in units of labor. Hence, the consumers maximize their utility (7.12) subject to a budget constraint given by

$$\sum_{i=1}^{N} p_i q_i \leq I \equiv L + \sum_{i=1}^{N} p_i q_i. \tag{7.13}$$

We form the Lagrangian

$$L(q_i, p_i, \lambda) \equiv \sum_{i=1}^{N} \sqrt{q_i} - \lambda \left[I - \sum_{i=1}^{N} p_i q_i \right].$$

The first-order condition for every brand i is

$$0 = \frac{\partial L}{\partial q_i} = \frac{1}{2\sqrt{q_i}} - \lambda p_i \quad i = 1, 2, \ldots, N.$$

Thus, the demand and the price elasticity (η_i) for each brand i are given by

$$q_i(p_i) = \frac{1}{4\lambda^2 (p_i)^2}, \quad \text{or} \quad p_i(q_i) = \frac{1}{4\lambda\sqrt{q_i}} \quad \eta \equiv \frac{\partial q_i}{\partial p_i} \frac{p_i}{q_i} = -2. \tag{7.14}$$

Finally, note that we assumed that λ is a constant. However, λ is not really a constant but a function of all prices and N. This procedure would be right had we assumed a continuum of brands indexed on the interval $[0, \infty)$. In this case, a rise in the price of a single brand would not have an effect on consumers' expenditure and hence on λ. The continuum version of (7.12) should be written as $u = \int_0^\infty \sqrt{q(i)}di$. However, in an attempt to avoid using integrals in this book, we provide the present approach as a good approximation for the continuous case.

Brand-producing firms

Each brand is produced by a single firm. All (potential) firms have identical technologies (identical cost structure) with increasing returns to scale (IRS) technologies. Formally, the total cost of a firm producing q_i units of brand i is given by

$$TC_i(q_i) = \begin{cases} F + cq_i & \text{if } q_i > 0 \\ 0 & \text{if } q_i = 0. \end{cases} \tag{7.15}$$

Defining a monopolistic-competition market structure

DEFINITION 7.3   *The triplet $\{N^{mc}, p_i^{mc}, q_i^{mc}, i = 1, \ldots, N^{mc}\}$ is called a Chamberlinian* **monopolistic-competition equilibrium** *if*

1. *Firms: Each firm behaves as a monopoly over its brand; that is, given the demand for brand i (7.14), each firm i chooses q_i^{mc} to $\max_{q_i} \pi_i = p_i(q_i)q_i - (F + cq_i)$.*

2. *Consumers: Each consumer takes his income and prices as given and maximizes (7.12) subject to (7.13), yielding a system of demand functions (7.14).*

$ATC_i(q_i), MC_i(q_i)$

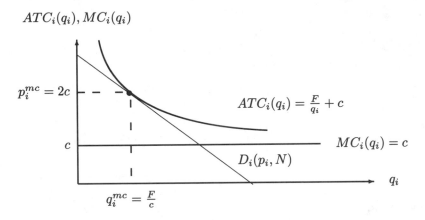

Figure 7.6: Decreasing average-cost technology

3. *Free entry: Free entry of firms (brands) will result in each firm making zero profits; $\pi_i(q_i^{mc}) = 0$ for all $i = 1, 2, \ldots, N$.*

4. *Resource constraint: Labor demanded for production equals the total labor supply; $\sum_{i=1}^{N}(F + cq_i) = L$.*

Definition 7.3 can be easily interpreted using Figure 7.6. The demand facing each (existing) brand-producing firm depends on the total number of brands in the industry, N. When N increases, the demand facing each brand-producing firm shifts downward, reflecting the fact that consumers partially substitute higher consumption levels of each brand with a lower consumption spread over a large number of brands. Therefore, free entry increases the number of brands until the demand facing each firm becomes tangent to the firm's average cost function. At this point, each existing brand-producing firm makes zero profit, and entry stops. The equilibrium condition in which demand becomes tangent to the average cost of each firm is known as *Chamberlin's tangency condition*.

Two important observations follow from the tangency condition displayed in Figure 7.6. First, in equilibrium the price of each brand equals average cost. Second, in equilibrium all brand-producing firms produce on the downward sloping part of the average cost curve. Thus, firms do not minimize average cost under a monopolistic-competition market structure.

Solving for a monopolistic-competition equilibrium

A firm's profit-maximization problem (item 1 of Definition 7.3) is the already familiar monopoly's problem analyzed in chapter 5. In that chapter we showed that if a monopoly produces a strictly positive amount of output, then the monopoly's price would satisfy

$$MR_i(q_i) = p_i \left(1 + \frac{1}{\eta}\right) = p_i \left(1 + \frac{1}{-2}\right) = \frac{p_i}{2} = c = MC(q_i).$$

Hence, the equilibrium price of each brand is given by $p_i^{mc} = 2c$ (twice the marginal cost).

The zero-profit condition (item 3 of Definition 7.3) implies that $0 = \pi_i(q_i^{mc}) = (p_i^{mc} - c)q_i^{mc} - F = cq_i^{mc} - F$. Hence, $q_i^{mc} = F/c$.

We are left to find how many brands will be produced in this economy. The resource-constraint condition (item 4 of Definition 7.3) implies that $N[F + c(F/c)] = L$. Hence, $N = L/(2F)$. Altogether, we have it that

Proposition 7.5

1. *In a monopolistic competition equilibrium with strictly positive fixed and marginal cost, only a finite number of brands will be produced. The equilibrium is given by*

$$p_i^{mc} = 2c; \quad q_i^{mc} = \frac{F}{c}; \quad N^{mc} = \frac{L}{2F}.$$

2. *When the fixed cost is large, there will be a low variety of brands, but each brand will be produced/consumed in a large quantity. When the fixed cost is low, there will be a large variety of brands, and each will be produced/consumed in a small quantity.*

7.2.2   Monopolistic competition in international markets

In the late 1970s trade theorists began applying the theory of monopolistic competition to international trade (see Helpman and Krugman 1985). The major motivation was that the neoclassical international trade theory failed to explain the data showing that most international trade consists of trade with similar products (intraindustry trade) rather of very different products (interindustry trade) as predicted by the traditional factor-proportion theory. That is, the application of monopolistic competition was needed in order to explain why countries trade in similar products. There are two (mutually dependent) ways for explaining gains from trade under increasing-returns production technologies: (a) trade increases specialization, thereby enabling firms to produce at a higher scale and therefore at a lower average cost; and (b) trade increases the world variety of brands facing each consumer in each country.

Consider a two-country world economy, in which each country is identical to the one analyzed above. Under autarky (no trade), each country is described by Proposition 7.5. Our first question is what would happen to the patterns of production and consumption when the two countries start trading (move to a free-trade regime)?

When the world is integrated into a single large economy, the labor resource and the number of consumers basically doubles. In view of the equilibrium described in Proposition 7.5, there will be no change in brand prices and the level of production of each brand. However, the number of brands under free trade will double and become $N^f = L/F = 2N^a$, where f and a denote equilibrium values under free trade and under autarky, respectively. Also, note that since the quantity produced of each brand remains unchanged ($q_i^f = q_i^a = F/c$), but the entire population has doubled, under free trade each consumer (country) consumes one-half of the world production ($F/(2c)$).

Our second question is whether there are gains from trade, given that we found that the consumption level of each brand has decreased to one-half the autarky level while the number of brands has doubled. In order to answer that, we should calculate the equilibrium utility levels under autarky and under free trade. Thus,

$$
\begin{aligned}
u^f &= N^f \sqrt{q_i^f} = \frac{L}{F}\sqrt{\frac{F}{2c}} = \frac{L}{\sqrt{2\sqrt{cF}}} \qquad (7.16)\\
&> \frac{L}{2\sqrt{cF}} = \frac{L}{2F}\sqrt{\frac{F}{c}} = N^a\sqrt{q_i^a} = u^a.
\end{aligned}
$$

Hence, each consumer in each country gains from trade. The intuition is quite simple. Comparing point a with point f in Figure 7.5 shows that a consumer is always better off if the variety doubles, despite the decline in the consumption level of each brand.

We conclude our analysis of the gains from trade with two remarks. First, we have shown that, under monopolistic competition, free trade yields a higher welfare level than autarky. However, Gros (1987) has shown that countries may benefit from imposing some import tariff on foreign-produced brands. Second, let us note that we have shown there are gains from trade when there is only one industry producing differentiated brands. Chou and Shy (1991) have shown that the gains from trade in monopolistic competition extend to the case where some industries produce nontraded brands; however, the remote possibility that trade may reduce the welfare of all countries (Pareto inferior trade) remains.

7.3 "Location" Models

In this section we present models in which consumers are heterogeneous. That is, due to different tastes or location, each consumer has a different preference for the brands sold in the market.

There could be two interpretations of "location" for the environment modeled in this section: Location can mean the physical location of a particular consumer, in which case the consumer observes the prices charged by all stores and then chooses to purchase from the store at which the price plus the transportation cost is minimized. Or, location can mean a distance between the brand characteristic that a particular consumer views as ideal and the characteristics of the brand actually purchased. That is, we can view a space (say, a line interval) as measuring the degree of sweetness in a candy bar. Consumers located toward the left are those who prefer low-sugar bars, whereas those who are located toward the right prefer high-sugar bars. In this case, the distance between a consumer and a firm can measure the consumers' disutility from buying a less-than-ideal brand. This disutility is equivalent to the transportation cost in the previous interpretation.

We analyze only horizontally differentiated products. That is, we analyze brands that are not uniformly utility ranked by all consumers. More precisely, horizontally differentiated brands are ones that, if sold for identical prices, elicit from different consumers choices of different brands (called ideal brands). The analysis of vertically differentiated brands, that is, brands that are uniformly ranked by all consumers, is postponed to section 12.2, where we discuss product differentiation with respect to quality (see more on these issues in Beath and Katsoulacos [1991] and Anderson, Palma, and Thisse [1992]; for a survey see Gabszewicz and Thisse [1992]).

7.3.1 The linear approach

Hotelling (1929) considers consumers who reside on a linear street with a length of $L > 0$. Suppose that the consumers are uniformly distributed on this interval, so at each point lies a single consumer. Hence, the total number of consumers in the economy is L. Each consumer is indexed by $x \in [0, L]$, so x is just a name of a consumer (located at point x from the origin).

Price game with fixed location

Suppose that there are two firms selling a product that is identical in all respects except one characteristic, which is the location where it is sold. That is, Figure 7.7 shows that firm A is located a units of distance from point 0. Firm B is located to the right of firm A, b units of distance from point L. Assume that production is costless.

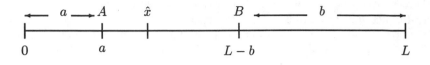

Figure 7.7: Hotelling's linear city with two firms

Each consumer buys one unit of the product. To go to a store, a consumer has to pay transportation cost of τ per unit of distance. Thus, a consumer located at some point x has to pay transportation cost of $\tau|x - a|$ for shopping at firm A, or $\tau|x - (L - b)|$ for shopping at firm B. The reader should note that distance here can have a different interpretation. We can think of a candy bar that can be produced with different degrees of sweetness. Thus, if we let x measure the percentage of sugar put into a candy bar, firm B produces a sweeter candy than firm A. A consumer located at x desires x degree of sweetness more than any other degree of sweetness. However the firms offer most consumers degrees of sweetness that differ from the most preferred one. With this interpretation, the equivalent of transportation costs is the monetary equivalent loss to a consumer who desires x degree of sweetness but instead has to purchase a candy bar with a different degree of sweetness.

Let us define the utility function of a consumer located at point x by

$$U_x \equiv \begin{cases} -p_A - \tau|x - a| & \text{if he buys from } A \\ -p_B - \tau|x - (L - b)| & \text{if she buys from } B. \end{cases} \tag{7.17}$$

Let $\hat{x}$ denote the consumer who is indifferent to whether he or she purchases from A or B. Formally, if $a < \hat{x} < L - b$, then

$$-p_A - \tau(\hat{x} - a) = -p_B - \tau(L - b - \hat{x}).$$

Hence,

$$\hat{x} = \frac{p_B - p_A}{2\tau} + \frac{(L - b + a)}{2},$$

which is the demand function faced by firm A. The demand function faced by firm B is

$$L - \hat{x} = \frac{p_A - p_B}{2\tau} + \frac{(L + b - a)}{2}.$$

We now look for a Bertrand-Nash equilibrium in price strategies. That is, Firm A takes p_B as given and chooses p_A to

$$\max_{p_A} \pi_A = \frac{p_B p_A - (p_A)^2}{2\tau} + \frac{(L - b + a)p_A}{2}. \tag{7.18}$$

The first-order condition is given by

$$0 = \frac{\partial \pi_A}{\partial p_A} = \frac{p_B - 2p_A}{2\tau} + \frac{(L - b + a)}{2}. \tag{7.19}$$

Firm B takes p_A as given and chooses p_B to

$$\max_{p_B} \pi_B = \frac{p_B p_A - (p_B)^2}{2\tau} + \frac{(L + b - a)p_B}{2}. \tag{7.20}$$

The first-order condition is given by

$$0 = \frac{\partial \pi_B}{\partial p_B} = \frac{p_A - 2p_B}{2\tau} + \frac{L + b - a}{2}.$$

Hence, the equilibrium prices are given by

$$p_A^h = \frac{\tau(3L - b + a)}{3} \quad \text{and} \quad p_B^h = \frac{\tau(3L + b - a)}{3}. \tag{7.21}$$

The equilibrium market share of firm A is given by

$$\hat{x}^h = \frac{3L - b + a}{6}. \tag{7.22}$$

Note that if $a = b$, then the market is equally divided between the two firms. The profit of firm A is given by

$$\pi_A^h = \hat{x}^h p_A^h = \frac{\tau(3L - b + a)^2}{18}, \tag{7.23}$$

which shows that the profit of each brand-producing firm increases with the transportation cost parameter, τ. This is not surprising in view of the fact that Propositions 7.1 and 7.2 showed firms reach higher profit levels when the brands they produce are more differentiated. In fact, Hotelling (1929, 50) states

> These particular merchants would do well, instead of orga-
> nizing improvement clubs and booster associations to better
> the roads, to make transportation as difficult as possible.

We leave it to the reader to determine whether such a behavior is observed or unobserved.

The above calculations were performed under the assumption that an equilibrium where firms charge strictly positive prices always exists. The following proposition describes the equilibria and provides precise conditions for existence. The proof of the proposition is given in the appendix (section 7.5).

Proposition 7.6

1. *If both firms are located at the same point $(a + b = L$, meaning that the products are homogeneous), then $p_A = p_B = 0$ is a unique equilibrium.*

2. *A unique equilibrium exists and is described by (7.21) and (7.22) if and only if the two firms are not too close to each other; formally if and only if*

$$\left(L + \frac{a - b}{3}\right)^2 \geq \frac{4L(a + 2b)}{3} \quad and \quad \left(L + \frac{b - a}{3}\right)^2 \geq \frac{4L(b + 2a)}{3}$$

the unique equilibrium is given by (7.21), (7.22), and (7.23).

When the two firms are located too closely, they start undercutting each other's prices, resulting in a process of price cuts that does not converge to an equilibrium. Proposition 7.6 shows that in order for an equilibrium to exist, the firms cannot be too closely located.

Location and price game

So far, we have assumed that the location of the firms is fixed, say, by the regulating (license-issuing) authority. It would be nice to have a theory under which firms can choose price and location. Unfortunately, we now show that there is no solution for this two-dimensional strategy game.

To show that, we ask what would firm A do if, given the price and location of its opponent, it would be allowed to relocate. To answer that, (7.23) implies that

$$\frac{\partial \pi_A}{\partial a} > 0,$$

meaning that for any locations a and b, firm A could increase its profit by moving toward firm B (obviously, to gain a higher market share). This case, where firms tend to move toward the center, is called in the literature the *principle of minimum differentiation* since by moving toward the center the firms produce less-differentiated products. However,

Proposition 7.6 shows that if firm A gets too close to firm B, an equilibrium will not exist. Also, if firm A locates at the same point where firm B locates, its profit will drop to zero, implying that it is better off to move back to the left. Hence

Proposition 7.7 *In the Hotelling linear-city game, there is no equilibrium for the game where firms use both prices and location as strategies.*

Quadratic transportation cost

Proposition 7.21 shows that even when the location is fixed, the linear-location model does not have an equilibrium in a price game when the firms are too close to each other. We also showed that there is no equilibrium in a game when firms choose both prices and location.

However, it is important to observe that so far, we have assumed linear transportation costs. The existence problem can be solved if we assume quadratic transportation costs. That is, let (7.17) be written as

$$U_x \equiv \begin{cases} -p_A - \tau(x-a)^2 & \text{if he buys from } A \\ -p_B - \tau[x-(L-b)]^2 & \text{if she buys from } B. \end{cases} \qquad (7.24)$$

To have even more fun, using the quadratic-transportation-cost setup, we can formulate a two-period game in which firms decide where to locate in the first period, and set prices in the second period. Since we look for a SPE (Definition 2.10), the reader who is eager to solve this game should follow the following steps:

Second period:

1. For given location parameters a and b, find the Nash-Bertrand equilibrium prices, following the same steps we used in order to derive (7.21).

2. Substitute the equilibrium prices into the profit functions (7.18) and (7.20) to obtain the firms' profits as functions of the location parameters a and b.

First period: Maximize the firms' profit functions which you calculated for the second period with respect to a for firm A and with respect to b for firm B. Prove that for a given b, $\frac{\partial \pi_A}{\partial a} < 0$, meaning that firm A would choose $a = 0$. Similarly, show that firm B would locate at point L.

This exercise shows that when there are quadratic transportation costs, firms will choose maximum differentiation. This result is consistent with Propositions 7.1 and 7.2, showing that profits increase with differentiation.

7.3.2   The circular approach

Proposition 7.7 shows that an equilibrium in games in which firms jointly decide on prices and location does not exist in the Hotelling model. One way to solve this problem is to let the city be the unit-circumference circle, where the consumers are uniformly distributed on the circumference.

As with the Hotelling model, this location model can also be given an interpretation for describing differentiated products that differs from the physical-location interpretation. Consider for example airline, bus, and train firms which can provide a round-the-clock service. If we treat the circle as twenty-four hours, each brand can be interpreted as the time where an airline firm schedules a departure.

Firms

This model does not explicitly model how firms choose where to locate. However, it assumes a monopolistic-competition market structure, in which the number of firms N is endogenously determined. All (infinitely many) potential firms have the same technology. Denoting by F the fixed cost, by c the marginal cost, and by q_i and $\pi_i(q_i)$ the output and profit levels of the firm-producing brand i, we assume that

$$\pi_i(q_i) = \begin{cases} (p_i - c)q_i - F & \text{if } q_i > 0 \\ 0 & \text{if } q_i = 0. \end{cases} \tag{7.25}$$

Consumers

Consumers are uniformly distributed on the unit circle. We denote by τ the consumers' transportation cost per unit of distance. Each consumer buys one unit of the brand that minimizes the sum of the price and transportation cost.

Assuming that the N firms are located at an equal distance from one another yields that the distance between any two firms is $1/N$. Figure 7.8 illustrates the position of firm 1 relative to the positions of firm 2 and firm N. Then, assuming that firms 2 and N charge a uniform price p, the consumer who is indifferent to whether he or she buys from firm 1 or firm 2 (similarly, firm N) is located at $\hat{x}$ determined by $p_1 + \tau\hat{x} = p + \tau(1/N - \hat{x})$. Hence,

$$\hat{x} = \frac{p - p_1}{2\tau} + \frac{1}{2N}. \tag{7.26}$$

Since firm 1 has customers on its left and on its right, the demand function facing firm 1 is

$$q_1(p_1, p) = 2\hat{x} = \frac{p - p_1}{\tau} + \frac{1}{N}. \tag{7.27}$$

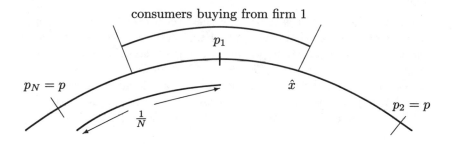

Figure 7.8: The position of firms on the unit circle

Defining and solving for the monopolistic-competition equilibrium

Let us begin with a definition:

DEFINITION 7.4 *The triplet $\{N^\circ, p^\circ, q^\circ\}$ is an equilibrium if*

1. *Firms: Each firm behaves as a monopoly on its brand; that is, given the demand for brand i (7.27) and given that all other firms charge $p_j = p^\circ, j \neq i$, each firm i chooses p° to*

$$\max_{p_i} \pi_i(p_i, p^\circ) = p_i q_i(p_i) - (F + cq_i) = (p_i - c)\left(\frac{p^\circ - p_i}{\tau} + \frac{1}{N}\right) - F.$$

2. *Free entry: Free entry of firms (brands) will result in zero profits; $\pi_i(q^\circ) = 0$ for all $i = 1, 2, \ldots, N^\circ$.*

The first-order condition for firm i's maximization problem is

$$0 = \frac{\partial \pi_i(p_i, p^\circ)}{\partial p_i} = \frac{p^\circ - 2p_i + c}{\tau} + \frac{1}{N}.$$

Therefore, in a symmetric equilibrium, $p_i = p^\circ = c + \tau/N$.
To find the equilibrium number of brands N, we set

$$0 = \pi_i(p^\circ, p^\circ) = (p^\circ - c)\frac{1}{N} - F = \frac{\tau}{N^2} - F.$$

Hence

$$N^\circ = \sqrt{\frac{\tau}{F}}, \quad p^\circ = c + \frac{\tau}{N} = c + \sqrt{\tau F}, \quad q^\circ = \frac{1}{N}. \qquad (7.28)$$

Welfare

We would like to investigate whether the "free market" produces a larger or a smaller variety than the optimal variety level. Before defining the economy's welfare function, we calculate the economy's aggregate transportation costs, denoted by T. Figure 7.8 shows that in equilibrium, all consumers purchasing from firm 1, say, are located between 0 and $1/(2N)$ units of distance from the firm (on each side). Since there are $2N$ such intervals, the economy's total transportation cost is given by

$$T(N) = 2N\tau \left(\int_0^{\frac{1}{2N}} x\,dx \right) = 2N\tau \left[\frac{x^2}{2} \right]_0^{\frac{1}{2N}} = \frac{\tau}{4N}. \qquad (7.29)$$

An alternative way to find the aggregate transportation cost without using integration is to look at the cost of the average consumer who is located half way between $\hat{x} = 1/(2N)$ and a firm. That is, the average consumer has to travel $1/(4N)$, which yields (7.29).

We define the economy's loss function, $L(F, \tau, N)$, as the sum of the fixed cost paid by the producing firms and the economy's aggregate transportation cost. Formally, the "Social Planner" chooses the optimal number of brands N^* to

$$\min_N L(F, \tau, N) \equiv NF + T(N) = NF + \frac{\tau}{4N}. \qquad (7.30)$$

The first-order condition is $0 = \frac{\partial L}{\partial N} = F - \tau/(4N^2)$. Hence,

$$N^* = \frac{1}{2}\sqrt{\frac{\tau}{F}} < N^\circ. \qquad (7.31)$$

Therefore, in a free-entry location model, too many brands are produced. Notice, that there is a welfare tradeoff between the economies of scale and the aggregate transportation cost. That is, a small number of brands is associated with lower average production costs but higher aggregate transportation costs (because of fewer firms). A large number of brands means a lower scale of production (higher average cost) but with a lower aggregate transportation cost. Equation (7.31) shows that it is possible to raise the economy's welfare by reducing the number of brands.

7.3.3 Sequential entry to the linear city

So far, we have not discussed any model in which firms strategically choose where to locate. In subsection 7.3.1 we have shown that the basic linear-street model does not have an equilibrium where firms choose both prices and location.

In this subsection, we discuss an example set forth by Prescott and Visscher (1977) in which prices are fixed at a uniform level set by the regulator. For example, in many countries, prices of milk, bread, and basic cheese products are regulated by the government. Thus, the only choice variable left to firms is where to locate (what characteristics—degree of sweetness in our example—the product should have).

Consider the unit interval (street) where there are three firms entering sequentially. In this three-period model, firm 1 enters in period 1, firm 2 in period 2, and firm 3 in period 3. We look for a SPE (see Definition 2.10) in location strategies, where each firm maximizes its market share.

We denote by $0 \le x_i \le 1$ the location strategy chosen by firm i (in period i), $i = 1, 2, 3$. Let ϵ denote a "very small" number, representing the smallest possible measurable unit of distance. Solving the entire three-period game is rather complicated. Instead, we shall assume that firm 1 has already moved and located itself at the point $x_1 = 1/4$. Figure 7.9 illustrates the location of firm 1.

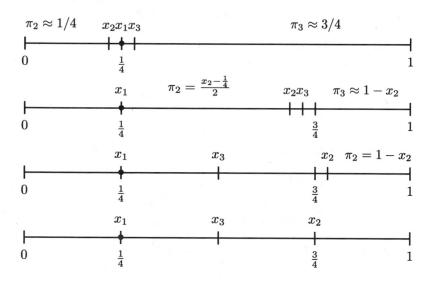

Figure 7.9: Sequential-location game

The third-period subgame

Firm 3 decides on its location x_3 after firm 1 and firm 2 are already located. There are three possible locations of firm 2 corresponding to the three upper parts of Figure 7.9.

$x_2 = \frac{1}{4} - \epsilon$: In this case firm 3 would locate at $x_3 = \frac{1}{4} + \epsilon$. Here, $\pi_3 \approx \frac{3}{4}$ while $\pi_2 = x_2 + \frac{1}{2}(\frac{1}{4} - x_2) < \frac{1}{4}$.

$\frac{1}{4} < x_2 < \frac{3}{4}$: In this case firm 3 would locate to the right of firm 2, at $x_3 = x_2 + \epsilon$. Here, $\pi_3 \approx 1 - x_2$ while $\pi_2 \approx \frac{x_2 - \frac{1}{4}}{2} < \frac{1}{4}$. That is, firm 2 shares the $[x_1, x_2]$ interval with firm 1.

$x_2 \geq \frac{3}{4}$: In this case firm 3 would locate between firm 1 and firm 2, at any point $x_1 < x_3 < x_2$. With no loss of generality, assume that $x_3 = \frac{\frac{1}{4} + x_2}{2}$. Here, $\pi_3 = \frac{x_2 - \frac{1}{4}}{2}$ and

$$\pi_2 = 1 - x_2 + \frac{x_2 - x_3}{2} = 1 - x_2 + \frac{1}{2}\left[x_2 - \frac{\frac{1}{4} + x_2}{2}\right] = \frac{15 - 12x_2}{16}.$$

The second-period subgame

Firm 2 knows that in the third period, the location decision of firm 3 will be influenced by its own choice of location. Thus, firm 2 calculates the best-response function of firm 3 (which we calculated above). Hence, firm 2 takes the *decision rule* of firm 3 as given and chooses x_2 that would maximize its profit. Clearly, firm 2 will not locate at $x_2 = \frac{1}{4} - \epsilon$ since this location yields a maximum profit of $\pi_2 \approx \frac{1}{4}$ (it will collect a higher profit by locating elsewhere, as described below).

If firm 2 locates at $\frac{1}{4} < x_2 < \frac{3}{4}$, we have shown that $x_3 = x_2 + \epsilon$ and $\pi_2 = \frac{x_2 - \frac{1}{4}}{2} < \frac{1}{4}$.

However, if firm 2 locates at $x_2 \geq \frac{3}{4}$ we have shown that $\pi_2 = \frac{15 - 12x_2}{16}$, which is maximized at $x_2 = \frac{3}{4}$. Located at $x_2 = \frac{3}{4}$, the profit of firm 2 is $\pi_2 = \frac{1}{4} + \frac{1}{8} = \frac{3}{8}$.

In summary, the SPE is reached where

$$x_2 = \frac{3}{4}, \quad \pi_2 = \frac{1}{4} + \frac{1}{8} \quad \text{and} \quad x_3 = \frac{1}{2}, \quad \pi_3 = \frac{1}{4}. \tag{7.32}$$

The bottom part of Figure 7.9 illustrates the location of the firms in a SPE.

7.3.4   Calculus-free location model

In this subsection we develop a calculus-free version of the Hotelling linear-city model analyzed in subsection 7.3.1.

Consider a city where consumers and producers are located only at the city's edges. Suppose that the city consists of N_0 consumers located at point $x = 0$ and N_L consumers located at the point $x = L$. There are two firms; firm A is located also at $x = 0$ and firm B is located at

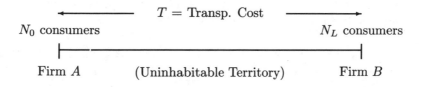

Figure 7.10: Discrete-location model

$x = L$. Assume that production is costless. Figure 7.10 illustrates the location of firms and consumers in this city.

Each consumer buys one unit either from the firm located where the consumer is, or from the firm located on the other side of town. Shopping nearby does not involve transportation cost, whereas shopping on the other side of town involves paying a fixed transportation cost of $T \geq 0$. Let p_A denote the price charged by firm A, and p_B the price charged by firm B. Thus, we assume that the utility of the consumer located at point $x = 0$ is given by

$$U_0 \equiv \begin{cases} -p_A & \text{buying from } A \\ -p_B - T & \text{buying from } B. \end{cases} \qquad (7.33)$$

Similarly, the utility of the consumer located at point $x = L$ is given by

$$U_L \equiv \begin{cases} -p_A - T & \text{buying from } A \\ -p_B & \text{buying from } B. \end{cases} \qquad (7.34)$$

Let n_A denote the number of consumers buying from firm A, and n_B denote the number of consumers buying from firm B. Then, (7.33) and (7.34) imply that

$$n_A = \begin{cases} 0 & \text{if } p_A > p_B + T \\ N_0 & \text{if } p_B - T \leq p_A \leq p_B + T \\ N_0 + N_L & \text{if } p_A < p_B - T \end{cases} \qquad (7.35)$$

$$n_B = \begin{cases} 0 & \text{if } p_B > p_A + T \\ N_L & \text{if } p_A - T \leq p_B \leq p_A + T \\ N_0 + N_L & \text{if } p_B < p_A - T. \end{cases}$$

Non-existence of a Nash-Bertrand equilibrium

A Nash-Bertrand equilibrium is the nonnegative pair $\{p_A^N, p_B^N\}$, such that for a given p_B^N, firm A chooses p_A^N to maximize $\pi_A \equiv p_A n_A$; and for a given p_A^N, firm B chooses p_B^N to maximize $\pi_B \equiv p_B n_B$, where n_A and n_B are given in (7.35).

Proposition 7.8 *There does not exist a Nash-Bertrand equilibrium in prices for the discrete version of Hotelling's location model.*

Proof. By way of contradiction, suppose that $\{p_A^N, p_B^N\}$ constitute a Nash equilibrium. Then, there are three cases: (i) $|p_A^N - p_B^N| > T$; (ii) $|p_A^N - p_B^N| < T$; and (iii) $|p_A^N - p_B^N| = T$.

(i) With no loss of generality, suppose that $p_A^N - p_B^N > T$. Then, (7.35) implies that $n_A^N = 0$, and hence $\pi_A^N = 0$. However, firm A can deviate and increase its profit by reducing its price to $\tilde{p}_A = p_B^N + T$ and by having $\tilde{n}_A = N_0$, thereby earning a profit of $\tilde{\pi}_A = N_0(p_B^N + T)$. A contradiction.

(ii) With no loss of generality, suppose that $p_A^N < p_B^N + T$. Then, firm A can deviate and increase its profit by slightly increasing its price to $\tilde{p}_A$, satisfying $p_A^N < \tilde{p}_A < p_B^N + T$ and maintaining a profit level of $\tilde{\pi}_A = N_0\tilde{p}_A > \pi_A^N$. A contradiction.

(iii) With no loss of generality, suppose that $p_A^N - p_B^N = T$. Then, $p_B^N = p_A^N - T < p_A^N + T$. Hence, as firm A did in case (ii), firm B can increase its profit by slightly raising p_B^N. A contradiction. ∎

Undercutproof equilibrium

Since a Nash equilibrium in prices for the discrete-location model does not exist, in this subsection we define, motivate, and solve for the undercutproof equilibrium.

In an undercutproof equilibrium, each firm chooses the highest possible price, subject to the constraint that the price is sufficiently low so that the rival firm would not find it profitable to set a sufficiently lower price in order to grab the entire market. That is, in an undercutproof equilibrium, firms set prices at the levels that ensure that competing firms would not find it profitable to completely undercut these prices. Thus, unlike behavior in a Nash-Bertrand environment, where each firm assumes that the rival firm does not alter its price, in an undercutproof equilibrium environment, firms assume that rival firms are ready to reduce their prices whenever undercutting prices and grabbing their rival's market are profitable to them. This behavior is reasonable for firms competing in differentiated products.

DEFINITION 7.5 *An undercutproof equilibrium for this economy is non-negative* n_A^U, n_B^U, *and* p_A^U, p_B^U *such that*

1. *For given* p_B^U *and* n_B^U, *firm A chooses the highest price* p_A^U *subject to*

$$\pi_B^U \equiv p_B^U n_B^U \geq (N_0 + N_L)(p_A^U - T).$$

2. *For given p_A^U and n_A^U, firm B chooses the highest price p_B^U subject to*

$$\pi_A^U \equiv p_A^U n_A^U \geq (N_0 + N_L)(p_B^U - T).$$

3. *The distribution of consumers between the firms is determined in (7.35).*

Part 1 of Definition 7.5 states that in an undercutproof equilibrium, firm A sets the highest price under the constraint that the price is sufficiently low to prevent firm B from undercutting p_A^U and grabbing the entire market. More precisely, firm A sets p_A^N sufficiently low so that B's equilibrium profit level exceeds B's profit level when it undercuts by setting $\tilde{p}_B = p_A^U - T$, and grabbing the entire market ($n_B = N_0 + N_L$). Part 2 is similar to part 1 but describes how firm B sets its price. We proceed with solving for the equilibrium prices.

Proposition 7.9 *There exists a unique undercutproof equilibrium for the discrete-location problem given by $n_A^U = N_0$, $n_B^U = N_L$, and*

$$p_A^U = \frac{(N_0 + N_L)(N_0 + 2N_L)T}{(N_0)^2 + N_0 N_L + (N_L)^2} \quad and \quad p_B^U = \frac{(N_0 + N_L)(2N_0 + N_L)T}{(N_0)^2 + N_0 N_L + (N_L)^2}.$$
$$(7.36)$$

Proof. First note that by setting $p_i \leq T$, each firm can secure a strictly positive market share without being undercut. Hence, in an undercutproof equilibrium both firms maintain a strictly positive market share. From (7.35), we have it that $n_A^U = N_0$ and $n_B^U = N_L$. Substituting $n_A^U = N_0$ and $n_B^U = N_L$ into the two constraints in Definition 7.5 and then verifying (7.35) yields the unique undercutproof equilibrium. ∎

Figure 7.11 illustrates how the undercutproof equilibrium is determined. The left side of Figure 7.11 shows how firm A is constrained in setting p_A to fall into the region where firm B would not benefit from undercutting p_A^U (compare with part 1 in Definition 7.5). The center of Figure 7.11 shows how firm B is constrained in setting p_B to fall into the region where firm A would not benefit from undercutting p_B^U (compare with part 2 in Definition 7.5). The right side of Figure 7.11 illustrates the region where neither firm finds it profitable to undercut the rival firm and the undercutproof equilibrium prices. It should be emphasized that the curves drawn in Figure 7.11 are not best-response (reaction) functions. The curves simply divide the regions into prices that make undercutting profitable or unprofitable for one firm.

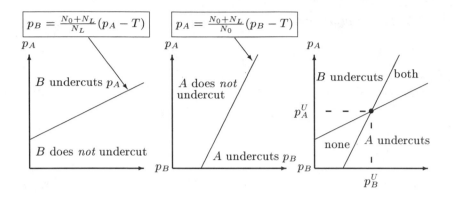

Figure 7.11: Undercutproof equilibrium for the discrete-location model

Properties of the undercutproof equilibrium

Clearly, prices rise with transportation costs and monotonically decline to zero as transportation costs approach zero, reflecting a situation in which the products become homogeneous. More interestingly,

$$\Delta p \equiv p_B - p_A = \frac{(N_0 + N_L)(N_0 - N_L)T}{(N_0)^2 + N_0 N_L + (N_L)^2}. \tag{7.37}$$

Hence, $\Delta p \geq 0$ if and only if $N_0 \geq N_L$. Thus, in an undercutproof equilibrium, the firm selling to the larger number of consumers charges a lower price. This lower price is needed to secure the firm from being totally undercut.

Finally, under symmetric distribution of consumers ($N_0 = N_L$), the equilibrium prices are given by $p_A^U = p_B^U = 2T$. That is, each firm can mark up its price to twice the level of the transportation cost without being undercut.

7.4 Appendix: Inverting Demand Systems

The demand system (7.1) can be written as

$$\begin{bmatrix} \beta & \gamma \\ \gamma & \beta \end{bmatrix} \begin{bmatrix} q_1 \\ q_2 \end{bmatrix} = \begin{bmatrix} \alpha - p_1 \\ \alpha - p_2 \end{bmatrix}.$$

Define Δ to be the determinant of

$$\Delta \equiv \det \begin{bmatrix} \beta & \gamma \\ \gamma & \beta \end{bmatrix} = \beta^2 - \gamma^2.$$

Then, using Cramer's Law we have it that

$$q_1 = \frac{1}{\Delta} \det \begin{bmatrix} \alpha - p_1 & \gamma \\ \alpha - p_2 & \beta \end{bmatrix} = \frac{\alpha(\beta - \gamma) - \beta p_1 + \gamma p_2}{\beta^2 - \gamma^2}$$

$$q_2 = \frac{1}{\Delta} \det \begin{bmatrix} \beta & \alpha - p_1 \\ \gamma & \alpha - p_2 \end{bmatrix} = \frac{\alpha(\beta - \gamma) - \beta p_2 + \gamma p_1}{\beta^2 - \gamma^2}.$$

This establishes equation (7.2).

7.5 Appendix: Existence of an Equilibrium in the Linear City

We now prove Proposition 7.6. (1) When $a + b = 1$, the products are homogeneous, so the undercutting procedure described in section 6.3 applies.

(2) For the general proof see d'Aspremont, Gabszewicz, and Thisse 1979. Here, we illustrate the argument made in their proof for the simple case where firms are located at equal distances along the edges. That is, assume that $a = b$, $a < L/2$. Then, we are left to show that the equilibrium exists if and only if $L^2 \geq 4La$, or if and only if $a \leq L/4$.

When $a = b$, the distance between the two firms is $L - 2a$. Also, if equilibrium exists, (7.21) is now given by $p_A = p_B = \tau L$. The profit level of firm A as a function of its own price p_A and a *given* B's price $\bar{p}_B = \tau L$ for the case of $a = b$ is drawn in Figure 7.12.

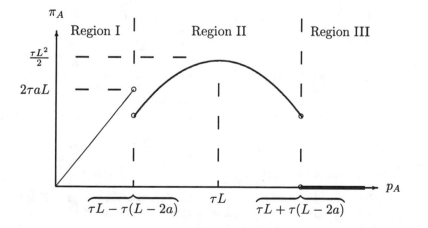

Figure 7.12: Existence of equilibrium in the linear city: The profit of firm A for a given $\bar{p}_B = \tau L$

Figure 7.12 has three regions:

Region I: Here, $p_A < \tau L - \tau(L - 2a)$. In this case, p_A is very low, so that even the consumer located at the same point where firm B is located would purchase from firm A. Thus, firm A has the entire market, and its profit is given by $\pi_A = p_A L$.

Region II: Here, both firms sell a strictly positive amount, so the profit of firm A as a function of p_A is given in equation (7.18). Substituting the equilibrium $p_B = \tau L$ into (7.18) yields

$$\pi_A = p_A L - \frac{(p_A)^2}{2\tau}, \qquad (7.38)$$

which is drawn in Region II of Figure 7.12. Maximizing (7.38) with respect to p_A yields $\pi_A = \tau L^2/2$, which corresponds to the peak drawn in Figure 7.12.

Region III: Here, p_A is high, so all consumers purchase from firm B. This is the polar case of Region I.

Now, for a given $p_B = \tau L$, Figure 7.12 shows that π_A has two local maxima. In one it has the entire market share ($p_A = \tau L - \tau(L - 2a) - \epsilon$), whereas in the other it shares the market with firm B ($p_A = \tau L$). For (7.21) to constitute the equilibrium prices, we must have it that in equilibrium, the globally profit-maximizing price for firm A would lie in Region II (and not Region I). Or, that for the equilibrium $p_B = \tau L$,

$$\pi_A^{II} = \frac{\tau L^2}{2} \geq \pi_A^I = [\tau L - \tau(L - 2a)]L = 2\tau a L,$$

implying that $a \leq L/4$. ∎

7.6   Exercises

1. Suppose that there are only two firms selling coffee, called firms 1 and 2. Let α_i denote the advertising level of firm i, $i = 1, 2$. Assume that the profits of the firms are affected by the advertising levels taken by the firms. Formally, assume that

    $$\pi_1(\alpha_1, \alpha_2) \equiv 4\alpha_1 + 3\alpha_1\alpha_2 - (\alpha_1)^2 \quad \text{and} \quad \pi_2(\alpha_1, \alpha_2) \equiv 2\alpha_2 + \alpha_1\alpha_2 - (\alpha_2)^2.$$

    Answer the following questions:

    (a) Calculate and draw the best-response function of each firm. That is, for any given advertising level of firm j, find the profit-maximizing advertising level of firm i.

    (b) Infer whether the strategies are strategically complements or strategically substitutes (see Definition 7.2).

(c) Find the Nash equilibrium advertising levels. Also, calculate the firms' Nash equilibrium profit levels.

2. Consider the Hotelling linear-city model analyzed in Subsection 7.3.1. Suppose that in the linear city there is only one restaurant, located at the center of the street with a length of 1 km. Assume that the restaurant's cost is zero. Consumers are uniformly distributed on the street, which is the interval $[0, 1]$, where at each point on the interval lives one consumer. Suppose that the transportation cost for each consumers is $1 for each unit of distance (each kilometer of travel). The utility of a consumer who lives a units of distance from the restaurant is given by $U \equiv B - a - p$, where p is the price of a meal, and B is a constant. However, if the consumer does not eat at the restaurant, her utility is $U = 0$. Answer the following questions:

   (a) Suppose that the parameter B satisfies $0 < B < 1$. Find the number of consumers eating at this restaurant. Calculate the monopoly restaurant's price and profit levels.

   (b) Answer the previous question assuming that $B > 1$.

3. University Road is best described as the interval $[0, 1]$. Two fast-food restaurants serving identical food are located at the edges of the road, so that restaurant 1 is located on the most left-hand side, and restaurant 2 is located on the most right-hand side of the road. Consumers are uniformly distributed on the interval $[0, 1]$, where at each point on the interval lives one consumer. Each consumer buys one meal from the restaurant in which the price plus the transportation cost is the lowest.

   In University Road, the wind blows from right to left, hence the transportation cost for a consumer who travels to the right is R per unit of distance, and only $1 per unit of distance for a consumer who travels to the left. Answer the following questions.

   (a) Let p_i denote the price of a meal at restaurant i, $i = 1, 2$. Assume that p_1 and p_2 are given and satisfy

   $$0 < p_1 - R < p_2 < 1 + p_1.$$

   Denote by $\hat{x}$ the location of the consumer who is indifferent to whether he or she eats at restaurant 1 or restaurant 2 and calculate $\hat{x}$ as a function of p_1, p_2, and R.

   (b) Suppose that the given prices satisfy $p_1 = p_2$. What is the minimal value of the parameter R such that all consumers will go to eat only at restaurant 1?

4. Consider the Hotelling model with quadratic transportation cost described in equation (7.24) and assume that both firms are located at the same distances from the edges of the unit interval (i.e., $a = b \geq 0$ in Figure 7.7).

(a) Assuming that firms produce the product with zero cost, calculate the (symmetric) Nash equilibrium in prices.

(b) Assuming that firm A is allowed to make a small adjustment in its location before both firms choose their prices; would firm A move inward or outward? Prove your answer!

7.7   References

Anderson, S., A. Palma, and J. Thisse. 1992. *Discrete Choice Theory of Product Differentiation*. Cambridge, Mass.: MIT Press.

Beath, J., and Y. Katsoulacos. 1991. *The Economic Theory of Product Differentiation*. Cambridge: Cambridge University Press.

Bulow, J., J. Geanakoplos, and P. Klemperer. 1985. "Multimarket Oligopoly: Strategic Substitutes and Complements." *Journal of Political Economy* 93: 488–511.

Chamberlin, E. 1933. *The Theory of Monopolistic Competition*. Cambridge, Mass.: Harvard University Press.

Cheng, L. 1985. "Comparing Bertrand and Cournot Equilibria: A Geometric Approach." *Rand Journal of Economics* 16: 146–152.

Chou, C., and O. Shy. 1991. "Intraindustry Trade and the Variety of Home Products." *Canadian Journal of Economics* 24: 405–416.

d'Aspremont, C., J. Gabszewicz, and J. Thisse. 1979. "On Hotelling's Stability in Competition." *Econometrica* 17: 1145–1151.

Dixit, A. 1979. "A Model of Duopoly Suggesting a Theory of Entry Barriers." *Bell Journal of Economics* 10: 20–32.

Dixit, A., and J. Stiglitz. 1977. "Monopolistic Competition and Optimum Product Diversity." *American Economic Review* 67: 297–308.

Eaton, B. C., and R. Lipsey. 1989. "Product Differentiation." In *Handbook of Industrial Organization,* edited by R. Schmalensee and R. Willig. Amsterdam: North-Holland.

Gabszewicz J., and J. Thisse. 1992. "Location." In *Handbook of Game Theory,* edited by R. Aumann and S. Hart. Amsterdam: North-Holland.

Gros, D. 1987. "A Note on the Optimal Tariff, Retaliation, and the Welfare Loss from Tariff Wars in a Model with Intra-Industry Trade." *Journal of International Economics* 23: 457–367.

Hotelling, H. 1929. "Stability in Competition." *Economic Journal* 39: 41–57.

Helpman, E., and P. Krugman. 1985. *Market Structure and Foreign Trade*. Cambridge, Mass.: MIT Press.

Lancaster, K. 1979. *Variety Equity, and Efficiency*. New York: Columbia University Press.

Prescott, E., and M. Visscher. 1977. "Sequential Location among Firms with Foresight." *The Bell Journal of Economics* 8: 378–393.

Salop, S. 1979. "Monopolistic Competition with Outside Goods." *Bell Journal of Economics* 10: 141–156.

Sattinger, M. 1984. "Value of an Additional Firm in Monopolistic Competition." *Review of Economic Studies* 51: 321–332.

Scherer, F. M. 1979. "The Welfare Economics of Product Variety: An Application to the Ready-To-Eat Cereals Industry." *Journal of Industrial Economics* 28: 113–133.

Schmalensee, R. 1978. "Entry Deterrence in the Ready-To-Eat Breakfast Cereal Industry." *Bell Journal of Economics* 9: 305–327.

Singh, N., and X. Vives. 1984. "Price and Quantity Competition in a Differentiated Duopoly." *Rand Journal of Economics* 15: 546–554.

Vives, X. 1985. "Efficiency of Bertrand and Cournot Equilibria with Product Differentiation." *Journal of Economic Theory* 36: 166–175.

Chapter 8

Concentration, Mergers, and Entry Barriers

> A prime reason for studying industrial organization is for understanding why concentration is observed very often.
> —Common statement

As we discussed in the introduction, the study of industrial organization is motivated mainly by the failure of the competitive market structure model, analyzed in chapter 4, to explain the commonly observed high concentration of firms in the same industry. Therefore, in this chapter we attempt to address the following questions:

1. Why do firms in some industries make pure profits?

2. When oligopolies make pure profits, how come entry of new firms does not always occur, thereby eliminating all pure profits?

3. What can explain mergers among firms in a given industry?

4. What is and what should be the regulators' attitudes towards concentrated industries? More precisely,

   (a) Should the regulator limit and control mergers among firms in the same industry?

   (b) Even if mergers do not occur, should the regulator attempt to control the degree of concentration in industries?

Section 8.1 (Concentration Measures) discusses and defines methods for measuring the degree of concentration in an industry. That is, we define indexes for measuring the distribution of market shares across firms in a given industry. Section 8.2 (Mergers) analyzes merger activities among firms and how those activities affect the industry's level of concentration. This section investigates the incentives of firms within various industries to merge with other firms in the same industry.

Section 8.3 (Entry Barriers) and section 8.4 (Entry Deterrence) provide a wide variety of explanations, classified into two related groups, for why entry does not always occur despite the fact that existing firms in the industry make strictly positive profits. By *entry barriers* we will refer to a long list of conditions that explain why entry does not occur. These conditions could be technological, such as economies of scale or sunk entry costs; legal, such as patent protection or exclusive rights given by other firms or regulators; or the result of market organization conditions, such as distribution channels, marketing networks; or consumer loyalty and goodwill. All these conditions are discussed in section 8.3.

By *entry deterrence* we will refer to strategic actions taken by incumbent firms when faced with a threat of actual entry into their industry. By *strategic actions* we mean actions that the incumbent firm would not find profitable to take in the absence of entry threats. Analyzing all possible such actions is the subject of section 8.4.

The distinction between entry-barrier arguments and entry-deterrence arguments is not without troubles, for several reasons: In many cases it is hard to find whether the conditions leading to no entry are external to the firms or are created by the incumbent firms. This in most cases makes antitrust litigation against monopoly firms very difficult because the monopoly firm can claim that the conditions that prevent entry are external to the firms. Furthermore, some of the conditions preventing entry can be augmented by the incumbent's behavior. More precisely, we will show that the existence of sunk (irreversible) costs may be sufficient to sustain one monopoly firm in the industry. Now, note that some sunk costs are external to the firms, such as entry taxes paid to the local authorities, initial market surveys required by the investors and so on. However, there are many sunk costs that are firm dependent. For example, the incumbent firm may spend on R&D to improve its product for the purpose of forcing R&D costs on the potential entrant. In addition, the incumbent may spend large sums of money on advertising for the purpose of forcing advertising sunk cost on the potential entrant.

In most of our analysis, sunk cost is either explicitly assumed or implicitly assumed to prevail as a consequence of having firms committing to certain capacity/output levels. Section 8.5 (Contestable Markets) introduces a *contestable market structure* which describes the behavior of an incumbent firm when potential entrants can enter without having to bear any sunk cost (generally called *hit-and-run entry*).

Finally, an appendix, section 8.6, provides an overview on how the

Department of Justice and the Federal Trade Commission decide whether to challenge a merger and the corresponding operating guidelines. Appendix section 8.7 discusses the legal approach to entry-deterrence behavior.

8.1 Concentration Measures

So far, our discussion of industry concentration regarded concentrated industry as one where there are few firms, and each firm maintains a high market share. In this section we eliminate the vagueness behind the concept of concentration and propose precise measures of concentration. There are two reasons why there is a need for these precise measures. First, to be able to compare concentration among different industries in the same or different countries. The compared industries need not share anything in common, but a proper concentration measure should be able to compare concentration despite the fact that different industries have different numbers of firms and different distributions of market shares. Second, in case the regulating authority would like to intervene and to prevent a change in concentration of a certain industry, the regulator must specify a general measure by which it decides that a certain industry is concentrated. These measures can then be used by the legal system that arbitrates conflicts between the firms and the regulator about mergers.

What is a concentrated industry? Clearly, the most concentrated industry is a monopoly which sells 100% of the industry's output. When the number of firms is greater than one, there are two factors that influence concentration: (a) the number of firms in the industry, and (b) the distribution of output among the firms in the industry. Thus, a measure of concentration should be sensitive to both the distribution of the industry's output across firms as well as the number of firms in the industry.

Let N be the number of firms in the industry, let Q denote the aggregate industry-output level (aggregate amount sold to consumers), and let q_i denote the output of firm i, $i = 1, 2, \ldots, N$. Thus, $Q = \sum_{i=1}^{N} q_i$. Obviously, there may be a problem with this summation if the industry is composed of firms producing differentiated products. In other words, can we add red cars and purple cars? What about adding large cars and small cars? We ignore these aggregation problems, which come up in almost every empirical work in industrial organization and international trade.

Let $s_i \equiv (100q_i/Q)$ denote the percentage of the industry's total output sold by firm i. We call s_i the *market share* of firm i. Observe that $0 \leq s_i \leq 100$ and that

$$\sum_{i=1}^{N} s_i = \frac{100 \sum_{i=1}^{N} q_i}{Q} = 100.$$

In what follows, we discuss two commonly used measures of concentration which, among other indicators, are used by the U.S. Federal Trade Commission for determining whether to approve a merger. For more measures and their interpretation, see discussions in Jacquemin 1987 and Tirole 1988, Chapter 5.

8.1.1   The four-firm concentration ratio

The four-firm concentration ratio was a measure was used for merger guidelines (see an appendix, section 8.6.2) purposes from 1968 to around 1982. It simply sums up the market shares of the four largest firms in the industry. Let us order all the firms in the industry (rename them) so that firm 1 would have the largest market share, firm 2 the second largest, and so on. That is, $s_1 \geq s_2 \geq s_3 \geq \ldots \geq s_N$. We define the four-firm concentration ratio by

$$I_4 \equiv \sum_{i=1}^{4} s_i. \tag{8.1}$$

Table 8.1 demonstrates the value of I_4 for four imaginary industries.

% share	s_1	s_2	s_3	s_4, s_5	$s_6 \ldots s_8$	s_9, s_{10}	I_4	I_{HH}
Industry 1	60	10	5	5	5	0	80	3,850
Industry 2	20	20	20	20	0	0	80	2,000
Industry 3	$\frac{100}{3}$	$\frac{100}{3}$	$\frac{100}{3}$	0	0	0	100	3,333
Industry 4	49	49	0.25	0.25	0.25	0.25	98.5	4,802

Table 8.1: Measures for industry's concentration (s_i in percentage)

You probably notice that there is something unsatisfactory about the four-firm concentration ratio. In industry 1, firm 1 has 60% of the market. Industry 2 has five firms, all have equal market shares of 20%. However, the four-firm concentration ratio yields $I_4 = 80\%$ for both industries. Thus, since the four-firm measure is linear, it does not differentiate between different firm sizes as long as the largest four firms maintain "most" of the market shares. Comparing industries 3 and 4 demonstrates the same problem where an industry equally shared by three firms is measured to be more concentrated than an industry dominated by only two firms.

8.1.2   The Herfindahl-Hirshman index

The Herfindahl-Hirshman index (denoted by I_{HH}) is a convex function of firms' market shares, hence it is sensitive to unequal market shares. We define this measure to be the sum of the squares of the firms' market shares. Formally,

$$I_{HH} \equiv \sum_{i=1}^{N}(s_i)^2. \qquad (8.2)$$

Table 8.1 shows that the I_{HH} for industry 1 is almost twice the I_{HH} for industry 2. This follows from the fact that squaring the market shares of the large firms increases this index to a large value for industries with significantly unequal market shares. Comparing industries 3 and 4 shows that while the I_4 measure indicates that industry 3 is more concentrated than industry 4, the I_{HH} measure indicates that industry 4 is more concentrated than industry 3. For this reason, the I_{HH} is found to be the preferred concentration measure for regulation purposes.

8.2   Mergers

The terms *mergers, takeovers, acquisitions,* and *integration* describe a situation where independently owned firms join under the same ownership. We will use the term *merger* to refer to any type of joining ownership and disregard the question of whether the merger is initiated by both firms, or whether one firm was taken over by another. Instead, we investigate the gains and incentives to merge and the consequences of mergers for the subsequent performance and productivity of the firms involved, for consumers' welfare, and for social welfare.

The Federal Trade Commission classifies mergers into three general categories:

Horizontal merger: This occurs when firms in the same industry, producing identical or similar products and selling in the same geographical market, merge.

Vertical merger: This occurs when a firm producing an intermediate good (or a factor of production) merges with a firm producing the final good that uses this intermediate good, or when two companies who have a potential buyer-seller relationship prior to a merger merge.

Conglomerate merger: This occurs when firms producing less related products merge under the same ownership. More precisely, conglomerate mergers are classified into three subclasses:

> *Product extension:* The acquiring and acquired firms are functionally related in production or distribution.
>
> *Market extension:* The firms produce the same products but sell them in different geographic markets.
>
> *Other conglomerate:* The firms are essentially unrelated in the products they produce and distribute.

Ravenscraft and Scherer (1987) provide a comprehensive study of merger activities in the United States and report four great merger "waves" that have marked American industrial history: one peaking in 1901; a milder one during the late 1920s; a third, with its peak in 1968; and the most recent one, a resurgence in the early 1980s. Looking at the types of mergers, we note that the data show a significant decline in horizontal and vertical activity and a rise in "pure" conglomerate mergers from the 1960s. The merger wave of the turn of the century was preponderantly horizontal. The wave of the 1920s saw extensive activity in the public-utility sector, in vertical and product-line extension, and in horizontal mergers that created oligopolies rather than monopolies. The wave of the 1960s was preponderantly conglomerate, reflecting a much more stringent antitrust policy against horizontal mergers.

Why do mergers occur? First, a merger may reduce market competition between the merged firms and other firms in the industry, thereby increasing the profit of the merged firms. However, note that section 8.8, exercise 2 demonstrates in a Cournot market structure that when there are more than two firms in the industry, the aggregate profit of the merged firms can be lower than the profit of the two firms separately before the merger occurs. Second, if the merger involves merging capital, assets, and other fixed factors of production, then the merged firms would be able to increase their size, possibly reduce cost, and thereby increase their market share, hence profit. Third, mergers and takeovers occur when there is a disparity of valuation judgments, given uncertainty about future business conditions: the buyer is for some reason more optimistic about the firm's future than the seller, or the buyer believes it can run the acquired entity more profitably as a part of this organization than the seller could by remaining independent. Fourth, those who control the acquiring entity seek the prestige and monetary rewards associated with managing a large corporate empire, whether or not the consolidation adds to the profits.

8.2.1   Horizontal merger

In subsection 6.1.3 we saw some theoretical basis for the presumption that under a Cournot market structure, a decrease in the number of firms in an industry (via, say, a merger) reduces social welfare. That is, we have shown that under a Cournot market structure, in the case of identical firms with no fixed costs, an increase in the number of firms increases the sum of consumer surplus and producers' profits despite the fact that profits decline.

However, there is still a question of whether a regulator should refuse to permit a merger to take place only on the basis of the associated sharp increase in concentration. The answer to this question is no! That is, in what follows, we construct an example where a merger of a high-cost firm with a low-cost firm increases overall welfare despite the increase in concentration (for a comprehensive analysis of mergers under the Cournot market structure for the case of n firms, see Salant, Switzer, and Reynolds 1983).

Consider the Cournot duopoly case, that of two firms producing a homogeneous product, analyzed in subsection 6.1.1 on page 98. Let the unit costs be $c_1 = 1$ and $c_2 = 4$ and the demand be $p = 10 - Q$. Equations (6.5), (6.6), and (6.7) imply that under the Cournot duopoly market structure: $q_1^c = 4$, $q_2^c = 1$, $p^c = 10 - (4 + 1) = 5$, $\pi_1^c = 16$, $\pi_2^c = 1$. Hence, in view of (3.3) (see subsection 3.2.3), the consumer surplus is $CS(5) = \frac{1}{2}(a - p^c)^2 = 25/2$. Hence, in view of (6.13), $W^c = CS(5) + \pi_1^c + \pi_2^c = 29.5$.

Now, allow a merger between the two firms. The new firm is a multiplant monopoly, and as shown in section 5.4, the newly merged firm would shut down plant number 2. Hence, the merged firm solves a simple single-plant monopoly problem analyzed in section 5.1, yielding an output level of $Q^m = 4.5$, and $p^m = 10 - 4.5 = 5.5$; hence, $\pi^m = (5.5 - 1)4.5 = 81/4$. Also, $CS(4.5) = \frac{1}{2}(10 - 5.5)^2 = 81/8$. Altogether, $W^m = CS(4.5) + \pi^m = 30.375$.

Comparing the premerger concentration level with the postmerger monopoly yields that

$$I_{HH}^c = (80\%)^2 + (20\%)^2 = 6,800 < 10,000 = (100\%)^2 = I_{HH}^m. \quad (8.3)$$

Observing that $W^m > W^c$, we can state the following:

Proposition 8.1 *Under a Cournot market structure, a merger among firms leading to an increase in concentration does not necessarily imply an overall welfare reduction.*

The intuition behind Proposition 8.1 is that when firms have different production costs, there exists a tradeoff between production efficiency and the degree of monopolization. In other words, a merger between a high-cost and a low-cost firm increases production efficiency since it eliminates the high-cost producer. However, the increase in concentration increases the market price and therefore reduces consumer welfare. Now, when the difference in production costs between the two firms is significant, the increase in production efficiency effect dominates the reduction in consumer welfare.

In view of the merger guidelines described in subsection 8.6.2 such a merger will not be approved, despite this example's demonstration that the merger would improve overall welfare. However, the reader is advised not to take this example too seriously for the following reason: It is possible that our methodology is wrong in the sense that we are making welfare judgments based on the Cournot market structure. Had the firms played Bertrand, the inefficient firm (firm 2) would not be producing in the duopoly case. In summary, conclusions about welfare that are based only on the Cournot market structure should be checked to determine whether they also hold under different market structures. Otherwise, such a welfare analysis is not robust.

The analysis of this subsection has a major shortcoming in that it is done without accounting for firms' size and therefore for the effects of changes in size associated with every merger. That is, under a Cournot market structure, when two firms with the same unit costs merge, their actual size merges into a single firm. Davidson and Deneckere (1984) develop a model that overcomes this shortcoming by introducing capacity to the analysis. In their model, when two firms with invested capacity merge, they merge with their entire stock of capacity, so the joint firm maintains a larger capacity level than each individual firm.

8.2.2 Vertical merger

A vertical merger is defined as a merger between a supplier (producer) of an intermediate good and a producer of a final good who uses this intermediate good as a factor of production. The common terminology used to describe these firms is to call the intermediate-good suppliers as *upstream firms*, and the final-good producers as *downstream firms*. Figure 8.1 illustrates an industry structure in which there are two upstream firms selling an input to two downstream firms. In Figure 8.1 the two input suppliers denoted by A and B sell identical inputs to both downstream firms denoted by 1 and 2. The left-hand side of Figure 8.1 shows the initial situation in which all firms are disjoint. The right-hand side illustrates the case in which the upstream firm A merges with downstream firm 1. We denote the merged firm by $A1$. There are several ways in which competition in the upstream and downstream markets could

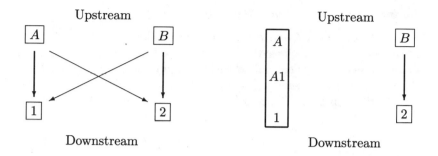

Figure 8.1: Upstream factor suppliers and downstream producers

be modeled (See for example Ordover, Saloner, and Salop 1990; Perry 1989; Salinger 1988; and Tirole 1988, Chap. 4). Clearly, if both the upstream and the downstream markets are characterized by a Bertrand price competition, then it is easy to show that profits of all firms are identically zero before and after vertical integration occurs. In order to solve this modeling problem we could assume that the downstream firms produce differentiated products (such as the Hotelling spatial competition analyzed in subsection 7.3.1) so that firms would make positive profits. Instead, we take an approach yielding similar results by assuming that the upstream market is characterized by a Bertrand price competition (section 6.3), whereas the downstream market is characterized by a Cournot quantity competition (section 6.1).

Downstream competition

We assume that the demand for the good marketed in the downstream market is given by the linear demand $p = \alpha - q_1 - q_2$, where $\alpha > 0$, and q_1 and q_2 are the output levels sold by downstream firms 1 and 2. Let the technology be such that one unit of input produces one unit of output, and denote by c_1 and c_2 the price of the input paid by firms 1 and 2, respectively. Hence, the firms' unit costs are given by c_1 and c_2, respectively. In section 6.1 we showed that under this demand and cost structure, a Cournot quantity competition yields the output and profit for each firm i given by

$$q_i = \frac{\alpha - 2c_i + c_j}{3} \quad \text{and} \quad \pi_i = \frac{(\alpha - 2c_i + c_j)^2}{9}. \qquad (8.4)$$

Hence, the aggregate downstream production and price levels are

$$Q \equiv q_1 + q_2 = \frac{2\alpha - c_1 - c_2}{3} \quad \text{and} \quad p = \alpha - Q = \frac{\alpha + c_1 + c_2}{3}. \qquad (8.5)$$

Upstream competition before the merger

The upstream firms A and B sell the intermediate product to the downstream firms 1 and 2. Since the two upstream firms engage in a Bertrand price competition, prices fall to their unit production cost which is assumed to be zero. Hence, $c_1 = c_2 = 0$, so the downstream firms have zero production costs. Thus, substituting into (8.4) yields

$$q_1 = q_2 = \frac{\alpha}{3}, \quad \pi_1 = \pi_2 = \frac{\alpha^2}{9} \quad \text{and} \quad \pi_A = \pi_B = 0. \tag{8.6}$$

Upstream and downstream merge

Suppose now that upstream firm A merges with downstream firm 1. We denote the merged firm by $A1$. Hence, the input cost of the merged firm $A1$ is zero. We assume that the merged firm $A1$ does not sell the intermediate good to firm 2; therefore, the upstream firm B is now a monopoly in the factor market and maximizes its profit by choosing the price for its intermediate product c_2 that equals the cost of production of downstream firm 2. Thus, the profit of upstream firm B is its price c_2 times the output level of downstream firm 2 given in (8.4). Formally, the upstream firm B chooses c_2 that solves

$$\max_{c_2} \pi_B = c_2 q_2 = \frac{c_2(\alpha - 2c_2 + c_1)}{3}. \tag{8.7}$$

The first-order condition yields $0 = \alpha - 4c_2 + c_1$, yielding that $c_2 = \alpha/4$. Clearly, the second-order condition is satisfied, so substituting $c_1 = 0$ and $c_2 = \alpha/4$ into (8.4) and (8.5) yields

$$q_1 = \frac{5\alpha}{12}, \quad q_2 = \frac{\alpha}{6}, \quad Q = \frac{7\alpha}{12}, \quad \text{and } p = \frac{5\alpha}{12}. \tag{8.8}$$

Hence, the profit of the two downstream firms is given by

$$\pi_{A1} = pq_{A1} = \frac{25\alpha^2}{144} \quad \text{and} \quad \pi_2 = (p - c_2)q_2 = \frac{\alpha^2}{36}. \tag{8.9}$$

Equation (8.8) yields the following proposition:

Proposition 8.2 *A merger between an upstream and a downstream firm increases the output level of the merged firm and reduces the output level of the downstream firm that does not merge.*

Proposition 8.2 is rather intuitive. The downstream firm that does not merge faces an increase in its input cost resulting from having to buy its input from a single monopoly firm B. Hence, the increase in firm 2's production cost and the reduction in firm 1's production cost would increase the output of firm 1 and reduce the output of firm 2.

We wish to investigate whether this vertical merger is profitable to the vertically merging firms. To see that, we need to compare the sum of profits of firms A and 1 prior to the merger to the profit of the merged firm $A1$. However, prior to the merger, firm A made zero profit, hence prior to merger their joint profit was $\pi_1 = \alpha^2/9$. Comparing this sum to π_{A1} in (8.9) implies that

Proposition 8.3

    1. The combined profit of the merging upstream and downstream firms increase after they merge.

    2. A merger between the upstream and the downstream firms will not foreclose the market of the disjoint downstream firm but will only reduce its profit.

Proposition 8.3 is important, since it is often argued that vertical mergers lead to a foreclosure of the disjoint downstream firms, which in our example means that firm B or firm 1 or both would go out of business. Note that this cannot happen in the present model since the upstream firm B will reduce the input price to prevent firm 2 from leaving the market (firm B sells only to firm 2 after the merger). Since vertical integration does not necessarily imply foreclosure, the FTC seems to be more forgiving to vertical mergers than to horizontal mergers. Moreover, many economists believe that vertical integration should be viewed as an increase in efficiency since most firms carry on several stages of production under a single plant anyway, with or without vertical integration. Thus, a firm is by definition a vertically merged entity and is believed to be an efficient form of organization.

Finally, the sum of the profits of the disjoint upstream firm B and downstream firm 2 is given by

$$\pi_B + \pi_2 = \frac{\alpha^2}{24} + \frac{\alpha^2}{36} = \frac{10\alpha^2}{144} < 0 + \frac{\alpha^2}{9}, \qquad (8.10)$$

which is the sum of profits of firm B and 2 prior to the merger between firm A and firm 1. Thus, despite the fact that the profit of the nonmerging upstream firm B increases with the merger of firm A with firm 1, the decline in the profit of the nonmerging final-good-producer firm 2 is larger than the increase in π_B, which is caused by the sharp drop in market share of firm 2.

8.2.3   Horizontal merger among firms producing complementary products

It was Cournot who realized that horizontal merger need not increase the equilibrium price level when two firms producing complementary products merge. The reader is probably familiar with the definition and examples of complementary products. Examples include coffee and milk or sugar, audio receivers and speakers, video players and cassettes, cameras and film, computers and monitors, computers and software, cars and tires, transportation and hotel services, and more. The reader is referred to section 10.3 for further analyses of the economics of systems that are composed of complementary components.

In this subsection we analyze an industry where firms produce two complementary products. Economides and Salop 1992, provide a more extensive analysis of complementary systems by considering several producers of each product.

Demand for systems

Consider a market for computer systems. A computer system is defined as a combination of two complementary products called computers (denoted by X), and monitors (denoted by Y). We denote by p_X the price of one computer and by p_Y the price of a monitor. Therefore, since a system consists of one computer and one monitor, the price of a system is given by $p_S = p_X + p_Y$. Let Q denote the quantity of systems purchased by all consumers, and assume that the aggregate consumer demand is given by

$$Q = \alpha - p_S = \alpha - (p_X + p_Y) \quad \text{or} \quad p_S = p_X + p_Y = \alpha - Q, \quad \alpha > 0. \quad (8.11)$$

We denote by x the amount of computers sold to consumers and by y, the amount of monitors sold. Since the two components are perfect complements, $x = y = Q$.

Independently owned producing firms

Suppose that computers and monitors are produced by different firms whose strategic variables are prices, and suppose that production of either product is costless. Consider the problem solved by the computer firm (X-producer). For a given p_Y, firm X chooses p_X that solves

$$\max_{p_X} \pi_X = p_X X(p_X) = p_X[\alpha - (p_X + p_Y)]. \quad (8.12)$$

The first-order condition yields $0 = \frac{\partial \pi_X}{\partial p_X} = \alpha - 2p_X - p_Y$. Clearly, the second-order condition is satisfied. Hence, firm X's price-best-response function to Y's price is $p_X = (\alpha - p_Y)/2$. Similarly, we can show that Y's price best response with respect to X's price is $p_Y = (\alpha - p_X)/2$. Altogether, when the complementary components are produced by independent firms, their prices, quantities, and firms' profit levels are given by

$$p_X = p_Y = \frac{\alpha}{3}, \quad Q = x = y = \alpha - (p_X + p_Y) = \frac{\alpha}{3} \quad \text{and} \quad \pi_X = \pi_Y = \frac{\alpha^2}{9}.$$
(8.13)

Monopoly producing all components

Now suppose that firms X and Y merge under a single ownership. Thus, computers are now sold as systems composed of a single monitor bundled with a single computer. Therefore, the monopoly systems producer chooses a system price p_S that solves

$$\max_{p_S} \pi_{XY} = p_S(\alpha - p_S)$$

yielding a first-order condition given by $0 = \frac{\partial \pi_{XY}}{\partial p_S} = \alpha - 2p_S$. Clearly, the second-order condition is satisfied. Hence, the price of a system under monopoly and the monopoly's profit are given by

$$p_S^M = \frac{\alpha}{2}, \quad Q^M = x^M = y^M = \alpha - p_S^M = \frac{\alpha}{2}, \quad \text{and} \quad \pi_{XY}^M = \frac{\alpha^2}{4}. \quad (8.14)$$

We conclude the discussion on mergers with the following proposition, which follows from the comparison of (8.13) and (8.14).

Proposition 8.4 *A merger into a single monopoly firm between firms producing complementary products would*

1. *reduce the price of systems (i.e., $p_S^M < p^S = p_X + p_Y$);*

2. *increase the number of systems sold (i.e., $Q^M > Q$); and*

3. *increase the sum of profits of the two firms (i.e., $\pi_{XY}^M > \pi_X + \pi_Y$).*

The significance of Proposition 8.4 is that a merger between two firms producing complementary products can increase social welfare, since consumers face lower prices, and firms gain a higher profit. The intuition behind Proposition 8.4 is as follows. Given that the two components are perfect complements, a rise in the price of one component reduces the demand for both components. Under price competition among independent component-producing firms, each firm overprices its component since each firm is affected by the reduced demand for its component and not the entire system. Thus, the negative externality on the other firm's demand is not internalized. However, when the firms merge, the joint ownership takes into consideration how the demand for both components is affected by an increase in the price of one component, and the negative demand externality is internalized.

We conclude our discussion of merger of firms producing complementary products with two remarks: First, Sonnenschein (1968) has shown that the Nash equilibrium were firms compete in price and sell perfect complements is isomorphic to the case where firms compete in quantity and sell perfect substitutes. One simply has to interchange the roles of price in the network case with the industry quantity in the perfect substitutes case. For example, Proposition 8.4 can be reinterpreted as showing that under quantity competition among firms selling perfect substitutes, a merger to monopoly would (1) reduce the aggregate quantity produced, (2) increase the price, and (3) result in strictly larger industry profits. Second, Gaudet and Salant (1992) show that the merger of firms producing complements and setting prices may be unprofitable if some members of the industry are not parties to the merger. Given Sonnenschein's observation, their result implies that mergers to less than monopoly may also be unprofitable if firms produce perfect substitutes and engage in Cournot competition, a point first noted in Salant, Switzer, and Reynolds 1983.

8.3   Entry Barriers

Why do we frequently observe that firms do not enter an industry despite the fact that the existing firms in the industry make above normal profits? In this section we investigate the following question: If oligopolies make pure profits, why does free entry not occur until competition brings down the price so that existing firms will no longer make above normal profits? Barriers to entry are considered an important structural characteristic of an industry. The competitiveness and the performance of an industry are generally assumed to be strongly influenced by its entry conditions.

There can be many reasons why entry may not occur. The primary explanation for entry barriers is the existence of entry cost. Bain's pioneering work (1956) specified three sources of entry barriers: absolute cost advantages of incumbent firms, economies of scale, and product-differentiation advantages of incumbent firms, such as reputation and goodwill. In addition politicians and all levels of governments may explicitly or implicitly support the existing firms (and the existing firms may in return support and contribute to the campaigns of politicians). Maintaining such connections seems impossible for new investors. Other reasons include the learning experience possessed by the existing firms, consumers' loyalty to brands already consumed, and availability of financing (banks are less eager to lend to new investors) (see also Geroski, Gilbert, and Jacquemin 1990).

In this section we briefly discuss entry barriers. As we mentioned earlier, we regard entry barriers as the conditions that are not controlled by the incumbent firms that explain why entry does not occur. Section 8.4 below will address issues of entry deterrence, which we regard as the strategic actions taken by incumbent firms when facing the entry into an industry of potential competitors. Subsection 8.3.1 demonstrates a technological explanation for entry barriers and shows how the degree of concentration is related to the fixed production costs. Subsection 8.3.2 demonstrates the role that the existence of sunk costs play in generating the conditions for entry barriers.

8.3.1 Concentration and fixed costs in a noncompetitive market structure: an example

Let us demonstrate the relationship between fixed costs and concentration by means of an example. Consider the monopolistic competition in the differentiated-products environment analyzed in section 7.2 on page 143. In that environment, firms have to bear a fixed cost, implying that in equilibrium there will be entry of a finite number of firms. More precisely, recall from Proposition 7.5 on page 147 that the number of firms is $N^{mc} = L/(2F)$, where L is the economy's resource endowment and F is the fixed cost of each firm, $(L > 2F)$. Hence, the industry described in Section 7.2 yields a concentration level given by

$$I_{HH} = N^{mc} \left(\frac{100}{N^{mc}} \right)^2 = \frac{100^2}{N^{mc}} = \frac{2F}{L} 10,000. \qquad (8.15)$$

Consequently, in a monopolistic-competition environment, the I_{HH} concentration ratio increases with the fixed cost. A similar calculation can be performed in a Cournot market structure, where firms have fixed cost, and therefore, only a finite number of firms would enter.

For the case of an industry producing a homogeneous product, von Weizsäcker (1980) demonstrates that if production technologies exhibit increasing returns to scale at low output levels (U-shaped average-cost functions), then the equilibrium number of firms is larger than the social optimum.

8.3.2 Sunk costs generate entry barriers

By *sunk costs* we mean costs that cannot be reversed or for which the investment associated with paying them cannot be converted to other causes, or resold in order to recapture part of the investment cost. Examples include legal (lawyers') fees and taxes that an entering firm must bear prior to the actual entry. If after paying this cost a firm reverses its decision to enter, the firm cannot recover these fees. Other forms of sunk costs include market surveys (almost always mandated by the investors), advertising costs, and expenditures on nontransportable, nonconvertible plant and equipment, such as the site preparation work for any plant.

Following Stiglitz (1987), we now demonstrate how in a market for a homogeneous product, the existence of even small sunk costs can serve as an entry barrier so that entry will not occur even if the incumbent continues to make a monopoly profit. There are two firms, A and B, both capable of producing an identical product with identical constant marginal costs. Firm B is the potential entrant. If firm B enters, it has to sink ϵ dollars into the process. Firm A is the incumbent monopoly firm earning a profit of $\pi^A = \pi^M - \epsilon$, where π^M denotes the monopoly's profit level, not including the entry cost it has already sunk in. This extensive-form game is illustrated in Figure 8.2.

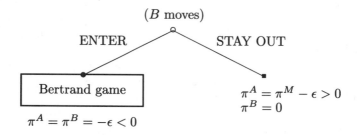

Figure 8.2: Sunk costs and entry barriers

In the game illustrated in Figure 8.2 the potential entrant (firm B) moves first by choosing whether to enter or not. In case firm B chooses not to enter, it saves the entry cost ϵ and therefore earns zero profit. In this case, firm A remains a monopoly and makes the monopoly profit less than the entry cost it sunk earlier. In contrast, if firm B enters, the firms are assumed to set their prices simultaneously, yielding a Bertrand equilibrium (see Definition 6.2 on page 108) where price equals marginal cost. In this case, both firms make a loss equal to the sunk cost. It is straightforward to establish the following proposition:

Proposition 8.5 *For any level of sunk entry cost satisfying $0 < \epsilon < \pi^M$, there exists a unique subgame perfect equilibrium where firm A is a monopoly earning $\pi^A = \pi^M - \epsilon$ and firm B stays out.*

That is, in a SPE, the entrant foresees that after entry occurs (the second stage of the game), the incumbent will switch from being a monopoly to being in an aggressive price competition and leading the marginal-cost pricing. Hence, in the first stage the potential entrant will choose not to enter since staying out yields zero profit.

Proposition 8.5 is rather disturbing because it means that entry will never occur as long as there are some (even infinitesimal) sunk costs associated with entry. However, the reader should notice that Proposition 8.5 applies only to homogeneous products. In fact, under these circumstances, it is likely that the entrant will engage itself in further investments (higher sunk costs) in order to develop a differentiated brand, in which case price competition need not yield zero or negative profits. However, Proposition 8.5 makes a point by stating that even small sunk cost can create all the conditions for entry barriers. In fact, the incumbent does not need to do anything to deter this entry and simply continues producing the monopoly output level. Proposition 8.5 highlights the role ex-post competition plays in creating entry barriers. What generates the entry barriers even for negligible sunk cost is the intensity of the postentry price competition. Had we assumed that the firms play Cournot after entry occurs, low sunk cost would not generate entry barriers. Assuming Bertrand price competition generates the postentry intense competition that makes entry unprofitable for even low entry costs.

We conclude this analysis be considering a situation where a firm could receive an amount of $\phi > 0$ upon exit. For example, if $\phi \leq \epsilon$, then we can view ϕ as the amount of its original expenditure the firm can recover upon exit. Figure 8.3 illustrates the modified game.

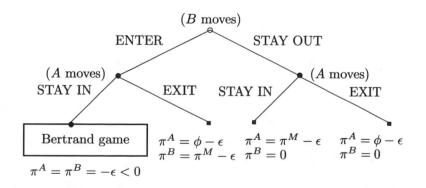

Figure 8.3: Sunk-cost entry barriers with partial cost recovery

In Figure 8.3 we added an additional stage enabling the incumbent (firm A) to exit after firm B makes its choice whether to enter or not. In fact, firm A's exit choice could have been included in the original game (Figure 8.2); however, in that game A's exit action was clearly dominated by other actions and was therefore ignored.

We now look for a subgame perfect equilibrium for this game. The subgame on the right (B does not enter) has a unique Nash equilibrium where the incumbent stays in and firm B earns zero profits. The subgame on the left (starting with the node where the incumbent makes a move) has a unique Nash equilibrium where the incumbent exits the industry and collects a profit of $\phi - \epsilon > -\epsilon$ it would collect if it stays in. In this case, the entrant becomes a monopoly. Therefore,

Proposition 8.6 *There exists a unique subgame perfect equilibrium for the game described in Figure 8.3, where firm B enters and firm A (incumbent) exits the industry.*

Proposition 8.6 states that the market for this product will remain dominated by a monopoly market structure despite the fact that entry (and exit) occur. One monopoly replaces another monopoly. Hence, from the consumers' point of view, this particular market will be regarded as one that has substantial entry barriers.

Finally, we can further modify the game described in Figure 8.3 by adding an initial stage in which firm A makes a choice whether to enter the game and become the incumbent firm. Clearly, if firm A would be able to recover only part of its sunk cost ($\phi < \epsilon$), then it would not enter at all, and no other firm would ever find it profitable to enter. This result makes our argument even stronger since in this case the entry barriers are so strong that entry is not profitable to any firm, because any entering firm would have to exit when another firm enters.

8.4   Entry Deterrence

We now turn to the strategic approach for explaining entry barriers. We assume that initially there is one firm, called the *incumbent* or the established firm, that is a monopoly in a certain market. In the second stage, we assume that another firm, called the *potential entrant* is entering the market if entry results in above normal profit.

Modifying Bain's classifications of entry deterrence, we use the following terminology:

Blockaded entry: The incumbent is not threatened by entry; no firm would find it profitable to enter, even if the incumbent produces the monopoly output level.

Deterred entry: The incumbent modifies its behavior (say, by lowering price or expanding capacity) in order to deter entry; if prices are lowered, then we say that the incumbent exercises *limit pricing.*

Accommodated entry: Entry occurs, and the incumbent firm modifies its action to take into account of entry that occurs.

Thus, blockaded entry corresponds to what we called entry barrier in section 8.3, where we discussed several conditions yielding entry barriers other than the behavior of incumbent firms. In contrast, we refer to entry deterrence and entry accommodation as actions taken by incumbent firms when faced with a threat of entry.

Earlier authors held that an incumbent firm may be able to deter entry by overproducing and selling at lower prices prior to the date at which entry is expected. These types of models relied on the *Bain-Sylos postulate,* under which the prospective entrant was assumed to believe that the established firm would maintain the same output after entry that it did before entry. Then the established firm naturally acquired a leadership role as described in the Leader-Follower model (section 6.2). In addition, some of the earlier models assumed that entrants have to sink (output-independent) costs in order to begin their operation, whereas incumbents do not.

Presently, most economists disregard these arguments for the following reasons: First, note that this cost asymmetry could be reversed, considering the fact that established firms may have to pay some costs that the entrant does not have to bear. For example, established firms may operate according to long-term contracts. Most notably, wage contractees and unions are hard to negotiate with, and the downward adjustment of wages needed to meet the competition with the entrant would invoke tough resistance from workers and unions. Yet in some instances, the potential entrant is free to choose workers and can decide on wages without having any prior obligation. The same argument holds for subcontracting and binding contracts with suppliers of raw material and parts. In addition, assuming asymmetric cost structure turns the problem of entry deterrence into an ad hoc problem since there always exists a level of entry cost that would prevent firms from entering the market. Moreover, even if the above asymmetry holds true in reality, it is likely that in the long run the entrant would be able to collect a high enough (duopoly) profit to more than cover the entry cost. In addition, banks observing that the entering firm would make such a profit would be willing to lend the entrant the entry cost since the firm would be able to pay back the loan (and interest) with its future profits.

Second, Friedman (1979) and Dixit (1980) question the validity of the Bain-Sylos postulate by raising some doubt regarding the logic behind the above entry-deterrence argument. They point out that the preentry price choice (or quantity in our case) of the established firm is irrelevant for the entry decision of the potential entrant. The only thing that should matter to the potential entrant is what the postentry market structure would be. After entry occurs and the entry cost is already paid, there is no reason to assume that the firms would play the Leader-Follower game. It would be more reasonable to assume that the firms would play Cournot or Bertrand where the firms have equal power and knowledge. Now, given that the entrant knows that the market structure would change after entry occurs, all the first-period entry-deterrence strategies (limit pricing) or overproduction are irrelevant to the postentry profits collected by all firms. Third, in modeling entry deterrence it is not clear why one firm gets to be the first to choose and commit itself to a certain production level, thereby obtaining what is commonly called a *first-mover advantage*?

The approach to modeling entry deterrence based on the Bain-Sylos postulate is given in subsection 8.4.1, where we sketch an analog to Spence (1977) and demonstrate that entry can be deterred if an incumbent firm builds an *irreversible capacity* prior to the period when entry is allowed, so that a potential entrant faces a saturated market if it decides to enter. Subsection 8.4.2 relaxes the Bain-Sylos postulate and assumes that the incumbent is aware of the possibility that the entrant may find it profitable to alter its actions after entry occurs.

Subsection 8.4.3 (Investment in capital replacement) introduces a dynamic entry-deterrence model showing how in the face of entry threats an incumbent with depreciating capital is forced to invest more frequently than what is needed to simply replace depreciated capital. Subsection 8.4.4 (Judo economics) focuses on the strategic choices of a potential entrant when an incumbent firm may find it more profitable to allow a small-scale entry rather than fighting it. Subsection 8.4.5 (Credible spatial preemption) analyzes an incumbent differentiated-good producer facing entry in one of its markets. We conclude our analysis of entry barriers with subsection 8.4.6, where we demonstrate that limit pricing can serve as an entry-deterring strategy when the entrant does not know the production cost of the incumbent.

8.4.1   Capacity commitment under the Bain-Sylos postulate

Earlier models analyzing entry deterrence adopted the Bain-Sylos postulate, under which the prospective entrant was assumed to believe that the incumbent firm would maintain the same output after entry as before. Spence (1977) explicitly distinguishes between capacity and quantity produced. In his model, the quantity produced is constrained by the amount of capacity firm 1 invests in the first period. Thus, as long as entry does not occur, the capacity is underutilized. However, in the event of a threat of entry, the incumbent can expand its output level and use all the capacity, thereby reducing the price to the level that makes entry unprofitable. In this subsection we refrain from making the distinction between capacity and output level and concentrate on analyzing how the incumbent determines how much capital to invest under the threat of entry.

Consider the two-period Leader-Follower game described in section 6.2. However, instead of assuming that firms decide how much to produce, let us assume that the firms' actions are confined to how much capacity (or capital) to accumulate (invest). Although this distinction is only a semantic one, it makes our story somewhat more convincing since capacity bears the sense of irreversibility (one is unable to discard it and to collect the costs already paid), thereby making capacity accumulation a credible strategic variable. Thus, in period 1, firm 1 has to choose its capacity-output investment, $k_1 \in [0, \infty)$; in period 2, firm 2 chooses whether to enter (choosing $k_2 > 0$) or to stay out ($k_2 = 0$).

We assume that the firms are identical in all respects, except that the potential entrant (firm 2) has to pay an entry cost. Such costs include an investment in new equipment, payments to lobbyists for facilitating the industry's control regulations, and so on. We denote the entry cost by $E, E \geq 0$. To completely describe the game, we define the profit of the firms (collected at the end of the second period) to be:

$$\pi_1(k_1, k_2) \equiv k_1(1 - k_1 - k_2) \quad \text{and} \tag{8.16}$$

$$\pi_2(k_1, k_2) \equiv \begin{cases} k_2(1 - k_1 - k_2) - E & \text{if entry occurs} \\ 0 & \text{otherwise.} \end{cases}$$

We solve this game backwards by first analyzing the last period, given the action taken in the preceding period.

The second period

In the second period, firm 2 takes $k_1 = \bar{k}_1$ as given and chooses k_2 to maximize its profit given in (8.16). There can be two cases: Firm 2 enters and pays the entry cost E, or it does not enter. Suppose for a moment that it enters. Then, firm 2 chooses k_2 to satisfy

$$0 = \frac{\partial \pi_2(\bar{k}_1, k_2)}{\partial k_2} = 1 - 2k_2 - k_1, \quad \text{hence} \quad k_2 = \frac{1 - \bar{k}_1}{2}. \tag{8.17}$$

Substituting into the profit function of firm 2 (8.16), we have it that if firm 2 enters, then

$$\pi_2 = \frac{1 - \bar{k}_1}{2} \left(1 - \bar{k}_1 - \frac{1 - \bar{k}_1}{2} \right) - E,$$

which is greater than zero if and only if $\bar{k}_1 < 1 - 2\sqrt{E}$.

We summarize the analysis for the second period by the best-response function of firm 2:

$$k_2 = R_2(\bar{k}_1, E) = \begin{cases} \frac{1 - \bar{k}_1}{2} & \text{if } \bar{k}_1 < 1 - 2\sqrt{E} \\ 0 & \text{otherwise.} \end{cases} \tag{8.18}$$

The first period

In the first period firm 1 has to set k_1 knowing how it will affect the capacity choice of firm 2. That is, firm 1 calculates (8.18). Firm 1 also knows that the best-response function of firm 2 is discontinuous when it sets $k_1 = 1 - 2\sqrt{E}$. Thus, firm 1 would take into consideration that small changes in its capacity around $k_1 = 1 - 2\sqrt{E}$ may induce firm 2 to alter its entry decision.

With this discontinuity in mind, our search for the profit-maximizing strategy for firm 1 would involve comparing the profit of firm 1 when firm 2 enters (the leader's profit level, denoted by π_1^s) with the profit of firm 1 when firm 2 does not enter (the monopoly profit level, denoted by π_1^m). Formally, these profit levels are given by

$$\pi_1^s = k_1 \left(1 - k_1 - \frac{1 - k_1}{2} \right) = k_1 \left(\frac{1 - k_1}{2} \right) \quad \text{and} \quad \pi_1^m = k_1(1 - k_1).$$
$$\tag{8.19}$$

Thus, for a given k_1, the monopoly's profit level is twice the leader's profit levels in the present formulation. The two profit functions are drawn in Figure 8.4. In Figure 8.4, the upper bell-shaped curves are the incumbent's monopoly profit (when entry does not occur). The lower bell-shaped curves are the leader's profit level (when entry occurs). Also, the entry-deterring capacity level of firm 1 (given by $k_1 = 1 - 2\sqrt{E}$) is marked by the vertical solid line with a rightward pointing arrow, indicating that for $k_1 \geq 1 - 2\sqrt{E}$ firm 1 is a monopoly (hence the upper bell-shaped profit curves apply).

Figure 8.4 is divided into three parts, indicating how firm 1 reacts for different levels of firm 2's entry cost.

1. *Blockaded entry:* This case is not displayed in Figure 8.4 but applies when $1 - 2\sqrt{E} < 1/2$ (high entry cost). In this case, choosing the monopoly capacity level is sufficient for deterring entry. That

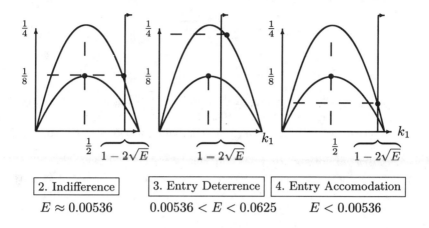

| 2. Indifference | 3. Entry Deterrence | 4. Entry Accomodation |

$E \approx 0.00536$ $0.00536 < E < 0.0625$ $E < 0.00536$

Figure 8.4: Incumbent's profit levels and capacity choices for different levels of entry cost.

is, when the entry cost is high, firm 2 will not enter when firm 1 plays its monopoly capacity level. Thus, substituting $k_2 = 0$ into (8.16), firm 1 chooses k_1 to maximize its monopoly profit. The first-order condition satisfies

$$0 = \frac{\partial \pi_1(k_1, 0)}{\partial k_1} = 1 - 2k_1.$$

Hence, $k_1 = 1/2$. Now, for having this output level deterring the entry of firm 2, (8.18) implies that E has to satisfy $k_1 = 1/2 \geq 1 - 2\sqrt{E}$, implying that $E \geq 1/16 = 0.0625$.

2. *Indifference between deterrence and accommodation:* We need to find the magnitude of the entry cost parameter E that would make firm 1 indifferent to whether it chooses to set $k_1 = 1 - 2\sqrt{E}$ to deter entry or to set $k_1 = 1/2$ and accommodate entry (it is clear that $k_1 = 1/2$ is the profit-maximizing capacity under monopoly as well as when entry occurs, since both profit curves peak at $k_1 = 1/2$).

Thus, we need to compare the leader's profit level under $k_1 = 1/2$ when entry occurs given in (8.19) to the profit level when firm 1 deters entry by setting $k_1 = 1 - 2\sqrt{E}$, denoted by π_1^d. Hence,

$$\pi_1^d = (1 - 2\sqrt{E})2\sqrt{E} = \frac{1}{8} = \pi_1^s. \qquad (8.20)$$

Thus, we need to solve $4E - 2\sqrt{E} + 1/8 = 0$, yielding

$$\sqrt{E} = \frac{16 - \sqrt{16^2 - 4 \times 32}}{64} \approx 0.07322,$$

implying that $E \approx 0.00536$.

3. *Entry deterrence:* From case 2 and case 3 of Figure 8.4, we have it that entry deterrence is profitable for firm 1 when the entry cost is at an intermediate level. That is, when $0.00536 < E < 0.0625$.

4. *Entry accommodation:* When the entry cost is very low, firm 1 would have to increase k_1 to a very high level in order to deter entry. Case 4 of Figure 8.4 shows that if $E < 0.00536$, deterring entry is not profitable, and that entry accommodation yields a higher profit level for firm 1.

8.4.2 Relaxing the Bain-Sylos postulate

So far, our analysis has relied on the Bain-Sylos postulate, under which the potential entrant is assumed to believe that the incumbent firm will maintain the same action after entry as before. Thus, under this postulate, the potential entrant is assumed to believe that upon entry, the incumbent will utilize its entire capacity to produce the highest possible output level in order to make entry unprofitable for the entrant. In this section, following Dixit 1980, we demonstrate that such an assumption is inconsistent with a strategic behavior under a subgame perfect equilibrium (Definition 2.10 on page 27). More precisely, we demonstrate that under a subgame perfect equilibrium, the incumbent firm will not find it profitable to utilize its entire capacity even when entry does occur. Thus, a rational potential entrant should be able to predict that a profit-maximizing incumbent will not find it profitable to utilize all its entire capacity. Therefore, we show that in a subgame perfect equilibrium, a profit-maximizing incumbent will not invest in excess capacity for the purpose of entry deterrence. In other words, overaccumulation of capacity will not occur.

Consider the following two-stage game. In the first stage firm 1 (incumbent) chooses a capacity level $\bar{k}$ that would enable firm 1 to produce without cost $q_1 \leq \bar{k}$ units of output in the second stage of the game. If, however, the incumbent chooses to expand capacity beyond $\bar{k}$ in the second stage, then the incumbent incurs a unit cost of c per each unit of output exceeding $\bar{k}$. Figure 8.5 illustrates the marginal-cost function facing the incumbent in the second stage of the game.

Intuitively speaking, we can say that any amount produced above the firm's capacity will require special inputs that are costly to the firm

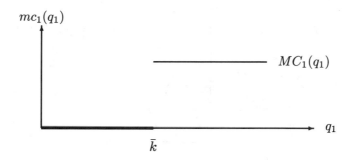

Figure 8.5: Capacity accumulation and marginal cost

when purchased at the last minute. Finally, to make our argument even stronger, we assume that capacity accumulation in the first stage is costless to the incumbent.

The entrant is assumed to make its entry decision in the second stage of the game. More precisely, in the second stage, both firms jointly choose their output levels and play a Cournot game (see section 6.1). We assume that firm 2 does not have any capacity and thus bears a unit cost of c, which is the same unit cost of the incumbent for producing beyond its capacity. If firm 2 chooses $q_2 = 0$, we say that entry does not occur. The game is illustrated in Figure 8.6.

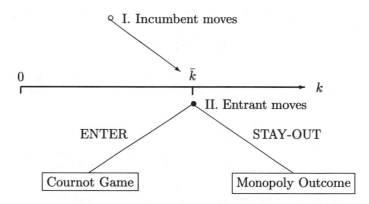

Figure 8.6: Relaxing the Bain-Sylos postulate

We now turn to the second stage after firm 1 has chosen its irrevocable capacity level given by $\bar{k}$. Figure 8.7 illustrates Cournot output best-response functions for three given choices of $\bar{k}$ by firm 1 in the first stage. The best-response functions drawn in Figure 8.7 are derived in the same way as that under the conventional Cournot market structure,

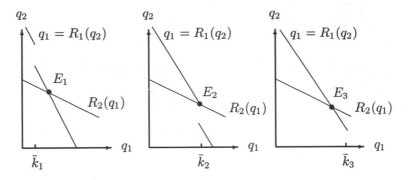

Figure 8.7: Best-response functions with fixed capacity: *Left:* low capacity; *Middle:* medium capacity; *Right:* High capacity

(see section 6.1, in particular Figure 6.1 on page 100). The only difference between the present case and the conventional Cournot case is that the incumbent's best-response function is discontinuous at an output level $q_1 = \bar{k}$, reflecting a jump in the unit cost associated with a production level beyond the firm's planned capacity.

Figure 8.7 has three drawings associated with having the incumbent investing in low, medium, and high capacity in the first period, thereby determining three Cournot equilibria denoted by E_1, E_2, and E_3, respectively. The most important observation coming from Figure 8.7 is that the equilibrium marked by E_2 is identical to the equilibrium marked by E_3, despite the fact that E_3 is associated with a higher capacity level invested in by firm 1 in the first stage. This proves our main proposition.

Proposition 8.7 *The incumbent cannot deter entry by investing in a large capacity. More generally, investing in excess capacity cannot serve as a tool for deterring entry.*

More interestingly, in our example the first-period cost of capital (capacity) is zero. Despite that cost, firm 1 cannot benefit by investing in $\bar{k}_3$ units of capital since after entry occurs, the incumbent's best response is to produce $q_1 = \bar{k}_2 < \bar{k}_3$. That is, the entrant can calculate that in the subgame of the second period, in a Cournot equilibrium, firm 1 will limit its production for the same reason that any firm limits its production under a Cournot market structure (preventing a price fall) and will therefore enter.

The main message conveyed by Proposition 8.7 is that investing in excess capital cannot provide the incumbent with a credible threat by which convince the potential entrant that entry is unprofitable. Thus, the Bain-Sylos postulate imposes an unrealistic belief on the potential entrant, namely, the belief that the incumbent will utilize all its capacity after entry occurs, despite the fact that this action does not maximize the incumbent's profit.

8.4.3 Investment in capital replacement

So far we have assumed that investment in capacity is sufficient to produce output for the desired period of production. However, plants and equipment are of finite duration. If investment in capital deters entry, then entry is unavoidable if capital depreciates and the incumbent does not invest in capital replacement. In what follows we construct a discrete-time version of the analysis found in Eaton and Lipsey 1980, and investigate how the threat of entry affects the frequency of capital investment by an incumbent firm in the presence of depreciating capital.

Consider an industry with two firms, firm 1 (incumbent) and firm 2 (potential entrant). Each firm can produce only if it has capital. The profit of each firm is as follows. If only firm 1 has capital in a certain period, then firm 1 earns a monopoly profit, given by H, in this particular period. If both firms have capital in a certain period, then each earns a duopoly profit, given by L, in this period.

Suppose that in each period t, $t = 0, 1, 2, \ldots$, each firm can invest $\$F$ in capital with finite duration, and that during the time period(s) of this capital, the firm can produce any amount of a homogeneous product. We denote the action taken by firm i in period t by a_t^i where $a_t^i \in \{INV, NI\}$ (Invest or Not Invest). Figure 8.8 illustrates the time path and the timing of actions taken by the two firms.

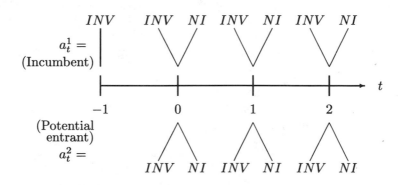

Figure 8.8: Capital replacement and entry deterrence

In Figure 8.8, firm 1 (the incumbent) is assumed to invest in capital in period $t = -1$, and then the game starts at $t = 0$, where both firms can invest in capital in any period $t = 0, 1, 2, 3 \ldots$. We make the following assumption on the parameters of the model:

ASSUMPTION 8.1

1. *Capital lasts for exactly two periods only. At the end of the second period the capital completely disintegrates, cannot be resold, and has a scrap value of zero.*

2. *The duopoly profit is insufficient to sustain two firms in the industry, whereas the monopoly profit level is sufficiently high relative to the capital investment cost. Formally, $2L < F < H$.*

Assumption 8.1 implies that if firm 1 invests in capital in period t, then using this capital the firm can produce in periods t and $t + 1$ where the capital completely disintegrates at the end of the second period after production is undertaken.

The game proceeds as follows: In period 0, if firm 2 (potential entrant) invests in capital, then each firm earns L in period 0. If firm 2 does not enter (does not invest in capital), then firm 1 earns H in period 0.

Let $0 < \rho < 1$ denote the discount parameter, and assume that each firm maximizes the sum of its discounted profit given by

$$ \Pi^i \equiv \sum_{t=0}^{\infty} \rho^t \left[R_t^i - C_t^i \right], $$

where $R_t^i = H$ if only firm i has capital in period t, and $R_t^i = L$ if both firms have capital in period t; and $C_t^i = F$ if firm i invests in capital in period t, and $C_t^i = 0$ if no investment is undertaken by firm i in period t.

Our purpose is to demonstrate the following:

Proposition 8.8 *Under Assumption 8.1:*

1. *If firm 2 is not allowed to enter, then firm 1 invests in capital in odd periods only. That is,*

$$ a_t^1 = \begin{cases} INV & for\ t = 1, 3, 5, \ldots \\ NI & for\ t = 0, 2, 4, 6 \ldots . \end{cases} $$

2. *If firm 2 is allowed to enter, and if the time discount parameter is sufficiently small and satisfies*

$$ \frac{F}{H} < \rho < \sqrt{\frac{F - L}{H - L}}, \tag{8.21} $$

then the following strategies constitute a subgame perfect equilib-
rium (Definition 2.10) for this game:

$$a_t^i = \begin{cases} INV & \text{if } a_{t-1}^j = NI \\ NI & \text{otherwise} \end{cases} \quad i, j = 1, 2, \ i \neq j, \ t = 0, 1, 2 \dots.$$

(8.22)

Hence, in this equilibrium entry is deterred by having firm 1 (in-
cumbent) investing in each period.

Proof. We look at equilibrium strategies where firm 1 invests in every t
and firm 2 does not invest.

First, observe that since firm 1 invests at t and still has capacity
at $t+1$, if firm 2 deviates and invests at t, it will earn $L - F$ at t, $L - F$
at $t + 1$, and $H - F$ in each period thereafter. Firm 2 will not deviate,
i.e., will not invest at t, if

$$\Pi^2 = (1 + \rho)(L - F) + \rho^2 \frac{H - F}{1 - \rho} < 0, \quad \text{or } \rho^2 < \frac{F - L}{H - L}.$$

Secondly, if firm 1 deviates, i.e., ceases investing at $t - 1$, then it has
no capacity at t and firm 2 will earn $H - F$ at t. Hence, firm 2 will
enter.

Thirdly, if firm 1 stops investing at $t - 1$, it will earn a profit of H
in period $t - 1$ and zero thereafter. Thus, in order for having firm 1
engaging in continuous investment, it must be that

$$H < \frac{H - F}{1 - \rho}, \quad \text{or } \rho > \frac{F}{H}.$$

Therefore, the strategies specified in (8.22) constitute a Nash equilibrium
when condition (8.21) holds. ∎

Proposition 8.8 conveys the very idea that in order to deter entry
the incumbent must carry out a costly activity, which is investing in
extra capital (capital that is not needed for production purposes). This
idea was suggested earlier by Schelling (1960), where he argued that in
games involving such conflicts, a threat that is costly to carry out can
be made credible by entering into an advanced commitment. That is,
we showed that despite the fact that capital lasts for two periods, an
incumbent monopoly must invest in each period in order to make entry
unprofitable for potential entrants. If the incumbent neglects to invest in
even one period, the entrant can credibly cause the exit of the incumbent
by investing in capital. Thus, the fact that capital lasts for more than
one period makes investing in capital a credible entry-deterring strategy
because it ensures the existence of a firm in a subsequent period.

8.4.4   Judo economics

So far, our discussion of entry deterrence has focused mainly on the incumbent firms. In this subsection, we analyze the strategic options available to the potential entrant prior to the time of entry into the industry. In particular, we analyze the entrant's choice of capacity when facing a large dominant incumbent firm that has the option to expand capacity and deter entry. We show that the potential entrant may profit by adopting a strategy of *judo economics* (Gelman and Salop 1983), which refers to having the entrant invest in only limited capacity—which would restrict the entrant's scale of entry and therefore its market share. We show that when the potential entrant limits its capacity sufficiently, it is the incumbent's best interest to accommodate entry rather than to fight it.

Consider a two-stage game in which in the first stage a potentially entering firm chooses: (a) whether to enter, (b) its capacity (maximum output) level, denoted by k and, (c) its price, denoted by p^e. In the second stage, the incumbent firm chooses its price, denoted by p^I. We assume that the incumbent firm is large in the sense that it has an unlimited capacity. Assume that production is costless and that the firms produce a homogeneous product for a single market with a demand curve given by $p = 100 - Q$. Also, assume that all consumers prefer the less expensive brand; however, consumers prefer the incumbent's brand at equal prices. Formally, let q^I denote the quantity demanded from the incumbent firm and q^e denote the quantity demanded from the entrant (if entering). Then, for a given sufficiently low capacity invested by the entrant, k, the demand facing each firm is given by

$$q^I = \begin{cases} 100 - p^I & \text{if } p^I \leq p^e \\ 100 - k - p^I & \text{if } p^I > p^e \end{cases} \quad \text{and} \quad q^e = \begin{cases} k & \text{if } p^e < p^I \\ 0 & \text{if } p^e \geq p^I. \end{cases}$$
$$(8.23)$$

That is, after the entrant sets p^e, the incumbent can always undercut the entrant by setting $p^I = p^e$. However, if the incumbent sets a price slightly above the entrant's price, the entrant gets to sell the first k units and then the incumbent faces the residual demand given by $q^I = 100 - k - p^I$.

Suppose now that in the first stage the entrant enters and sets a capacity k and a price p^e. Then, in the second stage, the incumbent can deter entry by setting $p^I = p^e$ or accommodate entry by setting $p^I > p^e$. If entry is deterred, then the incumbent's profit is given by $\pi_D^I = p^e(100 - p^e)$. In contrast, if the incumbent accommodates entry, then the incumbent's profit is $\pi_A^I = p^I(100 - k - p^I)$. Thus, under entry accommodation, the incumbent chooses $p^I > p^e$ to

$$\max_{p^I > p^e} \pi^I = p^I(100 - k - p^I),$$

yielding a first-order condition given by $0 = 100 - k - 2p^I$. Therefore, $p_A^I = (100 - k)/2$, hence $q_A^I = (100 - k)/2$ and $\pi_A^I = (100 - k)^2/4$. Comparing the incumbent's entry-deterring profit level to its profit under entry accommodation yields that

$$\pi_A^I \geq \pi_D^I \quad \text{and} \quad \frac{(100 - k)^2}{4} \geq p^e(100 - p^e). \qquad (8.24)$$

Under entry accommodation, the entrant earns $\pi^e = p^e k > 0$.

We now turn to the first stage, where the entrant sets its capacity level and its price. Figure 8.9, derived from (8.24), illustrates the range of k and p^e that would induce the incumbent to accommodate entry.

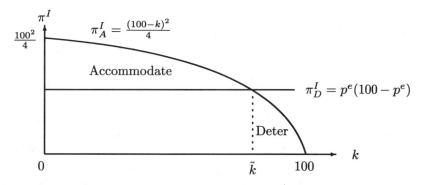

Figure 8.9: Judo economics: How an entrant secures entry accommodation

Figure 8.9 demonstrates that for a sufficiently low p^e, there always exists k small enough to induce the incumbent to accommodate entry according to the condition given in (8.24). More precisely, when the entrant reduces the price p^e, the horizontal line converges to the horizontal axis thereby increasing the area in which the incumbent accommodates the entry. Thus,

Proposition 8.9 *There exist a sufficiently limited capacity level k and a price p^e set by the entrant that ensure that the incumbent will find it profitable to accommodate the entry.*

The intuition behind this result is as follows. When the incumbent accommodates the entrant it does not match the entrant's price, but rather maintains an "umbrella" under which the entrant can prosper as long as it remains satisfied with its modest market share. In this case, the incumbent can maintain a higher price than the entrant and still sell since the entrant has a limited capacity that leaves a sufficiently profitable market share to the incumbent. Thus, when the entrant sets a sufficiently low capacity and price, entry deterrence (setting p^I to a very low level) yields a lower profit than entry accommodation to the incumbent firm.

The model presented in this subsection applies only to those situations in which the entrant can make credible capacity-limitation commitments. Such credibility can be enhanced by the use of contracts. For example, entry accommodation is sometimes observed in the airline industry, where large, established airline firms accommodate small carriers on some routes after observing that the entrant purchased a limited number of airport gates, a limited aircraft fleet, and low-capacity aircraft. Of course, as happens from time to time, some of these small entrants grow to become major carriers.

8.4.5 Credible spatial preemption

Our entry-deterrence analysis has concentrated so far on entry in a single market for a homogeneous product. In reality, firms produce differentiated, substitutable brands, so entry is likely to cause a head-to-head competition only on a subset of the incumbent's already produced brands. For example, in the airline industry where a monopoly airline is threatened by entry, it is likely to occur on a subset of the routes operated by the incumbent airline. The question raised in Judd 1985 is how would the incumbent firm react to partial entry, when entry into one market would affect the demand in a market for a substitute good, hence the incumbent's profit from the substitute good?

We demonstrate this entry problem by considering a monopoly firm (firm 1) which owns two restaurants, one Chinese (denoted by C) and one Japanese (denoted by J). Suppose that there are two consumers in town who are slightly differentiated with respect to the utility the receive from Chinese and Japanese food. More precisely, the utility of the consumer who is oriented toward Chinese food (U^C) and the utility of the consumer who is oriented toward Japanese food (U^J) are given by

$$U^C \equiv \begin{cases} \beta - p^C & \text{if eats Chinese food} \\ \beta - \lambda - p^J & \text{if eats Japanese food} \end{cases} \qquad (8.25)$$

$$U^J \equiv \begin{cases} \beta - \lambda - p^C & \text{if eats Chinese food} \\ \beta - p^J & \text{if eats Japanese food} \end{cases}$$

where β reflects the satisfaction from eating, and $\lambda > 0$ denotes the slight disutility a consumer has from buying his less preferred food. We assume that $\lambda < \beta < 2\lambda$, and normalize the restaurants' costs of operation to zero.

Suppose first that both restaurants are owned by a single firm (firm 1). Then, (8.25) implies that the monopoly owner would charge prices $p^C = p^J = \beta$ in each restaurant, and the monopoly's total profit would be $\pi_1 = 2\beta$.

Entry into the market for Chinese food

Suppose that a new restaurant (firm 2) with a different owner opens a new Chinese restaurant that serves food identical to the already existing Chinese restaurant owned by the monopoly. Assuming price competition, we see the price of Chinese food drop to zero (the assumed unit-production cost). Thus, $p_1^C = p_2^C = 0$. How would entry into the Chinese food market affect the price of a Japanese dinner? Well, clearly if the monopoly does reduce its price of a Chinese dinner to zero, all consumers including the one oriented toward Japanese food would purchase only Chinese food. Therefore, the maximum price the monopoly could charge for a Japanese dinner would be $p^J = \lambda$. Clearly, for this price the consumer oriented toward Japanese food would purchase Japanese since

$$U^J(J) = \beta - p^J = \beta - \lambda \geq \beta - \lambda - p^C = U^J(C).$$

That is, at $p^J = \lambda$ the Japanese-food-oriented consumer is indifferent to whether he or she buys Japanese (gaining a utility of $U^J(J)$) or Chinese (gaining $U^J(C)$). In this case the profit earned by the monopoly after the entry into the Chinese-food market occurs is $\pi_1 = \lambda$.

Incumbent withdraws from the Chinese restaurant

Now suppose that firm 1 (the initial monopoly on oriental food) shuts down its Chinese restaurant and keeps only the Japanese restaurant. In this event, after entry occurs, there are two restaurants, one serving Chinese food and the other serving Japanese food. Thus, the market structure is now a duopoly with firms selling differentiated products.

Lemma 8.1 *The unique duopoly price game between the Chinese and the Japanese restaurants results in the consumer oriented toward Japanese food buying from the Japanese restaurant, the consumer oriented toward Chinese food buying from the Chinese restaurant, and equilibrium prices given by* $p_1^J = p_2^C = \beta$.

Proof. We have to show that no restaurant can increase its profit by undercutting the price of the competing restaurant. If the Japanese restaurant would like to attract the consumer oriented toward Chinese food it has to set $p^J = p^C - \lambda = \beta - \lambda$. In this case, $\pi_2 = 2(\beta - \lambda)$. However, when it does not undercut, $\pi_2 = \beta > 2(\beta - \lambda)$ since we assumed that $\beta < 2\lambda$. A similar argument reveals why the Chinese restaurant would not undercut the Japanese restaurant.   ∎

We can now state our major proposition.

Proposition 8.10 *When faced with entry into the Chinese restaurant's market, the incumbent monopoly firm would maximize its profit by completely withdrawing from the Chinese restaurant's market.*

Proof. The profit of the incumbent when it operates the two restaurants after the entry occurs is $\pi_1 = \lambda$. If the incumbent withdraws from the Chinese restaurant and operates only the Japanese restaurants, Lemma 8.1 implies that $\pi_1 = \beta > \lambda$.   ∎

The intuition behind Proposition 8.10 is as follows. When entry occurs in one market, the price falls to unit cost. Given the reduction in this price, consumers buying a substitute good (Japanese food) would switch to buying Chinese food. Hence, the incumbent would have to reduce the price in its other market despite the fact that no entry occurred in the other market. Consequently, the incumbent would suffer a profit reduction in both markets. To avoid the latter, the incumbent would benefit from withdrawing and letting the entrant charge a higher price in the competing market. This would enable the incumbent to maintain the monopoly price in the remaining monopolized market (Japanese food). Thus, by withdrawing from competition, the incumbent differentiates itself from the entrant, so both firms could maintain a high price.

8.4.6   Limit pricing as cost signaling

Friedman's argument concerning the irrelevance of limit pricing raises the question whether incumbent firms would ever find it useful to exercise limit pricing during the preentry period. Milgrom and Roberts (1982) came up with an argument that limit pricing (or, expanded capacity or quantity produced) can serve as a cost-signaling device to the potential entrant who may not know the cost structure of the incumbent firm. We discuss here a simplified version of their model.

Demand, firms, and timing

There are two periods denoted by $t = 1, 2$. The market demand curve in each period is given by $p = 10 - Q$, where Q is the aggregate amount sold to consumers. Firm 1 is the incumbent and has to choose an output level in period 1 denoted by q_1^1. Firm 2 does not exist in $t = 1$ and chooses whether (or not) to enter only in the second period. Thus, firm 1 earns profits in the preentry period ($t = 1$) and in $t = 2$.

What about the output levels in the second period? Following Friedman's argument, we assume the following:

ASSUMPTION 8.2 *In the second period ($t = 2$), if entry occurs, then both firms play the Cournot game. If entry does not occur at $t = 2$, firm 1 produces the monopoly output level.*

This assumption highlights Friedman's argument in the sense that the incumbent's action at $t = 1$ has no influence on the market structure at $t = 2$, and therefore, we assume the most commonly used market structure for $t = 2$, which is Cournot if entry occurs and monopoly in the case of no entry.

Cost and information

Firm 2's unit-production cost is given by $c_2 = 1$. In addition, firm 2 has to pay an entry cost of $F_2 = 9$ if it enters at $t = 2$. The cost structure of firm 2 is assumed to be common knowledge.

In contrast, the cost structure of firm 1 (the incumbent) is known only to firm 1. The potential entrant does not exactly know the cost structure of the incumbent, but it knows the *probability distribution* of cost functions. Formally, firm 2 knows that the unit cost of firm 1 satisfies:

$$c_1 = \begin{cases} 0 & \text{with probability } 0.5 \\ 4 & \text{with probability } 0.5. \end{cases} \quad (8.26)$$

That is, firm 2 bases its decisions on the assumption that with 50% probability the incumbent is a low-cost firm ($c_1 = 0$), and with a 50% probability the incumbent is a high-cost firm ($c_1 = 4$).

Profits

The incumbent collects profits in periods 1 and 2 and maximizes the sum of the two periods' profits. The entrant collects profit only in the second period. In section 6.1, you have learned how to calculate the Cournot profit levels, so we avoid performing these simple calculations. These profit calculations are summarized in Table 8.2.

The two-period game

In the preentry era (period 1) firm 1 chooses its output level q_1^1. Thus, the profit of firm 1 in $t = 1$ is $\pi_1(c_1, q_1^1) = (10 - q_1^1)q_1^1 - c_1 q_1^1$.

In period 2, firm 2 observes q_1^1 and decides whether or not to enter. Its decision is based on the value of q_1^1 and on the estimated cost structure of firm 1, given in (8.26). Figure 8.10 illustrates this game.

Incumbent's cost:	Firm 2 (potential entrant)			
	ENTER		DO NOT ENTER	
Low $(c_1 = 0)$	$\pi_1^c(0) = 13$	$\pi_2^c(0) = -1.9$	$\pi_1^m(0) = 25$	$\pi_2 = 0$
High$(c_1 = 4)$	$\pi_1^c(4) = 1$	$\pi_2^c(4) = 7$	$\pi_1^m(4) = 9$	$\pi_2 = 0$

Table 8.2: Profit levels for $t = 2$ (depending on the entry decision of firm 2). *Note:* All profits are functions of the cost of firm 1 (c_1); π_1^m is the monopoly profit of firm 1; π_i^c is the Cournot profit of firm i, $i = 1, 2$.

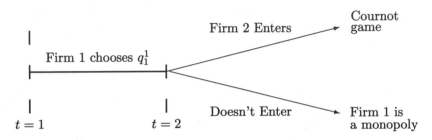

Figure 8.10: Two-period, signaling, entry-deterrence game

Solving the game assuming a high-cost incumbent

Without any further knowledge and assuming that firm 2 maximizes expected profit, we learn from (8.26) and Table 8.2 that upon entry firm 2's expected profit is

$$E\pi_2^c = \frac{1}{2}\pi_2^c(0) + \frac{1}{2}\pi_2^c(4) = \frac{1}{2}(-1.9) + \frac{1}{2}7 > 0,$$

hence, with no additional knowledge, firm 2 would enter. But why shouldn't the incumbent always state that it is a low-cost firm (rather than a high-cost firm)? Well, the incumbent can state whatever it wants, but firm 2 has no reason to believe the incumbent's statements.

Hence, given that entry occurs and the firms play Cournot in $t = 2$, the best firm 1 could do is to maximize the first-period profit by playing the monopoly's output in $t = 1$. That is, to set

$$q_1^1(4) = 5 \text{ and therefore earn } \pi_1(4) = \pi_1^m(4) + \pi_1^c(4) = 9 + 1 = 10.$$
$$(8.27)$$

Thus, if the incumbent is a high-cost firm, it would not attempt to limit its price and entry will occur.

Solving the game assuming a low-cost incumbent

Suppose that the incumbent (firm 1) is a low-cost firm ($c_1 = 0$). Then, if firm 2 were to know that firm 1 is a low-cost one, Table 8.2 shows that it would not enter since entry yields $\pi_2^c(0) < 0$. But since firm 2 does not know for sure that firm 1 is a low-cost one, the incumbent has the incentive to reveal it to firm 2. The purpose of this model is to demonstrate how limit pricing (or excess production) can serve as a means by which firm 1 can signal to firm 2 that it is a low-cost firm, thereby convincing firm 2 that entry is not profitable.

Proposition 8.11 *A low-cost incumbent would produce* $q_1^1 = 5.83$, *and entry will not occur in* $t = 2$.

Sketch of Proof. In order for the incumbent to convince firm 2 that it is indeed a low-cost firm, it has to do something "heroic." More precisely, in order to convince the potential entrant beyond all doubts that firm 1 is a low-cost one, it has to do something that a high-cost incumbent would never do—namely, it has to produce a first-period output level that is not profitable for a high-cost incumbent!

Now, a high-cost incumbent would not produce $q_1^1 = 5.83$ since

$$9.99 = (10-5.83) \times 5.83 - 4 \times 5.83 + \pi_1^m(4) < \pi_1^m(4) + \pi_1^c(4) = 9+1 = 10. \tag{8.28}$$

That is, a high-cost incumbent is better off playing a monopoly in the first period and facing entry in the second period than playing $q_1^1 = 5.83$ in the first period and facing no entry in $t = 2$.

Finally, although we showed that $q_1^1 = 5.83$ indeed transmits the signal that the incumbent is a low-cost firm, why is $q_1^1 = 5.83$ the incumbent's profit-maximizing output level, given that the monopoly's output level is much lower, $q_1^m(0) = 5$. Clearly, the incumbent won't produce more than 5.83 since the profit is reduced (gets higher above the monopoly output level). Also (8.28) shows that any output level lower than 5.83 would induce entry, and given that entry occurs, the incumbent is best off playing monopoly in $t = 1$. Hence, we have to show that deterring entry by producing $q_1^1 = 5.83$ yields a higher profit than accommodating entry and producing the monopoly output level $q_1^1 = 5$ in $t = 1$. That is,

$$\pi_1(0)|_{q_1^1=5} = 25+13 = 38 < 49.31 = (10-5.83) \times 5.83+25 = \pi_1(0)|_{q_1^1=5.83},$$

hence, a low-cost incumbent will not allow entry and will not produce $q_1^1 < 5.83$. ∎

8.4.7   Other entry-deterrence methods

The literature on entry deterrence explores various entry-deterring actions taken by incumbent firms (see survey articles by Neven [1989] and Wilson [1992]). One possible action referred to as *raising a rival's cost* is analyzed by Salop and Scheffman (1983). They suggest that incumbent firms may possess a variety of methods for raising the cost of entering firms. For example, one way of doing that is for the incumbent firm to sign high wage contracts, thereby raising the industry's labor cost. Another, is for the incumbent to lobby for higher tax rates. As noted earlier, potential entrants may be immune from these entry-deterring strategies since they may not be subjected to binding (wage and other cost) contracts. Note that in order for these actions to constitute entry-deterring methods, one needs to show that the these methods do not result in having the incumbent going bankrupt.

Another possible action analyzed in Aghion and Bolton 1987 suggests that incumbent firms rush to sign contracts with buyers in order to preempt entry. Gallini (1984) suggests that an incumbent can minimize its loss to firms producing potentially more advanced brands by simply licensing their own older technologies to potential entrants. The idea is that without licensing, potential entrants would develop superior technologies that would wipe out producers of older technologies. Finally, Spiegel (1993) demonstrates that incumbent firms can deter entry by subcontracting with other incumbent firms producing competing brands. Intuitively, if those firms have different cost structure, horizontal subcontracting reduces average costs of the incumbent firms, thereby reducing the likelihood that entry will occur.

Another way in which entry can be deterred is for the incumbent to deny access to a new technology by acquiring a patent right for its technology (see Gilbert and Newbery 1982). Finally, Scherer (1979) and Schmalensee (1978) analyze the FTC complaint that the four major cereal producers managed to deter entry by *proliferating* product varieties, thereby leaving insufficient room for the entry of new brands. Their result stems from the assumption of that the incumbent's decision to produce a brand is irreversible; however, subsection 8.4.5 demonstrates that incumbents may be better off to withdraw from the production of some brands in the presence of entry rather than fighting it.

8.5   Contestable Markets

Baumol, Panzar, and Willig (1982) proposed a market structure that describes the behavior of incumbent firms constantly faced by threats of entry. The main assumption underlying this market structure is that entry does not require any sunk cost. Note that with the absence of sunk cost incumbent firms are subject to a hit-and-run entry, meaning that potential entrants can costlessly enter and exit the industry without having to wait until they generate a sufficient amount of revenue to recover the sunk cost of entry. Therefore, if incumbent firms do not have any cost advantage over potential entrants, a contestable market equilibrium will result in having an incumbent firm making only normal (zero) profit.

Assume that in a homogeneous product industry there is one incumbent firm facing entry by potential competitors. Let all firms have identical and increasing returns-to-scale technologies summarized by the cost function $TC(q_i) = F + cq_i$, and assume that the inverse aggregate demand facing the industry is given by $p = a - Q^d$.

DEFINITION 8.1

1. An **industry configuration** is the incumbent's pair (p^I, q^I) of price charged and quantity produced.

2. An industry configuration is said to be **feasible** if

    (a) At the incumbent's price p^I, the quantity demanded equals the incumbent's quantity supplied. That is, if $p^I = a - q^I$.

    (b) The incumbent makes a nonnegative profit. That is, $p^I q^I \geq F + cq^I$.

3. An industry configuration is said to be **sustainable** if no potential entrant can make a profit by undercutting the incumbent's price. That is, there does not exist a price p^e satisfying $p^e \leq p^I$ and a corresponding entrant's output level q^e satisfying $q^e \leq a - p^e$, such that $p^e q^e > F + cq^e$.

4. A feasible industry configuration is said to be a **contestable-markets equilibrium** if it is sustainable.

Thus, an industry configuration is sustainable if no other firm could make a strictly positive profit by setting a lower or equal price while producing no more than the quantity demanded by the consumers.

A contestable-market equilibrium is illustrated in Figure 8.11, where the price p^I and quantity produced q^I satisfy the consumers' aggregate demand curve and, in addition, lie on the incumbent's average total-cost function thereby ensuring that the incumbent does not incur a loss. Hence, this configuration is feasible.

Now, given that all firms share the same cost structure, it is clear that under the industry configuration illustrated in Figure 8.11 no other

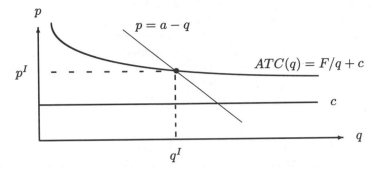

Figure 8.11: Contestable-markets equilibrium

firm could lower the price and make a strictly positive profit. Hence, this configuration is sustainable.

It should be noted that the contestable market structure can be used to describe an industry comprised of multiproduct firms, that is, firms producing a variety of different products (see Baumol, Panzar, and Willig 1982). Indeed, the advantage of using the contestable-markets market structure is that it can be applied to more realistic industries where firms produce more than one product, especially since all other market structures are defined for single-product firms that are rarely observed.

The contestable-market equilibrium defined in Definition 8.1 relies on the assumption that firms do not incur any sunk cost upon entry, and therefore can costlessly enter and exit the industry. This assumption is problematic since it is hard to imagine an industry where firms do not have to sink any irrevocable investment prior to entry. That is, firms generally conduct a market survey, place advertisements, and pay fees prior to entry, and these costs are definitely sunk and cannot be recovered. Moreover, Stiglitz (1987) pointed out the significance of this assumption by showing that if entrants face even tiny sunk costs prior to entry, then the only subgame perfect equilibrium is an incumbent charging a monopoly price and making a monopoly profit. In other words, although the contestable-market equilibrium yields a result that the incumbent makes zero profit, Proposition 8.5 showed that introducing even tiny sunk cost would imply that in a subgame perfect equilibrium of an entry-deterrence game, the incumbent makes pure monopoly profit. Therefore, the sensitivity of the market outcome to the existence of even small sunk cost is highly problematic because these two models have contradictory policy recommendations. On the one hand, contestable-market equilibrium implies that no intervention is needed by the antitrust authorities since even a single firm would charge the socially efficient price. On the other hand, the introduction of even a small sunk costs turns our model into a sustained monopoly, one which the antitrust authority would like to challenge. Finally, Schwartz (1986) has shown that, despite the assumed easy exit of potential entrants, hit and run entry is unprofitable if incumbent's price responses are sufficiently rapid.

8.6 Appendix: Merger and Antitrust Law

Section 7 of the Clayton Act (1914) states that

> No person engaged in commerce or in any activity affecting commerce shall acquire, directly or indirectly, the whole or any part of the stock or other share capital...shall acquire the whole or any part of the assets of another person engaged also in commerce or in any activity affecting commerce where in any line of commerce in any section of the country, the effect of such acquisition may be substantially to lessen competition, or to tend to create a monopoly.

Section 7 of the Clayton Act (amended in 1950) was needed because Sections 1 and 2 of the Sherman Act (1890) were not sufficient to halt mergers that would increase concentration and would reduce competition. Of course a question remains about why an increase in concentration would reduce competition and raise prices. This idea is built on two premises: First, that collusion or tacit coordination is less likely to succeed in less concentrated markets, where price cuts are less likely to be noticed by rival firms; and second, that antitrust should be viewed as consumer protection and that consumers tend to lose when faced by monopoly sellers. The discussion in this section is divided into two parts. We first discuss the procedure by which the FTC (Federal Trade Commission) and the DOJ (Department of Justice) can intervene in order to challenge a merger. Then, we proceed to the details, that the two agencies use to measure the effect of a merger. The interested reader is referred to Asch 1983; Fisher 1987; Gellhorn 1986; Salop 1987; and White 1987 for further reading and more references.

8.6.1 Challenging a merger

The monitoring of merger activities is in the hands of the FTC and the DOJ. The FTC issues guidelines to the DOJ recommending what types of mergers should be challenged. It is important to note that these guidelines do not constitute a law, but rather recommendations to the DOJ for starting to take actions against undesired mergers. In practice, firms with assets or sales in excess of $100 million must report acquisitions of assets valued in excess of $15 million. A merger does not take place until the FTC or the DOJ determines the competition effects of such an acquisition. With this procedure, very few cases are brought to courts since in most cases the FTC evaluation is sufficient for providing the signals to the acquiring firm about whether it should proceed with the acquisition or call it off.

8.6.2   Merger guidelines

The purpose of horizontal merger guidelines is to describe the analytical process that the agencies will employ to decide whether to challenge a merger; the guidelines are issued by the FTC and are suggestive rather than definitive. Salop (1987) summarizes five criteria that characterize those used by the FTC and the DOJ for evaluating a proposed merger: (1) the scope of the market upon which the merger may have anticompetitive effects; (2) the effect on concentration; (3) the ease of entry into the market; (4) other factors related to the ease of collusion in the market; and (5) efficiency gains (such as cost reduction) associated with the merger.

In 1982, the Reagan administration came up with new merger guidelines (released in 1984 and modified in 1992). The scope of the relevant market was defined in price terms. That is, the relevant antitrust market is defined as a set of products and a geographical area where firms could profitably raise prices by at least 5% above the premerger price for at least one year. These guidelines suggest that a merger should not be challenged if the postmerger Herfindahl-Hirshman concentration index I_{HH}, defined by (8.2), satisfies

1. $I_{HH} < 1000$;

2. $1000 < I_{HH} < 1800$, and $\Delta I_{HH} < 100$;

3. $I_{HH} > 1800$, and $\Delta I_{HH} < 50$.

Thus, a merger is more likely to be challenged when it results in a higher concentration ratio and when it results in a more significant change in concentration. More precisely, at low postmerger concentration levels, a merger resulting in a change in the I_{HH} of a less than 100 would not be challenged. However, at a high postmerger I_{HH}, a merger leading to a change of less than 100 but greater than 50 is likely to be challenged.

In the above, ΔI_{HH} measures the difference in the I_{HH} measure before and after the proposed merger. For example, if firm 1, maintaining a market share s_1, and firm 2, maintaining a market share of s_2, merge, then the market share of the newly merged firm is expected to be $s_1 + s_2$. In this case,

$$\Delta I_{HH} = (s_1 + s_2)^2 - [(s_1)^2 + (s_2)^2] = 2s_1 s_2.$$

The higher the concentration is, the more likely merger is to be challenged even if the merger causes only a small increase in the degree of concentration.

Several authors, for example Farrell and Shapiro (1990) and those found in their references, have criticized the use of the I_{HH} as a reliable measure of a merger-induced change in concentration because it assumes that the merged firms maintain the exact sum of the market shares the merged firms had prior to the merger. However, it is likely that the sum of the market shares of the merged firm would fall after the merger in the case where entry barriers do not prevail.

Finally, in 1992 the DOJ and the FTC released modified horizontal merger guidelines (see, Department of Justice and Federal Trade Commission Horizontal Merger Guidelines, April 2, 1992). The release marks the first time that the two federal agencies that share antitrust enforcement jurisdiction have issued joint guidelines. The new guidelines reflect the experience of the DOJ and the FTC in applying the 1984 merger guidelines. The 1992 guidelines modify the test for identifying the relevant market. The 1984 guidelines hypothesized a uniform price increase to identify the market. Under the 1992 guidelines the price increase is not necessarily uniform. Instead, the new guidelines assume that a hypothetical monopolist may increase prices for some localities more than for others.

Similar to the 1984 guidelines, a post merger concentration level of $I_{HH} < 1000$ classifies the market in the region as unconcentrated. A post merger concentration of $1000 \leq I_{HH} \leq 1800$ is regarded as moderately concentrated. Mergers producing $\Delta I_{HH} > 100$ raise significant competitive concerns depending on the factors set forth in Sections 2-5 of the 1992 guidelines. Post merger concentration level $I_{HH} > 1800$ is regarded as highly concentrated. Mergers yielding a change in concentration $50 < \Delta I_{HH} \leq 100$ raise significant competitive concerns depending on the factors set forth in Sections 2-5 of the 1992 guidelines. Mergers yielding $\Delta I_{HH} > 100$ are regarded as likely to create or enhance market power or facilitate its exercise. This presumption may be overcome by showing that the factors set forth in Sections 2-5 of the 1992 guidelines make it unlikely that the merger will enhance market power.

Sections 2-5 consider potential adverse competitive effects of mergers, in addition to market concentration measured by the I_{HH}. These effects include (i) the likelihood of coordination among firms; (ii) conditions revealing implicit or explicit coordination such as common price, fixed price differentials, stable market shares, or consumer or territorial restrictions; (iii) detection of conditions making punishments on deviations from collusion more effective, thereby increasing the likelihood of collusion; (iv) the likelihood that a merger between firms distinguished by differentiated products to cause a price increase for all differentiated brands; (v) ability of rival sellers to replace lost competition.

8.7   Appendix: Entry Deterrence and Antitrust Law

Single-firm conduct is covered by Section 2 of the Sherman Act (1890), under which it would be a violation of the antitrust law for an incumbent firm to engage in actions that would limit competition, as stated in Section 2 of the Sherman Act (1890):

> Every person who shall monopolize, or attempt to monopolize, or combine or conspire with any other person or persons, to monopolize any part of the trade or commerce among the several States, or with foreign nations, shall be deemed guilty of a felony.

Thus, Section 2 focuses on the unilateral conduct of a firm, whereas Section 1 focuses on the duality of actions among firms. More precisely, the essence of an offense under Section 1 is the act of joining together to conspire to limit competition, and therefore, the main concern is to find an agreement among firms. In contrast, Section 2 is concerned with the act of a monopoly that misuses its power by taking exclusionary actions.

Predatory prices are condemned, but there is little agreement on what defines predatory prices. A proof of pricing below average cost constitutes predatory pricing, and in this case the burden of proof is on the defendant to show that either the prices are not below average cost, or that the low prices are temporary, for promotional reasons only. However, prices that exceed average cost can still be considered as predatory if they are set in order to eliminate competition with other firms since any attempt to monopolize is a felony under Section 2.

Another violation of Section 2 is a *refusal to deal,* which refers to cases where a monopoly at one level of a chain of distribution refuses to deal with the next level in order to gain a monopoly position at both levels. Finally, product innovation is not considered to be a violation of Section 2 even if the introduction of the new product into the market makes it difficult for other firms to compete or even survive.

We conclude by discussing how the FTC handles anticompetitive behavior of incumbent firms. Section 5(a)(1) of the Federal Trade Commission Act (1914) states:

Unfair methods of competition in or affecting commerce, and
unfair or deceptive acts or practices in or affecting commerce,
are declared unlawful.

In earlier periods after the FTC was established, the FTC concentrated
on promoting "fair trade practices" among trade associations. Over the
years, the FTC extended its role in enforcing these laws by conduct-
ing repeated investigations for the purpose of finding violations of firms
that use a variety of anticompetitive methods, described earlier in the
chapter, in order to maintain their dominance in the market. When the
FTC suspects a violation, it opens an investigation against the suspected
firms and looks at the product's design and its distribution channels in
order to find a clue about whether these activities deter potential entrants from entering into the market. Investigations of these kinds are
generally made public and by themselves encourage more firms to enter
the market with competing brands, knowing that predatory activities
will not be sustained.

8.8   Exercises

1. The bicycle industry consists of seven firms. Firms 1, 2, 3, 4 each has
   10% market share, and firms 5, 6, 7 each has 20% market share. Using
   the concentration measures defined in Section 8.1, answer the following
   questions:

   (a) Calculate I_4 for this industry.

   (b) Calculate the I_{HH} for this industry.

   (c) Now, suppose that firms 1 and 2 merge, so that the new firm will
       have a market share of 20%.

       i. Calculate the post merger I_{HH}.

       ii. Calculate the change in the I_{HH} caused by the merger. That
           is, calculate ΔI_{HH}.

       iii. Using the merger guidelines described in subsection 8.6.2,
            evaluate the proposed merger and predict whether this merger
            will be challenged or not. Explain!

2. In an industry there are three firms producing a homogeneous product.
   Let q_i denote the output level of firm i, $i = 1, 2, 3$, and let Q denote the
   aggregate industry-production level. That is, $Q = q_1 + q_2 + q_3$. Assume
   that the demand curve facing the industry is $p = 100 - Q$. Solve the
   following problems:

   (a) Find the Cournot equilibrium output and profit level of each firm.

   (b) Now suppose that firms 2 and 3 merge into a single firm that we
       call firm 4. Calculate the profit level of firm 4 under a Cournot
       market structure.

(c) Do firms 2 and 3 benefit from this merger?

(d) Now suppose that firm 1 merges with firm 4. Does firm 4 benefit from the merger with firm 1?

(e) Explain why the first and the second mergers yield different results regarding the profitability of mergers.

3. Consider the merger among firms producing complementary components studied in subsection 8.2.3. Suppose that consumers desire computer systems composed of one computer (denoted as product X), and two diskettes (denoted as product Y). Thus, our consumers treat computers and diskettes as perfect complements where, for each computer, the consumers need two diskettes. Let p_X denote the price of a computer, and p_Y denote the price of a single diskette. Thus, the price of a computer system is $p_S = p_X + 2p_Y$. Formally, let the demand function for computer systems be given by

$$Q = \alpha - p_S = \alpha - (p_X + 2p_Y), \quad \text{where } Q = x = y/2, \ \alpha > 0.$$

Answer the following questions assuming that production is costless.

(a) Suppose that the X producer and the Y producer are independent. Solve for the Nash-Bertrand equilibrium in prices. Calculate the equilibrium prices, the quantity produced of each product, and firms' profit levels.

(b) Now suppose that firms X and Y merge under a single ownership. Calculate the monopoly equilibrium prices, the quantity produced of each product, and the monopoly's profit.

(c) Is this merger welfare-improving? Compare system prices and profits of the firms before and after the merger.

4. Consider the contestable-markets market structure defined in section 8.5. Suppose that in the industry there is one incumbent firm and several potential competitors all having identical technologies summarized by the cost function $TC(q_i) = 100 + (q_i)^2$, where q_i is the output of firm i. Solve for a contestable-markets equilibrium assuming that the (inverse) aggregate demand facing the industry is given by $p = 60 - 4Q^d$.

8.9   References

Aghion, P., and P. Bolton. 1987. "Contracts as a Barrier to Entry." *American Economic Review* 77: 388–401.

Asch, P. 1983. *Industrial Organization and Antitrust Policy*. New York: John Wiley & Sons.

Bain, J. 1956. *Barriers to New Competition*. Cambridge, Mass.: Harvard University Press.

Bain, J. 1972. *Essays on Price Theory and Industrial Organization*. Boston: Little, Brown.

Baumol, W., J. Panzar, and R. Willig. 1982. *Contestable Markets and the Theory of Industry Structure.* New York: Harcourt Brace Jovanovich.

Davidson, C., and R. Deneckere. 1984. "Horizontal Mergers and Collusive Behavior." *International Journal of Industrial Organization* 2: 117–132.

Dixit, A. 1979. "A Model of Duopoly Suggesting a Theory of Entry Barriers." *Bell Journal of Economics* 10: 20–32.

Dixit, A. 1980. "The Role of Investment in Entry-Deterrence." *Economic Journal* 90: 95–106.

Eaton, B. C., and R. Lipsey. 1980. "Exit Barriers are Entry Barriers: The Durability of Capital as a Barrier to Entry." *Bell Journal of Economics* 11: 721–729.

Economides, N., and S. Salop. 1992. "Competition and Integration Among Complements and Network Market Structure." *Journal of Industrial Economics* 40: 105–123.

Farrell, J., and C. Shapiro. 1990. "Horizontal Mergers: An Equilibrium Analysis." *American Economic Review* 80: 107–126.

Fisher, F. 1987. "Horizontal Mergers: Triage and Treatment." *Journal of Economic Perspectives* 1: 23–40.

Friedman, J. 1979. "On Entry Preventing Behavior and Limit Price Models of Entry." In *Applied Game Theory,* edited by S. Brams, A. Schotter, and G. Schwödiauer. Würzburg: Physica-Verlag.

Gallini, N. 1984. "Deterrence through Market Sharing: A Strategic Incentive for Licensing." *American Economic Review* 74: 931–941.

Gaudet, G., and S. Salant. 1992. "Mergers of Producers of Perfect Complements Competing in Price." *Economics Letters* 39: 359–364.

Gellhorn, E. 1986. *Antitrust Law and Economics.* St. Paul, Minn.: West Publishing Co.

Gelman, J., and S. Salop. 1983. "Judo Economics: Capacity Limitation and Coupon Competition." *Bell Journal of Economics* 14: 315–325.

Geroski, P., R. Gilbert, and A. Jacquemin. 1990. *Barriers to Entry and Strategic Competition.* Chur, Switzerland: Hardwood Academic Publishers.

Gilbert, R., and D. Newbery. 1982. "Pre-emptive Patenting and the Persistence of Monopoly." *American Economic Review* 72: 514–526.

Jacquemin, A. 1987. *The New Industrial Organization.* Cambridge, Mass.: MIT Press.

Judd, K. 1985. "Credible Spatial Preemption." *Rand Journal of Economics* 16: 153–166.

Milgrom, P., and J. Roberts. 1982. "Limit Pricing and Entry Under Incomplete Information: An Equilibrium Analysis." *Econometrica* 50: 443–459.

Neven, D. 1989. "Strategic Entry Deterrence: Recent Developments in the Economics of Industry." *Journal of Economic Surveys* 3: 213–233.

Ordover, J., G. Saloner, and S. Salop. 1990. "Equilibrium Vertical Foreclosure." *American Economic Review* 80: 127–141.

Perry, M. 1989. "Vertical Integration: Determinants and Effects." In *Handbook of Industrial Organization,* edited by R. Schmalensee, and R. Willing. Amsterdam: North-Holland.

Ravenscraft, D., and F. M. Scherer. 1987. *Mergers, Sell-offs, and Economic Efficiency.* Washington, D.C.: The Brookings Institution.

Salant, S., S. Switzer, and R. Reynolds. 1983. "Losses from Horizontal Merger: The Effects of an Exogenous Change in Industry Structure on Cournot-Nash Equilibrium." *Quarterly Journal of Economics* 98: 185–199.

Salinger, M. 1988. "Vertical Mergers and Market Foreclosure." *Quarterly Journal of Economics* 77: 345–356.

Salop, S. 1987. "Symposium on Mergers and Antitrust." *Journal of Economic Perspectives* 1: 3–12,

Salop, S., and D. Scheffman. 1983. "Raising Rival's Cost." *American Economic Review* 73, 267–271.

Schelling, T. 1960. *The Strategy of Conflict.* Cambridge, Mass.: Harvard University Press.

Scherer, F. M. 1979. "The Welfare Economics of Product Variety: An Application to the Ready-To-Eat Cereals Industry." *Journal of Industrial Economics,* 28: 113–133.

Schmalensee, R. 1978. "Entry Deterrence in the Ready-To-Eat Breakfast Cereal Industry." *Bell Journal of Economics* 9: 305–327.

Schwartz, M. 1986. "The Nature and Scope of Contestability Theory. *Oxford Economic Papers* 38(Suppl.): 37–57.

Sonnenschein, H. 1968. "The Dual of Duopoly in Complementary Monopoly: Or, Two of Cournot's Theories are One." *Journal Political Economy* 76: 316–318.

Spence, M. 1977. "Entry, Capacity, Investment and Oligopolistic Pricing." *Bell Journal of Economics* 8: 534–544.

Spiegel, Y. 1993. "Horizontal Subcontracting." *Rand Journal of Economics* 24: 570–590.

Stiglitz, J. 1987. "Technological Change, Sunk Costs, and Competition." *Brookings Papers on Economic Activity* 3 (Special Issue on Microeconomics: 883–937.

Tirole, J. 1988. *The Theory of Industrial Organization.* Cambridge, Mass.: MIT Press.

von Weizsäcker. 1980. "A Welfare Analysis of Barriers to Entry." *RAND Journal of Economics* 11: 399–420.

White, L. 1987. "Antitrust and Merger Policy: A Review and Critique." *Journal of Economic Perspectives* 1: 13–22.

Wilson, R. 1992. "Strategic Models of Entry Deterrence." In *Handbook of Game Theory,* edited by R. Aumann, and S. Hart. Amsterdam: North-Holland.

PART III

Technology and Market Structure

Chapter 9

Research and Development

> Innovation is an activity in which "dry holes" and "blind alleys" are the rule, not the exception.
> —Jorde and Teece, "Innovation and Cooperation: Implications for Competition and Antitrust"

Innovation is the search for, and the discovery, development, improvement, adoption, and commercialization of new processes, new products, and new organizational structures and procedures. Firms spend substantial amounts on research and development (R&D). In the developed countries, industries can be characterized according to the ratio of their R&D expenditure to output sales. Industries that exhibit high ratios include aerospace (23%), office machines and computers (18%), electronics (10%), and drugs (9%). Industries with R&D expenditure to output ratios of less than 1% include food, oil refining, printing, furniture, and textiles (OECD, 1980 data).

So far, in our analysis we have assumed that a production process or know-how can be characterized by a well-defined *production function* or by its dual the *cost function* (see section 3.1). Moreover, we have assumed that the production function is exogenous to the firms and viewed as a "black box" by the producers. In this chapter we analyze how firms can influence what is going on inside these black boxes by investing resources in innovation activities. We then analyze the methods by which society protects the right of innovators in order to enhance innovation activities in the economy.

Research and development is generally classified into two types: (a) *process innovation,* the investment in labs searching for cost-reducing technologies for producing a certain product, and (b) *product innovation,* the search for technologies for producing new products. It is often argued that from a logical point of view there is no difference between the two types of innovation since product innovation can be viewed as a cost-reducing innovation where the production cost is reduced from infinity (when the product was not available) to a finite level. However, many intuitively believe that there is a difference.

The concept of R&D is very difficult to understand and therefore to model, since the act of doing R&D means the production of knowledge or know-how (see Mokyr 1990 and Rosenberg 1994 for a historical overview of innovation, and Dosi 1988 and Freeman 1982 a survey of the literature and empirical evidence of innovation). Although we have so far always succeeded in avoiding discussion of the foundation of production functions and what know-how is, in this chapter we discuss precisely that by defining R&D as the act of creating (or changing) the production functions.

Section 9.1 (Process Innovation) classifies two types of process innovation. Section 9.2 (Innovation Race) analyzes how firms compete for discovering new technologies, and evaluates whether the equilibrium R&D level is below or above the socially optimal R&D level. Section 9.3 (Cooperation in R&D) analyzes how R&D is affected when firms coordinate their R&D efforts. Section 9.4 (Patents) analyzes how society encourages R&D by granting patent rights to innovators and suggests a method for calculating the optimal duration of patents. Section 9.5 (Licensing an Innovation) explains why firms tend to license their patented technologies to competing firms. Section 9.6 (International R&D Races) analyzes why governments subsidize R&D for exporting firms. In the appendix, section 9.7 analyzes patent law from historical and legal perspectives. Section 9.8 discusses the legal approach to cooperative R&D.

9.1   Classifications of Process Innovation

This section classifies process (cost-reducing) innovation according to the magnitude of the cost reduction generated by the R&D process. Consider an industry producing a homogeneous product, and suppose that the firms compete in prices (i.e., Bertrand competition, described in section 6.3 on page 107). Assume that initially, all firms possess identical technologies, meaning that they all produce the product with a unit production cost $c_0 > 0$. Then initially, there is a unique Bertrand equilibrium where all firms sell at unit cost $p_0 = c_0$, make zero profits, and produce a total of Q_0 units of output. This equilibrium is illustrated in Figure 9.1.

Suppose now that one and only one firm has the following R&D tech-

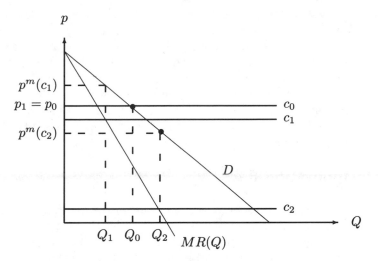

Figure 9.1: Classification of process innovation

nology: the firm can construct a research lab engaging in cost-reducing innovation that leads to a unit-cost technology of $c < c_0$. Now, recalling from chapter 5 that the pure monopoly's profit-maximizing output and price can be found by equating $MR(Q) = c$, we distinguish between a large and a small cost-reducing innovation in the following way:

DEFINITION 9.1 *Let $p^m(c)$ denote the price that would be charged by a monopoly firm whose unit production cost is given by c. Then,*

1. *Innovation is said to be* **large** *(or drastic, or major) if $p^m(c) < c_0$. That is, if innovation reduces the cost to a level where the associated pure monopoly price is lower than the unit production costs of the competing firms.*

2. *Innovation is said to be* **small** *(or nondrastic, or minor) if $p^m(c) > c_0$.*

Figure 9.1 illustrates the two types of process innovation. A cost reduction from c_0 to c_1 is what we call a small innovation. That is, the cost reduction is not large enough, implying that the innovating firm does not charge the pure monopoly price. In this case, the innovating firm will undercut all its rivals by charging a price of $p_1 = c_0 - \epsilon \approx c_0$, and will sell Q_0 units of output. In other words, a small innovation does not change the market price and the amount purchased by consumers. The only consequence of a small innovation is that the innovator sells to the entire market and makes strictly positive profit, equal to $(c_0 - c_1)Q_0$.

In contrast, a cost reduction from c_0 to c_2 in Figure 9.1 illustrates a large cost-reducing innovation, since the firm can undercut its rivals by simply charging the pure monopoly price associated with its new cost structure. That is, $p_2^m(c_2) < c_0$. Thus, a large innovation reduces the market price and increases quantity to Q_2.

Finally, note that Definition 9.1 connects the "physical" change of cost reduction with the market conditions (demand). That is, what we mean by small or large innovation depends on demand conditions and the market structure, in addition to the cost reduction itself.

9.2   Innovation Race

The timing of innovation plays a crucial role in the marketplace. There are two reasons why, in most cases, a firm that is first to discover a new technology or a new product gains an advantage over competing firms: First, the firm is eligible to obtain a patent protection that would result in earning monopoly profits for several years. Second, consumers associate the innovator with a higher-quality producer and will therefore be willing to pay a higher amount for the brand associated with the innovator.

Given the significance of becoming the first to discover, firms invest large sums in R&D, knowing that not discovering or discovering too late may result in a net loss from the innovation process. In this section we analyze the behavior of firms competing to discover a new product or a process, and we focus on the following questions: Do firms invest in R&D more or less than the socially optimal level? What is the impact of R&D competition on the expected date when the new product will be produced and marketed to consumers?

Assume that the discovery translates into a prize that can be viewed as the value of a patent associated with several years of earning monopoly profits.

Consider a two-firm industry searching for a new technology for producing a new product. The discovery of the product is uncertain. Each firm k, $k = 1, 2$, can engage itself in R&D by investing an amount of $\$I$ in a research lab. The payoff from R&D to a firm is as follows:

ASSUMPTION 9.1 *Once a firm invests $\$I$ in a lab, it has a probability α of discovering a technology that yields a profit of $\$V$ if the firm is the sole discoverer, $\$V/2$ if both firms discover, and $\$0$ if it does not discover.*

9.2.1   Equilibrium R&D in a race

We denote by $E\pi_k(n)$ the expected profit of firm k from investing in innovation when the total number of firms engaging in similar R&D is n,

$n = 1, 2$. Also, we denote by i_k ($i_k \in \{0, I\}$) the investment expenditure of firm k.

A single firm undertaking R&D

If only firm 1 invests in R&D, the firm discovers with probability α (therefore earning a profit of $V - I$) and does not discover with probability $1 - \alpha$ (earning a negative profit given by $-I$). Therefore, its expected profit is given by $E\pi_1(1) = \alpha V - I$. Hence, equating the expected profit to zero yields that the R&D investment decision of firm 1 is given by

$$i_1 = \begin{cases} I & \text{if } \alpha V \geq I \\ 0 & \text{otherwise.} \end{cases} \tag{9.1}$$

Two firms undertake R&D

The two-firm technology race highlights two important uncertainties facing firms engaging in R&D. First, there is *technological uncertainty*—whether or not the firm will discover the new product. Second, there is *market uncertainty*—whether or not the new product will be discovered by the rival firm.

When the two firms engage in R&D, the expected profit of each firm k is given by

$$E\pi_k(2) = \underbrace{\alpha(1 - \alpha)V}_{\text{only } k \text{ discovers}} + \underbrace{\alpha^2 V/2}_{\text{both discover}} - I. \tag{9.2}$$

Equating (9.2) to zero implies that the following is a sufficient condition for having both firms profitably undertaking R&D:

$$i_1 = i_2 = I, \quad \text{if} \quad \frac{\alpha(2 - \alpha)V}{2} \geq I. \tag{9.3}$$

Figure 9.2 illustrates the two conditions (9.1) and (9.3). When the combination of R&D cost and the success probability lies above the ray $E\pi_1(1) = 0$, no R&D is undertaken. That is, the combination of a low success probability or a high R&D cost yields the decision that innovation is not undertaken even under monopoly conditions.

Figure 9.2 also shows that when the R&D cost and probability combination lies between the curves $E\pi_k(2) = 0$ and $E\pi_1(1) = 0$, only one firm engages in R&D, whereas if this combination lies below $E\pi_k(2) = 0$, both firms undertake R&D.

9.2.2 Society's optimal R&D level

We now investigate what should be the number of firms that maximizes the society's welfare. In general, we should not expect that the equilib-

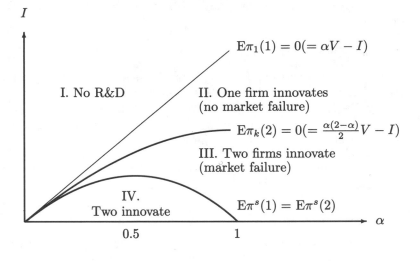

Figure 9.2: R&D race between two firms

rium number of firms calculated in the previous subsection is necessarily optimal since the action of undertaking R&D confers a negative externality on other firms engaging in the same R&D race. That is, from a social welfare point of view increasing the number of firms engaging in R&D will definitely increase the probability of discovery but will also increase the industry's aggregate R&D cost associated with R&D duplication. Therefore, without performing the actual calculation we find it hard to predict whether the equilibrium number of firms undertaking R&D is below or exceeds the optimal number.

We denote by $\mathrm{E}\pi^S(n)$ the industry's expected profit when n firms undertake R&D, and associate the industry's expected profit with the welfare of the society.

When only one firm undertakes R&D $(n = 1)$,

$$\mathrm{E}\pi^S(1) = \alpha V - I = \mathrm{E}\pi_1(1).$$

Thus, when there is only one firm, the social expected value of R&D coincides with the firm's expected profit from undertaking R&D.

When there are two firms undertaking R&D $(n = 2)$,

$$\mathrm{E}\pi^S(2) = \underbrace{2\alpha(1 - \alpha)V}_{\text{only one firm discovers}} + \underbrace{\alpha^2 V}_{\text{both discover}} - 2I.$$

Comparing $\mathrm{E}\pi^S(1)$ with $\mathrm{E}\pi^S(2)$ yields that

$$\mathrm{E}\pi^S(2) \geq \mathrm{E}\pi^S(1) \quad \text{if and only if } \alpha(1-\alpha)V \geq I.$$

Thus, in terms of Figure 9.2, any combination above the $\mathrm{E}\pi^S(1) = \mathrm{E}\pi^S(2)$ curve is associated with the situation where the socially optimal number of firms engaged in R&D is at most one.

Figure 9.2 is divided into four regions:

Region I: The combination of high innovation cost and a low probability of discovery makes it unprofitable for even a single firm to undertake innovation. It is obvious that if a single firm does not innovate, it is not beneficial for a society to engage in this R&D.

Region II: These combinations of cost and discovery probability leave room for only one firm to undertake R&D while still maintaining nonnegative expected profit. Since cost is relatively high (compared with the probability of discovery), there are no social benefits from having a second firm engaging in R&D.

Region III: A relatively low innovation cost makes it profitable for a second firm to engage in R&D. However, from the society's welfare point of view, the cost of duplicating the R&D effort ($2I$) is larger than the society's benefits from the increase in the likelihood of getting the discovery as a result of having a second firm engage in R&D. This a case of *market failure* which occurs because firms do not take into account how their R&D affect the profit of their rival firms.

Region IV: These combinations involve a low innovation cost, making it beneficial for both firms and the society to engage in the R&D race, despite the R&D cost duplication.

Proposition 9.1 *A market failure, a condition in which it is socially desirable to have at most one firm engaging in R&D but in equilibrium two firms engage in R&D, occurs only in Region III where the innovation cost, I, takes an intermediate value. Formally,*

$$\mathrm{E}\pi^S(2) < 0 \ \text{but } \mathrm{E}\pi_k(2) > 0, \quad \text{when } \alpha(1-\alpha)V < I < \frac{\alpha(2-\alpha)V}{2}.$$

In the literature, patent races are generally analyzed in continuous-time models, where the probability of discovery is a Poisson process that generates a constant probability of discovery at each point in time for a given R&D expenditure level (see Loury 1979; Lee and Wilde 1980; and Reinganum 1989 for such modeling). Fudenberg et al. (1983) analyze an industry where the probability of discovery increases with the length of time in which the R&D is conducted, and derive the conditions for having one firm preempt others from racing toward a discovery; see also Harris and Vickers 1985.

9.2.3 Expected date of discovery

Suppose that the race described in the previous subsection is repeated until one firm discovers the product. Then, what would be the expected date of discovery?

Before going to perform the calculations, we need the following lemma. The proof is given in an appendix (Section 9.9).

Lemma 9.1 *Let δ satisfy $0 < \delta < 1$. Then,*

$$\sum_{t=1}^{\infty} t\delta^{t-1} = \frac{1}{(1-\delta)^2}.$$

Let $T(n)$ denote the (uncertain) date when at least one firm discovers the product, given that n ($n \in \{1, 2\}$) firms are engaged in R&D for discovering the same product. Also, let $ET(n)$ denote the expected date at which at least one firm discovers it.

A single firm

When only one firm engages in R&D ($n = 1$), the probability that $T(1) = 1$, (discovery occurs at the first date) is α. Next, the probability that $T(1) = 2$, (discovery occurs at the second date) is $(1-\alpha)\alpha$. That is, the probability that the firm does not discover at the first date times the probability that it discovers at the second date. Next, the probability that the firm discovers at the third date is $(1-\alpha)^2\alpha$. Hence, the expected date of discovery is given by

$$
\begin{aligned}
ET(1) &= \alpha 1 + (1-\alpha)\alpha 2 + (1-\alpha)^2\alpha 3 + (1-\alpha)^3\alpha 4 + \dots \\
&= \alpha \sum_{t=1}^{\infty} t(1-\alpha)^{t-1} \stackrel{\text{Lem 9.1}}{=} \frac{\alpha}{[1-(1-\alpha)]^2} = \frac{1}{\alpha}.
\end{aligned}
\tag{9.4}
$$

Consequently, if the probability of discovery is $\alpha = 1/2$, then $ET(1) = 2$, and if $\alpha = 1/3$, then $ET(1) = 3$, and so on. Hence, as expected, an increase in the discovery probability α shortens the expected date of discovery.

Two firms

The probability that none of the firms discovers at a particular date is $(1-\alpha)^2$. Hence, the probability that at least one firm discovers at a particular date is $[1-(1-\alpha)^2]=\alpha(2-\alpha)$. Hence, $\text{prob}(T(2)=1)=\alpha(2-\alpha)$. Next, $\text{prob}(T(2)=2)=(1-\alpha)^2\alpha(2-\alpha)$ is the probability that none discovers at date 1 times the probability that at least one firm discovers at date 2. Therefore, the expected date of discovery when two firms engage in R&D is

$$
\begin{aligned}
ET(2) &= \alpha(2-\alpha)1+(1-\alpha)^2\alpha(2-\alpha)2+(1-\alpha)^4\alpha(2-\alpha)3+\ldots \\
&= \alpha(2-\alpha)\sum_{t=1}^{\infty}t(1-\alpha)^{2(t-1)}=\alpha(2-\alpha)\sum_{t=1}^{\infty}t\left[(1-\alpha)^2\right]^{t-1} \\
&= \frac{\alpha(2-\alpha)}{[1-(1-\alpha)^2]^2}=\frac{1}{\alpha(2-\alpha)},
\end{aligned} \tag{9.5}
$$

where the fourth equality sign follows from Lemma 9.1. Comparing (9.4) with (9.5) yields $ET(2)<ET(1)$, meaning that opening more independent research labs shortens the expected date of discovery.

9.3 Cooperation in R&D

The antitrust legislation prohibits firms from engaging in activities that reduce competition and increase prices. Any attempt at collusion is sufficient to provoke lawsuit against the cooperating firms. However, the antitrust legislation is less clear about how to handle cases where firms establish research joint ventures (RJV) or just decide jointly how much to invest in their (separated) labs. The legal approach to RJV is addressed in the appendix (Section 9.8).

In this section, we do not address problems such as how firms manage to implicitly or explicitly coordinate their research efforts and how the research information is shared by the participating firms (see Combs 1993 and Gandal and Scotchmer 1993). Instead, we analyze how firms determine their research efforts, taking into consideration that they compete in the final good's market after the research is completed. This problem has been the subject of many papers (see Choi 1993; d'Aspremont and Jacquemin 1988; Kamien, Muller, and Zang 1992; Katz 1986, and Katz and Ordover 1990).

In this section we analyze a two-stage game in which at $t=1$, firms determine (first noncooperatively and then cooperatively) how much to invest in cost-reducing R&D and, at $t=2$, the firms are engaged in a Cournot quantity game in a market for a homogeneous product, where the demand function is given by $p=100-Q$.

The process-innovation R&D technology

We denote by x_i the amount of R&D undertaken by firm i, $i = 1, 2$, and by $c_i(x_1, x_2)$ the unit production cost of firm i, which is assumed to be a function of the R&D investment levels of both firms. Formally, let

$$c_i(x_1, x_2) \equiv 50 - x_i - \beta x_j \ \ i \neq j, \ i = 1, 2, \ \ \beta \geq 0. \tag{9.6}$$

That is, the unit production cost of each firm declines with the R&D of both firms, where the parameter β measures the effect of firm j's R&D level on the unit production cost of firm i. Formally,

DEFINITION 9.2 *We say that R&D technologies exhibit (positive)* **spillover effects** *if $\beta > 0$.*

That is, if $\beta > 0$, the R&D of each firm reduces the unit cost of both firms. For example, spillover effects occur when some discoveries are made public during the innovation process (some secrets are not kept). Also, this positive externality can emerge from the labs investing in infrastructure or from research institutes and universities that benefit all other firms as well (see Jaffe 1986 for empirical evidence). Assuming $\beta > 0$ implies that R&D exhibits only positive spillover effects. However, note that in some cases β can be negative if the R&D of a firm also involves vandalism activities against competing firms, such as radar jamming or spreading false information and computer viruses.

Finally, to close the model we need to assume that R&D is costly to firms. Formally, denote by $TC_i(x_i)$ the cost (for firm i) of operating an R&D lab at a research level of x_i.

ASSUMPTION 9.2 (*Research labs operate under decreasing returns to scale. Formally,*

$$TC_i(x_i) = \frac{(x_i)^2}{2}.$$

Assumption 9.2 implies that the cost per unit of R&D increases with the size of the lab. That is, higher R&D levels require proportionally higher costs of lab operation. Note that this assumption heavily affects the results because if labs were to operate under increasing returns (say, by having to pay a high fixed cost for the construction of the lab), firms would always benefit from operating only a single lab (that serves both firms) when firms are allowed to cooperate in R&D.

Subsection 9.3.1 calculates the firms' profit maximizing R&D levels when firms do not cooperate. Subsection 9.3.2 calculates the R&D levels that maximizes the firms' joint profit when firms are allowed to coordinate their R&D levels while still maintaining two separate labs.

9.3.1   Noncooperative R&D

We look for a subgame perfect equilibrium (Definition 2.10) where firms choose their R&D expenditure levels in the first period and their output levels in the second periods. We find this equilibrium by first solving for the Nash equilibrium in the second period and then working backwards, we solve for the first-period R&D levels.

The second period

The second-period Cournot competition takes place after the cost reduction innovation is completed. Hence, the postinnovation c_1 and c_2 are treated as given. Thus, our Cournot analysis of section 6.1 on page 98 applies; so, if we recall (6.7), the Cournot profit levels are given by

$$\pi_i(c_1, c_2)|_{t=2} = \frac{(100 - 2c_i + c_j)^2}{9} \quad \text{for } i = 1, 2, \ i \neq j. \tag{9.7}$$

The first period

In the first period, each firm noncooperatively chooses its level of R&D given the R&D level of the rival firm. That is, we look for a Nash equilibrium (Definition 2.4 on page 18) in R&D levels. Formally, substituting (9.6) into (9.7), for a given level of x_j, firm i chooses x_i to

$$
\begin{aligned}
\max_{x_i} \pi_i &= \frac{1}{9}[100 - 2(50 - x_i - \beta x_j) + 50 - x_j - \beta x_i]^2 - \frac{(x_i)^2}{2} \\
&= \frac{1}{9}[50 + (2 - \beta)x_i + (2\beta - 1)x_j]^2 - \frac{(x_i)^2}{2}.
\end{aligned} \tag{9.8}
$$

The first-order condition yields

$$0 = \frac{\partial \pi_i}{\partial x_i} = \frac{2}{9}[50 + (2 - \beta)x_i + (2\beta - 1)x_j](2 - \beta) - x_i.$$

Given that the payoff functions are symmetric between the two firms, we look for a symmetric Nash equilibrium where $x_1 = x_2 \equiv x^{nc}$, where x^{nc} is the common noncooperative equilibrium R&D level invested by each firm when the firms do not cooperate. Thus,

$$x^{nc} = \frac{50(2 - \beta)}{4.5 - (2 - \beta)(1 + \beta)}. \tag{9.9}$$

9.3.2   Cooperative R&D

Under cooperative R&D, firms jointly choose R&D levels that will maximize their joint profits, knowing that in the second period they will compete in quantities.

The firms seek to jointly choose x_1 and x_2 to

$$\max_{x_1, x_2} (\pi_1 + \pi_2),$$

where π_i, $i = 1, 2$ are given in (9.7). The first-order conditions are given by

$$0 = \frac{\partial(\pi_1 + \pi_2)}{\partial x_i} = \frac{\partial \pi_i}{\partial x_i} + \frac{\partial \pi_j}{\partial x_i}.$$

The first term measures the marginal profitability of firm i from a small increase in its R&D (x_i), whereas the second term measures the marginal increase in firm j's profit due to the spillover effect from an increase in i's R&D effort. Hence,

$$
\begin{aligned}
0 = & \frac{2}{9}[50 + (2 - \beta)x_i + (2\beta - 1)x_j](2 - \beta) - x_i \\
+ & \frac{2}{9}[50 + (2 - \beta)x_j + (2\beta - 1)x_i](2\beta - 1).
\end{aligned}
$$

Assuming that second order conditions for a maximum are satisfied, the first order conditions yield the cooperative R&D level

$$x_1^c = x_2^c = x^c = \frac{50(\beta + 1)}{4.5 - (\beta + 1)^2}. \tag{9.10}$$

We now compare the industry's R&D and production levels under noncooperative R&D and cooperative R&D.

Proposition 9.2

1. Cooperation in R&D increases firms' profits.

2. If the R&D spillover effect is large, then the cooperative R&D levels are higher than the noncooperative R&D levels. Formally, if $\beta > \frac{1}{2}$, then $x^c > x^{nc}$. In this case, $Q^c > Q^{nc}$.

3. If the R&D spillover effect is small, then the cooperative R&D levels are lower than the noncooperative R&D levels. Formally, if $\beta < \frac{1}{2}$, then $x^c < x^{nc}$. In this case, $Q^c < Q^{nc}$.

Proof. For part 1, clearly, the firms could decide to set the R&D at the noncooperative levels. However, if they set $x^c \neq x^{nc}$, it means that their joint profit must increase. Parts 2 and 3 follow from comparing (9.9) with (9.10). The quantity comparisons follow from the simple fact that in a Cournot market structure, the aggregate quantity increases with a decline in unit production costs. ∎

The intuition behind parts 2 and 3 of Proposition 9.2 is as follows. First note that under noncooperation each firm sets its R&D level to reduce its own cost, ignoring that fact that it reduces the cost of the other firm as well. Now, if β is high, (the spillover effect is intense), then under cooperation the firms set R&D levels higher than the noncooperative levels since under cooperation firms take into account the effect of their R&D on their joint profits. When the spillover effect is small, the effect of each firm on the cost reduction of the other firm is small, hence, when firms do not cooperate each firm has a lot to gain from R&D since under small spillover effects, the R&D intensifies the cost advantage of the firm that undertakes a higher level of R&D.

Shaffer and Salant (1998) have pointed out some problems associated with the commonly used assumption that the two labs are engaged in an equal amount of R&D. They have shown that even though the aggregate R&D cost of identical firms in a research joint venture would be the lowest if they invested equally to reduce subsequent production costs, nonetheless members may enlarge their overall joint profit by instead signing agreements which mandate unequal investments. If we apply their analysis to our simple example, it turns out that unequal R&D levels maximize joint profit if the spillover parameter, β, is sufficiently low, $1 < 2(1 - \beta)^2$ or $\beta < 0.3$; implying that we need to assume that $\beta > 0.3$ in order to make the analysis of this section valid.

Finally, in the present analysis the profit of firms must be higher under cooperation than under noncooperation since under cooperation in the first stage the firms can always invest at the noncooperative R&D level and earn the same profit as under noncooperation. However, Fershtman and Gandal (1994) show that the profit of the firms may be lower under cooperation in a (different) game where firms compete in R&D in the first period but collude in the second period. This happens since, depending on the second-period profit-sharing rule, each firm may over-invest in R&D in order to negotiate a larger fraction of the (cooperative) profit in the second period.

9.4 Patents

A *patent* is a legal document, granted by a government to an inventor, giving the inventor the sole right to exploit the particular invention for a given number of years (see an appendix (Section 9.7) for a detailed analysis of patent law). It is widely accepted that the patent system is useful for encouraging new product development and process innovation despite the market distortion it creates by granting temporary monopoly rights to new firms. Thus, the patent system is essential to growing economies. Empirically, it is very hard to measure the social value of a patent since patented invention tend to be rapidly imitated (or be "patented around" the patented innovation), so the knowledge is diffused into many firms, into other industries (see Mansfield 1965), and into other countries. One way to solve the problem how to measure the social value of a patented innovation is to count the number of times the innovation is cited in other patented innovations (see Trajtenberg 1990).

Formally, the patent system has two social goals: To provide firms with the incentives for producing know-how, and to make the new information concerning the new discoveries available to the public as fast as possible. In other words, society recognizes that information dispersion is a key factor in achieving progress and that public information reduces duplication of R&D. Note that the information-dissemination goal of the patent may somewhat contradict the pure interpretation of the patent law stating that a future innovation is patentable only if it does not infringe on earlier patented inventions. That is, on the one hand, society desires to disclose the information behind the invention in order to enhance the research by other firms; on the other hand, other firms would not be able to patent a technology that infringes on older patents. However, providing the public with the information on patented technologies definitely reduces extra cost resulting from R&D duplication in the sense that it prevents the wheel from being reinvented.

The reason why innovators need extra protection lies in the fact that know-how is a very special entity, compared with other products such as chairs, cars, and cheese: know-how is easy to duplicate and steal. Once a firm makes its invention known to others, other firms would immediately start with imitation followed by intense competition, thereby reducing the price to unit cost. With zero profits, no firm would ever engage in R&D, and the economy would stagnate forever.

The goal of the patent system is to reward innovators. The drawback of the system is that it creates a price distortion in the economy since those goods produced under patent protection will be priced differently from goods under no patent protection.

There are different kinds of patents, such as patents given for a new product, a new process, or a substance and a design patent. In order for an invention to be classified as worthy of a patent it has to satisfy three criteria: it has to be novel, nontrivial, and useful. In practice, it is hard to measure whether an invention satisfies these criteria, and therefore, patents tend to be approved as long as they do not infringe on earlier patented innovations. For a discussion of the legal side of the patent system and intellectual property see the appendix (Section 9.7). This appendix discusses many important legal and economic aspects of patent protection.

In this section, we discuss only one important and difficult aspect of the patent system, the duration of patent protection. For example, in the United States, inventors are generally rewarded with seventeen years of patent protection, and in Europe with around twenty years of protection. Here, we wish to investigate what factors affect a society's optimal duration of patents.

We now provide a simple method for calculating the optimal duration of a patent that was proposed in Nordhaus 1969 and Scherer 1972. As in section 9.3, consider a firm that is capable of undertaking a process innovation R&D. An investment of x in R&D reduces the firm's unit cost from $c > 0$ to $c - x$. The cost of undertaking R&D at level x is the same as in Assumption 9.2. We assume that the innovation is minor (see Definition 9.1), so the innovating firm profit-maximizing price (assuming that the unit cost of all competing firms remain c) is $p = c$. Hence, there will be no change in output as a result of the innovation.

Figure 9.3 illustrates the market before and after the process innovation reduces the unit cost of the innovating firm by x, assuming a market demand given by $p = a - Q$, where $a > c$. Since there is no change in

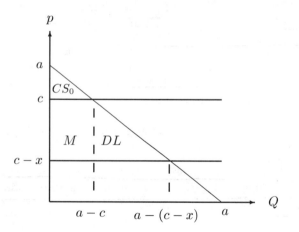

Figure 9.3: Gains and losses due to patent protection

price charged to the consumers, the area M in Figure 9.3 measures the innovator's gain in profit due to the innovation. Assuming that the government sets the patent life for $T \geq 0$ periods ($T = 17$ in the United States), we see that the innovator enjoys a profit of M for T periods, and zero profit from period $T + 1$ and on.

The area DL in Figure 9.3 is the *society's deadweight loss* resulting from the monopoly power held by the patent holder for T periods. That is, in periods $t = 1, 2, \ldots T$ the society's benefit from the innovation is only the monopoly's profits M (assuming that the profits are distributed to consumers, say, via dividends). In periods $t = T+1, T+2, \ldots$, after the patent expires, all firms have access to the new technology, and the equilibrium price falls to $c - x$. Hence, after the patent expires, the gain to the society is the sum of the areas, $M + DL$, since the removal of the monopoly rights expands output and increases consumer surplus by DL. It is clear from Figure 9.3 that

$$M(x) = (a-c)x \quad \text{and} \quad DL(x) = \frac{x^2}{2}. \tag{9.11}$$

Since the patent means monopoly rights for several periods, we need to develop a dynamic model in order to determine the optimal patent duration. Therefore, let ρ, $0 < \rho < 1$, denote the discount factor. Recall that the discount factor is how much a dollar next year is worth today. In perfect markets, the discount factor is also inversely related to the interest rate. That is, $\rho = 1/(1+r)$, where r is the market real-interest rate.

In what follows, we consider a two-stage game. In the first stage, the government sets the duration of the patent life T knowing how a firm would react and invest in cost-reducing R&D. In the second stage, at $t = 1$, the innovator takes the patent life as given, and chooses his or her R&D level. Then, during the periods $t = 1, \ldots T$, the innovator is protected by the patent rights and collects a monopoly profit for T periods.

9.4.1 Innovator's choice of R&D level for a given duration of patents

Denote by $\pi(x; T)$ the innovator's present value of profits when the innovator chooses an R&D level of x. Then, in the second stage the innovator takes the duration of patents T as given and chooses in period $t = 1$ R&D level x to

$$\max_x \pi(x; T) = \sum_{t=1}^{T} \rho^{t-1} M(x) - T \, C(x). \tag{9.12}$$

That is, the innovator chooses R&D level x to maximize the present value of T years of earning monopoly profits minus the cost of R&D. We need the following Lemma. The proof is given in an appendix, (Section 9.9).

Lemma 9.2

$$\sum_{t=1}^{T} \rho^{t-1} = \frac{1 - \rho^T}{1 - \rho}.$$

Hence, by Lemma 9.2 and (9.11), (9.12) can be written as

$$\max_{x} \frac{1 - \rho^T}{1 - \rho}(a - c)x - \frac{x^2}{2},$$

implying that the innovator's optimal R&D level is

$$x^I = \frac{1 - \rho^T}{1 - \rho}(a - c). \tag{9.13}$$

Hence,

Proposition 9.3

1. *The R&D level increases with the duration of the patent. Formally, x^I increases with T.*

2. *The R&D level increases with an increase in the demand, and decreases with an increase in the unit cost. Formally, x^I increases with an increase in a and decreases with an increase in c.*

3. *The R&D level increases with an increase in the discount factor ρ (or a decrease in the interest rate).*

The intuition behind Proposition 9.3 is as follows. When the duration of patents increases, the firm will be protected for a longer period and therefore will be selling more units over time. Thus, a higher R&D level would correspond to a unit-cost reduction for for a higher volume of production, which would make the process innovation even more profitable. The prediction of part 3 of Proposition 9.3 should remind you of your macroeconomics classes, where the Keynesian and ISLM approaches assumed that investment increases when interest rates fall. Here, we obtain this result: when the discount factor increases, say due to a drop in the real interest rate, the firm's present value of discounted profits increases, thereby making innovation more profitable.

9.4.2 Society's optimal duration of patents

We now turn to the first stage of the game, where the government legislates the duration of the patent to maximize social welfare, taking into account how the duration of patents affects the innovators' R&D level. As represented in Figure 9.3, the society's welfare is $CS_0 + M$ from the date the invention occurs, and $CS_0 + M + DL$ from the date when the monopoly's patent right expires.

Formally, the social planner calculates profit-maximizing R&D (9.13) for the innovator, and in period $t = 1$ chooses an optimal patent duration T to

$$\max_{T} W(T) \equiv \sum_{t=1}^{\infty} \rho^{t-1} \left[CS_0 + M(x^I) \right] + \sum_{t=T+1}^{\infty} \rho^{t-1} DL(x^I) - \frac{(x^I)^2}{2}$$

$$\text{s.t. } x^I = \frac{1 - \rho^T}{1 - \rho}(a - c). \tag{9.14}$$

Since

$$\sum_{t=T+1}^{\infty} \rho^{t-1} = \rho^T \sum_{t=0}^{\infty} \rho^t = \left(\frac{\rho^T}{1 - \rho} \right)$$

and using (9.11), (9.14) can be written as choosing T^* to maximize

$$W(T) = \frac{CS_0 + (a - c)x^I}{1 - \rho} - \frac{(x^I)^2}{2} \frac{1 - \rho^T}{1 - \rho} \quad \text{s.t. } x^I = \frac{1 - \rho^T}{1 - \rho}(a - c). \tag{9.15}$$

Thus, the government acts as a leader since the innovator moves after the government sets the patent length T, and the government moves first and chooses T knowing how the innovator is going to respond. We denote by T^* the society's optimal duration of patents. We are not going to actually perform this maximization problem in order to find T^*. In general, computer simulations can be used to find the welfare-maximizing T in case differentiation does not lead to an explicit solution, or when the discrete nature of the problem (i.e., T is a natural number) does not allow us to differentiate at all. However, one conclusion is easy to find:

Proposition 9.4 *The optimal patent life is finite. Formally, $0 < T^* < \infty$.*

Proof. It is sufficient to show that the welfare level under a one-period patent protection ($T = 1$) exceeds the welfare level under the infinite patent life ($T = \infty$).
When $T = 1$, $x^I(1) = a - c$. Hence, by (9.15),

$$W(1) = \frac{CS_0}{1 - \rho} + \frac{(a - c)^2}{1 - \rho} - \frac{(a - c)^2}{2}. \tag{9.16}$$

When $T = +\infty$, $x^I(+\infty) = \frac{a - c}{1 - \rho}$. Hence, by (9.15),

$$W(+\infty) = \frac{CS_0}{1 - \rho} + \frac{(a - c)^2}{(1 - \rho)^2} - \frac{(a - c)^2}{2(1 - \rho)^3}. \tag{9.17}$$

A comparison of (9.16) with (9.17) yields that

$$W(1) > W(\infty) \iff \frac{1}{1-\rho} - \frac{1}{2} > \frac{1}{(1-\rho)^2} - \frac{1}{2(1-\rho)^3}. \qquad (9.18)$$

To show that the last inequality in (9.18) holds for every $0 < \rho < 1$, define $\alpha \equiv 1 - \rho$. Hence, if we cross-multiply (9.18), it is sufficient to show that $2\alpha^2 - \alpha^3 > 2\alpha - 1$ for all $0 < \alpha < 1$. The latter holds if $(\alpha^2 - \alpha^3) + (\alpha^2 - 2\alpha + 1) = (\alpha^2 - \alpha^3) + (\alpha - 1)^2 > 0$. This inequality holds since each term is strictly positive. ∎

The result obtained in Proposition 9.4 is important because it is often argued in the literature that innovators should be granted an infinite patent life. The logic behind the infinite-patent-life argument is that in order to induce an innovator to undertake the optimal R&D level, the innovator should be rewarded with the entire profit stream from the innovation, which could last forever. That is, without the infinite patent protection, the innovator cannot capture all the rents from future sales associated with the innovation, and hence will not innovate at the optimal level. However, Proposition 9.4 shows that the monopoly distortion associated with an infinitely lived monopoly is larger than the innovation distortion associated with an insufficient reward to the innovator. Chou and Shy (1991, 1993) have found that this result also holds for patents given for product innovation (rather than for a process innovation in the present case). Also, Stigler (1968) provides an interesting calculation leading to an optimal patent life of seventeen years.

9.5 Licensing an Innovation

Licensing of technologies is common on both the national and the international scales. Over 80 percent of the inventions granted patents are licensed to other firms, where some are exclusively licensed and others are licensed to several manufacturers. Given this observation, we ask in this section why a firm that invested a substantial amount of resources in R&D would find it profitable to license its technology to a competing firm that has not invested in R&D. Several answers to this questions are given in the literature on patent licensing and surveyed in Kamien 1992. We answer this question by considering the following example:

Consider the simple two-firm Cournot example illustrated in Figure 9.3 and suppose that firm 1 has invented a (minor) cost-reducing process indicated by a lower unit cost $c_1 = c - x$, where c is the unit cost of the noninnovating firm 2 ($c_2 = c$).

No licensing

If firm 1 does not license its technology, the firms play Cournot, where in section 6.1 on page 98 we calculated that $\pi_1^c(c_1, c_2) > \pi_2^c(c_1, c_2)$ and $q_1^c(c_1, c_2) > q_2^c(c_1, c_2)$. That is, firm 1, with the lower unit cost, produces a higher amount and earns a higher profit than firm 2.

Licensing

Suppose that firm 1 negotiates with firm 2 for granting permission to firm 2 to use the less costly technology. There can be several types of licensing. For example, there can be a *fixed-fee* license (a fee that is independent of the output produced by firm 2), or firm 1 can charge firm 2 with a *per-unit fee* for every unit sold by firm 2.

Consider a per-unit fee case (that is very common in the electronics and entertainment industries, for example) in which firm 2 buys the technology for producing at unit cost of $c_1 < c_2$, and has to pay firm 1 the sum of \$$\phi$ for every unit it sells.

Although it is clear that the two firms have some surplus to divide between themselves, when firm 2 buys the cost-saving technology from firm 1, we take the simplest approach by assuming that firm 1 is a leader which offers firm 2 a take-it-or-leave-it contract to pay a per-unit fee of \$$\phi$. In other words, in the first stage firm 1 offers the technology to firm 2 for a per-unit fee. In the second stage, firm 2 can either reject the offer, or accept the offer and then choose how much to produce.

We now seek to find the profit-maximizing per-unit of output fee, ϕ, that firm 1 charges firm 2 for its cost-reducing technology. Clearly, firm 1 sets $\phi = (c_2 - c_1) - \epsilon \approx c_2 - c_1 = x$. That is, firm 1 charges a per-unit fee that is almost the size of the unit cost reduction associated with the licensed technology. Therefore, under this licensing contract, the (fee inclusive) per-unit cost facing firm 2 is now given by $c_{2\prime} = c_1 + \phi = c_2 - \epsilon \approx c_2$. Hence, in a Cournot equilibrium firm 2 would not change its quantity produced, and therefore, its profit level does not change.

In contrast, the profit of firm 1 is now given by $\pi_1 = \pi_1^c(c_1, c_2) + \phi q_2^c(c_1, c_2)$. That is, firm 1 gains all the surplus generated by the cost reduction in the production of firm 2. Therefore, we can state the following proposition.

Proposition 9.5

1. *In a Cournot environment, licensing a cost-reducing innovation can increase the profit of all firms.*

2. *In a Cournot environment, welfare increases when firms license cost-reducing innovations.*

The last part of the proposition follows from the fact that in our example, firms do not change their output levels and therefore the market price does not change. Hence, consumers' welfare remains unchanged. The profit of firm 1 increases, however, implying an aggregate welfare increase.

9.6 Governments and International R&D Races

We observe that governments never completely leave R&D to be performed by the free markets. Governments' intervention in R&D starts with the establishment of mandatory school systems and universities and ends with direct subsidies to firms or industries. In the developing countries, the gross estimation of the domestic R&D expenditure is around 3 to 3.5 percent of the GDP. Out of that, 30 to 60 percent is government financed.

In this section we analyze two examples in which international competition between firms located in different countries generates an incentive for each government to subsidize the R&D for the firm located in its country. Subsection 9.6.1 analyzes how a governmental subsidy to a domestic firm can secure the international dominance of the domestic firm in an international market for a new product. Subsection 9.6.2 analyzes governmental subsidies to process-innovation R&D.

9.6.1   Subsidizing new product development

Consider Krugman's (1986) illustration of how governments can enhance the international strategic position of the firms located in their countries. Suppose that there are only two civilian aircraft manufacturers in the entire world, and that the world consists of two countries, the United States and the European Community. Suppose that the U.S. manufacturer is called Boeing and the European firm is called Airbus. Each firm is considering developing the future super-large passenger plane, the "megacarrier," intended to transport six hundred passengers and having a flight range exceeding eighteen hours. Suppose further that each firm has a binary choice: develop (and produce) or don't develop (and don't produce). Table 9.1 demonstrates the profit levels of each firm under the four possible market outcomes.

Table 9.1 demonstrates what several civil aviation specialists frequently argue, that given the high development costs, a two-firm market is inconsistent with having positive profit levels. That is, in this kind of market, there can be at most one firm earning strictly positive profit. The Nash equilibrium (see Definition 2.4 on page 18) for this game is given in the following proposition.

AIRBUS

		Produce		Don't Produce	
BOEING	Produce	-10	-10	50	0
	Don't Produce	0	50	0	0

Table 9.1: Profits of Boeing and Airbus under no gov't intervention

Proposition 9.6 *In the Boeing-Airbus game, there exist exactly two Nash equilibria: (Produce, Don't Produce) and (Don't Produce, Produce).*

Now suppose that the EC subsidizes Airbus by providing fifteen units of money for the development of a European megacarrier. Table 9.2 illustrates the profit levels of the two aircraft manufacturers under the four possible outcomes.

AIRBUS

		Produce		Don't Produce	
BOEING	Produce	-10	5	50	0
	Don't Produce	0	65	0	0

Table 9.2: Profits of Boeing and Airbus under the EC subsidy

In this case, we can assert the following:

Proposition 9.7 *Under the EC subsidy, a unique Nash equilibrium is given by having Airbus play Produce and having Boeing play Don't Produce.*

Thus, by subsidizing product development, a government can secure the world dominance of the domestic firm in a product having large development costs relative to the potential market size. Although we have shown that the EC can guarantee its dominance in the megacarriers market by providing a subsidy to Airbus, it is not clear that the welfare of the EC residents increases with such a policy, since the EC residents will have to pay for this subsidy in one form or another!

9.6.2   Subsidizing process innovation

Following Brander and Spencer 1983 and 1985, consider two countries denoted by $i = 1, 2$, each of which has one firm producing a homogeneous product only for export, to be sold in the world market. The world's demand for the product is $p = a - Q$; assume that the preinnovation unit cost of each firm is c where $0 < c < a$.

Let x_i denote the amount of R&D sponsored by the government in country i. We assume that when government i undertakes R&D at level x_i, the unit production cost for the firm producing in country i is reduced to $c - x_i$, $i = 1, 2$. As in Assumption 9.2 on page 230 we assume that the total cost to government i of engaging in R&D at level x_i is $TC_i(x_i) = (x_i)^2/2$.

Since we assumed that the two firms play a Cournot quantity game in the world market, for given R&D levels x_1 and x_2, (6.5) and (6.7) (see section 6.1 on page 98) imply that the profit level of the firm located in country i is

$$\pi_i = \frac{[a - 2(c - x_i) + c - x_j]^2}{9} = \frac{(a - c + 2x_i - x_j)^2}{9}.$$

We denote by W_i the welfare of country i, which is defined as the sum of the profit earned by firm i minus the R&D cost. Altogether, each government i takes x_j as given and chooses an R&D level x_i, to maximize the welfare of its country. That is, government i solves

$$\max_{x_i} W_i \equiv \pi_i - TC_i(x_i) = \frac{(a - c + 2x_i - x_j)^2}{9} - \frac{(x_i)^2}{2}.$$

The first-order condition yields how the government of country i sets its R&D level in response to the R&D set is country j. Thus,

$$x_i \equiv R_i(x_j) = 4(a - c) - 4x_j \quad i, j = 1, 2; \quad i \neq j. \tag{9.19}$$

Note that the countries' best-response functions are strategic substitutes (see Definition 7.2 on page 140), reflecting the fact that if one country increases its R&D level, the other reduces it. Equation (9.19) shows that if country j does not subsidize its R&D ($x_j = 0$), then the government of country i sets a strictly positive R&D level, $x_i = 4(a - c) > 0$. Hence,

Proposition 9.8 *If initially the world is characterized by no government intervention, it is always beneficial for at least one country to subsidize R&D. That is, the increase in profit from export sales associated with the cost-reducing R&D dominates the cost of R&D.*

Solving (9.19) yields the unique symmetric Nash equilibrium R&D levels given by

$$x_1^n = x_2^n = \frac{4(a - c)}{5}.$$

Proposition 9.9 *In a Nash equilibrium of an R&D game between two governments, each government subsidizes the R&D for the firm located in its country. Also, the equilibrium levels of the R&D subsidies increase with a shift in the world demand (a) and decrease with the initial unit-production cost (c).*

Thus, when demand rises, governments increase their R&D subsidies since cost reduction is magnified by larger sales.

Finally, the reader should not interpret this model as the ultimate argument for having governments subsidize R&D of the exporting firms, because this model does not explain why the government itself should perform the R&D. In other words, why does the private sector not invest in R&D, given that the firms' increase in profit can more than cover the R&D cost? Why cannot banks finance this innovation? Also, it is unlikely that governments possess all the information needed to decide which R&D is profitable and which is not. For arguments against protection, see Baldwin 1967. For a comprehensive survey of strategic trade policy, see Krugman 1986.

The result obtained in this subsection has been mitigated in several papers. First, Dixit and Grossman (1986) have shown that in a general equilibrium model (as compared with our partial equilibrium framework) the incentive for protection becomes weaker. Second, Eaton and Grossman (1986) have shown that the choice of policy instrument for helping the domestic industry depends heavily on the assumed market structure. Hence, since governments never know exactly whether the market structure is Cournot or a different one, the optimal policy may simply be not to intervene. Third, Gaudet and Salant (1991) show that the Brander and Spencer result is a special case because if one country has a large number of exporting firms and one has a small number of exporting firm, the optimal policy for the government in the country with the large number of firms may be a tax (instead of a subsidy) that will induce some firms to exit.

9.7   Appendix: Patent Law

A patent application is submitted to the Patent Office. Then the Patent Office examines the application and does research to determine whether the claims made by the petitioner fulfill the criteria for granting a patent. In many cases patents are denied by the Patent Office, and the innovator resubmits the application. During this time, it often happens that other innovators apply for similar patents, and in this case, the question of who invented first has to be answered by the Patent Office.

After the patent is granted, the patentee is given exclusive rights to make, use, or sell the invention, to the absolute exclusion of others. In the United States, the patent is granted for seventeen years and cannot be renewed.

9.7.1 History of Patent Law

The history of the patent system can be traced to medieval times in Europe when commerce became controlled by various groups and guilds. The reader interested in more details is referred to Kaufer 1989 and Miller and Davis 1990. The earlier patents issued by the Crown in England were a method used by the monarch to control various sectors in return for some benefits. That is, early patent rights were not as concerned with inventions as with the protection of the monarchy itself. In 1623 the Statute of Monopoly ended the period of unrestricted granting of monopolies by the Crown. In fact, the development of patent law was needed to secure monopoly rights for special reasons, such as to reward the innovators, rather than for the unrestricted granting of monopoly rights. In 1624 England passed a statute to regularize previously arbitrary "letters of patents" issued by the Crown.

The life of a patent was set at fourteen years because fourteen is two times seven, and seven years was the normal length of an apprenticeship (the time needed to train a professional, say a doctor). Then, the patent could be extended for seven additional years, reaching a maximum number of twenty-one years of patent protection. It is possible that the current U.S. system of seventeen years represents a compromise between fourteen and twenty-one years.

In the New World the colonies began granting patents; the colonists recognized that society could benefit from rewarding the innovators. All this led to the statement in the U.S. Constitution that

> The Congress shall have the power...To promote the progress of science and useful arts, by securing for limited times to authors and inventors the exclusive right to their respective writings and discoveries.

Then, in 1836 the U.S. Patent Office was given the authority to examine proposed inventions and to determine whether they meet the criteria of the Patent Statute. In what follows, we will refer to the Patent Act of 1952 as the Patent Law.

9.7.2 Types of Patents

A patent can be granted for products, processes, plants, and design. However, any invention related to abstract ideas is not patentable. For example, the first person to prove Lemma 9.1 on page 228 (or any other lemma in this book) was not entitled to a patent right, since this "invention" is classified as an abstract idea, or a mathematical formula. However, note that applications for abstract ideas of theories may be patentable.

9.7.3   Criteria for granting a patent

In order for an invention to be entitled to a patent, it has to satisfy three requirements: novelty, nonobviousness, and usefulness. According to the patent law, novelty refers to the lack of prior domestic or foreign patenting, publication, use, or sale. Nonobviousness refers to the requirement that the invention must demonstrate some advance over "prior art" so that the ordinary mechanic skilled in prior art would not have been capable of making this advance. The purpose of the usefulness (or utility) requirement is to prevent patenting inventions that are based only on ingenuity and novelty but do not serve any purpose. This requirement also intends to steer the R&D towards inventing welfare-increasing inventions rather than useless ones.

9.7.4   First to invent versus first to file

The U.S. patent law differs from those of other countries in one major respect—the priority assignment given to one of several agents filing for the same patent. The general rule in the United States is that the innovator is the one who conceived first. However, one exception prevails, the case in which a second innovator reduces the invention into practice and the first innovator did not exercise continuous diligence. Thus, an innovator who is the first to conceive the innovation and the first to reduce it to practice has a definite priority in getting the patent.

The U.S. system is referred to as the *first-to-invent* system, which is not exercised by other countries. The EC and Japan use a different priority system, referred to as the *first-to-file* system. Obviously, the first-to-file system is easier to enforce. Problems arise nowadays when claiming a priority over international patents, since an invention could be recognized by one patent system but not the other.

9.7.5   Copyrights

Copyright gives an exclusive right to the copyright owner to reproduce the work and its derivatives in the form of copying or recording, and are given on the basis of pure originality, which refers to the act of authorship or artistic creativity, and not necessarily on novelty. The duration of the copyright ownership extends to the author's lifetime plus fifty years.

To obtain a copyright ownership, the author or the artist must demonstrate that he or she has contributed something to the final production or a reproduction. Thus, a reproduction of a book in modern style or with new decorations may be eligible for copyright protection because the author or artist has contributed something that did not exist in the earlier version. The Copyright Act also allows computer programs and sound recordings to receive copyright protection. Finally, the law permits reproduction of various works mainly for noncommercial purposes, such as education.

9.8   Appendix: The Legal Approach to R&D Joint Ventures

Two major questions are faced by the regulators regarding cooperative R&D: First, whether the act of joining together itself reduces competition, thereby violating antitrust laws. More precisely, should R&D joint ventures be considered as procompetitive or anticompetitive in the product's market? Second, even if R&D joint ventures are anticompetitive, are there efficiency gains associated with joint R&D that dominate the welfare loss resulting from anticompetitive behavior in the final-good market?

Clearly, unless the R&D joint ventures offer gains in efficiency associated with more productive and less costly R&D, there is no reason to permit it. For this reason, antitrust cases brought against firms cooperating in R&D are judged by the rule of reason rather than by the per se rule. The following discussion of the legal approach to cooperative R&D is based on Brodley 1990 and Jorde and Teece 1990.

The U.S. legal system seems to be less supportive of R&D joint ventures than the EC and Japan. According to the Clayton Act, allegations that firms use price fixing permit suing for treble damages. Therefore, there is a question of whether cooperation in R&D can open a channel of communication among firms to explicitly or implicitly collude on prices. Despite these suspicions, Congress has recognized the potential benefits associated with cooperative R&D and in 1984 enacted the National Cooperative Research Act (NCRA), which states that joint R&D ventures must not be held illegal per se. The NCRA established a registration procedure for joint R&D ventures. The firms that do follow the registration procedure are immune from paying treble damages on any antitrust violation. Instead, the maximum penalty for registered firms is limited to damages, interest, and costs.

In sum, the U.S. law attempts to distinguish between joint R&D and joint commercialization decisions by cooperating firms. The former is legal, and the latter is illegal. The reader should note that sometimes it is hard to distinguish between the two processes since the decision to commercialize an invention can be viewed as the last step of the R&D process. That is, it is possible that one firm has a comparative advantage in theoretical product development, while the other has one in making an innovation marketable. In this case, society may benefit from the formation of a joint venture despite the fact that joint commercialization may result in higher prices than those that obtain under pure competition, since otherwise, there might be no product at all. This approach is more common in Japan, where commercialization is an integral part of the R&D process.

9.9   Mathematical Appendix

Proof of Lemma 9.1   First, recall the (high school) identity given by

$$\sum_{t=0}^{\infty} \delta^t \equiv 1 + \delta + \delta^2 + \delta^3 + \ldots = \frac{1}{1 - \delta}.$$

Next,

$$
\begin{aligned}
\sum_{t=1}^{\infty} t\delta^{t-1} &= 1 + 2\delta + 3\delta^2 + 4\delta^3 + \ldots \\
&= (1 + \delta + \delta^2 + \delta^3 + \ldots) + (\delta + \delta^2 + \delta^3 + \ldots) + (\delta^2 + \delta^3 + \ldots) \\
&= \frac{1}{1 - \delta} + \frac{\delta}{1 - \delta} + \frac{\delta^2}{1 - \delta} + \ldots = \left(\frac{1}{1 - \delta}\right)\left(\frac{1}{1 - \delta}\right) = \frac{1}{(1 - \delta)^2}.
\end{aligned}
$$

∎

Proof of Lemma 9.2   Using the high school identity given at the beginning of this appendix section, we have it that

$$
\begin{aligned}
\sum_{t=1}^{T} \rho^{t-1} = \sum_{t=0}^{T-1} \rho^t &= \frac{1}{1 - \rho} - \rho^T - \rho^{T+1} - \rho^{T+2} - \ldots \\
&= \frac{1}{1 - \rho} - \rho^T (1 + \rho + \rho^2 + \rho^3 + \ldots) \\
&= \frac{1}{1 - \rho} - \frac{\rho^T}{1 - \rho} = \frac{1 - \rho^T}{1 - \rho}.
\end{aligned}
$$

∎

9.10   Exercises

1. Consider the classification of process R&D given in section 9.1. Suppose that the aggregate inverse-demand function is given by $p = a - Q$, and

that initially all the firms have identical unit costs measured by c_0, where $c_0 < a < 2c_0$. Suppose that one and only one of the firms is able to reduce its unit cost to $c_1 = 2c_0 - a$. Using Definition 9.1 infer whether this process innovation is considered to be minor or major.

2. Consider a three-firm version of the patent-race model studied in section 9.2. Suppose that each one of the three firms is capable of developing a product. Let V denote the monetary value of the patent associated with the new product. Each firm can construct a research lab provided that it invests $\$I$ in the lab. Assume that if a firm constructs a lab, it has a probability of $\alpha = 1/2$ of discovering the product.

   If only one firm discovers the product, it will earn a profit equal to the full value of the patent (i.e., $\$V$). If only two firms discover, then each will earn $\$V/2$, and if all three discover, then each will earn $\$V/3$. Answer the following questions.

   (a) Assuming that $I = 1$, calculate the minimal value of V that ensures that each firm will invest in constructing a lab.

   (b) Suppose now that firm 3 went out of business, and that a foreign firm purchased the two remaining firms. Calculate the minimal value of V that would induce the foreign owner of the two firms to run the two separate research labs instead of operating only one lab.

3. Consider the calculations of the expected time of discovery described in subsection 9.2.3. Suppose that n $(n \geq 2)$ firms are engaged in R&D, where the probability of discovery by each firm at each date is α, $0 < \alpha < 1$. Answer the following questions.

   (a) What is the probability that none of the firms discovers at a particular date?

   (b) What is the probability that at least one firm discovers at a particular date?

   (c) Calculate the expected date of discovery.

4. Consider the Boeing-Airbus game described in Table 9.1 on page 242.

   (a) Calculate the minimal subsidy to Airbus that will ensure that Airbus will develop the megacarrier. Explain!

   (b) Suppose that the EC provides Airbus with fifteen units of money as a subsidy. Which subsidy by the U.S. government to Boeing would guarantee that Boeing will develop this megacarrier?

   (c) Suppose that the EC provides Airbus with fifteen units of money as a subsidy. Is there any level of subsidy given by the U.S. government that would deter Airbus from developing this airplane?

   (d) From your answer to the previous question, conclude whether the world benefits by having both governments subsidizing their own aircraft manufacturing firms. Explain!

9.11   References

Baldwin, R. 1967. "The Case Against Infant-Industry Tariff Protection." *Journal of Political Economy* 77: 295–305.

Brander, J., and B. Spencer. 1983. "International R&D Rivalry and Industrial Strategy."*Review of Economic Studies* 50: 707–722.

Brander, J., and B. Spencer. 1985. "Export Subsidies and International Market Share Rivalry." *Journal of International Economics* 18: 83–100.

Brodley J. 1990. "Antitrust Law and Innovation Cooperation." *Journal of Economic Perspectives* 4: 97–112.

Choi, J. 1993. "Cooperative R&D with Product Market Competition." *International Journal of Industrial Organization* 11: 553–571.

Chou, C., and O. Shy. 1991. "New Product Development and the Optimal Duration of Patents." *Southern Economic Journal* 57: 811–821.

Chou, C., and O. Shy. 1993. "The Crowding-Out Effects of Long Duration of Patents." *RAND Journal of Economics* 24: 304–312.

Combs, K. 1993. "The Role of Information Sharing in Cooperative Research and Development." *International Journal of Industrial Organization* 11: 535–551.

d'Aspremont, C., and A. Jacquemin. 1988. "Cooperative and Noncooperative R&D in Duopoly with Spillovers." *American Economic Review* 78: 1133–1137.

Dosi, G. 1988. "Sources, Procedures, and Microeconomic Effects of Innovation." *Journal of Economic Literature* 26: 1120–1171.

Dixit, A., and G. Grossman. 1986. "Targeted Export Promotion With Several Oligopolistic Industries." *Journal of International Economics* 21: 233–249.

Eaton, J., and G. Grossman. 1986. "Optimal Trade and Industrial Policy under Oligopoly." *Quarterly Journal of Economics* 2: 383–406.

Fershtman, C., and N. Gandal. 1994. "Disadvantageous Semicollusion." *International Journal of Industrial Organization* 12: 141–154.

Freeman, C. 1982. "The Economics of Industrial Innovation." 2nd ed. Cambridge, Mass.: MIT Press.

Fudenberg, D., R. Gilbert, J. Stiglitz, and J. Tirole. 1983. "Preemption, Leapfrogging, and Competition in Patent Races." *European Economic Review* 22: 3–31.

Gandal, N., and S. Scotchmer. 1993. "Coordinating Research Through Research Joint Ventures." *Journal of Public Economics* 51: 173–193.

Gaudet, G., and S. Salant. 1991. "Increasing the Profits of a Subset of Firms in Oligopoly Models with Strategic Substitutes." *American Economic Review* 81: 658–665.

Harris, C., and J. Vickers. 1985. "Perfect Equilibrium in a Model of Race." *Review of Economic Studies* 52: 193–209.

Jaffe, A. 1986. "Technological Opportunity and Spillovers of R&D: Evidence from Firm's Patents, Profits, and Market Value." *American Economic Review* 76: 984–1001.

Jorde, M., and D. Teece. 1990. "Innovation and Cooperation: Implications for Competition and Antitrust." *Journal of Economic Perspectives* 4: 75–96.

Kamien M. 1992. "Patent Licensing." In *Handbook of Game Theory*, edited by R. Aumann, and S. Hart. Amsterdam: North-Holland.

Kamien, M., E. Muller, and I. Zang. 1992. "Research Joint Ventures and R&D Cartel." *American Economic Review* 82: 1293–1306.

Katz, M. 1986. "An Analysis of Cooperative Research and Development." *Rand Journal of Economics* 17: 527–543.

Katz, M., and J. Ordover. 1990. "R&D Cooperation and Competition." *Brookings Papers on Economic Activity: Microeconomics,* 137–203.

Kaufer, E. 1989. *The Economics of the Patent System.* New York: Hardwood Academic Publishers.

Krugman, P. 1986. *Strategic Trade Policy and the New International Economics.* Cambridge, Mass.: MIT Press.

Lee, T., and L. Wilde. 1980. "Market Structure and Innovation: A Reformulation." *Quarterly Journal of Economics* 94: 429–436.

Loury, G. 1979. "Market Structure and Innovation." *Quarterly Journal of Economics* 93: 395–410.

Mansfield, E. 1965. "Rates of Return from Industrial R&D." *American Economic Review,* Papers and Proceedings 55: 741–766.

Mokyr, J. 1990. *The Lever of Riches: Technological Creativity and Economic Progress.* Oxford: Oxford University Press.

Miller, A., and M. Davis. 1990. *Intellectual Property, Patents, Trademarks, and Copyright in a Nutshell.* 2nd ed. St. Paul, Minn.: West Publishing.

Nordhaus, W. 1969. *Invention Growth, and Welfare: A Theoretical Treatment of Technological Change.* Cambridge, Mass.: MIT Press.

Reinganum, J. 1989. "The Timing of Innovation: Research, Development, and Diffusion." In *Handbook of Industrial Organization*, edited by R. Schmalensee and R. Willig. Amsterdam: North-Holland.

Rosenberg, N. 1994. *Exploring the Black Box.* Cambridge: Cambridge University Press.

Scherer, F. M. 1972. "Nordhaus' Theory of Optimal Patent Life: A Geometric Reinterpretation." *American Economic Review* 62: 422–427

Shaffer, G., and S. Salant. 1998. "Optimal Asymmetric Strategies in Research Joint Ventures." *International Journal of Industrial Organization,* 16: 195–208.

Stigler, G. 1968. *The Organization of the Industry.* Homewood, Ill.: Richard
    D. Irwin.

Trajtenberg, M. 1990. "A Penny for Your Quotes: Patent Citations and the
    Value of Innovation." *Rand Journal of Economics* 21: 172–187.

Chapter 10

The Economics of Compatibility and Standards

> Standards are always out of date. That is what makes them
> standards.
> —Alan Bennet, *Forty Years On* (1969)

Perhaps the most easily observed phenomenon is that people do not
live alone. People (and all other animals) tend to live in groups (called
villages, towns, cities, or countries) since they benefit from interacting
with other people. In addition to the pure social observation that people
just enjoy being around other people, the benefits of being and working
together can be explained as follows:

Production: Most production processes involve teams or groups of people using other (complementary) intermediate products, such as
machinery and computers. Therefore, for the production to be efficient, machinery, computers, and all other equipment supporting
workers must be designed in a way that (a) different workers would
be able to use the same equipment, and (b) the output generated
by a certain machine would be able to be used by another worker
operating a different machine.

Consumption: People "enjoy" consuming goods that are also used by
other people. They like to watch the same movies, to exchange
books, and to listen to music of the same composers. People observe what others buy and try to match their consumption with
that of their neighbors.

Thus, we can conclude that product or brand *compatibility* affects both the productivity of workers and the welfare of consumers. In what follows, we start with some descriptive definitions. Later on in the chapter, we shall give more precise definitions.

DEFINITION 10.1

1. Brands of products are said to be **compatible**, *if they can work together, in the sense that the output of one brand can be operated or used by other brands. In this case, we say that the brands operate on the same* **standard**.

2. Brands are said to be **downward compatible** *if a newer model is compatible with an older model, but not necessarily the other way around.*

3. Consumers' preferences are said to exhibit **network externalities** *if the utility of each consumer increases with the number of other consumers purchasing the same brand.*

Examples for compatibility include products such as video and audio equipment (records and tapes), languages, railroad gauges, power supply, computer operating systems, computer software, communication equipment (the phone system, fax and telex machines, cellular and radio phones), keyboards (QWERTY versus DVORAK), and banks and automatic teller machines (ATMs).

More precisely, video tapes operate on various different standards such as VHS, Beta, and different sizes such as 8mm and VHS size. Music is recorded on LP's (long-play records), compact cassettes, and Compact Disks (CD). Cellular phones, which use airwaves instead of cables, are used in two different standards: analog or digital. The commonly used QWERTY (the first six letters on the upper row of the keyboard) English keyboard was designed so that it slows the typist, since fast typing is technically impossible on mechanical typewriters. The newer DVORAK system allows faster typing; however, people were reluctant to switch to it (see David 1985). Compatibility of automatic teller machines comes into effect when a customer carrying a bank card issued by one bank can withdraw cash from a machine servicing the clients holding a card issued by another bank. In fact, in Israel all the banks collude in the sense that any bank's card can be used on all teller machines. We will show later in this chapter that this behavior is indeed profitable to banks. Finally, extensions to the seven-bit ASCII code (the most widely used as a standard for saving and transmitting computer files) to eight-bit for the purpose of increasing the number of characters from 2^7 to 2^8

yielded several incompatible standards offered by MS-DOS, Macintosh, and other computers.

Downward compatibility is commonly observed in the software industry, where a newer version can read output files generated by the old version, but in many cases the older version cannot input files generated by the newer version.

An example for preferences exhibiting network externalities include all communication equipment. That is, it is unlikely that a person would purchase a phone knowing that nobody else uses it.

To illustrate the significance of the choice of standards on the profits of firms in a certain industry, Table 10.1 demonstrates a two-firm industry producing a product that can operate on two standards: standard α and standard β. Table 10.1 demonstrates a normal form game

		FIRM B		
		Standard α	Standard β	
FIRM A	Standard α	a	b	c	d
	Standard β	d	c	b	a

Table 10.1: Standardization game

where each firm can choose to construct its product to operate on standard α or standard β. The profits levels of the two firms are given by the nonnegative parameters a, b, c, and d, where the profit of each firm is affected by the standard choices of the two firms. We look for the Nash equilibria for this game (Definition 2.4 on page 18).

Proposition 10.1

1. If $a, b > \max\{c, d\}$, then the industry produces on a single standard, that is, (α, α) and (β, β) are Nash equilibria.

2. If $c, d > \max\{a, b\}$, then the industry produces on two different standards, that is, (α, β) and (β, α) are Nash equilibria.

Part 1 of Proposition 10.1 resembles the Battle of the Sexes game (see Table 2.2 on page 17), where the profit levels are high when the firms produce compatible brands (on the same standard). Industrywide compatibility is observed in the banking industry (ATM machines) and in many electronic appliances industries. Part 2 of the proposition demonstrates a polar case, where the firms can increase their profit by differentiating their brands and hence by constructing them to operate on different standards. Examples for this behavior include the computer industry's producing computer brands operating on different operating systems, and automobiles that are produced with model-specific parts. Thus, in this chapter we investigate firms' incentives to standardize and the effects of their choices on consumers' welfare.

There is a substantial amount of literature on compatibility issues. For a comprehensive discussion on the nature of standards see Kindleberger 1993. For literature surveys, see Farrell and Saloner 1987; David and Greenstein 1990; and Gabel 1991. Gandal 1994 provides some empirical evidence for the existence of network externalities in the computer software industry.

Our discussion of the economics of standardization is divided into three approaches: Section 10.1 (Network Externalities) analyzes an industry where consumer preferences exhibit network externalities. Section 10.2 (Supporting Services) shows that people's tendency to use products that are identical or compatible to the products purchased by others need not be explained by assuming that consumers' preferences exhibit network externalities. That is, it is possible that people will end up using compatible products even if their welfare is not directly affected by the consumption choice of other people. Section 10.3 (Components) analyzes interface compatibility of components that are to be combined into a single, usable system. Two applications of these theories are not discussed in this chapter. First, Conner and Rumelt 1991 provides an application of network externalities to explain why software firms do not always protect the software against copying. Second, an application is discussed in section 17.1, where we show that when the choice of restaurants depends on the choice of other consumers, a restaurant may refrain from raising its prices even when it faces a demand that exceeds its seating capacity.

10.1   The Network Externalities Approach

In this section we present the basic network-externality model, where consumers' valuation of a brand increases with the number of other consumers using the same brand.

10.1.1   The interdependent demand for communication services

One of the first attempts to model the aggregate demand for communication services is given in Rohlfs 1974.

The demand for phone services

Our point of departure is that the utility that a subscriber derives from a communication service increases as others join the system. Consider a group of a continuum of potential phone users indexed by x on the unit interval $[0, 1]$. Unlike the study of the Hotelling location model of subsection 7.3.1 in which we interpreted consumers indexed by a high x as consumers oriented toward brand B, and consumers indexed by a low x as consumers oriented toward brand A, here, since we have only one type of service, we interpret consumers indexed by a low x as those who love to subscribe to a phone system (high willingness to pay), and consumers indexed by a high x as those who have less desire for subscribing to a phone system (low willingness to pay).

We denote by n, $0 \leq n \leq 1$ the total number of consumers who actually subscribe to the phone system, and by p the price of subscribing to the phone system. Altogether, we define the utility of a consumer indexed by x, $0 \leq x \leq 1$, as

$$U^x = \begin{cases} n(1 - x) - p & \text{if he or she subscribes to the phone system} \\ 0 & \text{if he or she does not subscribe.} \end{cases}$$

$$(10.1)$$

Thus, the utility of each subscriber exhibits network externalities since it increases with n (the number of consumers subscribing to the phone system).

We now derive the consumers' aggregate demand for phone services. We first look at a particular consumer denoted by $\hat{x}$ who is at a given price p indifferent to the alternatives of subscribing to the phone system and not subscribing. In view of (10.1), the indifferent consumer is found by

$$0 = n(1 - \hat{x}) - p.$$

Since the number of consumers is given by $n = \hat{x}$, we have it that

$$0 = \hat{x}(1 - \hat{x}) - p \quad \text{or} \quad p = \hat{x}(1 - \hat{x}),$$

$$(10.2)$$

which is drawn in Figure 10.1. The price p_0 in Figure 10.1 intersects twice the 'flipped' U-shaped curve (at points $\hat{x}_0^L$ and $\hat{x}_0^H$). The interpretation for the two intersection points is that for a given price p_0 there can be two levels of demand: a low level, measured by $n = \hat{x}_0^L$, that is associated with a small number of subscribers, hence, by (10.1) with a low valuation by each subscriber, and therefore with a small number of users, and so forth. In contrast, at the given price p_0 there can be a high demand measured by $n = \hat{x}_0^H$, hence a high valuation by each subscriber, and therefore, a large number of subscribers, and so forth. However, only point $\hat{x}_0^H$ is a stable demand equilibrium, since at the intersection point $\hat{x}_0^L$ a small increase in the number of subscribers would make the phone subscription more desirable, thereby causing all the consumers indexed on $[\hat{x}_0^L, \hat{x}_0^H]$ to subscribe.

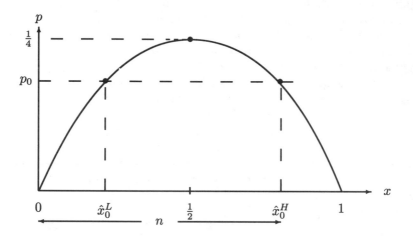

Figure 10.1: Deriving the demand for telecommunication services

The point $\hat{x}_0^L$ is defined in the literature as the *critical mass* for a given price p_0 to indicate that at a given price, any increase in the number of subscribers would shift the demand (number of subscribers) to the point $\hat{x}_0^H$.

The problem of the monopoly phone company

Now suppose that there is only one monopoly firm providing phone services, and suppose that the marginal cost of adding a subscriber is negligible, after the PTT (Public Telephone and Telegraph) company has already wired all the houses. We now ask what price maximizes the PTT's profit (equals revenue in our case)? To solve this problem, we formulate the PTT's profit-maximization problem, which is to choose $\hat{x}$ that solves

$$\max_{\hat{x}} \pi(\hat{x}) \equiv p(\hat{x})\hat{x} = \hat{x}(1 - \hat{x})\hat{x} = (\hat{x})^2(1 - \hat{x}). \qquad (10.3)$$

The profit function (10.3) is drawn in Figure 10.2. The first- and second-order conditions for (10.3) are given by

$$0 = \frac{\partial \pi}{\partial x} = 2x - 3x^2 \quad \text{and} \quad \frac{\partial^2 \pi}{\partial x^2} = 2 - 6x. \qquad (10.4)$$

Now, equation (10.4) and Figure 10.2 completely describe how the profit level is affected by changing the number of subscribers. Clearly, the profit is zero when there are no subscribers ($\hat{x} = 0$). The profit is

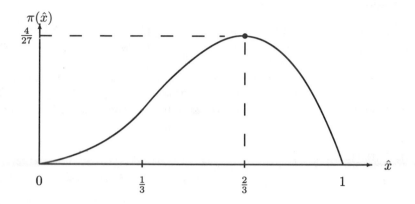

Figure 10.2: The PTT profit function in the presence of network externalities

also zero when the entire population subscribes, since in order to have the entire population subscribing, the PTT should set the price to zero.

The first-order condition shows that $\hat{x} = 0$ and $\hat{x} = 2/3$ are extremum points. In addition, the second-order condition shows that the second derivative is negative for $\hat{x} > 1/3$, implying that $\hat{x} = 2/3$ is a local maximum point. Since the first-order condition is positive for all $0 < \hat{x} < 2/3$, it must be that $\hat{x} = 2/3$ is a global maximum point. Hence,

Proposition 10.2 *A monopoly phone company's profit-maximizing subscription price is set such that the number of subscribers exceeds half of the consumer population but is less than the entire population.*

10.1.2   The standardization-variety tradeoff

In the previous subsection we confined the analysis to a single service. In this subsection we develop a different model in which we assume that there are two brands of the product and heterogeneous consumers, in the sense that each consumer prefers one brand over the other. There are two firms, each producing a different brand, brand A and brand B.

We assume a continuum of consumers, normalize the population size to 1, and assume that a $(0 < a < 1)$ consumers prefer brand A over brand B, whereas b $(0 < b < 1)$ consumers prefer brand B over brand A, where $a + b = 1$.

The Farrell and Saloner (1986) model assumes that the utility of each consumer type increases with the number of consumers buying the same brand. However, if a consumer purchases the less desired brand, his utility falls by $\delta > 0$. Formally, the utility functions of types A and

B consumers are given by

$$U^A = \begin{cases} x_A & \text{buys brand } A \\ x_B - \delta & \text{buys brand } B \end{cases} \qquad U^B = \begin{cases} x_A - \delta & \text{buys brand } A \\ x_B & \text{buys brand } B \end{cases}$$

(10.5)

where x_A denotes the number of consumers purchasing brand A and x_B denotes the number of consumers purchasing brand B, $x_A + x_B = 1$. The parameter δ also reflects the extra amount of money that a consumer is willing to pay to get his or her ideal brand.

DEFINITION 10.2

1. If $x_A = 1$ and $x_B = 0$, we say that the product is standardized on A.

2. If $x_A = 0$ and $x_B = 1$, we say that the product is standardized on B.

3. If $x_A > 0$ and $x_B > 0$, we say that the product is produced with incompatible standards.

4. An allocation of buyers between brands x_A and x_B is called an equilibrium, if no single buyer would benefit from switching to the competing brand, given that all other consumers do not switch from their adopted brand.

Equilibrium adoption of brands

We first seek necessary conditions for a single standard to be an equilibrium. Observe that in the following analysis, since we assume a continuum of consumers, each consumer is negligible in the sense that if a single consumer switches from buying brand A to buying brand B, then it will not affect the aggregate the number of A and B users measured by x_A and x_B. Now, if the industry is standardized on A ($x_A = 1$), then it must be that type B consumers would not benefit from switching from A to B, implying that $1 - \delta > 0$. That is, a consumer prefers to consume the same brand as the others rather than consuming alone his or her most preferred brand (i.e., if the network effect dominates the ideal good effect). Therefore,

Proposition 10.3

1. If $\delta < 1$, then two equilibria exist: one in which A is the standard ($x_A = 1$) and one in which B is the standard ($x_B = 1$).

2. If $\delta > 1$, no single-standard equilibrium exists.

We now investigate under what conditions the industry will produce two incompatible brands, that is, under what conditions $x_A = a$ and $x_B = b$ is an equilibrium. In this equilibrium, a type A consumer would not switch to B if $a > b - \delta$. Since $b = 1 - a$, we have it that $a > \frac{1-\delta}{2}$. Similarly, type B would not switch if $b > \frac{1-\delta}{2}$. Hence,

Proposition 10.4 *If the number of each type of consumers is sufficiently large, then there exists a two-standard equilibrium. Formally, if $a, b > \frac{1-\delta}{2}$, then $x_A = a$, $x_B = b$ is an equilibrium.*

Figure 10.3 illustrates the parameter range for which the two-standard equilibrium exists. As the utility loss from consuming the less preferred

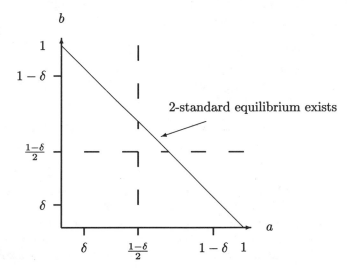

Figure 10.3: Two-standard (incompatibility) equilibrium

brand parameter δ increases, the parameter range for which incompatibility is an equilibrium increases. That is, if $\delta \geq 1$, a two-standard equilibrium always exists.

Efficiency of brand adoption

We define the economy's social welfare function as the sum of consumers' utilities. Formally, let $W \equiv aU^A + bU^B$. In view of the three possible outcomes described above, we have it that

$$W = \begin{cases} a + b(1 - \delta) & \text{if } A \text{ is the standard} \\ a^2 + b^2 & \text{if there are incompatible standards} \\ a(1 - \delta) + b & \text{if } B \text{ is the standard.} \end{cases} \quad (10.6)$$

Comparing these social welfare levels yields

Proposition 10.5 *If there are more consumers oriented toward brand A than there are consumers oriented toward brand B (a > b), then standardization on A is socially preferred to standardization on B.*

We now ask under what condition the incompatibility equilibrium outcome is socially preferred to a single-brand standardization. It follows from (10.6) that incompatibility is preferred over standardization on A, if $a^2 + b^2 > a + b - b\delta = 1 - b\delta$, or $\delta > \frac{1-a^2-b^2}{b}$. Using the fact that $b = 1-a$, we see that this last condition is equivalent to $\delta > 2a$, or $a < \frac{\delta}{2}$. Similarly, incompatibility is socially preferred over standardization on B if $b < \frac{\delta}{2}$. However, these conditions cannot both hold if $\delta < 1$ since in this case $a + b < \frac{\delta}{2} + \frac{\delta}{2} < 1$. Hence,

Proposition 10.6

1. *If the network preference effect is strong relative to the disutility from consuming the less preferred brand ($\delta < 1$), then the incompatibility equilibrium is socially inefficient.*

2. *If $\delta > 1$, incompatibility is socially optimal if $a < \frac{\delta}{2}$ and $b < \frac{\delta}{2}$.*

Is there a market failure?

We first ask whether standardization on a single-brand equilibrium may not be socially desirable. Proposition 10.3 shows that as long as $\delta < 1$, there are two equilibria in which the industry produces on a single standard. However, (10.6) implies that if there are more consumers oriented toward A, standardization on A socially dominates standardization on B. Hence,

Proposition 10.7 *An equilibrium in which the industry standardizes on the less socially preferred brand exists.*

However, note that in this case there is also a good equilibrium where the industry's standard is the more popular brand, so one can assume that with a minor coordination, consumers can choose the socially preferred standard.

How can it happen that an industry specializes on the wrong brand? Consider a dynamic scenario (which is not analyzed in this section) such that $a > b$ and brand B exists in the market before brand A attempts to enter the market. In this case, the firm producing brand A will not be able to enter the market. In the literature, this situation is generally described as a case where the existence of an *installed base* (brand B) has prevented the emergence of the more popular brand A.

We now seek to investigate whether a market failure can occur under the incompatibility equilibrium. Let us take an example: $a = b = 0.5$ and $\delta = 0.6$. Proposition 10.4 implies that incompatibility is an equilibrium since $1/2 > (1 - 0.6)/2 = 0.2$. However, since $\delta = 0.6 < 1$, Proposition 10.6 implies that incompatibility is inefficient. Hence,

Proposition 10.8 *An equilibrium in which the industry produces two incompatible brands need not be socially efficient.*

Finally, the opposite of Proposition 10.8 holds:

Proposition 10.9 *If incompatibility ($x_A = a$ and $x_B = b$) is efficient, then the incompatibility equilibrium exists and is unique.*

Proof. If incompatibility is efficient, then part 1 of Proposition 10.6 implies that $\delta > 1$. Since $a > 0$ and $b > 0$, Proposition 10.4 implies that incompatibility is an equilibrium. Also, Proposition 10.3 implies that an equilibrium where an industry is standardized on a single standard does not exist. ∎

10.2 The Supporting Services Approach

The analysis of the previous section was based on the assumption that consumers' value for a product increases when other consumers purchase a compatible or an identical brand. However, despite the fact that the network-externalities assumption is intuitive and appealing for modeling products such as telecommunication systems, where the utility of each consumer is directly related to the network size, the models themselves do not explain why people behave this way. So the remaining question is whether "network effects" can prevail even without assuming that consumers' preferences exhibit network externalities.

We therefore turn now to models describing consumers who do not derive satisfaction from the consumption of other consumers. Instead, consumers gain satisfaction from the product itself and the variety of (brand-specific) complementary products that we call *supporting services*. The literature utilizing this approach includes Chou and Shy 1990, 1993, and 1996, and Church and Gandal 1992a,b, 1993. In many instances, supporting services are incompatible across brands. For examples, most software packages are designed to operate on one operating system (such as UNIX, DOS, Macintosh, OS, etc.) and do not operate on the other operating systems. Videotapes recorded on the NTSC television system (used in North America and Japan) cannot be played in Europe or in the Middle East, where the dominant television standard is PAL. For a discussion of the newly emerging high-definition television standards see Farrell and Shapiro 1992 and the references therein.

10.2.1   Network effects without network externalities

Consider consumers who can freely choose between two computer brands named brand A (short for Artichoke computers) and brand B (short for Banana computers). Each consumer is endowed with Y dollars to be spent on one unit of hardware and the variety of software written for the specific hardware purchased. We denote by p_i the price of computer brand i, $i = A, B$. Hence, given a total budget of Y, a consumer purchasing brand i spends $E_i \equiv Y - p_i$ on i's specific software.

We denote by N_i the total number of software packages that can be run on an i machine. The utility of a consumer purchasing system i is defined as an increasing function of the number of software packages compatible with machine i, $i = A, B$. Consumers are uniformly indexed by δ on the interval $[0, 1]$ according to their relative preference towards computer brand B. We define the utility of a consumer type δ as

$$U^\delta \equiv \begin{cases} (1 - \delta)\sqrt{N_A} & \text{if she is an } A\text{-user} \\ \delta\sqrt{N_B} & \text{if she is a } B\text{-user.} \end{cases} \tag{10.7}$$

Thus, the utility function (10.7) describes preferences exhibiting "love for variety" of software. That is, a consumer's preferences toward a specific brand are affected by a fixed parameter, (δ or $(1 - \delta)$), and by the number of software packages available for each brand, (N_A and N_B). Figure 10.4 illustrates how consumers are distributed according to their preferences toward the two brands.

$\longleftarrow$ more A-oriented   more B-oriented $\longrightarrow$

0                                  $\hat{\delta}$ 1

Figure 10.4: Consumers' distribution of tastes

The consumer who is indifferent to the choice between system A and system B is denoted by $\hat{\delta}$, which is found from (10.7) by solving

$$(1 - \hat{\delta})\sqrt{N_A} = \hat{\delta}\sqrt{N_B}. \tag{10.8}$$

Thus, in equilibrium, a consumer indexed by $\delta < \hat{\delta}$ is an A-user whereas a consumer indexed by $\delta > \hat{\delta}$ is a B-user. The total number of A-users is denoted by $\delta_A \equiv \hat{\delta}$, and the total number of B-users is given by $\delta_B \equiv (1 - \hat{\delta})$. Altogether,

$$\frac{\delta_B}{\delta_A} = \frac{1 - \hat{\delta}}{\hat{\delta}} = \sqrt{\frac{N_B}{N_A}}. \tag{10.9}$$

Hence,

Proposition 10.10 *The brand with the higher market share is supported by a larger variety of software. Formally, $\delta_A \geq \delta_B$ if and only if $N_A \geq N_B$.*

Proposition 10.10 confirms widely observed phenomena, for example, the Intel-based machines (PCs) have the largest market share and are supported by the largest variety of software compared to machines based on other chips.

The software industry

We have not yet discussed how the variety (number) of each brand-specific software is being determined in each software industry. Instead of fully modeling the software industry, we conjecture that the number of software packages supporting each machine should be proportional to the aggregate amount of money spent on each type of software. We therefore make the following assumption:

ASSUMPTION 10.1 *The number of software packages (variety) supporting each brand is proportional to the aggregate expenditure of the consumers purchasing the brand-specific software. Formally,*

$$N_A = \hat{\delta}E_A = \hat{\delta}(Y - p_A) \quad and \quad N_B = (1 - \hat{\delta})E_B = (1 - \hat{\delta})(Y - p_B).$$

Substituting into (10.9) yields

$$\hat{\delta} = \frac{E_A}{E_A + E_B} = \frac{Y - p_A}{2Y - p_A - p_B}. \tag{10.10}$$

Network effects

The following proposition (part 4 in particular) demonstrates how network effects can prevail without assuming network externalities.

Proposition 10.11 *An increase in the price of hardware A (p_A) will*

1. *decrease the number of A-users (δ_A decreases);*

2. *increase the number of B-users (δ_B increases);*

3. *decrease the variety of software written for the A machine (N_A decreases) and increase the variety of B-software (N_B increases); and*

4. decrease the welfare of A-users and increase the welfare of B-users.

Proof. Part 1 follows from (10.10) since $\partial \hat{\delta}/\partial p_A < 0$. Part 2 immediately follows since $\delta_B = 1 - \delta_A$. Part 3 follows from Assumption 10.1 since as $\hat{\delta}$ decreases and p_A increases, it is implied that N_A must decrease while N_B must increase. Part 4 follows from (10.7), since a decrease in N_A decreases the utility of an A-user, whereas an increase in N_B increases the utility of a B-user.   ∎

When p_A increases, Assumption 10.1 implies that two factors exist that cause a reduction in the variety of A-software: First, the direct effect ($Y - p_A$ decreases), that is, A-users spend more on hardware and therefore less on software; and second, the indirect effect via a reduction in the number of A-users ($\hat{\delta}$ decreases). Assumption 10.1 also implies that N_B increases since there are more B-users.

Part 3 of Proposition 10.11 demonstrates the network effect generated by an increase in hardware price p_A on the welfare of B-users as follows:

$$p_A \uparrow \Longrightarrow \delta_A \downarrow \Longrightarrow \delta_B \uparrow \Longrightarrow N_B \uparrow \Longrightarrow U^{B-user} \uparrow.$$

That is, a decrease in the number of A-users causes an increase in the number of B-users, which in turn increases the variety of B-software, which increases the welfare and number of B-users, and so on.

10.2.2   Partial compatibility

Note that 100 percent compatibility is never observed. For example, you have probably noticed that sometimes you fail to transmit a fax to a remote fax machine because the other machine does not fully respond to all standards. You have probably also noticed that some record and tape players are not rotating at the same speed. Also, even when the manufacturer asserts that his computer (say) is DOS compatible, there are always some packages of software that can operate on one machine, but "refuse" to operate on another. In that sense, 100 percent compatibility is actually never observed.

Perhaps the main advantage of using the supporting-services approach to model network behavior is that it allows an easy interpretation for modeling the concept of partial compatibility.

DEFINITION 10.3 *A computer brand i is said to be* **partially compatible** *with a ρ_i ($0 \leq \rho_i \leq 1$) degree of compatibility with computer brand j if a fraction ρ_i of the total software written specifically for brand j can also be run on computer brand i.*

It should be pointed out that Definition 10.3 does not imply that compatibility is a symmetric relation. In other words, it is possible that a computer of a certain brand is designed to be able to read software developed for rival machines, but the rival machines are not designed to read software not specifically designed for them. In the extreme case, in which $\rho_i = 1$ but $\rho_j = 0$ (machine i can read j software, but machine j cannot read i software), we say that the machines are *one-way compatible*.

The number of software packages written specifically for machine i is denoted by n_i, $i = A, B$. The main feature of this model is that the machines can be partially compatible in the sense that in addition to its own software, each machine can also run a selected number of software packages written for its rival machine. That is, ρ_i measures the proportion of machine j software that can be run on an i machine, $i, j = A, B$ and $i \neq j$. Therefore, the total number of software packages available to an i-machine user is equal to

$$N_A = n_A + \rho_A n_B \quad \text{and} \quad N_B = n_B + \rho_B n_A. \tag{10.11}$$

We will not develop the complete model. The complete computer and software industry equilibrium is developed in Chou and Shy 1993. Instead, in what follows we merely illustrate the main insights of this model.

Suppose that the software industry produces a positive variety of both types of software. That is, $n_A > 0$ and $n_B > 0$. Now, for the sake of illustration, let N_A and N_B be kept constants. Figure 10.5 shows the equilibrium n_A and n_B levels associated with the given N_A and N_B.

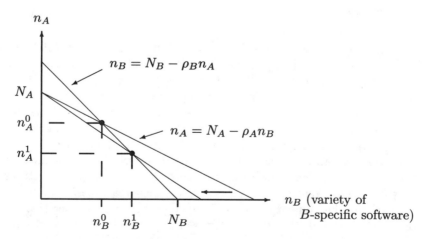

Figure 10.5: Equilibrium variety of brand-specific software

The line N_A shows the combinations of brand-specific software n_A and the rival brand-specific software n_B associated with a constant level N_A of A-usable software available to A-users, for a given level of compatibility ρ_A. Similarly, the line N_B shows all the n_A and n_B combinations associated with a constant level of B-usable software N_B. The point $\langle n_A^0, n_B^0 \rangle$ is the equilibrium variety of software written specifically for A and B machines.

Now, suppose that the producer of computer A makes its machine more compatible with B software (i.e., ρ_A increases). Hence, the line N_A tilts to the left because in order to keep the number of A-usable software at a constant level there is less need for A-specific software (since A-users can use more of B-software). Therefore, the new software-variety equilibrium is now given at the point $\langle n_A^1, n_B^1 \rangle$ in Figure 10.5. Consequently,

Proposition 10.12 *When there are two software industries, each producing brand-specific software, an increase in the degree of compatibility of the A-machine with the software written for the B-machine,*

1. *will reduce the variety of software specifically written for the A-machine (n_A decreases);*

2. *will increase the variety of software specifically written for the B-machine (n_B increases); and*

3. *will reduce the total variety of software available to A-users and will increase the total variety of software available to B-users (N_A decreases and N_B increases).*

The last part of the Proposition is proved in Chou and Shy 1993. The significance of the proposition (which was actually known to many computer makers a long time before it was known to economists) is that it shows that a computer manufacturer may refrain from making its machine more compatible with the software supporting the rival machine because compatibility with the rival machine's software will induce software writers to write more software for the rival machine (since part of it is usable for both machines), thereby making the rival machine more attractive to consumers. This result explains why computer manufacturers may choose different operating systems for their machines.

It should be pointed out that there could be reasons other than the one in Proposition 10.12 for why firms make their brand less compatible with other brands. For example, in subsection 12.2.2 we show other cases in which firms choose to differentiate themselves from other firms by producing products of different quality.

10.3   The Components Approach

In the previous sections we introduced two approaches to the economics of networks: (a) the network-externality approach, where a consumer's valuation of a certain brand is affected by the number of consumers purchasing a similar or an identical brand, and (b) the supporting-services approach, where a consumer's valuation of a brand is affected by the number of supporting services (supporting software) supporting the specific brand.

The components approach discussed in this section is similar to the supporting services approach in two aspects: First, it does not assume that consumers' preferences exhibit a consumption externality; second, it assumes complementarity, in the sense that just as computers yield no utility without the supporting software, the basic computer component does not yield utility without a complementary monitor component.

10.3.1   The basic model

The components models were first introduced in Matutes and Regibeau 1988 and Economides 1989.

The product

Consider a product that can be decomposed into two (perfect complements) components. For example, a computer system can be decomposed into a basic unit and a monitor. The basic unit and the monitor are perfect complements since a consumer cannot use one component without using the other. Another example is a stereo system, which is generally decomposed into an amplifier and speakers.

We denote the first component (the basic unit) by X and the second component (the monitor) by Y.

Firms and Compatibility

There are two firms capable of producing both components, which can be assembled into systems. We denote by X_A the first component produced by firm A, and by Y_A the second component produced by firm A. Similarly, firm B produces components X_B and Y_B. With no loss of generality, we simplify by assuming that production is costless.

Turning to compatibility, we can readily see that since the components are perfect complements, each consumer must purchase one unit of X with one unit of Y. The question of compatibility here is whether a consumer can combine components from different manufacturers when he or she purchases and assembles the system. Formally,

DEFINITION 10.4

1. *The components are said to be* **incompatible** *if the components produced by different manufacturers cannot be assembled into systems. That is, systems $X_A Y_B$ and $X_B Y_A$ do not exist in the market.*

2. *The components are said to be* **compatible** *if components produced by different manufacturers can be assembled into systems. That is, $X_A Y_B$ and $X_B Y_A$ are available in the market.*

Consumers

There are three consumers, denoted by AA, AB, and BB, with heterogeneous preferences toward systems. We denote by p_i^x and p_i^y the price of component X and component Y produced by firm i, respectively, $i = A, B$.

Each consumer has an ideal combination of components. That is, if $p_A^x = p_B^x$ and $p_A^y = p_B^y$, then consumer AA would always choose system $X_A Y_A$ over $X_B Y_B$, consumer BB would choose system $X_B Y_B$ over $X_A Y_A$, and if the systems are compatible (see Definition 10.4), then consumer AB would choose system $X_A Y_B$.

A consumer who purchases system $X_i Y_j$ would pay a total price of $p_i^x + p_j^y$ for this system, $i, j = A, B$. We denote by U_{ij} the utility level of consumer ij, whose ideal system is $X_i Y_j$, $ij \in \{AA, AB, BB\}$, and assume that for $\lambda > 0$

$$
U_{ij} \equiv
\begin{cases}
2\lambda - (p_i^x + p_j^y) & \text{if purchasing system } X_i Y_j \\
\lambda - (p_j^x + p_j^y) & \text{if purchasing system } X_j Y_j \\
\lambda - (p_i^x + p_i^y) & \text{if purchasing system } X_i Y_i \\
-(p_j^x + p_i^y) & \text{if purchasing system } X_j Y_i \\
0 & \text{if does not purchase any system.}
\end{cases}
\tag{10.12}
$$

Thus, in this simple model each consumer has a different ideal system (under equal prices). The utility function (10.12) shows that a consumer purchasing his ideal system gains a (net of prices) utility level of 2λ. If the system he buys has one component from his ideal system and one component from his less preferred system, his (net of prices) utility level is reduced by λ. Finally, a consumer who purchases a system in which both components are produced by his less preferred manufacturer has a (net of prices) utility level of 0. Clearly, given the threshold utility level of 0, no system will be purchased unless its total cost is lower than 2λ.

10.3.2 Incompatible systems

Suppose that the components produced by different manufacturers are incompatible (see Definition 10.4), so that only two systems are produced: system $X_A Y_A$ and system $X_B Y_B$. We denote by q_i the number of systems sold by firm i, and by p_i the price of system i (both components), $i = A, B$. That is, the price of system $X_A Y_A$ is $p_A \equiv p_A^x + p_A^y$ and the price of system $X_B Y_B$ is $p_B \equiv p_B^x + p_B^y$. Thus, the profit function of firm i is $\pi_i = p_i q_i$, $i = A, B$. We look for a Nash-Bertrand equilibrium in prices. Formally,

DEFINITION 10.5 *An incompatible-components equilibrium is a pair of price p_A^I and p_B^I, a pair of quantities q_A^I and q_B^I such that for a given p_j^I, firm i chooses p_i^I to $\max_{p_i} \pi_i(p_i, p_j^I)$ s.t. q_i = number of consumers maximizing (10.12) by choosing system i $(i, j = A, B, i \neq j)$.*

Before characterizing the equilibria we can show that

Lemma 10.1 *There does not exist an equilibrium where one firm sells to all consumers.*

Proof. If firm A sells to all customers, then it must set $p_A = 0$. But even at this price, if for $\epsilon > 0$ sufficiently small, firm B sets $p_B = \epsilon$, consumer BB would purchase system $X_B Y_B$. ∎

What Lemma 10.1 tells us is that if an equilibrium exists, then it must be that one firm sells to two consumers, while the other sells to one. Therefore,

Proposition 10.13 *There exist three equilibria:*
In one equilibrium firm A sells system $X_A Y_A$ to consumers AA and AB while firm B sells system $X_B Y_B$ to consumer BB. In this equilibrium, $p_A^I = \lambda$, $q_A^I = 2$, $p_B^I = 2\lambda$, $q_B^I = 1$.
In the second equilibrium, firm B sells system $X_B Y_B$ to consumers BB and AB while firm A sells system $X_A Y_A$ to consumer AA. In the second equilibrium, $p_A^I = 2\lambda$, $q_A^I = 1$, $p_B^I = \lambda$, $q_B^I = 2$.
In the third equilibrium, firm A sells system $X_A Y_A$ to consumer AA, firm B sells system $X_B Y_B$ to consumer BB, and consumer AB is not served. In this equilibrium, $p_A^I = p_B^I = 2\lambda$ and $q_A^I = q_B^I = 1$.
In any equilibrium the firms' profit levels are given by $\pi_A^I = \pi_B^I = 2\lambda$.

Proof. Since the first two equilibria are symmetric, it is sufficient to look at the first equilibrium. We have to show that firm A cannot increase its profit by reducing its price to a level at which it would sell to all three consumers (undercutting firm B). That is,

$$\pi_A^I = 2p_A^I \geq 3(p_B^I - 2\lambda). \qquad (10.13)$$

Similarly, we have to show that firm B cannot increase its profit by reducing its price p_B to p_A where it would sell to two consumers BB and AB.

$$\pi_B^I = p_B^I \geq 2p_A^I. \tag{10.14}$$

In fact, one should also check a third possibility in which firm B deviates by reducing the price to a level where all the three consumers purchase system $X_B Y_B$. However, such a deviation is not profitable since firm B has to set $p_B = p_A^I - 2\lambda = \lambda - 2\lambda < 0$.

First, note that our candidate equilibrium prices satisfy equations (10.13) and (10.14), so no firm would find it profitable to reduce its price.

Second, no firm could profitably deviate by raising its price since if firm B raises its price above 2λ, consumer BB will not purchase system $X_B Y_B$. Similarly, if firm A raises its price above λ, consumer AB will not purchase any system.

We still have to show that consumers AA, AB, and BA maximize their utility(10.12) by choosing system AA and that consumer BB maximizes utility by choosing system $X_B Y_B$. To do that, we need to calculate the equilibrium utility levels of all customers. Thus, in equilibrium we have it that

$$U_{AA}^I = 2\lambda - p_A^I = \lambda; \quad U_{BB}^I = 2\lambda - p_B^I = 0; \quad U_{AB}^I = \lambda - \lambda = 0. \tag{10.15}$$

It is easy to verify that consumer AA would not purchase system BB since system BB would yield a utility level of $-p_B = -2\lambda < U_{AA}^I$. Similarly, consumer BB would not purchase system AA since system AA would yield a utility level of $-p_A = -\lambda < U_{BB}^I$. Also, consumer AB would not purchase system BB since $p_B^I > p_A^I$, and both yield a (net of prices) utility level of λ.

Finally, to show that $p_A^I = p_B^I = 2\lambda$ constitute (the third) equilibrium, note that if, say, firm A reduces its price to $p_A = \lambda$, consumer AB buys system AA, and we have the first equilibrium. Since in all equilibria, firm A's profit level is $\pi_A^I = 2\lambda$, a deviation will not occur. ∎

We define the consumer surplus as the sum of consumers' utilities. Hence,

$$CS^I \equiv U_{AA}^I + U_{BB}^I + U_{AB}^I = \lambda. \tag{10.16}$$

We define the economy's welfare as the sum of firms' profit levels and consumer surplus. Thus,

$$W^I \equiv \pi_A^I + \pi_B^I + CS^I = 2p_A^I + p_B^I + CS^I = 2\lambda + 2\lambda + \lambda = 5\lambda. \tag{10.17}$$

The equilibrium social-welfare level given in (10.17) is simply the sum of the (net of prices) utility levels of all the consumers, which equals twice 2λ for consumers AA and BB, who consume their ideal systems, and λ for consumer AB, who purchases the system $X_A Y_A$ but whose ideal Y component is Y_B.

10.3.3 Compatible systems

When firms design their components to be compatible with components produced by the rival firm, two more systems become available to consumers: system $X_A Y_B$ and system $X_B Y_A$. We look for an equilibrium where each consumer buys (assembles) his ideal system. In this equilibrium, each firm i sells two units of component X_i and two units of component Y_i, $i = A, B$.

DEFINITION 10.6 *A compatible components equilibrium is the set of component prices $p_A^x, p_A^y, p_B^x, p_B^y$ and quantities of components sold by each firm $q_A^x, q_A^y, q_B^x, q_B^y$ such that for given p_j^x and p_j^y, firm i chooses p_i^x and p_i^y to max $\pi_i(p_i^x, p_i^y, p_j^x, p_j^y)$ s.t. q_i^x and q_i^y are the number of consumers maximizing (10.12) by choosing components X_i, Y_i, respectively.*

Proposition 10.14 *There exists an equilibrium where each consumer purchases his ideal system. In this equilibrium all components are equally priced at $p_A^x = p_A^y = p_B^x = p_B^y = \lambda$, and a firm's profit levels are $\pi_A^c = \pi_B^c = 3\lambda$.*

Proof. Since firm A sells two components of X and one component of Y, while firm B sells two components of Y and one component of X, equilibrium prices should be at levels so that firms could not profitably reduce the price of one component in order to sell this component to additional customers. For example, in equilibrium, firm A sells component X_A to consumers AA, and AB. Reducing the price of Y_A to $p_B^y - \lambda$ would induce consumer BB to buy component Y from firm A (note that in order to attract consumers from the competing firms, the price reduction should be at least λ). However, reducing a component price to zero cannot constitute a profit-maximizing deviation. By symmetry, firm B will not find it profitable to reduce its price to $p_A^x - \lambda = 0$.

Finally, since all prices are equal each consumer purchases his ideal brand, yielding equilibrium utility levels of

$$u_{AA}^c = u_{AB}^c = u_{BB}^c = 2\lambda - \lambda - \lambda = 0. \tag{10.18}$$

For this reason, no firm would find it profitable to increase a component's price since each consumer would not pay more than 2λ for a system. ∎

Hence, when all components are compatible, the (aggregate) consumer surplus, firms' profit levels, and the social welfare level are given by

$$CS^c = 0; \quad \pi_A^c = \pi_B^c = 3\lambda; \quad W^c \equiv \pi_A^c + \pi_B^c + CS^c = 6\lambda. \quad (10.19)$$

Like equation (10.17), equation (10.19) demonstrates that the social welfare is the sum of the (net of prices) utility levels.

10.3.4 Compatibility versus incompatibility

We now wish to examine the effects of components compatibility on firms' profit and consumers' utility levels, aggregate consumers' surplus, and the social welfare. Comparing (10.15) with (10.18) yields

Proposition 10.15 *Consumers are never better off when the firms produce compatible components than when firms produce incompatible components.*

However, comparing Propositions 10.13 with 10.14 yields

Proposition 10.16 *All firms make higher profits when they produce compatible components than when they produce incompatible components.*

Also, comparing (10.17) with (10.19) yields

Proposition 10.17 *Social welfare is higher when firms produce compatible components.*

In order to explain Proposition 10.15 we need to compare the systems' prices under the compatibility and incompatibility regimes (given in Propositions 10.13 and 10.14). Under the incompatibility regime, two consumers pay each λ for the system they buy. Under compatibility, each consumer pays 2λ for each system. Hence, total consumer expenditure under compatibility exceeds the expenditure under incompatibility by 2λ, but the (net of prices) utility level of consumer AB (the "mixing" consumer) rises by only λ. Thus, firms extract a surplus that exceeds the aggregate utility gains from compatibility, thereby reducing aggregate consumer surplus under the compatibility regime.

Proposition 10.16 can be explained by the following: First, under compatibility the mixing consumer is willing to pay more because he can now buy his ideal system. Second, compatibility reduces price competition between the component-producing firms since under incompatibility both firms are forced to lower the price of their system in order to attract the mixing consumer to choose their systems, given that the systems are not ideal for this consumer. This competition is relaxed when the components are compatible.

Finally, Proposition 10.17 shows that the welfare gains derived from having firms increase their profits by making their components compatible exceeds the welfare loss to consumers from the high component prices under compatibility.

10.3.5   How firms design their components

Proposition 10.16 shows that firms collect higher profits when all components are compatible with the components produced by the rival firms than they collect when firms produce incompatible components. We now ask whether an outcome where both firms choose to produce compatible components can be realized as an equilibrium for game in which firms choose both prices and the design of the components.

Consider a two-stage game where in period 1 firms choose whether to design their components to be compatible with the components produced by the rival firm. In period 2, given the design of the components, firms compete in prices, as described in subsections 10.3.2 and 10.3.3.

The subgame perfect equilibrium for this game turns out to be very simple because the compatibility decision by one firm forces an externality on the rival firm, in the sense that the compatibility of components is a symmetric relation, meaning that if component X_A is compatible with component Y_B, then component Y_B is compatible with component X_A. In other words, the market effect of having firm A make its X_A component compatible with component Y_B is equivalent to having firm B make its Y_B component compatible with X_A. Similarly, the outcome in which firm B makes its X_B component compatible with firm A's Y_A component is equivalent to firm A's making its Y_A component compatible with B's X_B component. It is important to note that this externality is a feature of the component approach discussed here, but it does not occur in the supporting-services approach (see Definition 10.3). That is, in the supporting-services approach we can have it that machine A reads B's software, but not the other way around.

Thus, given this externality feature of the components approach, it is sufficient for one firm to decide on compatibility to produce a market outcome identical to that which would result from both firms deciding on compatibility. Therefore, Proposition 10.16 implies that

Proposition 10.18 *In the two-stage game, a subgame perfect equilibrium yields compatible components.*

10.4 Exercises

1. Consider the supporting-services approach model developed in subsection 10.2.

    (a) For a given hardware price of brand A, p_A, what is the price of computer B beyond which firm B would have a zero market share?

    (b) Suppose that $p_A > p_B$, and suppose that the income of each consumer doubles to $2Y$, while hardware prices remain unchanged. Calculate the effect this increase in incomes on (i) the market shares (δ_A and δ_B), and on (ii) the ratio of the number of software packages written for computer A to the number of software packages written for computer B.

2. Consider the component approach analyzed in subsection 10.3, but assume that there are four consumers: consumer AA, consumer BB, consumer AB, and consumer BA.

    (a) If the components are incompatible, prove that no Nash-Bertrand equilibrium in system prices p_A and p_B (as defined in Definition 10.5) exists.

    (b) If the components are compatible, calculate the symmetric equilibrium prices of all components, firms' profit levels, and consumers' surplus.

10.5 References

Chou, C., and O. Shy. 1990. "Network Effects without Network Externalities." *International Journal of Industrial Organization* 8: 259–270.

Chou, C., and O. Shy. 1993. "Partial Compatibility and Supporting Services." *Economics Letters* 41: 193–197.

Chou, C., and O. Shy. 1996. "Do Consumers Gain or Lose When More People Buy the Same Brand?" *European Journal of Political Economy* 12: 309–330.

Church, J., and N. Gandal. 1992a. "Integration, Complementary Products and Variety." *Journal of Economics and management Strategy* 1: 651–676.

Church, J., and N. Gandal. 1992b. "Network Effects, Software Provision, and Standardization." *Journal of Industrial Economics* 40: 85–104.

Church, J., and N. Gandal. 1993. "Complementary Network Externalities and Technological Adoption." *International Journal of Industrial Organization* 11: 239–260.

Conner, K., and R. Rumelt. 1991. "Software Piracy: An Analysis of Protection Strategies." *Management Science* 37: 125–139.

David, P. 1985. "Clio and the Economics of QWERTY." *American Economic Review* 75: 332–336.

David, P., and S. Greenstein. 1990. "The Economics of Compatibility Standards: An Introduction to Recent Research." *Economics of Innovation and New Technology* 1: 3–42.

Economides, N. 1989. "Desirability of Compatibility in the Absence of Network Externalities." *American Economic Review* 79: 1165–1181.

Farrell, J., and G. Saloner. 1986. "Standardization and Variety." *Economics Letters* 20: 71–74.

Farrell, J., and G. Saloner. 1987. "The Economics of Horses, Penguins, and Lemmings." In *Production Standardization and Competitive Strategies,* edited by L. G. Gable. Amsterdam: North-Holland.

Farrell, J., and C. Shapiro. 1992. "Standard Setting in High-Definition Television." *Brookings Papers on Economic Activity: Microeconomics,* 1–93.

Gabel, L. 1991. *Competitive Strategies for Product Standards.* London: McGraw Hill.

Gandal, N. 1994. "Hedonic Price Indexes for Spreadsheets and an Empirical Test of Network Externalities." *RAND Journal of Economics* 25: 160–170.

Katz, M., and C. Shapiro. 1985. "Network Externalities, Competition, and Compatibility." *American Economic Review* 75: 424–440.

Katz, M., and C. Shapiro. 1986. "Technology Adoption in the Presence of Network Externalities." *Journal of Political Economy* 94: 822–841.

Kindleberger, C. 1983. "Standards as Public, Collective and Private Goods." *KYKLOS* 36: 377–396.

Matutes, C., and P. Regibeau. 1988. "Mix and Match: Product Compatibility Without Network Externalities." *RAND Journal of Economics* 19: 221–234.

Rohlfs, J. 1974. "A Theory of Interdependent Demand for a Communication Service." *Bell Journal of Economics* 5: 16–37.

PART IV

Marketing

Chapter 11

Advertising

> Hardly any business practice causes economists greater
> uneasiness than advertising.
> —L. Telser, "Advertising and Competition"

Advertising is an integral part of our life. Each one of us is constantly
bombarded by advertising for products and services in a wide variety of
forms. We watch advertising on TV, listen to advertising on the radio,
read ads in newspapers, in magazines, on outdoor billboards, on buses
and trains, receive a large amount of so-called junk mail, and we transmit
advertising via word-of-mouth and by wearing brand-name labels on our
clothes.

   Despite this basic observation, very little is understood about the
effects of advertising. Advertising is generally defined as a form of providing information about prices, quality, and location of goods and services. Advertising differs from other forms of information transmissions
(like stock-exchange data and guidebooks) in two respects: First, the
information is transmitted by the body who sells the product, and second, the buyer does not always have to pay to receive the information
(or pays a little with his or her value of time of watch a TV ad or to
sort out the relevant ads in the Sunday newspaper).

   What is the purpose of advertising? We first need to acknowledge
that advertising must serve a purpose for some agents in the economy
since—as a matter of fact—firms, governments, and individuals spend
large sums of money on advertising. It is generally estimated that developed economies spend more than 2 percent of their GNPs on advertising
(see Schmalensee 1972, 1986). The expenditure of firms on advertising
is generally measured in terms of advertising expenditure divided by the
value of sales. These ratios vary drastically across products and industries. The ratio of advertising expenditure to sales of vegetables may

be as low as 0.1 percent, whereas for cosmetics or detergents, this ratio may be as high as 20 to 60 percent.

There have been many attempts to correlate industry types, product characteristics, geographical locations, and other characteristics with advertising-to-sales ratios. However, in most cases advertising still remains a mystery since neither empirically nor theoretically can we explain why different firms spend different amounts on advertising. For example, Adams and Brock (1990) report that the Big Three car producers in the United States, which are ranked among the largest advertisers in the country, happen to have different advertising-to-sales ratios. In 1986 the largest producer, GM (which spent $285 million on advertising), spent $63 per car, whereas Ford spent $130 and Chrysler spent $113 per car (though they spent less overall than GM). This may hint of economies of scale in car advertising.

Earlier modern authors, e.g. Kaldor (1950), held the idea that advertising is "manipulative" and reduces competition and therefore reduces welfare for two reasons: First, advertising would persuade consumers to believe wrongly that identical products are differentiated because the decision of which brand to purchase depends on consumers' perception of what the brand is rather than on the actual physical characteristics of the product. Therefore, prices of heavily advertised products would rise far beyond their cost of production. Second, advertising serves as an entry-deterring mechanism since any newly entering firm must extensively advertise in order to surpass the reputation of the existing firms. Thus, existing firms use advertising as an entry-deterrence strategy and can maintain their dominance while keeping above-normal profit levels.

More recent authors, Telser (1964), Nelson (1970, 1974), and Demsetz (1979), proposed that advertising serves as a tool for transmitting information from producers to consumers about differentiated brands, thereby reducing consumers' cost of obtaining information about where to purchase their most preferred brand.

Nelson (1970) distinguishes between two types of goods: *search goods* and *experience goods*. Consumers can identify the quality and other characteristics of the product before the actual purchase of search goods. Examples include tomatoes or shirts. Consumers cannot learn the quality and other characteristics of experience goods before the actual purchase. Examples include new models of cars and many electrical appliances with unknown durability and failure rates. Note that this distinction is not really clear-cut, since we cannot fully judge the quality of a tomato until we eat it, and we cannot fully judge the quality of a shirt until after the first wash!

What Nelson claims is that the effects of advertising may vary between these two groups of products, because consumers do not depend on information obtained from the manufacturers concerning search products (since consumers find it by themselves). However, consumers do rely on advertisements when they purchase experience goods. Several tests have also confirmed that advertising of experienced products is more intensive (in terms of the ratio of advertising expenditure to sales) than advertising of search goods.

The economics literature distinguishes between two types of advertising: *persuasive advertising* and *informative advertising*. Persuasive advertising intends to enhance consumer tastes for a certain product, whereas informative advertising carries basic product information such as characteristics, prices, and where to buy it. In the following two subsections we analyze these two types of advertising and ask whether from a social welfare point of view, firms engage in too little or too much advertising.

11.1 Persuasive Advertising

In this subsection we analyze persuasive advertising. That is, advertising that boosts the industry demand for the advertised product(s). We first investigate what the optimal advertising level is, assuming that the demand for the good is monotonically increasing with the firm's advertising level. Then, we ask whether from a social welfare point of view there is too much or too little advertising.

11.1.1 The monopoly's profit-maximizing level of advertising

Consider a monopoly firm selling a single product in a market where the demand curve is given by

$$Q(A,p) = \beta A^{\epsilon_A} p^{\epsilon_p}, \quad \text{where } \beta > 0, \ 0 < \epsilon_A < 1, \ \text{ and } \ \epsilon_p < -1.$$
(11.1)

The parameter A denotes the firm's expenditure on advertising, Q and p denote the quantity demanded and the price for this product. Thus, the quantity demanded is monotonically increasing with the level of advertising (A) but at a decreasing rate (since $\epsilon_A < 1$).

Denoting by $\eta_A(A,p)$ and $\eta_p(A,p)$ the demand advertising elasticity and price elasticity respectively, and recalling subsection 3.2.1, where we showed the exponents of the variables in an exponential demand function (illustrated in Figure 3.4) are the elasticities of the corresponding variables, the reader can verify that

$$\eta_A \equiv \frac{\partial Q(A,p)}{\partial A} \frac{A}{Q} = \epsilon_A \quad \text{and} \quad \eta_p \equiv \frac{\partial Q(A,p)}{\partial p} \frac{p}{Q} = \epsilon_p. \qquad (11.2)$$

Let c denote the unit cost of the product. The monopoly has two choice variables: the price (p) and the advertising expenditure (A). Thus, the monopoly solves

$$\max_{A,p} \pi(A,p) \equiv pQ - cQ - A = \beta A^{\epsilon_A} p^{\epsilon_p + 1} - c\beta A^{\epsilon_A} p^{\epsilon_p} - A. \quad (11.3)$$

The first-order condition with respect to price is given by

$$0 = \frac{\partial \pi(A,p)}{\partial p} = \beta A^{\epsilon_A}(\epsilon_p + 1)p^{\epsilon_p} - c\beta A^{\epsilon_A}\epsilon_p p^{\epsilon_p - 1}, \quad (11.4)$$

implying that

$$p^M = \frac{\epsilon_p}{\epsilon_p + 1}c \quad \text{and hence} \quad \frac{p^M - c}{p^M} = \frac{-1}{\epsilon_p}. \quad (11.5)$$

The first-order condition with respect to advertising level is given by

$$0 = \frac{\partial \pi(A,p)}{\partial A} = \beta \epsilon_A A^{\epsilon_A - 1} p^{\epsilon_p}(p - c) - 1, \quad (11.6)$$

implying that

$$\frac{p^M - c}{p^M} = \frac{1}{\beta \epsilon_A A^{\epsilon_A - 1} p^{\epsilon_p + 1}}. \quad (11.7)$$

Equating equations (11.5) with (11.7) yields

$$\frac{\epsilon_A}{-\epsilon_p} = \frac{1}{\beta A^{\epsilon_A - 1} p^{\epsilon_p + 1}} = \frac{A^M}{p^M Q^M}, \quad \text{where} \quad Q^M \equiv Q(p^M). \quad (11.8)$$

Equation (11.8) is known as the Dorfman-Steiner (1954) condition. Therefore,

Proposition 11.1 *A monopoly's profit-maximizing advertising and price levels should be set so that the ratio of advertising expenditure to revenue equals the (absolute value of the) ratio of the advertising elasticity to price elasticity. Formally,*

$$\frac{A^M}{p^M Q^M} = \frac{\epsilon_A}{-\epsilon_p}.$$

Thus, a monopoly would increase its advertising-to-sales ratio as the demand becomes more elastic with respect to the advertising (ϵ_A is close to 1), or less elastic with respect to price (ϵ_p is close to zero).

11.1.2 Too much or too little persuasive advertising?

Persuasive advertising was defined as a method of information transmission that boosts the demand for the advertised product. Thus, persuasive advertising makes the good attractive to consumers and therefore has the potential to increase welfare. This does not imply that persuasive advertising must be truthful. All that persuasive advertising does is to provide an image for the product that would induce the consumer to purchase the product in order to identify with the message or people portrayed in the ads.

Dixit and Norman (1978) have proposed an extremely simple method for evaluating the welfare effect of persuasive advertising. Consider a simplified version of the demand function (11.1) where $\beta = 64$, $\epsilon_A = 0.5$, and $\epsilon_p = -2$. For this case, we assume that

$$Q = 64\sqrt{A}p^{-2} \quad \text{or} \quad p = \frac{8A^{1/4}}{Q^{1/2}}. \tag{11.9}$$

Taking the unit production cost to equal $c = 1$, the monopolist chooses p^M and A^M to maximize

$$\max_{A,p} \pi(A,p) = pQ - 1Q - A = 64A^{1/2}p^{-1} - 64A^{1/2}p^{-2} - A. \tag{11.10}$$

The first-order condition with respect to p is given by

$$0 = \frac{\partial \pi(A,p)}{\partial p} = \frac{-64\sqrt{A}}{p^2} + \frac{128\sqrt{A}}{p^3}, \tag{11.11}$$

implying that $p^M = 2$ and hence, $Q^M = 16\sqrt{A}$. Since the demand function has a constant elasticity, the monopoly price is independent of the level of advertising. The first-order condition with respect to A is given by

$$0 = \frac{\partial \pi(A,p)}{\partial A} = \frac{64}{2\sqrt{A}p} - \frac{64}{2\sqrt{A}p^2} - 1, \tag{11.12}$$

implying that $A^M = 64$ and hence, $Q^M = 16\sqrt{64} = 128$.

In order to check whether the monopoly advertises at the socially optimal level we first need to calculate the consumer surplus associated with each advertising level. The shaded area in Figure 11.1 shows the consumer surplus associated with a given advertising level A and the monopoly price $p^M = 2$. Hence, for a given advertising level A, the consumer surplus is given by

$$
\begin{aligned}
CS(A) &= \int_0^{16\sqrt{A}} 8\frac{\sqrt[4]{A}}{\sqrt{Q}}dQ - 2 \times 16\sqrt{A} \tag{11.13}\\[2mm]
&= 2 \times 8\sqrt[4]{A}\left[Q^{1/2}\right]_0^{16\sqrt{A}} - 32\sqrt{A} = 32\sqrt{A}.
\end{aligned}
$$

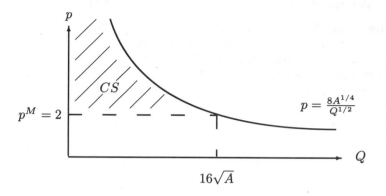

Figure 11.1: Consumer surplus for a given persuasive-advertising level

Assuming a monopoly price of $p^M = 2$, the firm's profit level as a function of the level of advertising is given by

$$\pi(A, 2) = 2Q(A) - Q(A) - A = 32\sqrt{A} - 16\sqrt{A} - A = 16\sqrt{A} - A. \quad (11.14)$$

The social planner takes the monopoly price $p^M = 2$ as given and chooses an advertising level A^* to

$$\max_A W(A) \equiv CS(A) + \pi(A, 2) = 48\sqrt{A} - A. \quad (11.15)$$

The first-order condition is given by

$$0 = \frac{\partial W(A)}{\partial A} = \frac{24}{\sqrt{A}} - 1. \quad (11.16)$$

Hence, the socially optimal advertising level is $A^* = 24^2 > 64 = A^M$. Notice that this social optimum is not a "first-best" optimum, since a first-best optimum requires marginal cost pricing. Hence,

Proposition 11.2 *Given a monopoly market structure, the equilibrium level of persuasive advertising is below the socially optimal level.*

Finally, the model presented in this section is very special and is given for the purpose of introducing one method for evaluating the welfare effects of persuasive advertising. We note here several problems concerning the robustness of Proposition 11.2. First, is it appropriate to use the consumer surplus as a welfare measure when the demand (utility) is affected by the advertising level? Second, even if this measure is appropriate, since the model is a partial equilibrium one, the measure does not capture the entire welfare effect associated with an increase in the demand for the advertised product. That is, an increase in the demand for one product would decrease the demand for other products (say, for substitute products). Hence, the change in consumers' surplus in other markets should be taken into account.

11.2   Informative Advertising

Consumers often rely on information for their purchases. Without advertising, few consumers would be exposed to the variety of existing products, the price distribution, and the location of specific products. As Nelson points out, advertising can serve as a tool for transmitting this information to consumers and therefore should not be considered as an unnecessary activity. In fact, Benham (1972) has shown that prices are lower in markets where prices of eyeglasses are advertised than in markets where prices are not advertised.

The literature investigating the welfare effects of informative advertising concentrates on the conventional question of whether there is too little or too much informative advertising. Butters (1977) develops a model in which firms advertise the price of a homogeneous product and finds that the aggregate advertising level determined in a monopolistic competition equilibrium is socially optimal. Thus, Butters shows that informative advertising need not always be detrimental. Grossman and Shapiro (1984) consider a world of product differentiation where consumers who are located on the circumference of a circle (see subsection 7.3.2) are able to recognize a brand only if the producer advertises. This model provides ambiguous results about the excessiveness of informative advertising. Thus, the literature demonstrates that whether informative advertising is excessive or not depends on the specific functional form used for describing the industry. Recently, Meurer and Stahl (1994) developed a model in which some consumers are informed about two differentiated products and some are not, and in which both advertising and prices are choice variables. They show that social welfare may increase or decrease, depending on the level of advertising.

We proceed by developing a very simple model to analyze this question. Obviously, the answer that will be given here is not robust. However, the purpose of developing this model is to present one approach for how to model this type of question.

Consider a single-consumer, single-product market. Let p be the price of the product and assume that p is exogenously given (e.g., p is regulated). Let m denote the consumer's benefit from purchasing one unit of the product. Altogether, we assume that the utility function of the consumer is given by

$$u = \begin{cases} m - p & \text{if he purchases the product} \\ 0 & \text{if does not purchase.} \end{cases} \qquad (11.17)$$

There are two firms producing the same product and offering it for sale at a price of p. With no loss of generality, assume that production is costless so that the only cost firms have to bear is the cost of sending an advertisement to the consumer. Formally, assume that each firm has a single decision variable, which is whether or not to advertise. The cost of advertising is given by a constant denoted by A.

The consumer may receive a total of 0, 1, or 2 ads from the firms. If the consumer receives one ad, he buys the product from the firm that sent it. If he receives no ads, he buys none, and if he receives two ads, he splits the transaction equally between the firms, that is, he pays $p/2$ to each firm. Note that this assumption is similar to the assumption that the consumer flips a coin when he receives two ads, thereby yielding an expected revenue of $p/2$ to each firm. Therefore, the profit of firm i, $i = 1, 2$ is given by

$$\pi_i = \begin{cases} p - A & \text{if only firm } i\text{'s ad is received} \\ \frac{p}{2} - A & \text{if both firms' ads are received} \\ -A & \text{if firm } i \text{ sends an ad, but the ad is not received} \\ 0 & \text{if firm } i \text{ does not advertise (and hence does not sell).} \end{cases}$$
$$(11.18)$$

The fact that a firm sends an ad does not imply that the consumer will indeed receive it. For instance, even if the firm invests $\$A$ in a TV ad, it is possible that the consumer will not be watching TV at the time that the ad runs on the air. Formally, let δ, $0 < \delta < 1$, be the probability that a message sent by a certain firm would be received by the consumer. Therefore, the expected profit of firm i, $i = 1, 2$, is given by

$$E\pi_i = \begin{cases} \delta(1 - \delta)(p - A) + \delta^2(\frac{p}{2} - A) - (1 - \delta)A & \text{both advertise} \\ \delta(p - A) - (1 - \delta)A & \text{only } i \text{ advertises} \\ 0 & i \text{ does not.} \end{cases}$$
$$(11.19)$$

Comparing the expected profits in the first and second rows in (11.19) to the reservation profit of 0 yields:

Proposition 11.3 *For a given value of p, $p \leq m$,*

1. at least one firm will engage in advertising if and only if

$$\frac{p}{A} \geq \frac{1}{\delta};$$

2. two firms will engage in advertising if

$$\frac{p}{A} \geq \frac{2}{\delta(2-\delta)}.$$

Figure 11.2 illustrates the combinations of the receiving probability parameter(δ) and the ratio of price to advertising cost (p/A) associated with having no firm, one firm, or two firms placing ads. Clearly,

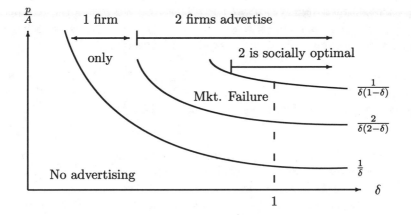

Figure 11.2: Equilibrium number of firms placing ads

for a low receiving probability δ, or for a high advertising cost relative to the price (low p/A), no firm would place an ad. As either δ or p/A increase, the number of firms placing ads also increases.

We now turn to the welfare analysis. The problem solved by the social planner is to choose the number of firms that advertise in order to maximize the expected sum of consumer surplus and firms' profits. First, observe that if both firms advertise, the probability that at least one firm would sell is $2\delta(1-\delta) + \delta^2 = \delta(2-\delta)$ (which is twice the probability that one ad will be received while the other will not, plus the probability that both ads are received). Formally, the expected social welfare as a function of the number of ads is given by

$$EW = \begin{cases} \delta(2-\delta)m - 2A & \text{if both firms advertise} \\ \delta m - A & \text{if only one firm advertise} \\ 0 & \text{both do not advertise.} \end{cases} \quad (11.20)$$

If we observe that p does not appear in (11.20), it is easy to infer that as long as $p < m$, a market failure is likely to occur. This happens because firms do not capture the entire consumer surplus and therefore will underadvertise compared with what a social planner would choose. Therefore, in order to check whether too many firms engage in advertising from a social viewpoint, we set $p = m$, implying that all consumer surplus is absorbed in the firms' profits. In this case, (11.20) implies that it is socially optimal to have two firms sending ads (rather than a single firm) if and only if $m/A = p/A > 1/[\delta(1-\delta)]$. However, Proposition 11.3 implies that a weaker parameter restriction is needed for having an equilibrium where two firms send ads. That is, $m/A = p/A > 2/[\delta(2-\delta)]$. Hence, in Figure 11.2 the area between the curves given by $2/[\delta(2-\delta)] < p/A < 1/[\delta(1-\delta)]$ represents the parameter range where both firms advertise in equilibrium, but it is socially optimal to have only one firm engaged in advertising.

Proposition 11.4 *In a model where some placed ads do not reach the consumer, there exists a parameter range $(2/[\delta(2-\delta)] < p/A < 1/[\delta(1-\delta)])$ where too many firms engage in advertising, from a social welfare point of view.*

Finally, what happens when the advertising technology improves, in the sense that there is a higher probability ads sent to consumers arrive? Figure 11.2 shows that when $\delta \to 1$, the upper curve shifts upward with no bounds, implying that for high values of δ, it is never socially optimal to have two firms engage in advertising. The intuition is as follows: Since sending ads is costly, and since $\delta \to 1$ implies that ads are always received, then one firm advertising is sufficient to have the consumer receive the information about the product.

11.3 Targeted Advertising

The literature on advertising assumes that advertising is either persuasive or informative. That is, the nature of advertising is always treated as exogenously given, thereby ignoring the question of how firms choose the content for their advertising.

The underlying observation is that societies are composed of heterogeneous consumers with different rankings (preferences) over products. Thus, firms are unable to advertise and sell their brands to all types of consumers and therefore must limit the scope of their advertising by choosing a narrow group of consumers to which their advertising appeals. There may be three reasons for that: First, it is impossible to classify products' attributes that are (highly) valued by all consumers. Second, given the high cost of advertising, firms and advertising agencies may find it profitable to narrow the scope of advertising to a limited group of consumers. Third, ignoring advertising costs, since product differentiation may facilitate price competition, firms may intentionally choose to target a limited consumer group.

The purpose of this section is to propose a framework for modeling firms' choice of advertising methods and the resulting targeted consumer group, where firms' advertising must be confined to choosing a single advertising method and therefore a single consumer target group. For example, a firm may choose to advertise its brand by emphasizing one attribute of the product that is preferred by at least one consumer group but is not found in a competing brand. Alternatively, instead of advertising the product's attributes, a firm may target its advertising to a certain age group (young or old) or to inexperienced consumers and ignore the (attributes) quality differences among the competing brands.

11.3.1 Firms and consumers

There are two firms denoted by i, $i = 1, 2$, producing differentiated brands, which we will refer to as brand 1 and brand 2, respectively.

There are two types of buyers: There are N consumers, who are first-time buyers that we call the inexperienced consumers. In addition, there are E consumers, who have purchased the product before and whom we call *experienced* consumers. Figure 11.3 illustrates how the consumer population is divided between consumer types. We assume that the

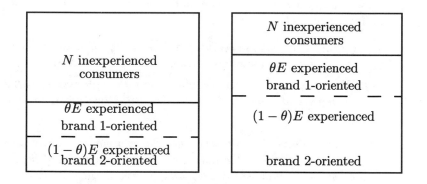

Figure 11.3: Targeted advertising: Experienced versus inexperienced consumers out of total population: *Left: $E < N$; Right: $E > N$*

group of experienced consumers is divided into two subgroups: those who prefer to purchase brand 1 over brand 2, and those who prefer brand 2 over brand 1. Let θ, $0 < \theta < 1$, be the fraction of brand 1-oriented consumers (among experienced consumers). Therefore, $(1 - \theta)$ is the fraction of brand 2-oriented consumers (among experienced consumers). Thus, out of a total of E experienced consumers, there are θE brand 1-oriented and $(1 - \theta)E$ brand 2-oriented consumers.

11.3.2   Advertising methods

There are two advertising methods: A firm can use persuasive advertising, a strategy denoted by P. Alternatively, a firm can use informative advertising, a strategy denoted by I. Thus, each firm i chooses s^i from an action set given by $S \equiv \{P, I\}$. For our purposes, we assume that no firm can employ more than one advertising method, that is, a firm can choose P or I but not both! One justification for such a strong assumption would be that advertising agencies tend to specialize in a single advertising method (or philosophy). Therefore, if a firm would like to use both advertising methods, it has to employ two advertising agencies, which may increase cost more than profit.

To simplify our model, we assume that choosing advertising methods is the only strategic variable available to firms. Thus, in this model, we ignore prices and assume that firms seek to maximize the number of consumers buying their brand. We denote by $\Pi \equiv \langle \pi^1, \pi^2 \rangle$ the vector of profit levels (which equals the number of customers buying from each firm.) We make the following assumption:

ASSUMPTION 11.1

1. *Persuasive advertising attracts only inexperienced consumers. Formally, if firm i chooses $s^i = P$, then*

   (a) *if firm j does not use persuasive advertising, then all inexperienced consumers purchase brand i, that is, $\pi^i = N$ if $s^j \neq P$;*

   (b) *if both firms use persuasive advertising, then all inexperienced consumers are equally divided between the two firms, that is, $\pi^i = N/2$ if $s^j = p$.*

2. *Informative advertising attracts only the experienced consumers who are oriented toward the advertised brand. Formally, if firm 1 chooses $s^1 = I$, then $\pi^1 = \theta E$, and if firm 2 chooses $s^2 = I$, $\pi^2 = (1 - \theta)E$.*

Table 11.1 demonstrates the profit level of each firm and the industry aggregate profit under all four possible outcomes $\langle s^1, s^2 \rangle$. We look for a Nash equilibrium (see Definition 2.4) in the above strategies.

Profit \ Outcome	$\langle P,P \rangle$	$\langle P,I \rangle$	$\langle I,P \rangle$	$\langle I,I \rangle$
π^1	$N/2$	N	θE	θE
π^2	$N/2$	$(1-\theta)E$	N	$(1-\theta)E$
$\pi^1 + \pi^2$	N	$N + (1-\theta)E$	$\theta E + N$	E

Table 11.1: Profits for firms under different advertising methods

Proposition 11.5

1. *A necessary condition for having both firms using persuasive advertising is that the number of inexperienced consumers exceeds the number of experienced consumers $(N > E)$. In this case, $\langle P,P \rangle$ is a unique equilibrium if $1 - \frac{N}{2E} < \theta < \frac{N}{2E}$.*

2. *A necessary condition for having both firms using informative advertising is that the number of experienced consumers is more than twice the number of inexperienced consumers $(E > 2N)$. In this case, $\langle I,I \rangle$ is a unique equilibrium if $\frac{N}{E} < \theta < 1 - \frac{N}{E}$.*

3. *If brand 1 is unpopular among experienced users, then firm 1 uses persuasive advertising and firm 2 uses informative advertising. Formally, $\langle P,I \rangle$ is an equilibrium if $\theta < \min\{\frac{N}{E}; 1 - \frac{N}{2E}\}$.*

4. *If brand 1 is sufficiently popular among experienced users, then firm 1 uses informative advertising and firm 2 uses persuasive advertising. Formally, $\langle I,P \rangle$ is an equilibrium if $\theta > \max\{\frac{N}{2E}; 1 - \frac{N}{E}\}$.*

Proposition 11.5 is illustrated in Figure 11.4. The upper part of Figure 11.4 corresponds to part 1 of Proposition 11.5, where the number of experienced consumers is lower than the number of inexperienced consumers. Both firms use persuasive advertising when the brands have similar popularity among experienced users. As the number of experienced consumers gets below $E < N/2$, the entire θ range corresponds to $\langle P,P \rangle$ where both firms use persuasive advertising. That is, for every popularity parameter θ, the unique equilibrium is $\langle P,P \rangle$.

The lower part of Figure 11.4 corresponds to part 2 of Proposition 11.5, where the number of experienced consumers is more than twice the number of inexperienced consumers. In this case both firms use informative advertising unless one brand is very popular among the experienced consumers compared with the other brand. Then, a firm would use persuasive advertising only if its brand is very unpopular among the experienced consumers. Finally, as the number of experienced

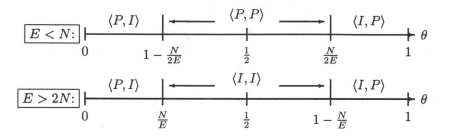

Figure 11.4: Informative versus persuasive advertising

consumers increases with no bounds, the entire popularity parameter θ range corresponds to having both firms using only informative advertising.

Proof of Proposition 11.5.
Part 1: We look at firm 1. In this equilibrium, $\pi^1(P, P) = N/2$. If firm 1 deviates and chooses $s^1 = I$, then $\pi^1(I, P) = \theta E$. Therefore, a deviation is not profitable for firm 1 if $N/2 > \theta E$, or if $\theta < N/(2E)$. Similarly, firm 2 will not deviate if $1 - \theta < N/(2E)$, or $\theta > 1 - N/(2E)$. In order for this region to be nonempty, we must have it that $1 - N/(2E) < N/(2E)$, implying that $E < N$.

Part 2: In this equilibrium, $\pi^1(I, I) = \theta E$. If firm 1 deviates and chooses $s^1 = P$, then $\pi^1(I, P) = N$. Hence, firm 1 will not deviate if $\theta E > N$, or if $\theta > N/E$. Similarly, firm 2 will not deviate if $1 - \theta > N/E$, or $\theta < 1 - N/E$. In order for this region to be nonempty, we must have it that $N/E < 1 - N/E$, implying that $E > 2N$.

Part 3: For firm 1, $\pi^1(P, I) = N$. If firm 1 deviates to $s^1 = I$, then $\pi^1(I, I) = \theta E$. Hence, firm 1 will not deviate if $N > \theta E$ or if $\theta < N/E$. For firm 2, $\pi^2(P, I) = (1 - \theta)E$. If firm 2 deviates to $s^2 = P$, then $\pi^2(P, P) = N/2$. Hence, firm 2 will not deviate if $(1 - \theta)E > N/2$, or $\theta < 1 - N/(2E)$. Altogether, $\theta < \min\{N/E; 1 - N/(2E)\}$.

Finally, Part 4 can be proved in a similar way, and we leave it as an exercise to the reader.   ∎

11.4   Comparison Advertising

Comparison advertising is defined as one in which the advertised brand and its characteristics are compared with those of the competing brands.

11.4.1   Comparison advertising: an overview

In the United States, no law ever prevented the use of comparison advertising. However, advertisers were reluctant to use it (Boddewyn and Marton 1978). Only in the early 1970s, did television networks begin to (extensively) broadcast comparison advertisements. Since then, comparison ads have become popular in the printed media as well as in the broadcast media.

The EEC also began to address the issue of comparison advertising in the late 1970s, suggesting that comparison advertising should be legal as long as it compares material and verifiable details and is neither misleading nor unfair.

The principle advantage of comparison advertising is that the information contained in a comparison advertisement provides consumers with low-cost means of evaluating available products (Barnes and Blakeney 1982). In addition, comparison advertising makes the consumers more conscious of their responsibility to compare before buying. It also forces the manufacturer to build into the products attributes consumers want and eventually to produce a better product. There are arguments suggesting that comparison advertising does not assist consumer comparisons because the comparison will lack objectivity since the advertiser will select only those aspects of his brand that are superior to those of the competitors. The critics consider that the risk of consumer confusion and deception is great in comparison advertising, partly because of information overload.

In most countries where comparative advertising is legal, it is closely monitored and regulated by government agencies. Different studies suggest different figures on the relative use of comparative advertising. Muehling, Stoltman, and Grossbart note that around 40 percent of all advertising is comparative. Others (Pechmann and Stewart 1990, and references) suggest that the majority of all ads are indirectly comparative (60 percent, as opposed to 20 percent that contain direct comparative claims; the rest are noncomparative).

11.4.2   Strategic use of comparison advertising

The model developed in section 11.3 can be modified to capture the effects of comparative advertising. Assume that each firm has an action set given by $S \equiv \{A, C\}$, where C means that a firm uses comparison advertising, and A means that the firm advertises its product without comparing it to the competing brand.

Following Assumption 11.1, we assume that

ASSUMPTION 11.2

1. *Plain (noncomparative) advertising (A) attracts only the inexperi-enced consumers.*

2. *Comparison advertising (C) attracts only the experienced consumers who are oriented toward the advertised brand.*

Thus, plain (noncomparative) advertising is intended to inform consumers about the existence of the product by informing the consumer about a specific brand. The drawback of plain advertising is that it also attracts new consumers of the wrong type.

In contrast, comparison advertising informs the experienced misplaced consumers (wrong-brand users) about the difference between the brand they have purchased in the past and their ideal brand. Thus, a firm uses the comparison-advertising strategy to attract experienced users who are oriented toward its brand.

The intuition behind Assumption 11.2 is simple. It is likely that a comparison advertisement is meaningless for the inexperienced consumer simply because a nonuser may not understand the way the product and its features operate. Thus, an inexperienced consumer will not comprehend an ad involving a comparison of the brands' attributes. Assumption 11.2 suggests that the relevance of comparison advertising is a consequence of prior experience with the product itself. Assumption 11.2 also suggests that plain advertising is not very relevant (irrelevant in our extreme case) to the experienced user, since an experienced user definitely knows about the existence of the product and its basic features. Although Assumption 11.2 sounds very intuitive, it has not been tested. In fact, many experiments cited in the references (e.g., chapter 7 of Boddewyn and Marton 1978) tend to find very little difference in the effects produced by comparative and by noncomparative advertising. However, none of these tests attempted to test them on experienced and first-time buyers separately.

Applying Proposition 11.5 to the present case yields

Proposition 11.6

1. *Comparison advertising is used by both firms when the majority of the potential consumers are experienced. That is, when $E > 2N$.*

2. *Comparison advertising will not be used if the number of inexperienced consumers is larger than the number of inexperienced consumers. That is, when $E < N$.*

3. *Comparison advertising is used by the popular firm producing the more popular brand among the experienced consumers. That is, a firm would use comparison advertising when the fraction of experienced consumers oriented toward its brand is large.*

11.5 Other Issues Concerning Advertising

11.5.1 Advertising and quality

Information about prices of products is often easier to acquire than information about the quality of products. It is relatively easy (although costly) to find out the distribution of prices for TV sets. However, it is difficult to find out the frequency of repair of various TV brands, for the simple reason that producers do not release these data to consumers.

Several authors questioned whether information on quality can be transmitted via advertising. That is, can advertising correctly inform consumers on the quality of the product? If the answer is yes, then one should ask what the exact relationship is between advertising and the quality of the advertised product.

Advertising a search good (if it occurs) is likely to be honest because lies will be detected immediately. Thus, false advertising of search goods may hurt firms' reputations rather than enhance them. This need not be the case for experience goods, for which producers may gain from false advertising (at least in the short run). Producers of experience goods will attempt to develop all kinds of persuasive methods to get consumers to try their products.

There are few analytical models attempting to find the link between advertising and quality. Schmalensee (1978) finds that low-quality brands are more frequently purchased, and that firms producing low-quality products advertise more intensively. Thus, there is a negative correlation between the intensity of advertising and the quality of the advertised product.

Kihlstrom and Riordan (1984) develop a two-period model in which high- and low-quality products are sold and high quality firms have an incentive to advertise in order to "trap" the consumers seeking to purchase high-quality products in the second period, (i.e., trap repeat buyers). Their model finds a positive correlation between advertising intensity and the quality of the advertised product. On this line, which is similar to the signaling model of subsection 8.4.6, Milgrom and Roberts (1986) develop a signaling model in which a high level of advertising is used as a signal sent by high-quality-producing firms to those consumers who desire to purchase high-quality products. Bagwell (1994) and Bagwell and Ramey (1994) argue that efficient firms operating under increasing

returns tend to spend large amount on advertising to convince buyers
that large sales will end up with lower prices (due to lower cost). Thus,
efficient firms would spend more on advertising than less efficient firms
to reveal their cost identity to the buyers.

11.5.2 Advertising and concentration

Basic intuition may lead us to think that in a (near) competitive industry with a large number of firms, no firm would have an incentive to
advertise, since (persuasive) advertising may boost the demand facing
the industry, but may have only a small effect on the demand facing
the advertising firm. Thus, a "free rider" effect will generate little advertising. Recognizing this effect leads advertising associations in some
countries to advertise how good advertising can be.

This kind of argument generates the testable hypothesis that intensive advertising (high advertising-expenditure-to-sales ratio) is associated with the more concentrated industries, (concentration measures
are analyzed in section 8.1). Orenstein (1976) summarized early empirical tests that attempted to investigate a connection between advertising
and concentration. From a theoretical point of view, this hypothesis can
be explained by an increasing-returns type of argument. Kaldor claimed
that if one takes an industry in which advertising is prohibited, and
then allows advertising, the larger firms would increase their advertising
expenditure at a faster rate than the smaller firms, thereby increasing
industry concentration. However, Telser (1964) demonstrated very little
empirical support for an inverse relationship between advertising and
competition. In addition, Orenstein (1976) tested for increasing returns
in advertising (say, resulting from a falling advertising cost associated
with an increase in advertising volume) but showed very little evidence
in favor of this hypothesis. For a very comprehensive recent empirical and theoretical study of the association between industry structure,
concentration, and advertising intensity, the reader is referred to Sutton
1991.

Several authors, including Sutton (1974), suggested that the relationship between advertising and concentration need not be always monotonically increasing and that there can exist a certain concentration level
at which advertising is most intensive. That is, the relation between
advertising and concentration may take the form of an (upside-down)
U-shaped function. Sutton suggested that industries with low concentration are associated with low incentives to advertise together with low
opportunity, (by "incentive" Sutton meant the extra profit generated
by extra advertising; whereas, by "opportunity" he meant the success
of the advertising). However, Sutton suggested that in highly concen-

trated industries both the incentives and the opportunity are lower than in medium-level concentrated industries because profit expectations tend to be higher in medium-concentration industries.

11.5.3 Advertising and prices

Despite the fact that there is no significant evidence for the association between concentration and advertising intensity, there is, however, some evidence on how advertising affects prices. Benham (1972) found that the average price of eyeglasses in states where advertising eyeglasses is prohibited is around twice the average price of eyeglasses in states where eyeglasses are advertised. A similar test regarding the introduction of toy advertising on television suggests a sharp price reduction following this introduction.

How can we explain this observation that high advertising intensity is associated with lower price, but not necessarily in a reduced market concentration? We demonstrate it by the following simple example. Let us first assume that there is only one firm (monopoly) selling a particular good, whose period 0 demand is given by $Q = a_0 - p$, where a_0 is (or is positively related to) the period 0 level of advertising by the monopoly. Let A denote the advertising cost. We assume a simple form of increasing-returns technology represented by the following cost function:

$$TC(A, Q) = \begin{cases} A + c_H Q & \text{if } Q \leq Q^* \\ A + c_L Q & \text{if } Q > Q^* . \end{cases} \tag{11.21}$$

Thus, for a given advertising level A, the variable cost is discontinuous at the output level Q^*. Figure 11.5 illustrates that the marginal production cost falls to c_L at output levels exceeding Q^*, reflecting a situation where at high output levels, the firm uses a different production method, say employing assembly lines to assemble products or shipping production overseas to low-wage countries. We saw in section 5.1 that the period 0 monopoly equilibrium is at a production level of $Q_0^M = (a_0 - c_H)/2$ and a price level of $p_0^M = (a_0 + c_H)/2$.

Now, suppose that in period 1, the monopoly intensifies its advertising effort and spends $A_1 > A_0$ on advertising. We assume that a higher level of advertising shifts the demand to $Q = a_1 - p$, where $a_1 > a_0$. Figure 11.5 shows that the new equilibrium is associated with an output level $Q_1^M = (a_1 - c_L)/2$ and a price of $p_1^M = (a_1 + c_L)/2$. Comparing the prices associated with the two advertising levels yields

Proposition 11.7 *Monopoly price $p_1^M < p_0^M$ if and only if $c_H - c_L > a_1 - a_0$. That is, advertising reduces the monopoly price if and only if the reduction in marginal cost associated with a higher production level exceeds the level of change in the demand.*

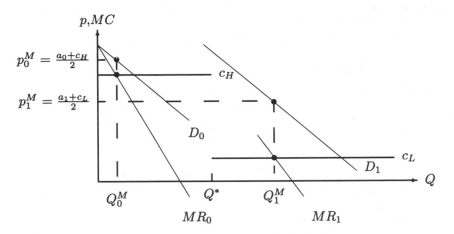

Figure 11.5: Advertising-induced demand increase and falling prices

We have ignored the question of whether advertising is profitable for this monopoly, since it simply depends on how the period 1 advertising expenditure relates to the period 0 advertising level (i.e., on the magnitude of $A_1 - A_0$). If this difference is relatively low, then the monopoly will advertise and price will fall if the condition in Proposition 11.7 is fulfilled. If the difference in advertising expenditure is large, then the monopoly may choose not to increase its advertising level. In any case, we have shown that it is possible to have a situation where prices fall (or rise) when advertising increases but the industry concentration level remains unchanged (in this case concentration remains at the level of 100 percent).

The conclusion from this experiment demonstrates a very well known econometric problem in which looking at data on prices and quantities cannot reveal what has happened to concentration, since prices and quantities may be affected by demand and production cost changes at the same time.

11.6   Appendix: Advertising Regulations

Advertising regulation has two purposes:

1. Regulation prevents firms from using advertising in a way that limits the competition among the firms in the industry.

2. Regulation is intended to protect consumers from false advertising and misrepresentations. In addition, some (negative) advertising,

such as the labels on clothes, or smoking-alert labels on cigarettes, is sometimes mandated by governments.

The main difficulty in establishing advertising regulations stems from the fact that these two goals may in some cases conflict with one another. That is, in order to protect the consumer against misrepresentations, the FTC or the local government have to limit the scope of advertising. However, restricting advertising may hamper the operation of the competitive process. A second difficulty in regulating advertising stems from the fact that many countries allow free speech (including commercial free speech), implying that producers are free to advertise their products and services. Yet producers of product or services tend to misrepresent their products and services, thereby leading some consumers to believe that they buy what they want, although they actually do not.

In the following subsections we discuss some advertising regulations in two large markets: The United States and the EC. The interested reader is referred to Barnes and Blakeney 1982, McManis 1988, and Maxeiner and Schotthöfer 1992 for extensive discussions and analysis of country-specific advertising regulations.

11.6.1 The United States

We focus most of our discussion on the United States since advertising is used most intensively in the United States, and (paradoxically) advertising is heavily regulated in the United States. In the United States, federal, state, and local governments independently regulate advertising. Concurrent regulation is not contradictory, since state laws should not conflict with federal laws. In practice, advertising laws differ from state to state.

Federal advertising legislation is found in two major laws: the Federal Trade Commission Act and the Trademark (Lanham) Act. In practice, the FTC issues advertising guidelines to the industry. States create their own versions of the FTC Act. Finally, the private sector is also active as a self-regulator by imposing many rules via organizations such as the Consumers' Union and Better Business Bureaus.

Under the First Amendment to the U.S. Constitution, freedom of speech is protected. However, freedom of speech applies only to truthful advertising; that is, false advertising is not protected.

The Trademark (Lanham) Act prohibits the use of false designations of origin and false or misleading descriptions of fact and the representation of a fact. This includes the prohibition of the creation of confusion about the origin, sponsorship, and approval of goods and services. The FTC Act prohibits any unfair methods of competition, including dissemination of false advertisements. There is the question of which ads constitute false or misleading advertising. First, misleading advertising has to be material (i.e., it should affect the consumers' decisions). Second, the claims (or implied claims) made in the ad have to be false, where omissions do not constitute false advertising. Third, the ads have to mislead a substantial fraction of the audience, where the audience is expected to have a "reasonable" interpretation.

The FTC requires that the advertisers (advertising agencies) will have bases for their advertised objective claims. Subjective claims such as "this product has changed my life (for the good or for the bad)" need not be substantiated. This guide is particularly important for the case of comparison advertising, which is perfectly legal (even somewhat encouraged) in the United States, but all claims must be substantiated.

Finally, in the United States there are special federal laws that address special products and services. For example, advertising cigarettes on TV is prohibited. Special regulations prevail for advertising financial investments and drugs.

11.6.2   The European Community

Advertising in Europe is generally regulated by national laws. Regulation by the EC takes the form of directives to governments, meaning that the member countries would have to adopt their own laws in order to achieve the (directed) results.

The EC Treaty guarantees the freedom of movement of goods and services across member states. This implies the freedom of transnational advertising. Thus, the idea is to promote a market favorable to all member states' products. The EC directive toward TV and radio advertising is intended to limit the ads separable from the programs to a maximum of 20 percent of the broadcasting time. The ads should not be discriminative on the basis of nationality or any other basis. Cigarette advertising is prohibited, and advertising alcoholic beverages on TV is restricted. In addition, comparison advertising is legal as long as it is based on substantiated grounds. (Australia also allows comparison advertising based on testable claims [see Barnes and Blakeney 1982]).

Finally, the EC has also issued some directives concerning misleading advertising, thereby encouraging member states to adopt measures in order to prevent it.

11.7   Exercises

1. Congratulations! You have been appointed to become a CEO of UGLY, Inc., the sole producer of facial oil skin-life extender. Your first as-

signment is to determine the advertising budget for next year. The marketing department provides you with three important information items: (a) The company is expected to sell $10 million worth of the product. (b) It is estimated that a 1 percent increase in the advertising budget would increase quantity sold by 0.05 percent. (c) It is also estimated that a 1 percent increase in the product's price would reduce quantity sold by 0.2 percent.

(a) How much money would you allocate for advertising next year?

(b) Now, suppose that the marketing department has revised its estimation regarding the demand price elasticity to 1 percent increase in price, resulting in a reduction in quantity sold by 0.5 percent. How much money would you allocate to advertising after getting the revised estimate?

(c) Conclude how a change in the demand price elasticity affects advertising expenditure.

2. In Future City there are two fortune-tellers: Ms. α and Mr. β. Each fortune-teller charges a fixed (regulated) fee of $10 for one visit. Let A_i denote the advertising expenditure of fortune-teller i, $i = \alpha, \beta$. The number of clients visiting each teller (per unit of time) is denoted by n_i, $i = \alpha, \beta$. We assume that n_i depends only on the advertising expenditure of both tellers. Formally, let

$$n_\alpha \equiv 6 - 3\left(\frac{A_\beta}{A_\alpha}\right) \quad \text{and} \quad n_\beta \equiv 6 - 3\left(\frac{A_\alpha}{A_\beta}\right).$$

Thus, the number of clients visiting teller α increases with α's advertising expenditure and decreases with β's advertising expenditure. Altogether, assume that each fortune-teller i has only one choice variable, which is the advertising level, and therefore chooses A_i to maximize the profit given by

$$\pi_i(A_\alpha, A_\beta) = 10n_i - A_i = 10\left[6 - 3\frac{A_j}{A_i}\right] - A_i, \quad i = \alpha, \beta.$$

(a) Compare the number of visitors and the profit level of each fortune-teller when $A_\alpha = A_\beta = \$1$ and for $A_\alpha = A_\beta = \$2$. What can you conclude about the role of advertising in this city?

(b) Calculate and draw the best-response function of teller β as a function of the advertising expenditure of teller α. (In case you forgot how to define best-response functions, we first used them in section 6.1).

(c) Calculate the tellers' advertising level in a Nash equilibrium.

(d) In view of your answer to (a), is the Nash equilibrium you found in (c) optimal for the fortune-teller industry?

(e) Is the equilibrium you found stable?

3. Prove part 4 of Proposition 11.5. *Hint:* Follow the same steps as in the proof of part 3.

11.8   References

Adams, W., and J. Brock. 1990. "The Automobile Industry." In *Structure of American Industry*, edited by W. Adams. New York: Macmillan Publishing Company.

Bagwell, K. 1994. "Advertising and Coordination." *Review of Economic Studies* 61: 153–172.

Bagwell, K., and G. Ramey. 1994. "Coordination Economics, Advertising, and Search Behavior in Retail Markets." *American Economic Review* 84: 498–517.

Barnes, S., and M. Blakeney. 1982. *Advertising Regulation.* Sydney: The Law Book Company.

Benham, L. 1972. "The Effects of Advertising on the Price of Eye-Glasses." *Journal of Law and Economics* 15: 337–352.

Boddewyn, J. J., and K. Marton. 1978. *Comparison Advertising.* New York: Hastings House Publishers.

Butters, G. 1977. "Equilibrium Distributions of Sales and Advertising Prices." *Review of Economic Studies* 44: 465–491.

Demsetz, H. 1979. "Accounting for Advertising as a Barrier to Entry." *Journal of Business* 52: 345–360.

Dixit, A., and V. Norman. 1978. "Advertising and Welfare." *The Bell Journal of Economics* 9: 1–17.

Dorfman, R., and P. Steiner. 1954. "Optimal Advertising and Optimal Quality." *American Economic Review* 44: 826–836.

Grossman, G., and C. Shapiro. 1984. "Informative Advertising With Differentiated Products." *Review of Economic Studies* 51: 63–81.

Kaldor, N. 1950. "The Economic Aspects of Advertising." *Review of Economic Studies* 18: 1–27.

Kihlstrom, R., and M. Riordan. 1984. "Advertising as a Signal." *Journal of Political Economy* 92: 427–450.

Maxeiner, J., and P. Schotthöfer. 1992. *Advertising Law in Europe and North America.* Deventer, The Netherlands: Kluwer Law and Taxation Publishers.

McManis, C. 1988. *Unfair Trade Practices in a Nutshell.* St. Paul, Minn.: West Publishing Co.

Meurer, M., and D. Stahl. 1994. "Informative Advertising and Product Match." *International Journal of Industrial Organization* 12: 1-9.

Milgrom P., and J. Roberts. 1986. "Price and Advertising Signals of Product Quality." *Journal of Political Economy* 94: 796–821.

Muehling, D., J. Stoltman, and S. Grossbart. 1990. "The Impact of Comparative Advertising on Levels of Message Involvement." *Journal of Advertising* 19: 41–50.

Nelson, P. 1970. "Information and Consumer Behavior." *Journal of Political Economy* 78: 311–329.

Nelson, P. 1974. "Advertising as Information." *Journal of Political Economy* 82: 729–754.

Orenstein, S. 1976. "The Advertising - Concentration Controversy." *Southern Economic Journal* 43: 892–902.

Pechmann C., and D. Stewart. 1990. "The Effects of Comparative Advertising on Attention, Memory, and Purchase Intentions." *Journal of Consumer Research* 17: 180–191.

Schmalensee, R. 1972. *The Economics of Advertising.* Amsterdam: North-Holland.

Schmalensee, R. 1978. "A Model of Advertising and Product Quality." *Journal of Political Economy* 86: 485–503.

Schmalensee, R. 1986. "Advertising and Market Structure." In *New Developments in the Analysis of Market Structure,* edited by J. Stiglitz and G. Frank Matthewson. Cambridge, Mass.: MIT Press.

Shapiro, C. 1980. "Advertising and Welfare: Comment." *Bell Journal of Economics.* 11: 749–752.

Sutton, J. 1974. "Advertising Concentration, Competition." *Economic Journal* 56–69.

Sutton, J.. 1991. *Sunk Costs and Market Structure.* Cambridge, Mass.: MIT Press.

Telser, L. 1964. "Advertising and Competition." *Journal of Political Economy* 72: 537–562

Chapter 12

Quality, Durability, and Warranties

> Anybody can cut prices, but it takes brains to make a better article.
> —Philip D. Armour (1832-1901)

We observe that products within the same category are distinguished by a wide variety of characteristics. Cars, for example, are differentiated by engine size, horse power, gas consumption, body size, number of doors, body shape (sedan vs. hatchback), transmission (manual vs. automatic), and luxurious components such as air conditioning, radio, seat covers, electric windows, electric seats.

We tackled the issue of product differentiation in chapter 7, where we analyzed markets with firms' target brands for different consumer populations and showed that product differentiation facilitates price competition. In this chapter, we wish to focus on one aspect of product differentiation that we call *quality*. The only aspect of quality not explicitly analyzed is the risk (health hazard) involved in using the product (see Oi 1973).

We also confine part of the analysis in this chapter to one particular aspect of quality that we call *durability*. The reason for focusing on durability separately from quality is that durability is related to the time dimension, which has a direct impact on the frequency of repeated purchase by consumers. For this reason some economists have argued that market structure has a strong effect on the durability aspect of the product but not necessarily on other quality aspects of the product.

In general, it is hard to point out what constitutes the quality of a certain product since quality has many dimensions. Using the example of the car, we note that quality could mean acceleration, frequency of maintenance, frequency of repair, comfort, and safety. Any reader of the consumer magazines will notice that consumer magazines rarely recommend one brand over all others for the simple reason that quality has many dimensions. That is, recommendations for choosing a certain brand are generally given conditionally on the specific needs of the user. In most cases, consumer magazines provide the readers with tables for comparing from ten to thirty features among the popular brands. Hence, in general, brands are noncomparable on the basis of quality since each brand can be highly ranked because it has some features that are not available with other brands.

For this reason, since multidimensional modeling of quality is very difficult, we will follow the literature and assume that quality can be measured by a real number. Thus, we assume that a higher-quality product is indexed by a higher real number. Using this simplified measure of quality, we analyze in section 12.1 (Personal Income and Quality Purchase) the relationship between consumer-income distribution and the quality of products they purchase. Section 12.2 (Quality as Vertical Product Differentiation) explains why firms produce brands with different qualities. Section 12.3 (Market Structure, Quality, and Durability) discusses a thirty-year-old, still ongoing debate, about whether monopoly firms produce a less durable product than firms under competition. Section 12.4 (The Innovation-Durability Tradeoff) analyzes the effect of product durability on the frequency of introduction of new, improved products. Section 12.5 (The Market for Lemons) analyzes the market for used cars and demonstrates how the existence of bad cars can drive good cars from the used-car market. Section 12.6 (Quality-Signaling Games) demonstrates how high-quality firms can set their price structure in order to signal the quality of their products. Section 12.7 (Warranties) analyzes the role that warranties can play when the quality of the product is unknown prior to the actual purchase. In the appendix, section 12.8 provides a short summary of products-liability laws.

12.1   Personal Income and Quality Purchase

We provide now a short illustration of how the level of personal income affects the quality of brands purchased by different-income consumers. In a series of models, Gabszewicz and Thisse (1979, 1980) and Shaked and Sutton (1982) use the following model to determine what the levels of qualities are and the number of different quality brands that are produced in an industry with free entry and exit. For the sake of brevity, we skip the analysis of the firms and concentrate only on consumers.

Consider an industry with two firms producing brands with different qualities: quality level $k = H$ and quality level $k = L$, $(H > L > 0)$. There are two consumers denoted by i, $i = 1, 2$. The income of consumer 1 is given by I_1, and the income of consumer 2 by I_2, where $I_1 > I_2 > 0$. Thus, consumer 1 is the high-income consumer and consumer 2 is the low-income consumer. Each consumer buys only one unit of the product. The utility level of consumer i, $i = 1, 2$ is given by

$$U_i \equiv \begin{cases} H(I_i - p_H) & \text{if he buys the high-quality brand} \\ L(I_i - p_L) & \text{if he buys the low-quality brand.} \end{cases} \tag{12.1}$$

This utility function has the property that for given prices, the marginal utility of quality rises with an increase in the consumer's income.

The following proposition demonstrates how different-income consumers are assigned to different quality products under the utility function given in (12.1).

Proposition 12.1

1. If the low-income consumer buys the high-quality brand, then the high-income consumer definitely buys the high-quality brand.

2. If the high-income consumer buys the low-quality brand, then the low-income consumer definitely buys the low-quality brand.

Proof. To prove part 1, let $U_i(k)$ denote the utility level of consumer i when he buys the brand with quality k. We want to show that

$$U_1(H) = H(I_1 - p_H) > L(I_1 - p_L) = U_1(L).$$

From (12.1) we have it that since consumer 2 buys the high-quality brand then it must be that

$$U_2(H) = H(I_2 - p_H) > L(I_2 - p_L) = U_2(L).$$

Hence,

$$(H - L)I_2 > Hp_H - Lp_L.$$

Since $I_1 > I_2$, we have it that

$$(H - L)I_1 > (H - L)I_2 > Hp_H - Lp_L.$$

Therefore,

$$H(I_1 - p_H) > L(I_1 - p_L).$$

This concludes the proof for the first part. The second part is left as an exercise in section 12.9. ∎

There have been several applications for the model presented above. Gabszewicz and Thisse (1979, 1980) and Shaked and Sutton (1982) present models based on the utility function (12.1) with more than two possible quality levels and show that even under free sequential entry, only a small number of different-quality brands will be produced.

12.2　Quality as Vertical Product Differentiation

In subsection 7.3.1 we introduced the Hotelling location (address) approach to product differentiation. We interpreted the location of each consumer as his preference for, say, a certain degree of sweetness desired in a chocolate bar, where distance between a consumer and the firm is proportional to the consumer's disutility from the specific brand it sells. Another interpretation for the Hotelling model is simply the physical location of two stores, where consumers must bear per-unit-of-distance transportation cost. In this section we modify the Hotelling model to capture quality differences among differentiated brands.

12.2.1　Vertical differentiation in the basic Hotelling model

The Hotelling model developed in subsection 7.3.1 was classified as a model of horizontal differentiation for the simple reason that, given that the firms are located in the same street as the consumers, there always exist consumers who would rank the two brands differently. That is, in the Hotelling model, assuming that all brands are equally priced, the consumer who is closer to firm A than to firm B would purchase brand A, whereas a consumer who is closer to firm B would purchase brand B. Thus, given equal prices, brands are not uniformly ranked among all consumers, and for this reason we say that the brands are horizontally differentiated.

Phlips and Thisse (1982) emphasized the distinction between horizontal and vertical product differentiation in the following way:

DEFINITION 12.1

1. Differentiation is said to be **horizontal** if, when the level of the product's characteristic is augmented in the product's space, there exists a consumer whose utility rises and there exists another consumer whose utility falls.

2. Differentiation is said to be **vertical** if all consumers benefit when the level of the product's characteristic is augmented in the product space.

Figure 12.1 illustrates a simple diagrammatic comparison between horizontal and vertical-quality differentiation (for a comprehensive discussion of horizontal and vertical differentiation see Beath and Katsoulacos 1991). In Figure 12.1 all consumers are located between points 0 and 1.

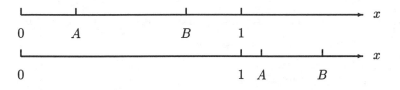

Figure 12.1: Horizontal versus vertical differentiation. *Up:* horizontal differentiation; *Down:* vertical differentiation

The upper part of Figure 12.1 is the same as the Hotelling horizontal-differentiation model displayed in Figure 7.7. In this case, given equal prices, the consumers located near firm A prefer brand A over brand B, whereas consumers located near brand B prefer brand B over brand A. In contrast, the lower part of Figure 12.1 illustrates an industry with vertically differentiated brands where all consumers prefer brand A over brand B (since all consumers are located closer to A than to B).

12.2.2 A modified Hotelling vertical-differentiation model

The basic Hotelling model developed in subsection 7.3.1 is based on preferences given in (7.17) and refers to the "street" illustrated in Figure 12.1. In what follows, we modify the utility function (7.17) so that instead of having consumers gain a higher utility from the nearby brand, all consumers would have their ideal brand located at point 1 on the $[0, 1]$ interval. This modification would allow us to model product differentiation where firms still locate on the $[0, 1]$ interval (and not outside this interval).

There is a continuum of consumers uniformly distributed on the interval $[0, 1]$. There are two firms, denoted by A and B and located at points a and b ($0 \leq a \leq b \leq 1$) from the origin, respectively. Figure 12.2 illustrates the location of the firms on the $[0, 1]$ interval.

The utility of a consumer located at point x, $x \in [0, 1]$ and buying brand i, $i = A, B$ is defined by

$$U_x(i) \equiv \begin{cases} ax - p_A & i = A \\ bx - p_B & i = B \end{cases} \qquad (12.2)$$

where p_A and p_B are the price charged by firm A and B, respectively.

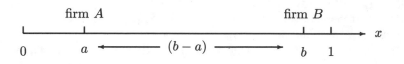

Figure 12.2: Vertical differentiation in a modified Hotelling model

We seek to define a two-period game, where firms choose location in the first period, and choose price in the second period, after locations have been fixed. Before defining the game, let us solve for a Nash-Bertrand equilibrium in prices, assuming fixed locations as illustrated in Figure 12.2.

Let $\hat{x}$ denote a consumer who is indifferent to whether he or she buys from firm A or firm B. Assuming that such a consumer exists, and that consumer $\hat{x}$ locates between the two firms, that is $a \leq \hat{x} \leq b$, the location of the indifferent consumer is determined by

$$U_{\hat{x}}(A) = a\hat{x} - p_A = b\hat{x} - p_B = U_{\hat{x}}(B). \qquad (12.3)$$

Thus, the utility of consumer indexed by $\hat{x}$ from buying brand A equals his utility from buying brand B. Therefore, assuming that $a \leq \hat{x} \leq b$, the number of consumers buying from firm A is $\hat{x}$, whereas the number of consumers buying from firm B is $(1 - \hat{x})$. Solving for $\hat{x}$ from (12.3) yields

$$\hat{x} = \frac{p_B - p_A}{b - a} \quad \text{and} \quad 1 - \hat{x} = 1 - \frac{p_B - p_A}{b - a}. \qquad (12.4)$$

Figure 12.3 provides a graphic illustration of how $\hat{x}$ is determined. The left-hand side of Figure 12.3 illustrates the utility for a consumer located at any point $0 \leq x \leq 1$ when he or she buys brand A and when he or she buys brand B, assuming that $p_B > p_A$. By definition, for the consumer located at $\hat{x}$, the utility from buying A equals the utility from buying B. Moreover, Figure 12.3 shows that all consumers located on $[0, \hat{x}]$ gain a higher utility from purchasing brand A (lower quality) than from purchasing brand B. Similarly, all consumers located on $[\hat{x}, 1]$ gain a higher utility from purchasing brand B (higher-quality brand) than from purchasing brand A.

Note that, as in subsection 7.3.1, we assume here that consumers always buy one unit from firm A or from firm B. In contrast, assuming a reservation utility of zero would generate a group of consumers who do not purchase any brand. Formally, if a reservation utility of zero is assumed, all consumers indexed on $[0, z]$ (where consumer z, $z = p_A/a$ is drawn in Figure 12.3) will not purchase any brand. In this case, the

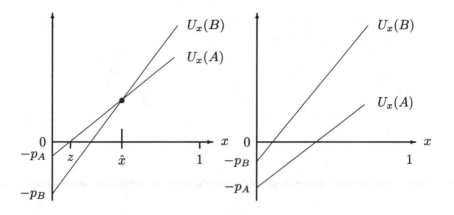

Figure 12.3: Determination of the indifferent consumer among brands vertically differentiated on the basis of quality. *Left: $p_A < p_B$, Right: $p_A > p_B$*

number of A buyers would be reduced to the size of the interval $[z, \hat{x}]$. Exercise 1 in Section 12.9 addresses the case of reservation utility.

It is also clear from the right-hand side of Figure 12.3 that if the price of the lower-quality brand (brand A) is higher than the price of the high-quality brand (brand B), $(p_A > p_B)$, then all consumers purchase only the high-quality brand (brand B).

For given locations of firms (a and b), in the second period each firm takes the price set by its rival firm as given and chooses its price to maximize its profit level. Formally, firm A and B solve

$$\max_{p_A} \pi_A(a, b, p_A, p_B) \;=\; p_A \hat{x} = p_A \left[\frac{p_B - p_A}{b - a} \right] \tag{12.5}$$

$$\max_{p_B} \pi_B(a, b, p_A, p_B) \;=\; p_B (1 - \hat{x}) = p_B \left[1 - \frac{p_B - p_A}{b - a} \right].$$

After introducing all the assumptions for this model, we now pause to give a precise definition for this two-period game. We simply look for a subgame perfect equilibrium as described in Definition 2.10 on page 27.

DEFINITION 12.2 *The quadruple $< a^e, b^e, p_A^e(a, b), p_B^e(a, b) >$ is said to be a vertically differentiated industry equilibrium if*

Second period: *For (any) given locations of firms (a and b), $p_1^e(a, b)$ and $p_2^e(a, b)$ constitute a Nash equilibrium.*

First period: *Given the second period-price functions of locations $p_A^e(a, b)$, $p_B^e(a, b)$, and $\hat{x}(p_A^e(a, b), p_B^e(a, b))$, (a^e, b^e) is a Nash equilibrium in location.*

Definition 12.2 is a subgame perfect equilibrium (see Definition 2.10 on page 27) in which, in the first period, firms choose locations taking into account how their choice of location will affect the second-period equilibrium prices and hence profit levels. It is important to note that the equilibrium actions of the firms in the second periods are functions (not scalars) of all possible given locations of firms.

We now proceed to solve the model, starting from the second period. The first-order conditions to (12.5) are given by

$$0 = \frac{\partial \pi_A}{\partial p_A} = \frac{p_B - 2p_A}{b - a} \quad \text{and} \quad 0 = \frac{\partial \pi_B}{\partial p_B} = 1 - \frac{2p_B - p_A}{b - a}. \quad (12.6)$$

Hence,

$$p_A^e(a,b) = \frac{b - a}{3} \quad \text{and} \quad p_B^e(a,b) = \frac{2(b - a)}{3}. \quad (12.7)$$

Note that both equilibrium prices exceed marginal cost despite the fact that one firm produces inferior quality.

Equation (12.7) reveals that

Proposition 12.2 *The firm producing the higher-quality brand charges a higher price even if the production cost for low-quality products is the same as the production cost of high-quality products.*

Substituting (12.7) into (12.5) yields that

$$\pi_A(a,b) = \frac{1}{b-a}\left[\frac{2(b-a)^2}{9} - \frac{(b-a)^2}{9}\right] = \frac{b-a}{9} \quad (12.8)$$

$$\pi_B(a,b) = \frac{1}{b-a}\left[\frac{4(b-a)^2}{9} - \frac{2(b-a)^2}{9}\right] = \frac{4(b-a)}{9}.$$

We now move to the first period, where firm A takes b^e as given and maximizes $\pi_A(a, b^e)$ given in (12.8), whereas firm B takes a^e as given and maximizes $\pi_B(a^e, b)$.

It is easy to see that firm A would choose to produce the lowest possible quality and locate at $a^e = 0$, whereas firm B would choose to produce the highest possible quality and locate at $b^e = 1$. This result is known as the *principle of maximum differentiation*. Formally,

Proposition 12.3 *In a vertically differentiated quality model each firm chooses maximum differentiation from its rival firm.*

Are you confused? Well, you should be confused since in the horizontal differentiation model of subsection 7.3.1 we showed that when transportation costs are linear, firms tend to move toward the center (minimum differentiation). However, in a vertical (quality) differentiation model the principle of maximum differentiation applies. The reason for this difference is that in a vertically differentiated products model firms specialize in the production of quality for a certain consumer group. Maximum differentiation implies that firms can increase their market power in their targeted consumer group.

12.3   Market Structure, Quality, and Durability

There is an extensive literature debating the relationship between the degree of a firm's monopoly power and the quality or durability it chooses to build into a product (see a survey article by Schmalensee [1979]). That is, the main question is whether a monopoly firm that is known to distort prices and quantity produced (see chapter 5) also builds a shorter durability or a lower quality into its product than does a competitive industry.

Earlier writers on this subject, Kleiman and Ophir (1966) and Levhari and Srinivasan (1969), concluded that firms with monopoly power have the incentives to produce goods of lower durability than would be produced by firms in a competitive market.

Contrary to this literature, Swan (1970a, b, 1971) has demonstrated that there is actually no implied relationship between monopoly power and durability. Swan's novel result is known in the literature as the *Swan's independence result*. This result gave rise to an extensive literature examining the robustness of the independence result. Levhari and Peles (1973) demonstrated that durability built in a product produced by a monopoly can be longer or shorter than under competition. In addition, they have shown that partial regulation of a monopoly that chooses strategies of quantity produced (or price) and durability (or quality) can reduce welfare, where partial regulation is defined as a restriction by the regulating authority on either the quantity produced or the quality but not on both.

Kihlstrom and Levhari (1977) examine the robustness of Swan's result by analyzing the effect of increasing returns-to-scale (IRS) technologies on the production of durability. Spence (1975) developed a fixed-cost (implying an IRS technology) model to measure the divergence between the socially optimal quality level and the monopoly's equilibrium quality level.

The debate on Swan's independence result will probably continue forever. However, the reader is advised to learn the arguments given by the authors participating in this long debate.

In this section we provide a simple illustration of the Swan's independence result by considering a monopoly firm selling light bulbs with variable durability. Let us consider a consumer who lives for two periods who desires light services for two periods. Assume that the consumer is willing to pay an amount of V ($V > 0$) per each period of light services.

On the supply side, assume that light bulb-producing firms possess the technology for producing two types of light bulbs: a short-durability light bulb yielding light services for one period only, and a long-durability light bulb yielding light services for two periods. The unit cost of producing the short-durability light bulb is denoted by c^S, and the unit cost of producing a long-durability light bulb is denoted by c^L, where $0 < c^S < V$, $0 < c^L < 2V$, and $c^S < c^L$.

For simplicity we ignore discounting and analyze market equilibria under extreme market structures: monopoly and perfect competition.

Monopoly firm producing light bulbs

The monopoly firm has the option of selling short- or long-durability light bulbs and to charge a monopoly price for either type of bulbs. First, suppose that the monopoly sells short-durability light bulbs. Then, since the consumer is willing to pay V per period of light services, the monopoly would charge $p^S = V$ per period and would sell two units (one unit each period). Hence, the profit of a monopoly selling short-durability light bulbs is given by

$$\pi^S = 2(V - c^S). \tag{12.9}$$

Now, suppose that the monopoly sells long-durability light bulbs. Since the light bulb lasts for two periods, the monopoly charges a price of $p^L = 2V$. Hence, the profit of the monopoly firm selling long-durability light bulbs is given by

$$\pi^L = 2V - c^L. \tag{12.10}$$

We would like to know under what condition the monopoly produces long- or short-durability light bulbs. Clearly, the monopoly produces short-durability bulbs if $\pi^S \geq \pi^L$. Comparing (12.9) with (12.10) yields

Proposition 12.4 *A monopoly producer of light bulbs would minimize the production cost per unit of duration of the light bulb. Formally, the monopoly would produce short-durability light bulbs if $2c^S < c^L$, and would produce long-durability bulbs if $2c^S > c^L$.*

Proposition 12.4 illustrates Swan's argument that despite the fact that there is only one seller, the monopoly's decision about which type of bulb to produce depends only on cost minimization and not on the market conditions, such as the demand structure. However, to show Swan's complete argument, we investigate which type of light bulbs are produced in a competitive industry.

Competitive light bulb industry

Under perfect competition, the price of each type of light bulb drops to its unit cost. Hence, $p^S = c^S$ and $p^L = c^L$. The consumer who desires two periods of light services would purchase a short-duration light bulb if $2(V - p^S) > 2V - p^L$, or, if, $2c^S < c^L$. Similarly, consumers purchase long-durability light bulbs if $2V - p^L > 2(V - p^S)$, or if $c^L < 2c^S$.

Hence, we can state Swan's independent result by the following proposition:

Proposition 12.5

1. *The durability of light bulbs is independent of the market structure.*

2. *The firms would choose the level of durability that minimizes the production cost per unit of time of the product's services.*

It is important to note that this analysis assumes that our consumer is only concerned with the length of time service is provided by the product and does not attach any other value for durability per se. This is rather an extreme assumption since if, for example, cost minimization yields the decision that light bulbs with durability of five minutes are produced, then this means that our consumer has to replace a light bulb every five minutes. Given that our consumer may attach value for the time it takes to buy and replace a light bulb, it is unlikely that consumers will purchase short-duration light bulbs. Similarly, if cost minimization yields the decision that only single-shave razor blades are produced, then consumers will have to buy a stock of 365 razor blades each year. In this case, it is clear that consumers would be willing to pay more than five times the amount they are willing to pay for a single shave blade for a five-shave blade.

12.4 The Innovation-Durability Tradeoff

All of us often wonder what to do with our old washing machine, black-and-white TV, typewriter, personal computer, turntable, or stereo. When technologies keep changing rapidly, consumers desire new-technology products while they still receive some benefits from the older-technology product that they still own. If all consumers have similar preferences, and hence all desire the new-technology products, old-technology products cannot be sold in a market for used products. Hence, we sometimes get the feeling that with a rapidly changing technology, goods are too durable. That is, we often say to ourselves some variation of: "My old computer does not want to break down, so I don't know what to do with it once I replace it with a newer model."

The question we investigate in this section is whether and under what conditions firms may produce products with excess durability, from a social point of view. In other words, under what conditions do firms find it profitable to produce goods that will last for a very long time so that firms entering with new technologies will not be able to introduce and sell new products owing to the large existing supply of durable old-technology products.

This problem is analyzed in Fishman, Gandal, and Shy 1993 in an infinite-horizon overlapping-generations framework. Here, we merely illustrate their argument in a two-period model, with a simplifying assumption that in each period there is only one firm.

Consumers

In period $t = 1$, there is only one consumer who seeks to purchase computer services for the two periods of his or her life, $t = 1, 2$. In period $t = 2$, one additional consumer enters the markets and seeks to purchase one period of the product's services.

Let V_t denote the per period gain from the quality of the technology imbedded into the product a consumer purchases in period t, and let p_t be the corresponding price. Altogether, the per period utility of each consumer purchasing period t technology is

$$U_t \equiv \begin{cases} V_t - p_t & \text{if purchasing the period } t \text{ technology product} \\ 0 & \text{if not purchasing.} \end{cases}$$

(12.11)

Firms

There are two firms. Firm 1 (operating in period 1 only) is endowed with an old technology providing a (per period) quality level of v^O to consumers. Firm 2 (a potential entrant in period 2) can produce the old-technology product (v^O); however, in addition, firm 2 is endowed with the capability of upgrading the technology to a level of v^N, $v^N > v^O$ for an innovation cost of $I > 0$.

On the production side, we assume that the production cost is independent of the technology level but depends on the durability built into the product. Durability affects production costs since long-lasting products are generally made with more expensive material (say, more metal relative to plastic cases and moving parts). We say that the product is nondurable if it lasts for one period only. That is, a nondurable product is assumed to completely disintegrate after one period of usage. We say that the product is durable if it lasts for two periods. The unit production cost of a nondurable is denoted by c^{ND}, whereas the unit production cost of a durable is denoted by c^D, where we assume that $c^D > c^{ND}$. That is, we assume that durable goods are more costly to produce than nondurables. With no loss of generality, we also assume that the production of a nondurable product is zero $(c^{ND} = 0)$.

The two-period, two-firm game is described as follows: In period 1 firm 1 sells the old-technology product and therefore has to decide which price to charge, (p_1) and whether to produce a durable (D) or a nondurable (ND) product. In this second period, firm 2 obviously chooses to produce a nondurable (since the world ends at the end of period 2) and hence has to decide whether to invest in adopting the newer (v^N) technology and the price (p_2). Figure 12.4 illustrates this two-period game.

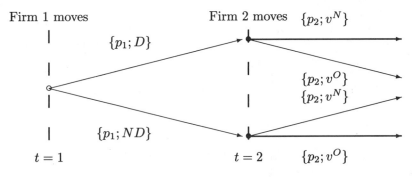

Figure 12.4: Innovation and durability

Below, we analyze two situations based on whether firm 1 produces a durable or a nondurable in period 1.

Second-period pricing, given that first-period production is nondurable

In the second period firm 2 offers either the old-technology v^O product for sale, or invests I for the adoption of its new-technology v^N product. The pricing and innovation decision of firm 2 are summarized by

$$p_2 = \begin{cases} v^N & \text{if } 2(v^N - v^O) \geq I \\ v^O & \text{if } 2(v^N - v^O) < I \end{cases} \qquad \pi_2 = \begin{cases} 2v^N - I & \text{if } 2(v^N - v^O) \geq I \\ 2v^O & \text{if } 2(v^N - v^O) < I. \end{cases} \tag{12.12}$$

That is, when firm 1 produces a nondurable in period 1, then in period 2 both the old and the new consumers seek to purchase the product. If the innovation cost is sufficiently low, firm 2 invests in the improved technology and sells it to the old and new consumers. However, if I

is high, firm 2 sells the old technology to both the old and the new consumers.

Second-period pricing, given that the first-period product is durable

Now, suppose that firm 1 sells a durable in period 1. Then, in period 2, the old consumer already possesses the v^O technology product. In this case, firm 2 has two possibilities: It can price its new-technology product low enough at $p_2^L = v^N - v^O$, which induces the old consumer to discard his old-technology durable and purchase the new product (v^N); in this case, $\pi_2^L = 2(v^N - v^O) - I$. Or, it can price it high at $p_2^H = v^N$, so that only the new consumer purchases the new-technology product, while the old keeps using the old durable product. In this case, $\pi_2^H = v^N - I$.

Comparing π_2^L with π_2^H yields:

Proposition 12.6 *Suppose that firm 1 sells a durable to period 1 consumer. Then, in period 2, firm 2 sells the new-technology product if $I \leq \max\{2(v^N - v^O); v^N\}$. In this case,*

1. *if $v^N > 2v^O$, firm 2 sells its new-technology product to both the old and new consumers;*

2. *if $v^N < 2v^O$, firm 2 sells its new-technology product to the new consumer only.*

First-period durability choice

In period $t = 1$, firm 1 chooses a price (p_1) and whether to produce a durable or a nondurable. If firm 1 sells a nondurable, (12.11) implies that the maximum price firm 1 can charge for selling one period of the product service is $p_1^{ND} = v^O$. In this case, $\pi_1^{ND} = v^O - c^{ND} = v^O$.

In contrast, if firm 1 sells a durable, (12.11) implies that the maximum it can charge is given by $p_1^D = 2v^O$, since in this case the product provides a service of v^O for two periods. In this case, $\pi_1^D = 2v^O - c^D$. Therefore, comparing π_1^{ND} with π_1^D yields

Proposition 12.7 *Firm 1 produces a durable if $v^O > c^D$. Otherwise, it produces a nondurable.*

Proposition 12.7 is rather simple. Firm 1 would produce a durable if the extra profit from charging for second-period product service exceeds the difference in cost between producing a durable and a nondurable $(c^D - c^{ND} = c^D)$.

Durability, innovation, and welfare

We define the social-welfare function as the sum of consumers' utility levels and the firms' profits over the two periods given by

$$W \equiv U_1^1 + U_2^1 + U_2 + \pi_1 + \pi_2 \tag{12.13}$$

where U_1^1 and U_2^1 are the utility levels of period 1 consumer in periods 1 and 2 respectively; U_2 is the utility level of the consumer who lives in period 2 only, and π_t is the profit of the firm operating in period t.

We conclude from the previous analysis that there could be three types of equilibria: (1) firm 1 produces a durable or a nondurable; (2) firm 2 innovates and adopts the new technology or does not innovate; (3) the combination of the two possibilities. The type of equilibrium that obtains is determined by the exact parameter values. In order to restrict the parameter range to interesting cases, we assume that

ASSUMPTION 12.1 $v^O > c^D$, and $\max\{2(v^N - v^O); v^N\} < I < 2v^N$.

The first part of Assumption 12.1 implies that the first-period firm would find it profitable to produce a durable product. The second part implies that the innovation cost for the new technology is at an intermediate range.

We now state our main proposition:

Proposition 12.8 *Under Assumption 12.1,*

1. *firm 1 produces a durable, innovation will not occur, and only the old-technology product will be sold; and*

2. *this outcome is dominated, from a social-welfare viewpoint, by an outcome where firm 1 produces a nondurable instead of a durable.*

Proof. Since $v^O > c^D$, Proposition 12.7 implies that firm 1 produces a durable in period 1. Now, by way of contradiction suppose that firm 2 innovates. Then, if firm 2 sells to both consumers, $\pi_2^L = 2(v^N - v^O) - I < 0$ by Assumption 12.1. Similarly, if firm 2 innovates and sells only to the young consumer, $\pi_2^H = v^N - I < 0$, also by Assumption 12.1: a contradiction. Hence, firm 2 will not innovate, which proves part 1 of the proposition.

To prove part 2, we first calculate the social welfare under this outcome (firm 1 produces a durable and firm 2 does not innovate). In this case, $p_1 = 2v^O$, $\pi_1 = 2v^O - c^D$, $p_2 = v^O$, $\pi_2 = v^O$, and $U_1^1 = U_1^2 = U_2 = 0$. Hence, using (12.13)

$$W^D = 3v^O - c^D. \tag{12.14}$$

Now, suppose that for some reason, firm 1 is forced to produce a non-durable. Then Assumption 12.1 implies that firm 2 does not innovate. In this case, $p_1 = v^O$, $\pi_1 = v^O$, $p_2 = v^O$, $\pi_2 = 2v^O$, and $U_1^1 = U_1^2 = U_2 = 0$. Hence, using (12.13)

$$W^{ND} = 3v^O. \qquad (12.15)$$

Comparing (12.14) with (12.15) implies that $W^{ND} > W^D$.   ∎

The intuition behind part 2 of Proposition 12.8 is as follows: Durability in this model serves as a strategic means to capture future market share. However, durability per se does not serve any purpose to consumers and therefore to the social planner. Since durability is costly to the economy, the social planner can increase welfare by supplying a product of the same quality with no durability.

What policy conclusions can we derive from this model? One recommendation would be for quality-regulating institutions such as standards institutes to allow short durability products into a market with rapidly changing technologies.

12.5   The Market for Lemons

So far, we have analyzed markets where sellers could control the quality of the product they sell. However, there are many markets in which products with predetermined qualities are sold, and therefore sellers are constrained to sell a product with a given quality.

If consumers can determine the precise quality by simply inspecting the product prior to the purchase (if the product is a search good), then the market will be characterized by a variety of qualities of the same product sold at different prices, where higher quality brands will be sold for a higher price. However, in most cases buyers cannot determine the quality before the actual use (the product is an experience good). A natural question to ask is whether markets can function when buyers cannot observe qualities prior to purchase and when experience goods with different qualities are sold. The reason the answer may be negative is that in such markets sellers need not adjust prices to reflect the actual quality of the specific product they sell.

In this section we analyze markets where sellers and buyers do not have the same amount of information about the product over which they transact. That is, we analyze markets with *asymmetric information,* where sellers who own or use the product prior to the sale have a substantial amount of information concerning the particular product they own. By contrast, a buyer does not possess the knowledge about the quality of the particular product he wishes to purchase.

A second feature of the particular markets we analyze here is that reputation does not play a role. This assumption is unrealistic for certain markets where sellers generate most of their sales from returning customers. In fact, almost all the large retail stores in the United States are now allowing consumers to return the products for a full refund, thereby guaranteeing satisfactory quality. Reputation effects are also present in expensive restaurants where most sales are generated from fixed clientele. Still, there is a substantial number of markets in which reputation does not play a role. For example, our analysis will focus on the market for used cars. Whether the seller is a private owner or a dealer, the issue of reputation is of not of great interest to the seller. Therefore, if the seller possesses a low-quality product, the seller has all the incentives to sell it as a high-quality product.

The problem of asymmetric information between buyers and sellers is perhaps most noticeable in the market for used cars. A buyer has a short time to inspect the car, to check the engine's compression and oil consumption, and to perform other tests that can partially reveal the quality of the car. Since full warranties are not observed in the market for used cars, a buyer has to assume that with some probability the used car he buys may be a lemon. Of course, lemon cars need not be just old cars, since all lemon cars have been initially sold as new cars. However, the difference between new lemon cars and used lemon cars is that the seller of a new car (new-car dealer) does not know the quality of the particular car he sells to a particular customer, whereas a seller of a used car knows whether the particular car is a lemon or a good car. Thus, the markets for used and new cars have substantially different information structures.

12.5.1   A model of used and new car markets

Following Akerlof (1970), let us consider an economy with four possible types of cars: brand-new good cars, brand-new lemon cars (bad cars), used good cars, and used lemon cars. All individuals in this economy have the same preferences for all the four types of cars. We let

N^G = value of a new good car;

N^L = value of a new lemon car;

U^G = value of a used good car; and

U^L = value of a used lemon car.

We make the following assumptions:

ASSUMPTION 12.2

   1. *The value of new and old lemon cars is zero; that is,* $N^L = U^L = 0$.

2. *Half of all cars (new and old) are lemons, and half are good cars.*

3. *New good cars are preferred over used good cars; that is, $N^G > U^G > 0$.*

The first and the second items of Assumption 12.2 are merely for the sake of simplifying the model. The third item is clear and is intended to induce good used-car owners to purchase new cars under certain price structure. Assumption 12.2 implies that the expected values of new and used cars are given by

$$EN \equiv 0.5N^G + 0.5N^L = 0.5N^G, \quad \text{and} \quad EU \equiv 0.5U^G + 0.5U^L = 0.5U^G. \tag{12.16}$$

Clearly, the expected value of a new car exceeds the expected value of a used car, $EN > EU$.

There are four types of agents in this economy: (1) new car dealers who sell new cars for an *exogenously given* uniform price denoted by p^N. Clearly, since there is no knowledge of the quality of new cars, all new cars are sold for the same price; (2) individuals who do not own any car, whom we call buyers in what follows; (3) owners of good used cars, whom we call sellers; and (4) owners of lemon used cars, whom we also call sellers.

We denote by p^U the price of a used car. Since used-car buyers cannot distinguish between lemon used cars and good used cars, all used cars are sold for the same price p^U.

We assume that each buyer maximizes the expected value of a car minus a price, in case the agent is a buyer. Formally, the utility of a buyer (who does not own any car) is assumed to be

$$V^b \equiv \begin{cases} EN - p^N & \text{if he buys a new car} \\ EU - p^U & \text{if he buys a used car.} \end{cases} \tag{12.17}$$

The utility of a seller of a good used car who sells his used car for p^U and buys a new car for p^N is given by

$$V^{s,G} \equiv \begin{cases} EN - p^N + p^U & \text{if he buys a new car (and sells his used car)} \\ U^G & \text{if he maintains his (good) used car.} \end{cases} \tag{12.18}$$

Finally, the utility of a seller of a lemon car who sells his used lemon for p^U and buys a new car for p^N is given by

$$V^{s,L} \equiv \begin{cases} EN - p^N + p^U & \text{if he buys a new car (and sells his used car)} \\ U^L & \text{if he maintains his lemon used car.} \end{cases} \tag{12.19}$$

That is, each used-car owner has the option to maintain his car, thereby gaining a utility of U^G or U^L, depending on whether he owns a good or a lemon used car, or to buy a new car for p^N and, in addition, get paid p^U for selling his used car.

The problem of the buyers

The buyers do not own any car and therefore have the option of either buying a new car or buying an old car. Thus, in view of (12.17) buyers will buy a used car if $\mathrm{E}U - p^U \geq \mathrm{E}N - p^N$, or if p^U satisfies

$$p^U \leq \mathrm{E}U - \mathrm{E}N + p^N = \frac{U^G - N^G}{2} + p^N. \qquad (12.20)$$

The problem of the lemon used-car seller

An owner of lemon used car has the option of keeping his car (gaining zero utility), or selling his used car and buying a new car. In view of (12.19) an owner of a lemon used car sells his car if $0 \leq \mathrm{E}N - p^N + p^U$ or

$$p^U \geq p^N - \mathrm{E}N = p^N - 0.5N^G. \qquad (12.21)$$

The problem of the good used-car seller

An owner of a good used car has the option of keeping his car, or selling his used car and buying a new car. In view of (12.18) an owner of a good used car sells his car if $U^G \leq \mathrm{E}N - p^N + p^U$, or

$$p^U \geq p^N + U^G - \mathrm{E}N = p^N + U^G - 0.5N^G. \qquad (12.22)$$

Figure 12.5 summarizes the cases given in (12.20), (12.21), and (12.22) in the (p^N, p^U) space, where used cars are either demanded or offered for sale. The two regions of interest are the upper one, corresponding to (12.22) where p^U is sufficiently high so that an owner of a good used car offers his or her car for sale, and the lower region, corresponding to (12.20) where buyers (those who do not own cars) find p^U to be sufficiently low and decide to purchase a used car.

Figure 12.5 shows that the combinations of p^N and p^U satisfying the condition in which good used cars are sold do not satisfy the condition in which buyers would demand used cars. That is, the region in which p^U is high enough to induce an owner of a good used car to sell his or her good car does not intersect with the region in which p^U is low enough to induce a buyer to purchase a used car instead of a new car. This proves our main proposition, known as the *Lemons' Theorem*.

Proposition 12.9 *Good used cars are never sold. That is, lemon used cars drive good used cars out of the market.*

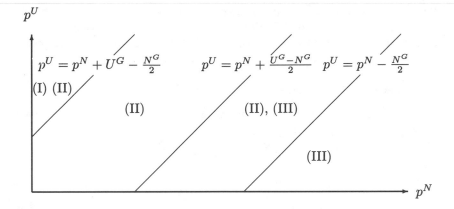

Figure 12.5: The market for lemons: Bad cars drive out the good cars. The prices of new and used cars corresponding to cases where used cars are demanded or offered for sale. (I) Good used-car seller sells. (II) Bad used-car seller sells. (III) Buyers demand used cars. (*Note:* The Figure assumes $U^G > N^G/2$).

A reader who may have purchased a good used car may wonder how it happened. That is, we sometimes observe that good used cars are sold in the market despite what Proposition 12.9 predicts. The reason this happens follows from our assumption that used-car owners may sell their cars only if they wish to buy a new one. However, it often happens that used-cars owners sell their cars for different reasons, such as moving to another state or abroad. Thus, the observation that sometimes good used cars are sold does not contradict Proposition 12.9.

12.5.2   Applications of the lemon problem

The model described in the previous subsection can be applied to describe a wide variety of other markets as well. Consider the health insurance market, where both healthy and sick people wish to purchase health insurance from an insurance company or an HMO. The buyer of an insurance policy knows whether he is healthy. However, the insurance company has no prior information on the particular buyer, unless it requires that all buyers go through an extensive medical checkup. If the insurance price reflects the average treatment costs for a certain period, then by the same argument as in the previous subsection, it is clear that only sick people would purchase health insurance. So, the remaining question is how can insurance companies or HMOs make a profit? The answer is probably that insurance companies attempt to discriminate on the basis of price (charge different rates) according to age and according to health problems the patient had prior to filing the insurance applications. A similar problem occurs in other insurance coverage, namely, risky drivers tend to buy extended coverage for their car. Insurance companies can partially solve this problem by charging different rates according to age, location, and distance to work, following the data they collect on accident frequencies.

Consider now the market for all-you-can-eat restaurants. The buyers are divided into two groups of people, those who eat a lot, and those who eat very little. If the price of a meal reflects the food cost of the average eaters, then it is clear that only very hungry people would go to all-you-can-eat restaurants, whereas less hungry people would generally prefer to pay for each specific dish they order. The question is, then, how can all-you-can-eat restaurants earn a profit? The answer is perhaps that many all-you-can-eat restaurants also serve regular meals, and, as with most restaurants, they earn the profit on side dishes, such as drinks and desserts.

Consider now a labor market in which firms cannot distinguish between productive workers and lazy ones. If the ongoing market wage reflects the average productivity of a worker, it is clear that a good worker who has an alternative wage which does reflect his productivity will not apply for a job at the ongoing wage rate. Thus, the lemon theorem suggests that only less productive workers apply for jobs. Spence (1974) suggests that good workers may take some acts that will distinguish them from the less productive workers, thereby signaling to the firms that they are productive (signaling is discussed in subsections 8.4.6, 12.6, and 12.7). One act would be to go to college. Although college does not necessarily improve the skill of the worker, going to college may signal to firms that the graduate is a productive worker since unproductive workers may not be able to graduate and therefore would not benefit from investing in education.

12.6 Quality-Signaling Games

Consumers are often unable to recognize the quality of a product before they actually purchase and use the product, even if they are aware that both high-quality and low-quality brands are sold in the market. We refer to such goods as experience goods. Producers, however, have more information regarding the brands they sell and in most cases are fully aware of their product. This creates a problem of asymmetric information that we first analyzed in subsection 8.4.6. In that section, we analyzed an entry-deterrence problem in which the potential entrant did not know the production cost of the incumbent, and the incumbent had to signal its production cost by the price it charged prior to the threat of entry.

In this section we analyze a technically similar problem, in which a monopoly firm knows the quality of the brand it sells, but consumers are unable to learn the brand's quality prior to the actual purchase. Our goal is to demonstrate that a monopoly firm can signal the quality it sells by choosing a certain price and by imposing a quantity restriction on the brand it sells. We should note that signaling models are derived from Spence (1974) (for an application to quality signaling, see Wolinsky 1983).

Suppose that there is a continuum of identical consumers. With no loss of generality we normalize the number of consumers to equal 1. Each consumer buys, at most, one unit and knows that the product can be produced in two quality levels: high $(k = H)$ and low $(k = L)$, where $H > L > 0$. For a given price denoted by p, the utility function of each consumer is given by

$$U \equiv \begin{cases} H - p & \text{if the brands happens to be of high quality} \\ L - p & \text{if the brands happens to be of low quality} \\ 0 & \text{if he does not purchase the product.} \end{cases} \quad (12.23)$$

Suppose that each consumer goes to the monopoly's store and observes a price level of p dollars. Will consumers purchase the product if they find that $p = H$? Clearly not, since there is a possibility that the product may be of low quality, and in this case (12.23) implies that such a purchase results in a utility level below zero (which is the reservation utility level).

We now describe the monopoly producer side. Denote by c_H the unit production cost of the monopoly if it is a high-quality producer, and by c_L if it is a low-quality one, where $c_H > c_L \geq 0$. That is, the unit production cost of a high-quality product exceeds that of a low-quality product. We make the following assumptions:

ASSUMPTION 12.3

1. *The monopolist is a high-quality producer.*

2. *Production costs are sufficiently low relative to consumers' valuation of the two qualities. Formally, $L > c_H$.*

The second part of Assumption 12.3 ensures that a high-quality producer can charge $p = L$ for a high-quality product without making a loss.

We assume that the strategy available to the monopolist is two-dimensional so that it can choose the price (p) and the quantity produced (q). Clearly, $0 \leq q \leq 1$ (since the total number of consumers is normalized to equal 1). We wish to solve the problem how a high-quality monopolist can sell a high-quality product, given that consumers are not sure whether the brand they buy is a high-quality one. In other words, how can a high-quality producer convince the consumers that he or she does not cheat by selling a low-quality brand for a high price? Hence, in choosing the price and quantity levels, the producer needs to signal his or her high quality to the consumer.

Proposition 12.10 *There exists a pair of a price and a quantity level that convinces consumers (beyond all doubts) that the brand they buy is a high-quality one. Formally, if the monopolist sets*

$$p^m = H \quad and \quad q^m = \frac{L - c_L}{H - c_L},$$

then (a) consumers can infer that the brand is of high quality, (b) q^m consumers will purchase the product and $(1 - q^m)$ consumers will not purchase the brand due to the lack of supply.

Before proving this proposition, we think it is worthwhile to repeat that the essence of signaling is the firm's to choosing a price-quantity combination that would signal to the consumer that the product is of high quality. In order to do that, the monopoly must choose both a price and a quantity produced that a low quality producer would not find profitable to set! Using this action, the monopoly can convince the consumer that it is not a low-quality producer.

Proof. The monopoly has to show that a low-quality producer would not choose p^m and q^m as the profit-maximizing price and quantity. If the monopolist were a low-quality producer, then he or she could clearly sell to all consumers for the price $p = L$ and make a profit of $\pi^L(L, 1) = 1(L - c_L)$. Let us note that this profit level is attainable by a low-quality producer. Clearly, at this price all consumers would purchase the product.

Now, the question is whether a low-quality monopoly could profitably choose p^m and q^m as the profit-maximizing price and quantity? Suppose it does! Then,

$$\pi^L(p^m, q^m) = (p^m - c_L)q^m = (H - c_L)\frac{L - c_L}{H - c_L} = L - c_L = \pi(L, 1).$$

Thus, using these price and quantity levels, a high-quality monopolist is able to demonstrate that, had he or she been a low-quality producer, he or she could earn the same profit by setting $p = L$ and selling to all consumers instead of setting p^m and q^m. That is, by cutting the profit level to that of what a low-quality monopolist could collect under perfect information, the high-quality producer convinces the consumers that he or she is not a low-quality one, since if he or she were a low-quality producer, he or she could make the same profit level. ∎

So far, we have showed that a high-quality producer can signal his or her quality level to the consumer by using the price and quantity instruments, so that consumers' uncertainty is completely resolved. However, this signaling mechanism raises two questions: What is the cost paid by the monopoly to resolve consumers' uncertainty? Would this high-quality monopoly find it profitable to signal its (high) quality level to the consumers?

To answer these questions, we need to calculate the profit level of a high-quality monopolist when he or she sets p^m and q^m. Hence,

$$\pi^H(p^m, q^m) = p^m q^m = (H - c_H)\frac{L - c_L}{H - c_L} < H - c_H.$$

Hence, comparing this profit level to the profit under perfect information $(H - c_H)$ yields the cost of revealing information. The answer to our second question depends on whether

$$(H - c_H)q^m = (H - c_H)\frac{L - c_L}{H - c_L} \geq (L - c_H)1. \qquad (12.24)$$

Cross-multiplying (12.24) yields that this inequality always holds, since $H > L > c_H > c_L$.

Criticism of the quality-signaling model

The quality-signaling model developed in this section is used only for the sake of illustration. Note that if a firm can choose whether to become a low-quality or a high-quality producer, it would choose to be a low-quality producer. That is, since a high-quality producer needs to signal his quality, and since production cost is higher, it becomes more profitable to be a low-cost producer. This model can be modified to capture profitable signaling by adding consumers who purchase only high quality goods.

12.7 Warranties

One common method of insuring the consumer against defects in the product is to bundle the product with a warranty. There are many kinds of warranties. Some warranties restrict the manufacturer's liability only to parts, others to labor and parts, in case that repair is needed. Most warranties are limited to a certain time period after the purchase, whereas few provide a lifetime warranty. We shall not discuss in the present section why most warranties are limited. The reason has to do with the *moral hazard* phenomenon, a situation where a full warranty will provide the consumer with the incentives to misuse the product, or not to take proper care or it (see Cooper and Ross 1985). Therefore, in order to demonstrate the role of warranty in market behavior, we make the following assumption:

ASSUMPTION 12.4

1. *The product can be either fully operative or fully defective. A defective product has no value to the buyer and cannot be resold for scrap.*

2. *At the time of purchase neither sellers nor buyers know whether the specific product is defective.*

3. *The manufacturer/seller has two options regarding the sale of the product:*

   (a) *He or she can sell the product without a warranty. In this case, if the specific product is found to be defective, the buyer loses the entire value of the product.*

   (b) *He or she can sell the product with a full replacement warranty, which guarantees full replacement of a defective product with no loss of value to the buyer. That is, if the replacement product is also found to be defective, the monopoly is obligated to replace the replacement product, and so on.*

In the literature, Grossman (1980) provides a comprehensive analysis of a monopoly that can offer a warranty for the product it sells. Spence (1977) builds on a signaling argument and shows that higher-quality firms offer a larger warranty than do low-quality firms. In what follows, we confine our analysis to a monopoly selling a product to a competitive consumer, where the product has a certain probability of being defective. The next subsection discusses the monopoly optimal provision of warranty under symmetric information between the buyer and the seller. A subsequent subsection analyses a market in which warranties can serve as a (partial) signal of the product's quality.

12.7.1 Warranties under symmetric information

Consider a product whose value to the consumer is V if the product is operative, and 0 if the product is defective, where $V > 0$. Suppose that there is a known probability for products of this type to be functional. We denote this probability by ρ, where $0 < \rho < 1$. Thus, with probability

$(1 - \rho)$, the product produced by the monopoly will be found to be defective. In this subsection we assume that the seller and the buyer have symmetric information regarding the product's reliability, meaning that both the seller and the buyer know the product is reliable with an exogenously given probability ρ.

Let p denote the monopoly price and $c > 0$ denote the unit production cost of the product. We assume that the utility function of the consumer is the expected value of the product minus the product's price, if he buys the product, and zero if he does not buy the product. Formally,

$$U \equiv \begin{cases} V - p & \text{if he buys the product with full replacement warranty} \\ \rho V - p & \text{if he buys the product without any warranty} \\ 0 & \text{if he does not buy.} \end{cases}$$

$$(12.25)$$

Finally, we assume that $\rho V > c$, which implies that the expected utility from the product exceeds the unit production cost. Assuming otherwise would yield that the product will not be produced since the monopoly will not be able to get consumers to pay a price exceeding unit cost.

The profit-maximizing monopoly has the option of selling the product with or without a warranty.

No warranty

With no warranty, (12.25) implies that the maximum price the monopoly can charge is the expected value of the product. Thus, if we assume one consumer, then under no warranty the monopoly price and profit level are given by

$$p^{NW} = \rho V \quad \text{and} \quad \pi^{NW} = \rho V - c. \tag{12.26}$$

Warranty

When the monopoly provides the consumer with a full replacement warranty, under Assumption 12.4 the consumer is assured of gaining a value of V from the product. We need the following Lemma.

Lemma 12.1 *The expected unit production cost for a firm providing a full replacement warranty is c/ρ.*

Proof. The cost of producing the product is c. If the product is defective, expected cost increases by $(1 - \rho)c$. If the replacement product is defective, then expected cost increases again by $(1 - \rho)^2 c$, and so on. Hence, expected cost is given by

$$c + (1 - \rho)c + (1 - \rho)^2 c + (1 - \rho)^3 c + \cdots = \frac{c}{1 - (1 - \rho)} = \frac{c}{\rho}. \tag{12.27}$$

∎

Thus, Lemma 12.1 implies that the expected production cost is c when $\rho \to 1$ (zero failure probability), and becomes infinite as $\rho \to 0$ since in this case the product is produced and replaced infinitely many times. Altogether, the maximum price a monopoly can charge and the profit level are given by

$$p^W = V \quad \text{and} \quad \pi^W = V - \frac{c}{\rho}. \tag{12.28}$$

Will the monopoly sell with a warranty?

Comparing (12.26) with (12.28) yields the conclusion that $\pi^W > \pi^{NW}$ if $V > c/\rho$, which must hold for the monopoly to make profit under any warranty policy. Hence, we can conclude the analysis with the following proposition:

Proposition 12.11 *Under symmetric information where the reliability parameter ρ is common knowledge, a monopoly will always sell the product with a warranty.*

The intuition behind Proposition 12.11 is as follows. When the monopoly provides a warranty, the monopoly can increase the price by $(1 - \rho)V$ above the price selling with no warranty. The associated increase in cost is

$$\frac{c}{\rho} - c = \frac{(1 - \rho)c}{\rho} < (1 - \rho)V = p^W - p^{NW}$$

by assumption. Hence, by providing a warranty, and given that the monopoly extracts all consumer surplus, the monopoly can increase its price by more than its increase in the cost associated with replacing the products with a certain probability of failure. In other words, consumers are willing to pay more for the warranty than what it costs the seller.

12.7.2   The role of warranties under asymmetric information

In section 12.5 we encountered the problem of asymmetric information between sellers and buyers, where we assumed that sellers are generally better informed about the product's quality than the buyers. Since consumers are not informed, they cannot distinguish between highly reliable products (products with a high probability of not breaking down) and products with a high defective rate.

In this subsection, we continue with the exploration of markets with asymmetric information and analyze a duopoly in which one firm produces a reliable product (high probability of being operative) and one firm produces an unreliable product (with a low probability of being operative). However, the consumer does not have any way of knowing which one of the firms produces the more reliable product. That is, the consumer cannot distinguish between the two products. We show that by providing a warranty with the product and choosing a certain price, the high-quality firm can signal to the consumer that it is selling the more reliable product. In this case, the consumer can conclude beyond all doubt that the high-quality firm is indeed a high-quality producer and not a low-quality producer masquerading as a high-quality firm.

The signaling principle always remains the same: if a high-quality producer wants to prove to the consumer that he or she is a high-quality producer, he or she has to carry an act that is unprofitable for a low-quality producer. From this act, the consumer will conclude that the producer does produce a high-quality product and will be willing to pay for the product accordingly.

Consider an economy with two producers. A high-quality producer selling a product with probability ρ_H of being operative, and a low-quality producer producing a product with probability ρ_L of being reliable, $0 < \rho_L < \rho_H < 1$.

No warranties

Since the consumer cannot distinguish between the producers before the purchase, both products (high and low reliability) are sold for the same price. In this case, since from the consumer's point of view the products are homogeneous before the purchase, a Bertrand price competition (see section 6.3) leads to a unique equilibrium where prices equal the unit cost, hence, zero profits. That is, $p^{NW} = c$ and $\pi_i^{NW} = 0$, $i = H, L$. Therefore, with equal production cost, both high- and low-quality products are produced and the high quality manufacturer cannot be identified by the consumer.

Warranty as a signal

We now show that by providing a warranty and choosing an appropriate price, the high-quality producer can signal to the consumer that he or she sells a reliable product.

Proposition 12.12 *Let $V > c$. The high-quality producer can push the low quality producer out of the market by setting $p^W = c/\rho_L$ and providing a warranty. In this case the consumer will buy only the more reliable product, and the high-quality producer will make a strictly positive profit.*

Proof. We first show that a low-quality producer will not find it profitable to sell his or her product with a warranty at this price. To see that, using (12.27), we calculate that

$$\pi_L^W(p^W) = p^W - \frac{c}{\rho_L} = 0.$$

This concludes the main part of the proof. To complete the proof, we need to verify that first, the consumer will indeed prefer purchasing the more reliable product with a warranty instead of the less reliable product at the lowest possible price, $p = c$; and second, the high-quality producer makes an above zero profit. To see this, observe that the profit of the high-quality firm is given by

$$\pi_H^W = p^W - \frac{c}{\rho_H} = \frac{c}{\rho_L} - \frac{c}{\rho_H} > 0.$$

Finally, the utility of a consumer buying the more reliable product exceeds the utility of buying the less reliable product without a warranty even if the less reliable product has the lowest possible price, c, since

$$U_H^W = V - p^W = V - \frac{c}{\rho_L} > U_L^{NW} = \rho_L V - c.$$

■

12.8 Appendix: The Legal Approach to Products Liability

In this section, we briefly describe the legal approach to products liability, which is concerned with defective products and trades. The reader interested in learning all the legal issues concerning liability should consult Howard 1983 and Phillips 1988 for a comprehensive analysis of product liability. *Liability* refers to the obligation of the producer or the merchant seller to those who were damaged as a result of a defective product. Note that those damaged need not be only the buyers, but could also be bystanders and owners of property.

12.8.1 Defects and liability

In general, there are four types of defects: production defects, design defects, erroneous operating instructions and warnings, and mislabeling and misrepresentations of products. Thus, liability law extends the liability beyond what are purely understood as manufacturing flaws. Clearly, these distinctions are hard to make, but they seem to be important in deciding what standard of liability (strict liability or negligence) is assumed for the manufacturer. For example, it seems more likely that strict liability is generally imposed for production defects than for design defects. Misrepresentation defects may or may not be judged under strict liability.

Under these classifications, it is necessary to determine whether the product is defective. The most common way to make that determination is to rely on consumer expectations, meaning that the product sold must be more dangerous than the "ordinary consumer" with the "ordinary" knowledge common to the community would expect it to be. A problem may arise when the consumer buys products known to be dangerous, since an ordinary consumer should expect the danger associates with this product. Another way of determining defectiveness is to ask whether the seller would have sold the product had he or she known the potential harm resulting from the sale. Thus, in this case, defectiveness is defined as a presumed knowledge by the seller about the quality of the product. Defectiveness can also be determined by determining whether the producer invested a sufficient amount in preventing a risk, where sufficiency estimated by balancing the cost of preventive investment and the monetary value of the inflicted damage or risk caused by the product in the condition it was sold.

Liability is not limited solely to the producer. Liability may be assumed to rest on any commercial seller such as dealers, vendors, constructors, stores, and so on. However, strict liability is less likely to be imposed on them, since the presumed knowledge of the seller is smaller than that of the maker of the product.

12.8.2 Warranties

The Uniform Commercial Code states that unless excluded or modified, a warranty is implied in the contract of sale. However, a warranty is not implied if the seller is not a merchant. The implied warranty, which attaches strict liability to the seller is important since it reduces the chances that written agreements (such as warranty certificates or disclaimers) would always be effective in reducing the seller's liability. In order for the seller to reduce his or her liability to a level below that assumed in the implied warranty, he or she has to provide a disclaimer; however, a disclaimer is not always accepted by courts. A disclaimer is generally accepted in the case of negligence on the part of the consumer. Also, a disclaimer is valid only with respect to the trading parties (buyers), not, for example, with respect to bystanders.

Since warranties have been recognized as a special source of the deception of consumers, the FTC has issued several rules, some of which have been adopted as laws, that require that the terms of the guarantee will be clear and presented in a clear fashion. All of us who have been given warranties can imagine that the amount of information that has to be included in a warranty must be enormous. For example, what is the time interval corresponding to a life time warranty that we often see on back of our packages? What is meant by full warranty? Does a full warranty include labor cost, parts, freight, or the loss of time associated with the loss of use?

12.9   Exercises

1. Consider the modified Hotelling vertical-differentiation model of subsection 12.2.2, but suppose that consumers have a reservation utility, in the sense that a consumer prefers not to buy any brand if his or her utility falls below zero. Recall that the preferences exhibited in (12.2) imply that there is no lower bound on utility from consumption. Figure 12.3 implies that this modification in preferences would not affect the number of high-quality-brand buyers, since all consumers indexed on $[\hat{x}, 1]$ gain a strictly positive utility from buying the high-quality brand. However, point z in Figure 12.3 shows that no consumers indexed on $[0, z]$ will purchase any brand, since otherwise their utility falls below zero.

   Perform the following exercises:

   (a) Show that for given a, b, p_A and p_B, the number of consumers who do not purchase any brand equals to $z = p_A/a$.

   (b) Conclude that the market share of firm A is

   $$\hat{x} - z = \frac{p_B - p_A}{b - a} - \frac{p_A}{a}.$$

   (c) Using the same procedure as in (12.5), show that for given a and b, the second-period equilibrium prices (and profit levels) are given by

   $$p_A(a,b) = \frac{a(b-a)}{4b-a}, \quad \text{and} \quad p_B(a,b) = \frac{2b(b-a)}{4b-a}$$

   $$\pi_A(a,b) = \frac{ab(b-a)}{(4b-a)^2} \quad \text{and} \quad \pi_B(a,b) = \frac{4b^2(b-a)}{(4b-a)^2}.$$

   (d) Show that in the first period, firm A would choose to locate at $a^e = 4/7$, whereas firm B would locate at $b^e = 1$.

2. Prove the second part of Proposition 12.1 using the same procedure as the one used in the proof of the first part.

3. Consider the lemon model described in section 12.5 and suppose that the owner of the good used car must sell his or her car because he or she is leaving the country. Assume that the market prices of used and new cars are exogenously given by $0 < \bar{p}^U < U^G/2$, and $\bar{p}^N = N^G/2$, respectively. Characterize the demand and supply patterns of the four types of agents under these prices.

4. Consider the monopoly's warranty problem under symmetric information analyzed in subsection 12.7.1 but assume that for some reason the monopoly cannot guarantee more than one product replacement in case the product purchased is found defective. That is, if the product is found defective, the monopoly can provide a warranty to replace the product with a new product; however, if the replacement product fails, then the monopoly cannot replace the replacement product.

   (a) What is the monopoly's expected cost if it provides this type of warranty?

   (b) What is the maximum price the monopoly can charge for the product sold with this type of warranty?

   (c) Conclude whether Proposition 12.11 holds for this type of warranty.

12.10   References

Akerlof, G. 1970. "The Market for 'Lemons': Qualitative Uncertainty and the Market Mechanism." *Quarterly Journal of Economics* 89: 488–500.

Beath, J., and Y. Katsoulacos. 1991. *The Economic Theory of Product Differentiation.* Cambridge: Cambridge University Press.

Cooper, R., and T. Ross. 1985. "Product Warranties and Double Moral Hazard." *Rand Journal of Economics* 16: 103–113.

Fishman, A., N. Gandal, and O. Shy. 1993. "Planned Obsolescence as an Engine of Technological Progress." *Journal of Industrial Economics* 41: 361–370.

Gabszewicz, J., and J. Thisse. 1979. "Price Competition, Quality and Income Disparities." *Journal of Economic Theory* 20: 340–359

Gabszewicz, J., and J. Thisse. 1980. "Entry (and Exit) in a Differentiated Industry." *Journal of Economic Theory* 22: 327–338.

Grossman, S. 1980. "The Role of Warranties and Private Disclosure about Product Quality." *Journal of Law and Economics* 24: 461–483.

Howard, M. 1983. *Antitrust and Trade Regulation Selected Issues and Case Studies.* Englewood Cliffs, N.J.: Prentice-Hall.

Kihlstrom, R., and D. Levhari. 1977. "Quality, Regulation, Efficiency." *KYKLOS* 30: 214–234.

Kleiman, E., and T. Ophir. 1966. "The Durability of Durable Goods." *Review of Economic Studies* 33: 165–178.

Levhari, D., and Y. Peles. 1973. "Market Structure, Quality, and Durability." *Bell Journal of Economics* 4: 235–248.

Levhari, D., and T. N. Srinivasan. 1969. "Durability of Consumption Goods: Competition versus Monopoly." *American Economic Review* 59: 102–107.

Oi, W. 1973. "The Economics of Product Safety." *Bell Journal of Economics* 4: 3–28.

Phillips, J. 1988. *Products Liability in a Nutshell.* 3rd ed. St. Paul, Minn.: West Publishing Co.

Phlips, L., and J. Thisse. 1982. "Spatial Competition and the Theory of Differentiated Products: An Introduction." *Journal of Industrial Economics* 31: 1–11.

Schmalensee, R. 1979. "Market Structure, Durability, and Quality: A Selective Survey." *Economic Inquiry* 17: 177–196.

Shaked, A., and J. Sutton. 1982. "Relaxing Price Competition Through Product Differentiation." *Review of Economic Studies* 49, 1–13.

Spence, M. 1974. *Market Signaling.* Cambridge, Mass.: Harvard University Press.

Spence, M. 1975. "Monopoly, Quality, and Regulation." *Bell Journal of Economics* 6: 417–429.

Spence, M. 1977. "Consumer Misperceptions, Product Failure, and Producer Liability." *Review of Economic Studies* 44: 561–572.

Swan, P. 1970. "Durability of Consumer Goods." *American Economic Review* 60: 884–894.

Swan, P. 1970. "Market Structure and Technological Progress: The Influence of monopoly on Product Innovation." *Quarterly Journal of Economics* 84: 627–638.

Swan, P. 1971. "The Durability of Consumer Goods and the Regulation of Monopoly." *Bell Journal of Economics* 2: 347–357.

Wolinsky, A. 1983. "Prices as Signals of Product Quality." *Review of Economic Studies* 50: 647–658.

Chapter 13

Pricing Tactics: Two-Part Tariff and Peak-Load Pricing

> People want economy, and they'll pay any price to get it.
> —Attributed to Lee Iacocca

> You'd be surprised how much it costs to look this cheap.
> —Attributed to Dolly Parton

The pricing techniques discussed in this chapter are generally studied under the subject of public-utility pricing, where a regulating agency (such as the state, city, or any other local government) controls the prices and quality of service provided by the public utility. However, as the reader will discover, these pricing techniques are also used by unregulated and privately owned firms. The major difference between regulated public-utility pricing and prices chosen by privately owned firms is that a regulator attempts to choose prices intended to maximize consumer welfare, whereas unregulated firms choose prices to maximize profit. As it turns out, in many cases the regulator and an unregulated monopoly will choose to set similar price structures that may differ only by a lump-sum transfer from consumers to firms.

In what follows we study several pricing techniques employed by unregulated, profit-maximizing firms. Section 13.1 (Two-Part Tariff) analyzes why sports clubs tend to charge annual membership fees instead of (or in addition to) fixing a price per visit. Two-part tariffs are also charged by some cable TV companies and by wholesale club stores. Section 13.2 (Nonuniform Pricing) generalizes the two-part tariff to the case of heterogeneous consumers and demonstrates how quantity discounts can increase firms' profit by extracting higher surplus from different consumer groups. Section 13.3 (Peak-Load Pricing) analyzes firms' choices of capacity and prices when the demand is seasonal, for example, the choices of airline firms, car rental companies, hotels, resorts, regulated and unregulated phone and electricity companies, universities (day versus evening classes), movie theaters, restaurants, and many others. Section 13.4 (Can Firms "Control" the Seasons?) concludes with an extension of the peak-load pricing problem by having firms set prices to manipulate the relative quantity demanded between seasons.

13.1   Two-Part Tariff

It has been observed that many commercial enterprises charge annual membership dues instead of (or in addition to) pricing each unit of consumption separately. This phenomenon is observed mostly in entertainment industries—such as amusement parks, most sports clubs, and some theaters—and recently in wholesale clubs. Oi (1971) proposed an explanation for this observation. Given downward-sloping demand, when a monopoly charges a fixed price per unit of consumption, if consumers purchase the product, then they gain positive consumer surplus (see subsection 3.2.3 on page 52). Thus, even when a monopoly charges its profit-maximizing price, it is unable to extract the entire consumer surplus. Therefore, in addition to the per unit price, a monopoly firm needs to set a second pricing instrument in order to be able to extract the entire consumer surplus.

13.1.1   Club-visiting consumers

Suppose that a consumer gains satisfaction from club visits and from other goods which we term as money. We denote by Q the number of club visits, and by m the amount of money spent on other goods. Let the consumer earn a fixed income of $\$I$ to be spent entirely on club visits and other goods. We denote by ϕ the membership dues and by p the price per visit. Thus, the consumer's budget constraint is given by

$$m + \phi + pQ \leq I. \tag{13.1}$$

The utility of our fun-loving consumer is a function of the number of club visits (Q) and the consumption of other goods (m). We assume a *quasi-linear* utility function given by

$$U \equiv m + 2\sqrt{Q}. \tag{13.2}$$

Figure 13.1 illustrates a set of indifference curves derived from this utility function. In Figure 13.1, the indifference curve U_0 originating

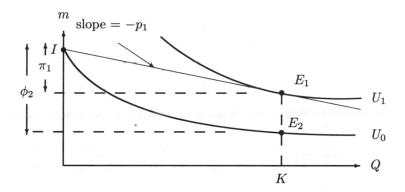

Figure 13.1: Quasi-linear utility indifference curves

from the income level I is associated with the initial utility from spending all the income I on other goods. This indifference curve shows the combinations of club visits and spending on other goods that leave the consumer neither better off nor worse off than spending all the income on other goods.

We now derive the consumer's demand curve for club visits. Substituting (13.1) into (13.2) for m yields the consumer-utility-maximization problem. Hence, for given p and ϕ at a sufficiently low level, the consumer chooses the number of visits Q that solves

$$\max_Q U = I - \phi - pQ + 2\sqrt{Q} \qquad (13.3)$$

yielding a demand function

$$p = \frac{1}{\sqrt{Q^d}}, \quad \text{i.e.} \quad Q^d = \frac{1}{p^2}. \qquad (13.4)$$

13.1.2 No club annual membership dues

Suppose that the club has a limited capacity. Formally, assume that the club's capacity is limited to K visitors, $K > 0$. We now suppose that the club has only one method of collecting money from the club visitors, which is charging a price p per visit where club membership is not required. That is, the club sets the annual membership dues to $\phi = 0$.

When $\phi = 0$ the monopoly club chooses Q to maximize

$$\pi \equiv pQ = \frac{1}{\sqrt{Q}}Q = \sqrt{Q}. \tag{13.5}$$

Proposition 13.1 *Under the preferences given in (13.2), the monopoly club sets the price so that the demand for club visits equals its capacity. Formally,*

$$p_1 = \frac{1}{\sqrt{K}}, \quad and \;\; Q_1 = K, \quad and \; hence \;\; \pi_1 = \sqrt{K}.$$

Proof. The preferences (13.2) yield an elastic demand curve (13.4), implying that the club's profit rises with the number of visits. Therefore, the club will operate under full capacity. The consumption point is illustrated in Figure 13.1 at the point E_1, where the price line (budget constraint) is tangent to the indifference curve labeled U_1, $U_1 > U_0$. Hence, under a price-per-visit structure with no membership fees, the welfare of the consumer must increase compared with the no-club-visits allocation. As we show below, this is not necessarily the case when club charges involve annual fixed dues.   ∎

13.1.3   Annual membership dues

Annual membership fees (fixed-part tariff) is in fact a bundling method discussed in section 14.1, in which the club offers the consumer the opportunity to pay a fixed amount of $\phi > 0$ and to receive a package containing a fixed number of "free" visits.

Figure 13.1 shows that for a package containing $Q = K$ number of visits, the consumer is willing to pay a maximum amount of ϕ_2. That is, consuming a package of K visits for a fixed fee of $\phi \leq \phi_2$ would leave the consumer no worse off than he or she would be with the no-club-visits case.

We now calculate the maximum annual fee that the club can charge for K number of visits that make it worthwhile for the consumer to purchase. To do that, let us observe that in Figure 13.1, by construction, the point E_2 lies on the initial indifference curve U_0. That is, the club sets ϕ just about the level where the consumer is neither better off nor worse off by joining the club. Formally, the club sets ϕ_2 that solves

$$\max_{\phi} \pi(\phi) = \phi \;\; \text{s.t.} \;\; I - \phi + 2\sqrt{K} \geq I = U_0, \tag{13.6}$$

implying that $\phi_2 = 2\sqrt{K}$ and hence $\pi_2 = 2\sqrt{K}$. Hence,

Proposition 13.2 *A fixed fee for a bundle of visits yields a higher profit to the club than any profit generated with a per unit price with no annual fee. Formally,*

$$\pi_2 \equiv \pi(\phi = \phi_2, p = 0) = 2\sqrt{K} > \sqrt{K} = \pi(\phi = 0, p = 1/\sqrt{K}) = \pi_1.$$

13.1.4　Two-part tariff

In practice, a club would hesitate charging exactly ϕ_2 as a membership fee mainly because a small mistake in estimating the exact location of the indifference curve U_0 or the consumer's income may result in no sales at all. A second reason why a firm would not use only a fixed membership fee is that consumers may have heterogeneous preferences so that a high membership fee may induce only a partial participation. We therefore conclude that clubs would generally charge a lower fee than the maximum fee calculated in the earlier subsection. For example, Figure 13.2 demonstrates a possible "package" of Q_3 club visits for an annual fee equal to ϕ_3. Clearly, the consumer buys such a package.

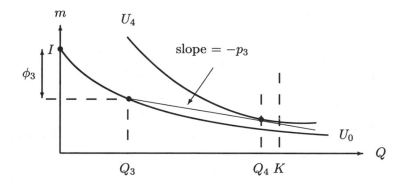

Figure 13.2: Pure two-part tariff club charges

However, Figure 13.2 also shows that the club can further increase its profit by supplementing the membership fee ϕ_3 with an option to purchase additional visits for a price of p_3 per unit. In this case, for p_3 that is not too high, the consumer purchases additional visits, bringing the total number of visits to Q_4, as illustrated in Figure 13.2.

13.2   Nonuniform Pricing

Section 13.1 demonstrated how a two-part tariff can increase firms' profit above the monopoly's per-unit-price profit level by employing two price instruments: the conventional per unit price and the lump-sum (consumption independent) fixed membership dues. The profit gains from using the two-part tariff are due to the monopoly's ability to extract higher surplus from a given group of homogeneous consumers.

In this section we demonstrate a price strategy commonly used by firms to price discriminate among heterogeneous groups of consumers. The *nonuniform price schedule* is a tariff for one or more goods in which the consumer's total outlay does not simply rise proportionately with the amounts of goods the consumer purchases. That is, a nonuniform price schedule consists of quantity discounts and quantity premiums, (for extensive analysis of nonuniform pricing, see Brown and Sibley 1986).

Figure 13.3 illustrates the (inverse) demand for local phone calls by two different groups: households and business, given by $p_H = 12 - 2q_H$ and $p_B = 6 - q_B/2$, respectively, where prices are given in cents. Assuming zero marginal cost in providing phone services, section 5.3

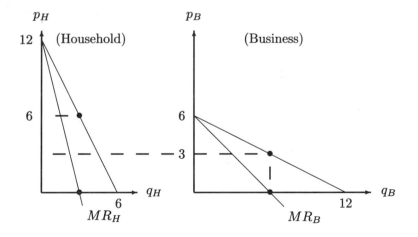

Figure 13.3: Nonuniform pricing and price discrimination

on page 75 shows that a monopoly selling in two segmented markets (markets in which arbitrage cannot take place), would set quantity produced in each market by equating $MR_H(Q_H) = MC(Q_H + Q_B) = MR_B(Q_B) = 0$, thereby charging different prices in the two markets given by $p_H = 6$ and $p_B = 3$ and producing $q_H = 3$ and $q_B = 6$. Therefore, if the monopoly can price discriminate, it would charge business lower rates than it would charge households for local phone calls.

The problem facing the monopoly is how to set the price schedule in a way that would induce the two different groups of consumers to pay different prices and to consume different quantities. In general, there are many reasons why a firm may not be able to charge different prices to different groups of consumers, for example, price discrimination is illegal under the Clayton Act (see subsection 5.6.3); also a monopoly may not be able to identify the consumers belonging to a particular group. Altogether, we now demonstrate that nonuniform pricing can generate the price discrimination monopoly outcome even when the monopoly does not directly discriminate among the different groups of consumers or cannot simply identify these groups.

We now investigate the price schedule illustrated in Figure 13.4.

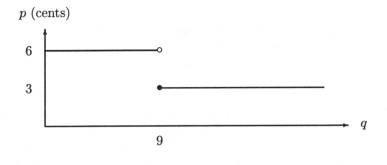

Figure 13.4: Nonuniform price schedule

Proposition 13.3 *Consider the price-per-call schedule illustrated in Figure 13.4 and formally given by*
Regular Rate Program: *Pay 6 cents per phone call.*
Quantity Discount Program: *Pay a reduced rate of 3 cents per phone call but be charged for at least 9 phone calls.*
Then, this price schedule yields the same market prices as those charged by a discriminating monopoly.

Proof. Clearly, Figure 13.3 implies that when $p_H = 6$, households demand $Q_H = 3$ phone calls, and given $p_B = 3$, business customers demand $Q_B = 6$ phone calls. We need to show to show that households will not benefit from adopting the quantity-discount price scheme. If households adopt the regular rate, their consumer surplus (subsection 3.2.3 on page 52) is $CS(6) = (6 \times 3)/2 = 9$.

If households adopt the discount rate, then they are "forced" to buy 9 phone calls (and actually use only 6), which makes the gross-consumer surplus equals the entire area under the demand curve given by $(12 \times 6)/2$. Since households are required to pay for 9 phone calls, their net consumer surplus is

$$CS_H(\text{discount}) = \frac{12 \times 6}{2} - 3 \times 9 = 9 = CS_H(6).$$

Given that the households are indifferent between the two plans, we can assume that they do not purchase the discount plan.

Clearly, when $p = 6$, businesses will purchase zero on the regular payment program. However, when they choose the discount plan

$$CS_B(\text{discount}) = \frac{(6 - 1.5)9}{2} + 1.5 \times 9 - 3 \times 9 = 6.75 > 0.$$

Hence, businesses will choose the discount plan.

Finally, it can be shown that this monopoly phone company makes a higher profit under nonuniform pricing than under uniform pricing. ■

13.3   Peak-Load Pricing

The problem of peak-load pricing is generally studied in the context of optimal governmental regulations for public companies such as public utilities, including phone, transportation and electricity companies (see Brown and Sibley 1986; Joskow 1976; Sherman 1989; and Steiner 1957). However, it should be emphasized that unregulated firms also benefit from setting peak-load pricing, simply because peak-load pricing tends to be efficient and profitable when demand is periodic, and when the investment in capacity is irrevocable in the short run. For example, private firms such as hotels, restaurants, sports clubs, movie theaters, and airlines and other transportation companies are all subject to seasonal demand schedules that vary between yearly seasons, days of the week, or the hours of the day. We therefore focus our analysis on a private-sector monopoly firm (which could represent an airline, a hotel, or a restaurant) and then conclude with a discussion on the role of the regulator in controlling the prices.

Three factors characterize the peak-load pricing problem: First, the levels at which demand varies between periods. Second, capital has to be rented or leased for a long period. That is, since the firm must commit in advance to the level of the plant's capacity, and since this commitment cannot be reversed between periods, the duration of these contracts affect firms' seasonal pricing decisions. Third, the firm's output (products or services) is too costly or impossible to store. Otherwise, if the output is storable, then the firm could produce equal amounts in each period (or all the output in a single period) and then allocate the output across periods according to demands.

Consider a monopoly airline company flying on a single route during high (H) and low (L) seasons.

13.3.1   Seasonal passengers

We let p^H, Q^H, p^L, and Q^L denote the price and quantity of tickets in the high and low seasons, respectively. The demand for flights in each season is given by

$$p^H = A^H - Q^H \quad \text{and} \quad p^L = A^L - Q^L, \quad A^H > A^L > 0. \qquad (13.7)$$

Figure 13.5 illustrates the seasonal demand structure.

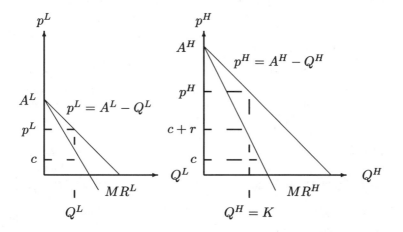

Figure 13.5: Seasonal demand structure and monopoly peak-load pricing

13.3.2   Seating capacity and the airline's cost structure

The monopoly airline faces two types of costs: Capacity cost, which is the number of airplane seats the airline rents for the entire year, and variable cost, which is the cost associated with handling each passenger, which includes check-in, luggage, and food services. For simplicity we ignore other costs commonly associated with airline operations, such as airport charges (see section 17.2 of an analysis of the airline industry).

We denote by r, $r > 0$, the unit capacity cost. Thus, if the airline rents aircraft capacity that can fly K passengers throughout the year, its total capacity investment cost is rK. We denote by c the operational (variable) cost per passenger. Thus, assuming that seating capacity cannot be rented for less than one year (high and low seasons together), the airline's total cost when it flies Q^H passengers in the high season, and Q^L in the low season is

$$TC(Q^H, Q^L, K) = c(Q^H + Q^L) + rK \quad \text{for} \quad 0 < Q^L, Q^H \leq K. \quad (13.8)$$

Equation (13.8) highlights the difference between a two-market, discriminating monopoly analyzed in section 5.3 and the present problem, in which a monopoly airline faces two independent seasonal markets. The difference between the analysis of section 5.3 and this problem follows from the fact that investment in capacity for the high season implies that no investment in seating capacity is needed for the low season. Thus, (13.8) implies that the airline monopoly cost structure exhibits *joint production* where production cost in one market also (partially) covers the cost of producing in a different market (different season).

13.3.3 Profit-maximizing seasonal airfare structure

In section 5.3 we proved that a monopoly discriminating between markets determines the price charged and quantity produced for each market by equating the marginal revenue in each market to its marginal cost. However, how should we calculate the airline's marginal cost in the present case? Clearly, the operational cost (c) is part of the unit cost, but how do we allocate the unit-capacity cost between the markets? The following proposition assumes that the low-season demand is significantly lower than the high-season demand, see Steiner (1957).

Proposition 13.4 *The monopoly's profit-maximizing seasonal pricing and output structure is determined by*

$$MR^H(Q^H) = c + r \quad \text{and} \quad MR^L(Q^L) = c, \quad \text{where} \quad Q^H > Q^L; \quad \text{and}$$

$$p^H = \frac{A^H + c + r}{2} > \frac{A^L + c}{2} = p^L.$$

That is, capacity is determined only by the high-season demand, where the high-season marginal revenue equals the sum of the operational and capacity (marginal) costs.

Proof. Clearly, given the linear shift of demand between the seasons, the profit-maximizing output levels satisfy $Q^H > Q^L$. Hence, $K \geq Q^H > Q^L$, meaning that in the low season the airline does not fly at full capacity. Consequently, the marginal cost of flying one additional passenger in the low season is independent of k. Hence, according to section 5.3, the profit-maximizing low-season number of serviced passengers is determined by is $MR^L(Q^L) = c$. Therefore, investment in capacity is determined only by the high-season demand, so if we follow section 5.3, the monopoly sets is $MR^H(Q^H) = c + r$. ∎

13.3.4 Peak-load pricing and efficiency

Many utility companies (gas, local phone, electricity, and transportation) are regulated in most states, and they have to adhere to price schedules determined by the corresponding government. Most states require that utility companies (especially electricity) submit variable-load price structures based on the (efficient) marginal-cost pricing principle. If we move to the regulator's problem, we discover that the fact that the monopoly faces periodic demand schedules does not complicate the problem beyond the regulator's problem when the monopoly faces a stable demand. Thus, given that marginal-cost pricing is efficient, Proposition 13.4 tells us that the regulator should set the price in the high season to $p^H = c + r$ and in the low season to $p^L = c$. Thus, efficient pricing requires that high-season consumers pay the marginal operational plus the marginal capacity costs, whereas low-season consumers pay only the marginal operational cost.

13.3.5 Peak-load pricing over longer periods

So far our analysis has concentrated on a time period where there is only one low season and only one high season. Suppose that the airline firm is required to invest in capacity for n years, $n > 1$, so that capacity holds for n low seasons and n high seasons. In this case, what would be the profit-maximizing pricing structure for this monopoly airline?

Proposition 13.5 *The monopoly's profit-maximizing seasonal pricing and output structure over n low and n high seasons is determined by*

$$MR^H(Q^H) = c + r/n \quad and \quad MR^L(Q^L) = c.$$

Thus, if the monopoly expects that the capacity would be maintained for n high seasons, the effective unit capacity cost in each period should be taken as k/n.

13.3.6 Limitation of our peak-load pricing analysis

Some limitations of the traditional approach to peak-load pricing analysis are listed in Bailey and White 1974 and Bergstrom and MacKie-Mason 1991. A serious limitation of this analysis is that we neglected to analyze the markets with periodic demand schedules when the different seasonal prices induce consumers to substitute high-season consumption for low-season consumption. High substitutability between peak and off-peak hours is most noticeable in the telephone industry, where individuals postpone making personal phone calls until late at night, early in the morning, and on weekends. Thus, our analysis is incomplete, since it assumes that the demand for peak-season service is independent of the off-peak price.

13.4   Can Firms "Control" the Seasons?

Peak-load prices are generally calculated by assuming that peak and off-peak periods are exogenously given. Although this assumption may describe some public utilities where the regulating authority decides on which periods are considered peak and which off-peak (such as electricity and the telephone), most firms get to control the quantity demanded in each period by simply adjusting the relative prices in the different periods/seasons. For example, by substantially reducing winter airfare, airline firms can potentially turn a low season into a high season. Restaurants control the flow of customers by substantially reducing the price of lunch compared with the price of a dinner. Car rental companies can turn the weekend into a high-demand period by substantially reducing weekend rents to attract nonbusiness-related renters during the weekends.

All these examples lead to one conclusion, namely, peak and off-peak periods should be regarded as economic variables and therefore should not be assumed.

In this section we calculate peak-load prices in an environment where the selling firm can use the pricing structure to manipulate which period will be the peak and which will be off-peak. We analyze what would be the profit-maximizing pricing structure chosen by a service-providing monopoly. There are two reasons why we should analyze the monopoly case: First, analyzing the monopoly case helps us to capture the intuition about the tradeoff between consumers' preferences towards certain period services and the cost of maintaining capacity. Second, many utility and transportation companies are (regulated or unregulated) monopolies. Examples include most transportation companies (buses, trains, and airline), PTTs (public telegraph and telephone companies), and gas and electric utility companies.

Let us consider an industry selling a particular service in two time periods, say, during the day (denoted by D), or during the night (denoted by N). We denote by p_D the price of the service sold during the day and by p_N the price of the service sold during the night.

Consumers and seasonal demand

Let us consider a continuum of consumers indexed and uniformly distributed on the closed interval $[a, b]$, where $b > a \geq 0$ and $b > 1$. We denote by δ a particular consumer indexed on $[a, b]$. The utility of consumer δ, $\delta \in [a, b]$, is assumed to be given by

$$U^\delta \equiv \begin{cases} \beta\delta - p_D & \text{if she buys a day service} \\ \beta - p_N & \text{if she buys a night service} \\ 0 & \text{if she does not buy any service} \end{cases} \tag{13.9}$$

where $\beta > 0$ is the reservation utility for a night service.

Recalling Definition 12.1 on page 310, we can use the following definition to provide the terminology for characterizing consumers' attitudes toward purchasing the service in the different periods (seasons).

DEFINITION 13.1 *Day service and night service are said to be*

1. **vertically differentiated** *if, given equal prices $(p_D = p_N)$, all consumers choose to purchase only the day service;*

2. **horizontally differentiated** *if, given equal prices $(p_D = p_N)$, consumers indexed by a high δ choose to purchase the day service whereas consumers indexed by a low δ choose to purchase the night service.*

Using (13.9), we can see that all day and night services are vertically differentiated if $a \geq 1$, since in this case $\delta\beta \geq \beta$. In contrast, when $0 \leq a < 1$, the two services are horizontally differentiated according to Definition 13.1.

Finally, the consumer indexed by $\hat{\delta}$ denotes the consumer who is indifferent about whether to buy a day service or a night service at the given market prices for these services. Clearly, from (13.9), $\hat{\delta}$ is determined by

$$\hat{\delta} = \frac{\beta + p_D - p_N}{\beta}. \tag{13.10}$$

Thus, given prices, all consumers indexed by $\delta \in [a, \hat{\delta})$ purchase the night service, whereas all the consumers indexed by $\delta \in (\hat{\delta}, b]$ buy the day service.

Production of services

We denote by n_D the number of consumers buying a daytime service and by n_N the number of consumers buying a nighttime service. Clearly, $n_D + n_N \leq b - a$, which is the total number of consumers in the economy.

Production of services requires an investment in capacity and, in addition, bears operation costs. For example, in transportation industries, capacity determines the upper limit on the number of passengers that can be transported in each of the time periods. In the telecommunication industry, capacity determines the upper limit on the number of phone calls (switchboards) that can be simultaneously made in each time period.

Therefore, we denote by K the capacity of a service-producing firm. Then, the number of day or night users cannot exceed this capacity; that is, $n_D \leq K$ and $n_N \leq K$. We denote by r the cost of a unit capacity facing the firm(s).

In addition to capacity cost (number of aircraft seats, etc.), service-producing firms bear operation costs. Therefore, we denote by c_D the per customer operation cost of producing a day service, and by c_N the per customer operation cost of producing a night service. With no loss of generality we assume that $c_D \geq c_N \geq 0$. That is, the operation-per-customer cost of producing a night service is not higher than the operation-per-customer cost of producing a day service.

Clearly, by varying the relative price of the daytime service and the nighttime service, the monopoly service-producing firm can shift the peak demand from day to night or night to day. For this reason, we refrain from using the terminology *peak* and *off-peak* periods (commonly used in the literature) and confine the terminology to *daytime* or *nighttime* periods. That is, peak and off-peak periods are endogenously determined by the selling firm.

In order to find the profit-maximizing pricing scheme set by the monopoly firm, in what follows we decompose the analysis into a cost analysis and a revenue analysis.

The monopoly's cost structure

Assuming that all consumers are served (either by day or night service), we have it that $n_N = \hat{\delta} - a$, and $n_D = b - \hat{\delta}$. Then, the total cost as a function of the indifferent consumer defined in (13.10), is given by

$$TC(\hat{\delta}) = r \max\{\hat{\delta} - a, b - \hat{\delta}\} + \hat{\delta} c_N + (1 - \hat{\delta}) c_D. \tag{13.11}$$

Figure 13.6 illustrates the monopoly's production cost as a function of the location of the indifferent consumer. Figure 13.6 shows that the cost is minimized when the market is equally divided between daytime users and nighttime users, that is, $\hat{\delta} = (a + b)/2$, because when the market is equally divided, half of the total population buys a day service and the other half buys a night service, which implies that the amount of capacity needed by the firm is $K = (a + b)/2$, which is at minimum

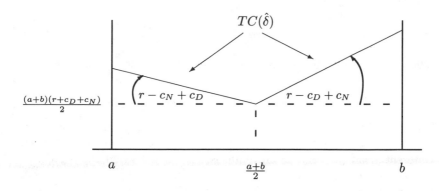

Figure 13.6: Cost structure of a monopoly selling services in two periods. *Note:* $(r > |c_D - c_N|)$

under this equal division. As $\hat{\delta}$ increases, the amount of capacity must increase to accommodate a larger number of nighttime users. Hence, any deviation from the equal division of consumers, either by increasing the number of night users (an increase in $\hat{\delta}$), or by increasing the number of day users (a decrease in $\hat{\delta}$), will result in an additional investment in building capacity.

If we assume that all consumers are served, an increase in $\hat{\delta}$ means that the monopoly switches consumers from day service to night service. Hence, for each consumer switching from day to night, the monopoly saves an operation cost of $c_D - c_N$. Similarly, for each consumer being switched from night to day service (a decrease in $\hat{\delta}$), the operation cost increases by the difference $c_D - c_N$.

Altogether, in view of (13.11), the marginal cost as a function of the indifferent consumer is given by

$$MC(\hat{\delta}) = \begin{cases} -r + c_N - c_D & \text{if } \hat{\delta} < (a+b)/2 \\ +r + c_N - c_D & \text{if } \hat{\delta} > (a+b)/2. \end{cases} \qquad (13.12)$$

Monopoly's revenue

The monopoly seeks to extract maximum surplus from consumers. Hence, in view of (13.9), the monopoly would charge a price of $p_N = \beta$ for a night service. Then, according to (13.10), determining the price for the day service, p_D is equivalent to determining the location of the indifferent consumer, $\hat{\delta}$. Hence, we can assume that the monopoly's choice variable is $\hat{\delta}$, while p_D is determined according to $p_D = \beta\hat{\delta}$. Consequently, we can define the monopoly's revenue as a function of the location of the indifferent consumer by

$$TR(\hat{\delta}) \equiv p_N n_N + p_D n_D = \beta(\hat{\delta} - a) + \beta\hat{\delta}(b - \hat{\delta}). \qquad (13.13)$$

The marginal revenue as a function of the indifferent consumer is given by

$$MR(\hat{\delta}) = \beta(1 + b) - 2\beta\delta. \qquad (13.14)$$

Figure 13.7 illustrates the revenue functions for the cases of vertical and horizontal differentiation. The bottom figure shows that under vertical differentiation ($a > 1$), the revenue is maximized when the indifferent consumer locates to the left of the midconsumer. This is because when the products are vertically differentiated, all consumers prefer day over night services, and given that they are willing to pay more for a daytime service, the monopoly will choose prices so that the majority of the consumers will be daytime users.

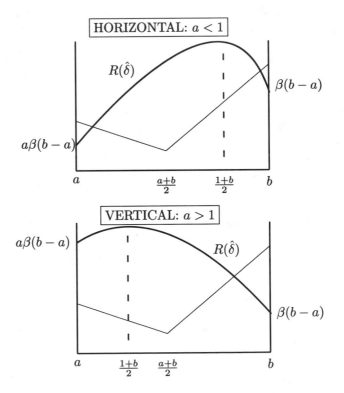

Figure 13.7: Revenue functions for the vertical and horizontal differentiation cases

The top figure shows that when the products are horizontally differentiated ($a < 1$), revenue is maximized when the indifferent consumer locates to the right of the midconsumer. The last case, when $a = 1$, is not illustrated, but in this case the revenue is maximized when the indifferent consumer locates exactly at the midpoint, implying that the monopoly allocates half of the consumers to day services and half to night services.

Monopoly's profit-maximizing pricing structure

Before we proceed with the calculations of the profit-maximizing pricing structure, let us note that the monopoly's profit is measured by the distance between the revenue and the cost functions in Figure 13.7. Figure 13.7 (bottom) reveals that under vertical differentiation the monopoly will never choose to price the service, so that the indifferent consumer would locate to the right of the midconsumer. Figure 13.7 (top) reveals that under horizontal differentiation the monopoly will never choose to price the service, so that the indifferent consumer would locate to the left of the midconsumer.

DEFINITION 13.2 *The daytime period is called a* **peak period** *if $\hat{\delta} < (a + b)/2$, and* **off-peak** *otherwise. Similarly, the nighttime period is called a peak period if $\hat{\delta} > (a + b)/2$, and off-peak otherwise.*

Hence, Figure 13.7 and Definition 13.2 imply that

Proposition 13.6 *If the two time-period services are vertically differentiated, then the monopoly will turn the daytime period into the peak period. If the two time-period services are horizontally differentiated, then the monopoly will turn the nighttime period into the peak period.*

We therefore can state the main proposition concerning monopoly behavior:

Proposition 13.7 *Given that $r > |c_D - c_N|$, a monopoly that maximizes profit will set prices so that services are purchased in both periods such that*

1. *under vertical differentiation*

$$\hat{\delta} = \min\left\{\frac{\beta(1 + b) - r + c_D - c_N}{2\beta}; \frac{a + b}{2}\right\}, \text{ and}$$

2. *under horizontal differentiation*

$$\hat{\delta} = \max\left\{\frac{\beta(1 + b) + r + c_D - c_N}{2\beta}; \frac{a + b}{2}\right\}.$$

Proof. The monopoly seeks to choose $\hat{\delta}$ to maximize $TR(\hat{\delta}) - TC(\hat{\delta})$. By Proposition 13.6, under vertical differentiation $\hat{\delta} < (a+b)/2$. Hence, (13.12) and (13.14) imply that

$$\beta(1+b) - 2\beta\hat{\delta} = r + c_N - c_D.$$

Under horizontal differentiation $\hat{\delta} > (a+b)/2$. Hence, (13.12) and (13.14) imply that

$$\beta(1+b) - 2\beta\hat{\delta} = -r + c_N - c_D.$$

∎

13.5 Exercises

1. Congratulations! You have been appointed to be the chairperson of the Economics department at Wonderland University. Since that old photocopy machine broke down three years ago, the department has been deprived of copying services, and therefore, your first task as a chairperson is to rent copying services from KosKin Xeroxing Services, Inc.. The KosKin company offers you two types of contracts: The Department can simply pay 5 cents per page, or, the department can pay a yearly fee of $300 and in addition pay 2 cents per page.

   (a) Draw the department's total photocopying expenses as a function of the number of copies made each year under the two types of contracts.

   (b) Conclude which contract is less costly, given the number of copies made each year.

2. SouthNorthern Airlines is the sole provider of flights between City A and City B. During the winter, the inverse demand for flights on this route is given by $p_W = 10 - q_W$, where p_W is the airfare charged during the winter and q_W is the number of passengers flown on this route during the winter. Similarly, during the summer the inverse demand function is given by $p_S = 5 - q_S/2$. Denote by K the airline's capacity, defined by the number of airplane seats SouthNorthern intends to acquire, and assume that the average cost of an airplane seat is $r > 0$. Also, suppose that the cost of flying each passenger is $c > 0$.

   (a) Calculate the number of passengers flown in each season and SouthNorthern's profit level, assuming that $r = c = 1$.

   (b) Calculate the number of passengers flown in each season and SouthNorthern's profit level, assuming that $r = 3$ and $c = 1$.

13.6 References

Bailey, E., and L. White. 1974. "Reversals in Peak and Off-Peak Prices." *Bell Journal of Economics* 5: 75–92.

Bergstrom, T., and J. MacKie-Mason. 1991. "Some Simple Analytics of Peak-Load Pricing." *Rand Journal of Economics* 22: 241–249.

Brown, S., and D. Sibley. 1986. *The Theory of Public Utility Pricing.* Cambridge: Cambridge University Press.

Joskow, P. 1976. "Contributions to the Theory of Marginal Cost Pricing." *Bell Journal of Economics* 7: 197–206.

Oi, W. 1971. "A Disneyland Dilemma: Two-Part Tariffs for a Mickey Mouse Monopoly." *Quarterly Journal of Economics* 85: 77–96.

Sherman, R. 1989. *The Regulation of Monopoly.* Cambridge: Cambridge University Press.

Steiner, P. 1957. "Peak-Loads and Efficient Pricing." *Quarterly Journal of Economics* 585–610.

Tirole, J. 1988. *The Theory of Industrial Organization.* Cambridge, Mass.: MIT Press.

Chapter 14

Marketing Tactics: Bundling, Upgrading, and Dealerships

> You can automate the production of cars but you cannot automate the production of consumers.
> —Walter Reuther

In chapter 11 we analyzed advertising as a major marketing tool for firms. Chapter 12 analyzed quality, durability, and warranties as additional strategic tools available to firms. Chapter 13 introduced pricing techniques firms use to extract more surplus from the consumers. In this chapter we proceed to analyze other important strategic marketing tools available to firms. Section 14.1 (Bundling and Tying) analyzes the conditions under which a monopoly finds it profitable to sell two or more units of the product bundled in a single package. We then proceed to analyze the conditions under which a monopoly finds it profitable to tie the purchase of one product to the purchase of another. Next, we show that tying can serve another purpose, as a tool that a firm employs for the purpose of differentiating itself from competing firms (products). Section 14.2 (Used-Books Market) analyzes the textbook market and the incentives publishers have for coming out with yearly new editions. Section 14.3 (Dealerships) analyzes various distribution systems and marketing channels and optimal contracts between producers and distributors.

14.1 Bundling and Tying

Bundling refers to a marketing method in which firms offer for sale packages containing more than one unit of the product. Thus, a firm is said to bundle if consumers have to choose between buying a number of units of the product at a given price, or not buying at all. We sometimes say that a firm that bundles is engaged in *nonlinear pricing,* meaning that each unit of the product is not sold for the same price. Examples of bundling include all quantity discounts (buy one unit, and get the second one for free), volume discounts on phone calls, and frequent-flyer mileage earned by passengers who convert them to free tickets.

Tying refers to firms that offer for sale packages containing at least two different products. For example, a car dealer may offer cars with an already installed car radio, and a computer dealer may include some software packages with the sale of computer hardware. In this case, we say that the seller ties complementary products. However, not every instance of tying involves complementary products; for example, a book store may provide a T-shirt to a customer who purchases a book.

14.1.1   How can bundling be profitable?

Consider a monopoly selling a product to a single consumer whose demand curve is given by $Q(p) = 4 - p$, where p is the monopoly's price and Q is the quantity purchased. Assuming that production is costless, we showed in chapter 5 that the monopoly will set $p^m = 2$ and sell $Q^m = 2$, yielding a profit level of $\pi^m = 2 \times 2 = 4$. Figure 14.1 illustrates the monopoly profit-maximizing price and quantity sold. Clearly, since this monopoly cannot price discriminate with respect to quantities, the consumer surplus is positive and is equal to 2.

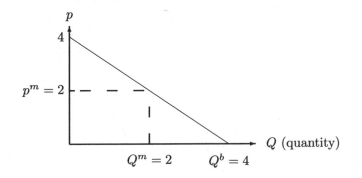

Figure 14.1: Bundling monopoly

Recall from subsection 3.2.3 on page 52 that consumer surplus is defined by the area of the triangle above p^m in Figure 14.1.

Now, suppose that the monopoly bundles four units of the product in a single package and offers it for sale for \$8 (minus 1 cent) per package of four units. The consumer's problem now is whether to purchase the package for \$8 (minus 1 cent) or not to purchase at all. Since purchasing the package of four yields a consumer surplus of $4 \times 4/2 = 8$, it is clear that a consumer faced with this decision would prefer to purchase the package of four rather than not purchasing at all. Therefore, in the case of bundling, the monopolist's profit is $\$8 > \$4 = \pi^m$. Hence,

Proposition 14.1 *A monopoly engaging in bundling would extract all consumer surplus and will therefore make a higher profit than a non-bundling monopolist. Therefore, a bundling monopolist earns the same profit as a perfectly discriminating monopoly.*

14.1.2   How can tying be profitable?

We now show that if consumers are heterogeneous, in the sense that they have different valuations for different products, firms can increase their profits by selling the different products in one package. The gain in profit from tying is analyzed in Burstein 1960; Adams and Yellen 1976; Lewbel 1985; and McAfee, McMillan, and Whinston 1989. We analyze the gains from tying by examining the following monopoly example.

Consider a monopoly selling two goods labeled X and Y. There are two consumers denoted by i, $i = 1, 2$, who buy at most one unit of each product and have different valuations for the different products. We denote by V_X^i the consumer i's valuation of product X (the maximum price consumer i is willing to pay for product X). Similarly, V_Y^i denotes consumer i's valuation of product Y. Table 14.1 shows the different valuations of the two consumers. Table 14.1 shows that consumer 1 is good X-oriented, whereas consumer 2 is good Y-oriented; however, both consumers gain utility from both goods.

	Product	
	X	Y
Consumer 1:	$V_X^1 = H$	$V_Y^1 = L$
Consumer 2:	$V_X^2 = L$	$V_Y^2 = H$

Table 14.1: Consumers' valuations for tied products $(H > L > 0)$

Finally, we assume that the consumers purchase the products only for consumption and therefore do not trade with each other.

No tying

When tying is not allowed, the monopoly has two options: First it can set a low price and sell both products to both consumers. Second, it can set a high price for both goods, and sell one unit to each consumer.

Formally, suppose that the monopoly sets $p_X = p_Y = L$. Then, both consumers purchase both goods, yielding a profit of $\pi^{NT}(L) = 4L$.

Now suppose that the monopoly sets $p_X = p_Y = H$. In this case, consumer 1 buys only good X and consumer 2 buys only good Y. Hence, $\pi^{NT} = 2H$. Comparing the two profit levels yields the monopoly price decision for the case of no tying:

$$p_X^{NT} = p_Y^{NT} = \begin{cases} H & \text{if } H > 2L \\ L & \text{if } H < 2L \end{cases} \quad \text{and} \quad \pi_X^{NT} = \begin{cases} 2H & \text{if } H > 2L \\ 4L & \text{if } H < 2L. \end{cases}$$
$$(14.1)$$

Thus, when H is high, a monopoly would increase the price to a high level and sell only two units. When H is close to L, the monopoly would reduce the price and sell four units.

Tying

Now suppose that the monopoly decides to sell only packages that contain one unit of good X and one unit of good Y for a price of p^T. Clearly, the monopoly sets $p^T = H + L$ in order to extract all surplus from the consumers. In this case, the monopoly sells two packages and earns a profit of $\pi^T = 2(H + L)$. Therefore, we can state the following proposition:

Proposition 14.2 *A monopoly selling two products to heterogeneous consumers (whose preferences are negatively correlated) makes a higher profit from selling a tied package than from selling the components separately. Formally, for every $H > L > 0$, $\pi^T > \pi^{NT}$.*

Proposition 14.2 demonstrates that bundling enables a monopolist to earn the profit level of a price discriminating monopolist as long as the preferences of consumers are negatively correlated. In addition, the gains from tying increase when the preferences become more diverse, $(H - L)$ increases).

14.1.3   Mixed tying

Adams and Yellen (1976) demonstrated that a tying monopoly can further increase its profit if, in addition to pure tying (the monopoly sells only packages composed of both products), the monopoly sells the two products separately.

Following the example of Table 14.1, let us consider the three-consumer example given in Table 14.2. We now investigate the monopoly's marketing options under no tying (NT), pure tying (T), and mixed tying (MT).

Product

	X	Y
Consumer 1:	$V_X^1 = 4$	$V_Y^1 = 0$
Consumer 2:	$V_X^2 = 3$	$V_Y^2 = 3$
Consumer 3:	$V_X^3 = 0$	$V_Y^3 = 4$

Table 14.2: Consumers' valuations for the mixed-tying example

No tying

There are two possibilities under no tying:

(1) If $p_X = p_Y = 3$, then consumer 1 buys good X, consumer 3 buys good Y, and consumer 2 buys one unit of X and one unit of Y. Therefore, the monopoly profit is $\pi^{NT} = 3 \times 4 = 12$.

(2) If $p_X = p_Y = 4$, then consumer 1 buys good X, consumer 3 buys good Y, and consumer 2 does not purchase any good. Therefore, the monopoly profit is $\pi^{NT} = 4 \times 2 = 8$.

It is clear that option (1) will be chosen by the monopolist, since this option yields a profit of $\pi^{NT} = 12$.

Pure tying

In the case of pure tying the monopoly sells packages that contain one unit of X with one unit of Y for a single price, denoted by p^T. Again, there are two possibilities:

(1) The monopoly sets $p^T = 4$. In this case, all three consumers purchase the tied package. Hence, $\pi^T = 3 \times 4 = 12$.

(2) The monopoly sets $p^T = 6$. This price exceeds the package valuations of consumers 1 and 3, and only consumer 2 buys this package. Hence, $\pi = 1 \times 6 = 6$. It is clear that the monopoly will choose option (1) since it yields a profit level of $\pi^T = 12$.

Mixed tying

We now assume that the monopoly markets the two products in two forms. It sells a package of one unit of X and one unit of Y for the price of $p^{MT} = 6$; in addition, the monopoly offers the individual products for sale: thus, mixed tying. Suppose that the monopoly sets the price of the individual products to $p_X = p_Y = 4$.

Clearly, consumer 2 will not buy the individual products since each product is priced at 4 which is above his valuation level. However, consumer 2 will purchase the tied package for $p^{MT} = 6$. In addition, consumer 1 will purchase good X and consumer 2 will purchase good Y, each priced at 4. Thus, the total monopoly profit under mixed tying is given by $\pi^{MT} = 1 \times 6 + 4 + 4 = 14 > 12 = \pi^T$. Hence,

Proposition 14.3 *Mixed tying may yield strictly higher profit levels than pure tying and no tying marketing tactics.*

The intuition behind Proposition 14.3 is as follows: Consumer 2 can be viewed as a consumer who treats the two products as complements, since he attaches a relatively low valuation to each product, but values the two products together at 6, which exceeds the valuation of a package by consumers 1 and 3. In contrast, consumers 1 and 3 do not attach any extra value to the package, but attach a high value to one of the products. By using mixed tying, the monopoly can extract maximum surplus from consumer 2 by selling him his desired package and can extract all surplus from consumers 1 and 3 by selling them their most desired product.

Finally, as pointed out in Adams and Yellen 1976, it is possible to show that mixed tying is not always as profitable as pure tying.

14.1.4   Tying and foreclosure

As we will discuss in section 14.4, antitrust laws prohibit bundling or tying behavior whenever it leads to a reduced competition in the industry. Following Seidmann 1991 and Whinston 1990, we ask why does antitrust law assume that bundling and tying may reduce competition? That is, what is the connection between tying and reduced competition?

To see this connection, we look at two consumers (type 1 and type 2) and a two-system example. Suppose that consumers desire to purchase a system that combines one unit of a computer hardware and one monitor. There are two firms producing computers, which we denote as brand X and brand Y, and one firm producing monitors, denoted by Z. We assume that monitors are compatible with both brands X and Y, (see section 10.3 for an analysis of components' compatibility).

The consumers preferences are given by

$$U^1 \equiv \begin{cases} 3 - p_X - p_Z & \text{buys } X \text{ and } Z \\ 1 - p_Y - p_Z & \text{buys } Y \text{ and } Z \\ 0 & \text{Otherwise} \end{cases} \tag{14.2}$$

$$U^2 \equiv \begin{cases} 1 - p_X - p_Z & \text{buys } X \text{ and } Z \\ 3 - p_Y - p_Z & \text{buys } Y \text{ and } Z \\ 0 & \text{Otherwise.} \end{cases}$$

Thus, (14.2) assumes that consumer 1 is brand X-oriented whereas consumer 2 is brand Y-oriented.

Three independent firms

Suppose now that the firms producing brands X, Y, and Z are independently owned. We look for a Nash-Bertrand equilibrium. Unfortunately, there is more than one equilibrium corresponding to a high monitor price and low computer prices or a low monitor price and high computer prices. Therefore,

Proposition 14.4 *When the industry is decomposed into three independent firms:*

1. *The following prices constitute a Nash-Bertrand equilibrium: $p_X = p_Y = 2$, $p_Z = 1$. In this equilibrium the firm producing X sells one unit to consumer 1, the firm producing Y sells one unit to consumer 2, and the firm producing Z sells two units (one unit to each consumer); the firms earn profit levels of $\pi_X = \pi_Y = \pi_Z = 2$.*

2. *The above equilibrium is not unique.*

Proof. If firm Z raises its price no consumer would buy any system. Also, since all consumers already buy a unit of Z, firm Z cannot increase its profit by lowering its price. In order for the X-producing firm to undercut the Y-producing firm it must set $p_x = 0$, and hence cannot increase its profit. Therefore, undercutting is not profitable to firms X and Y. This establishes part 1.

To establish part 2, observe that the following triplets are also equilibria: $(p_X, p_Y, p_Z) = (1, 1, 2)$, $(p_X, p_Y, p_Z) = (0, 0, 3)$, and $(p_X, p_Y, p_Z) = (3, 3, 0)$. ∎

Firm X takes over firm Z

We now show that firm X can drive firm Y out of business when it buys firm Z and sells products X and Z tied in a single package. Suppose that the newly merged firm, denoted by XZ, offers the package containing one unit of X with one unit of Z for a price of p_{XZ}. We now state our main proposition:

Proposition 14.5

1. *By setting the package price to $p_{XZ} = 3$, the firm selling the package XZ drives firm Y out of business. Thus, tying can serve as a tool for foreclosing a competing firm.*

2. *Foreclosing is not profitable for the bundling firm. The profit of the merged firm XZ when engaged in foreclosing firm Y is lower than the sum of the two premerged firms X and Z.*

Proof. Suppose that firm Y sets $p_Y = 0$. When $p_{XZ} = 3$, the utility for consumer 2 when buying system XZ and product Y for $p_Y = 0$ is $U^2 = 3 - p_{XZ} - 0 = 0$. Hence, firm Y will not produce, and consumer 2 is not served. This proves part 1. Under this foreclosure equilibrium, $\pi_{XZ} = 3$. However, the sum of the profits of firms X and Z before the merger was larger than 3. ∎

Proposition 14.5 shows that tying for the purpose of foreclosing a horizontally competing firm is too costly to the foreclosing firm and is therefore unlikely to be used. The proposition also showed that the act of foreclosing the market reduces aggregate industry profit, since the foreclosure causes one consumer not to be served. Thus, a foreclosed industry may be serving a reduced number of consumers, and hence earns a lower aggregate industry profit. However, in what follows, we show that when firm X buys firm Z, then it is profitable for the merged firm not to completely foreclose on the competing firm, but to leave it a small market share. We therefore define the concept of ϵ-foreclosure.

DEFINITION 14.1 *Suppose that firm X buys firm Z. Then, firm X is said to be ϵ-**foreclosing** firm Y, if for any given small ϵ, $\epsilon > 0$, there exists a Nash equilibrium in prices p_{XZ} and p_Y that would leave firm Y with a profit of $\pi_Y = \epsilon$.*

Definition 14.1 states that ϵ-foreclosure implies that firm Y can still profitably sell units of product Y. However, the merged XZ firm could set p_{XZ} so that it can bring the profit of firm Y to as low as it wishes.

Proposition 14.6

1. *Let $\epsilon > 0$ be a small number. The prices $p_{XZ} = 3 - \epsilon$ and $p_Y = \epsilon$ constitute an ϵ-foreclosure equilibrium.*

2. An ε-foreclosure equilibrium yields a higher profit level to the fore-closing firm than does the total foreclosure equilibrium given in Proposition 14.5.

Proof. Clearly, these prices constitute a Nash equilibrium. To demonstrate the profit advantage of this equilibrium over the total foreclosure equilibrium, let us observe that firm XZ sells to both consumers and therefore earns $\pi_{XZ} = 2(3 - \epsilon)$. However, under the total-foreclosure equilibrium, firm XZ sells to only one consumer, thereby earning $\pi_{XZ} = 3$. Thus, for a sufficiently small ϵ, the ε-foreclosure equilibrium is more profitable for the foreclosing firm.   ∎

The intuition behind the profitability of the ε-foreclosure equilibrium is that the foreclosing firm manages to provide the Y-oriented consumer his or her most preferred system. That is, under the ε-foreclosure equilibrium consumer 2 buys system XZ for $p_{XZ} = 3 - \epsilon$, and then discards the X component and buys the Y component for a negligible price $p_Y = \epsilon$. However, under the total foreclosure equilibrium described in Proposition 14.5, consumer 2 does not get his most preferred system, and therefore, since his willingness to pay falls to 1, consumer 2 does not buy any product.

14.1.5   Tying and international markets segmentation

Firms selling in different markets will generally find it profitable to price discriminate among the markets in which they sell. The profitability from price discrimination has already been discussed in section 5.3. The problem is that in order to price discriminate, the markets should be segmented in the sense that consumers or merchants should not be able to buy the product in the low-price market and then sell it in the high-price market. That is, in order for price discrimination to be feasible, agents should be prevented from engaging in *arbitrage* activities.

In the international economy, arbitrage is weakened by heavy trade restrictions imposed by all governments. Restriction methods include tariffs, quotas, value-added taxes, foreign exchange (dollar holdings) restrictions, safety regulations, and the usual bureaucracy. These government restrictions help firms to engage in price discrimination across international boundaries.

The question that we ask in this section is whether the removal of trade barriers (such as that practiced in the European Community and the North America) would imply that the prices of products would necessarily equalize across markets. We show that since market integration (such as that in the EC) cannot remove all differences of language, culture, and location among consumers, firms may have at their disposal means for making international arbitrage costly to consumers even after integration. Whenever the regional markets differ in some aspects, firms may find it possible and profitable to segment the markets themselves to exploit these differences, especially after government trade restrictions are removed.

Consider a two-country world economy with one consumer in each country. There is only one product produced and distributed by a single manufacturer. This world-monopoly producer has two marketing options: It can sell directly to the consumer in each country, or it can open a dealership in each country selling the product tied with service to the consumer.

Let p_k^S and p_k^{NS} denote the prices of the product when tied or not tied with services, respectively. The utility function of the consumer in country k, $k = 1, 2$, is given by:

$$U_k = \begin{cases} B_k + \sigma - p_k^S & \text{if he or she buys the product with service} \\ B_k - p_k^{NS} & \text{if he or she buys with no service} \\ 0 & \text{if he or she does not purchase the product} \end{cases}$$
(14.3)

where B_k measures the maximum amount a consumer in country k is willing to pay for the basic (without service) product. Thus, each consumer treats a product tied with domestic service and the product with no service as *vertically differentiated* (see section 12.2 for a definition), since for equal prices, $p_k^S = p_k^{NS}$, each consumer would purchase only the serviced product.

The following assumption would make price discrimination profitable for the international monopoly.

ASSUMPTION 14.1 *The consumer in country 1 is willing to pay a higher price for the basic product than the consumer in country 2. Formally,* $B_1 > B_2$.

Finally, with no loss of generality we assume that the product itself is costless to produce but that there may be costs associated with each dealership providing services in each country, which we denote by w, $w \geq 0$.

In the next two subsections we compare two marketing strategies available to the international monopoly.

No attempts to segment the market

Suppose that the monopoly sells the product directly to each consumer (say, via international mail order) and hence does not tie any local service with the product. Then, given zero transportation costs, there is perfect arbitrage between the countries, and therefore, the monopoly would charge identical prices in both countries. Otherwise, a consumer living in the low-price country would make a profit by buying the product in his country and selling it in the high-price country. Altogether, the international monopoly's world uniform price and profit levels under no segmentation (NS) are given by

$$p_k^{NS} = \left\{ \begin{array}{ll} B_2 & \text{if } B_1 < 2B_2 \\ B_1 & \text{if } B_1 > 2B_2 \end{array} \right. \quad \pi^{NS} = \left\{ \begin{array}{ll} 2B_2 & \text{if } B_1 < 2B_2 \\ B_1 & \text{if } B_1 > 2B_2. \end{array} \right. \quad (14.4)$$

Thus, if consumers' valuations are not too diverse $(B_1 < 2B_2)$, then the monopoly would find it profitable to lower the price to B_2 and sell two units. If the consumers' valuations are substantially diverse $(B_1 > 2B_2)$, then the international monopoly would raise the price and sell the product only in country 1.

Segmenting the market

We now suppose that the international monopoly opens dealerships in each country selling the product tied with local service. That is, the local dealer may produce manuals, provide training using the local language, and provide a repair service for the product. Since local services are not internationally traded, the monopoly can charge a different price in each country. Thus, under segmentation (S) the price in each country k, $k = 1, 2$ and the international monopoly profit level are given by

$$p_k^S = B_k + \sigma \quad \text{and} \quad \pi^S = B_1 + B_2 + 2(\sigma - w). \quad (14.5)$$

Thus, by tying services with the product, the international monopoly is able to segment the markets and hence to price discriminate between the markets. Comparing the profit levels given in (14.5) and (14.4) yields

Proposition 14.7 *A sufficient condition for the international monopoly to segment the international market into two national markets by providing local services is that $B_1 > B_2 + 2(w - \sigma)$.*

Is there room for arbitrage after segmentation?

The prices given in (14.5) differ by country. That is, $p_1^S > p_2^S$. However, in order to prove that this segmentation is sustainable, we still need to prove that under these prices arbitrage will not occur. In other words, following Horn and Shy (1996), we need to show that the high-valuation consumer (consumer 1) will not benefit from traveling to country 2, buying the product for $B_2 + \sigma$, then taking it to country 1, and consuming it without the service part.

Now, the consumer in the high-price country (consumer 1) will not benefit from purchasing the product with service in country 2 and then using it without service in country 1 if

$$B_1 - p_2 < B_1 + \sigma - p_1, \quad \text{implying that} \quad p_1 - p_2 < \sigma,$$

that is, if the utility from doing that is lower than the utility of buying from the local dealer with service at a high price. Substituting (14.5) into this condition yields

$$B_1 - B_2 < \sigma, \tag{14.6}$$

that is, if the difference in basic valuation of the product between the countries does not exceed the value of local service. Equation (14.6) yields our major proposition:

Proposition 14.8 *If consumers' valuation of service is higher than the differences between the two consumers in the basic product valuation (i.e., $B_1 - B_2 < \sigma$), then the international monopoly will succeed in segmenting the international market into two national markets in the sense that equilibrium price differentials between the two national markets will not generate arbitrage activities.*

14.1.6   Tying as product differentiation

So far, we have analyzed how a monopoly can increase its profit by using tying and mixed tying. In this subsection we analyze how tying tactics are used by firms competing in prices in a market for a homogeneous product. We show that under oligopoly, firms may use tying tactics in order to differentiate themselves from the competing brands. Put another way, we show that firms engaging in a Bertrand competition in homogeneous products can increase their profit by tying their product with another product or a service in order to differentiate itself from the competing firm. This strategy may lead to market segmentation where the market is split into a group of consumers buying the homogeneous product and another group buying a product tied to a service contract.

Following Carbajo, de Meza, and Seidmann (1990) and Horn and Shy (1996), we consider two firms that produce identical products. However, the firms can sell the product with or without service. By service, we mean service repair contracts, warranties, help in learning how to operate the product, and so on. Examples of firms that sell products without service include some mail-order firms that sell products via the mail without providing substantial training or assembling services to the customers.

Let us consider a single market for a homogeneous product sold by two firms. The firms have the option of selling the product with or without supporting services. Let p^S denote the product's price when tied with services, and p^N the price when sold untied.

Consumers attach the same value B to the basic product. Services, however, yield different benefit to different consumers. To capture this variable, let consumers be uniformly distributed with a unit density on the unit interval according to an increasing valuation for services. A consumer indexed by $s = 0$ derives the least benefit from services, whereas the consumer indexed by $s = 1$ derives the most. Each consumer buys at most one unit of the product, and we assume that B is large enough, relative to consumers' reservation utilities, so that in equilibrium everyone buys a unit. The utility of consumer s, $0 \leq s \leq 1$, is given by

$$U^s = \begin{cases} B - p^N & \text{if the product is bought without services} \\ B + s - p^S & \text{if bought tied with services.} \end{cases}$$

(14.7)

Thus, the service-tied product is vertically differentiated from the basic product in the sense that if both are sold for the same price, each consumer prefers to have the service bundled with the product; (see Definition 12.1 on page 310 for a definition of vertical differentiation).

Let $m > 0$ denote the unit production cost of the basic product, and let $w > 0$ denote the production cost of services (influenced, say, by the wage rate in the services sector). For the rest of this analysis assume that $w < 2$; as we will see, this is a necessary and sufficient condition to guarantee that each firm will have a nonzero market share.

The interaction between the firms takes place in two stages (it is a two-stage game). First, each firm decides whether to sell the product with or without a unit of services. In the second stage, the firms compete in prices.

Solving for a subgame perfect equilibrium (Definition 2.10 on page 27), we first characterize the second-stage price-competition equilibrium under three types of outcomes arising in the first stage of the game.

Both firms tie services, or neither does

Suppose now that neither firm ties its product with services. Since the products are homogeneous, they are sold at a uniform price of $p^N = m$, both firms make zero profits, and the market can be arbitrarily divided between the firms.

If both firms tie the product with services, the products become homogeneous again and will be sold at a price $p^S = m + w$. Hence, both firms make zero profits, and the market can be arbitrarily divided between the two firms.

One firm ties services

If one firm sells the good tied with services and the other without services, and if each firm sells a positive amount, then the market-dividing condition is given by $B + \hat{s} - p^S = B - p^N$, where $\hat{s}$ is the market size and share of the nonserviced product, whereas $1 - \hat{s}$ is the market size and share of the firm that ties. Hence,

$$\hat{s} = \begin{cases} 1 & \text{if } p^S - p^N \geq 1 \\ p^S - p^N & \text{if } 0 < p^S - p^N \leq 1 \\ 0 & \text{if } p^S \leq p^N. \end{cases} \qquad (14.8)$$

Thus, a firm that ties-in has a profit $(p^S - m - w)(1 - \hat{s})$, and a firm that does not tie-in has a profit $(p^N - m)\hat{s}$, where $\hat{s}$ is defined by (14.8).

We define an equilibrium in the second stage when one firm ties and the other does not as the pair $(\bar{p}^S, \bar{p}^N)$, such that for a given $\bar{p}^N$, the bundling firm chooses $\bar{p}^S$ to maximize $\pi^S = (p^S - m - w)(1 - \hat{s})$, subject to $\hat{s}$ satisfying (14.8); and for a given $\bar{p}^S$, the nontying firm chooses $\bar{p}^N$ to maximize $\pi^N = (p^N - m)\hat{s}$, subject to $\hat{s}$ satisfying (14.8).

Substituting $\hat{s}$ from (14.8) into the profit functions and then maximizing with respect to corresponding prices yield first-order conditions (for the interior solution) given by

$$0 = \frac{\partial \pi^S}{\partial p^S} = 1 - 2p^S + p^N + m + w \quad \text{and} \quad 0 = \frac{\partial \pi^N}{\partial p^N} = p^S - 2p^N + m. \quad (14.9)$$

Therefore, the reaction functions are given by, respectively,

$$p^S = \begin{cases} p^N & \text{if } p^N > m + w + 1 \\ \frac{1}{2}(1 + m + w + p^N) & \text{if } m + w - 1 \leq p^N \leq m + w + 1 \\ [p^N + 1, \infty) & \text{if } p^N < m + w - 1 \end{cases}$$
$$(14.10)$$

$$\text{and} \quad p^N = \begin{cases} p^S - 1 & \text{if } p^S > m + 2 \\ \frac{1}{2}(m + p^S) & \text{if } m \leq p^S \leq m + 2 \\ [p^S, \infty) & \text{if } p^S < m. \end{cases}$$

Solving the "middle" parts of the reaction functions given in (14.10) shows that an interior solution exists and is given by

$$\bar{p}^S = \frac{2}{3}(1 + w) + m; \quad 1 - \bar{s} = \frac{1}{3}(2 - w); \quad \bar{\pi}^S = \frac{1}{9}(2 - w)^2 \quad (14.11)$$

$$\bar{p}^N = \frac{1}{3}(1 + w) + m; \quad \bar{s} = \frac{1}{3}(1 + w); \quad \bar{\pi}^N = \frac{1}{9}(1 + w)^2.$$

The first stage: Tying versus not tying

Equations (14.11) imply that when one firm ties with services and the other does not, both firms make positive profits (in contrast to the case where both bundle or both do not). Hence,

Proposition 14.9

1. *In a two-stage game where firms choose in the first period whether to tie their product with services, one firm will tie-in services while the other will sell the product with no service.*

2. *An increase in the wage rate (in the services sector) would*

   (a) *increase the market share of the nontying firm (the firm that sells the product without service) and decrease the market share of the tying firm (decreases $1 - \bar{s}$).*

   (b) *increase the price of the untied good and the price of the tied product (both $\bar{p}^S$ and $\bar{p}^N$ increase).*

Part 2a of Proposition 14.9 is intuitively clear: An increase in the wage rate (the cost of providing services) would reduce the market share of the firm that ties service with the product. Part 2b is interesting since it implies that an increase in the wage rate would raise all prices including the price of the firm that does not provide services (the firm that does not pay the w). This happens because prices are strategic complements (see Definition 7.2), meaning that when the cost (and therefore the price) of the tying firm increases, the price of the nontying firm also increases.

The socially optimal provision of service

We now turn to ask whether from a social point of view this duopoly equilibrium results in too much or too little service marketed to consumers. That is, the interesting question is whether the amount nonserviced products is too high or too low from a social welfare perspective. The socially optimal number of consumers purchasing the product without service, denoted by $s^\star$, is obtained under marginal-cost pricing. Thus, let $p^S = m + w$ and $p^N = m$. Then, $s^\star \equiv p^S - p^N = w$. It can easily be verified that $\bar{s} < s^\star$ if and only if $w < \frac{1}{2}$. Hence,

Proposition 14.10

1. *If the wage rate in the services sector is high, that is, when $w > \frac{1}{2}$, the equilibrium number of consumers purchasing the product tied with service exceeds the socially optimal level. That is, $\bar{s} > s^\star$.*

   2. If the wage rate is low, that is, when $w < \frac{1}{2}$, the equilibrium number
   of consumers purchasing the product tied with service is lower than
   the socially optimal level. That is, $\bar{s} < s^{\star}$.

Proposition 14.10 is easy to interpret. When the cost of service production (w) is high, a smaller number of the serviced product is socially
desirable; that is, the firm that ties the product with service overpro-
duces from a social view point. This is interesting since under a high
wage rate one would expect the sales of the service-tying firm to over-
taken by the (discount) firm that sells with no service. However, as we
show below, the nonservicing firm takes an advantage of the servicing
firm's high service-production cost and raises its price thereby losing
market share to the high-cost servicing firm.

   To support the last argument, let us investigate which firm charges
a higher markup, the service-tying firm, or the discount, nonservicing
firm? We define a firm's price markup by the ratio of selling price, minus
the unit production cost, divided by the unit production cost. Hence,
for $w > 1/2$,

$$\frac{\bar{p}^S - (m + w)}{m + w} = \frac{2 - w}{3(m + w)} < \frac{1 + w}{3m} = \frac{\bar{p}^N - m}{m}. \qquad (14.12)$$

Therefore,

Proposition 14.11 *When $w > 1/2$ and when one firm ties its product*
with services while the competing firm sells an identical product without
services, the firm that sells without service (say, the discount or mail-
order firm) charges a higher markup.

Proposition 14.11 provides the key intuition behind this price competition, since it shows that it is the discount or mail-order firm that over-
charges relative to cost. In other words, it demonstrates that the discount stores use the fact that they have a monopoly on those consumers
who do not desire services (low s consumers). Thus, the nonservicing
firm pushes the price up to the point where the price of a nonserviced
product is close to the price of a service-inclusive product.

14.2   Killing Off Markets for Used Textbooks

Perhaps the most challenging marketing task is to market a new product in a market flooded with perfectly functioning used products. The
reason for this is that marketing often relies on advertising the sustained
quality and durability of the product; hence, if consumers believe that
the advertising is reliable, then consumers will be convinced that old

products need not be replaced. Thus, advertising the quality of the product may be counterproductive for a firm trying to sell new products. Since markets for used products often kill off the market for new products, manufacturers are forced into special marketing techniques to convince consumers to drop their used products and replace them with new ones.

A notable example of this process is the market for light private aircraft. Light aircraft happen to be extremely durable because the airframe rarely degrades, and engines are routinely replaced. This reduction in demand caused several aircraft makers to stop the production of small aircraft (e.g., of the two-seater Cessna 152).

It is often thought that textbook publishers come up with yearly revisions in order to prevent the used-books market from taking sales away from the publishers. Benjamin and Kormendi (1974), Liebowitz (1982), Miller (1974), and Rust (1986) have all analyzed the market for used and new textbooks. We investigate this problem by considering a simple two-period model.

The students

Suppose that in each period t, $t = 1, 2$, there are n students who are requested by their professor to purchase a textbook for their class, which will conclude at the end of the same year. That is, in period 1 there are n students who purchase a new textbook; the students graduate at the end of period 1 and offer the books for sale to the n period 2 newly entering students. We assume that the value of new and used book to an entering student is V. We postpone to an exercise in section 14.6 analyzing the case where used books are less valuable to students than new ones.

We denote by p_t the period t price of a book, $t = 1, 2$. Thus, the utility of a "generation t" student is given by

$$U_t \equiv \begin{cases} V - p_t & \text{if the student buys a book} \\ 0 & \text{if the student does not buy the book.} \end{cases} \tag{14.13}$$

We assume that students have *perfect foresight,* meaning that they are able to calculate the profitable actions taken by the book publisher in the second period.

The textbook monopoly

We assume that there is only one textbook publisher for this particular course, and that in period 1 the publisher sells a brand-new textbook. We denote the unit production cost of a book by c, $c > 0$. In addition, in the second period, the monopoly can invest an amount of F to revise the textbook and to introduce a new edition that may be required by the professor.

Altogether, in period 1 the monopoly chooses the price for the new book p_1, and in period 2 the monopoly chooses whether or not to introduce a new edition and the corresponding price p_2^N or p_2^U.

14.2.1 Second-period actions taken by the textbook publisher

Suppose that all the n period 1 students have purchased a textbook in period 1, and that they offer them for sale (as used books) in period 2. The monopoly seller has to decide whether to invest F in order to introduce a new edition (in this case the value of a used textbook drops to zero), or to sell new copies of the old edition.

Introduction of a new edition

If a new edition is introduced (and adopted by the professor), the value of used books drops to zero, so none of the n period 1 students are able to sell their used books. Hence, all the n period 2 students purchase new books for the monopoly price $p_2^N = V$. In this case, the second-period profit of the monopoly publisher is given by

$$\pi_2^N|_{p_2^N=V} = n(V - c) - F. \qquad (14.14)$$

Selling the old edition

When a new edition is not introduced, the publisher and the n period 1 students compete in homogeneous products. However, given that the n period 1 students already own the used books, their production cost is zero, compared with a unit production cost of $c > 0$ for the monopoly. Hence, Bertrand price competition (see section 6.3) drives the used-books price to unit cost. Formally,

$$p_2^U = c \quad \text{and} \quad \pi_2^U = 0. \qquad (14.15)$$

Thus, the fact that period 1 students do not desire their used textbooks, enables period 1 students to undercut the publisher and to sell the used books to period 2 students. Note that the assumption that the number of students does not vary between generations is critical.

14.2.2 Profit of the publisher

We now calculate the monopoly's sum of profits both for when a new edition is introduced in the second period and for when it is not. Clearly, from (14.14) and (14.15) we know that a new edition is introduced in period 2 if

$$F < n(V - c). \tag{14.16}$$

Hence, if condition (14.16) is not satisfied, the monopoly calculates that the textbook sold in the first period will be sold as used in period 2 for a price of $p_2^U = c$. In this case the monopoly charges $p_1 = V + c$, which is the value of the book plus the resale value in period 2.

If condition (14.16) holds, then a new edition will be introduced in period 2, so the first-period monopoly price is only $p_1 = V$ (since textbooks will not have a resale value in period 2).

Altogether, the sum of the two-period profits is

$$\pi = n(p_1 - c) + \pi_2 = \begin{cases} n(V - c) + n(V - c) - F & \text{if } F < n(V - c) \\ n(V + c - c) + 0 & \text{if } F > n(V - c). \end{cases} \tag{14.17}$$

Equation (14.17) shows the profit of the publisher under the two possible outcomes: a new edition is introduced or it is not introduced in period 2.

14.2.3 Welfare in the textbook market

We now wish to compare the welfare under the two outcomes. Table 14.3 shows the utility of each generation of students under the two textbooks outcomes. Table 14.3 shows that the publisher absorbs all consumer

Publisher's Action	Generation t's Utility	
	$t = 1$	$t = 2$
New Edition	0	0
No Revision	$n[\dot{V} - (V + c) + c]$	$n(V - c)$

Table 14.3: Consumers' utility under the new and used textbooks outcomes

surplus when he introduces a new edition. However, when the publisher does not revise the book, period 2 students gain a strictly positive surplus since competition with used books reduces the price to cost $(p_2 = c)$.

We define the economy's social welfare as the sum of utility and profit levels over the two periods. Summing up Table 14.3 and (14.17) yields

$$W \equiv U_1 + U_2 + \pi = \begin{cases} n(V - c) + n(V - c) - F & \text{new edition} \\ nV + n(V - c) & \text{no revision.} \end{cases} \tag{14.18}$$

Thus,

Proposition 14.12 *A new edition is socially undesirable.*

The result given in Proposition 14.12 is not surprising, since in our model new editions do not serve any social purpose. However, given that the used-books market introduces competition to publishers, the publisher introduces new editions in order to "disconnect" from the used-books market.

14.3   Dealerships

Manufacturers are often not involved with direct marketing to consumers (generally referred to as *end users*). Instead, manufacturers sell their products to dealers and distributors, who offer the products for sale at retail prices. In the literature, the types of arrangements between manufacturers and retailers are referred to as *vertical restraints* and are surveyed in Mathewson and Winter 1986 and Tirole 1988, chap. 4. The common arrangements between manufactures and distributors are: (1) *exclusive territorial arrangements,* where a dealer is assigned a territory of consumers from which other dealers selling the manufacturer's product are excluded; (2) *exclusive dealership,* which prohibits the dealer from selling competing brands; (3) *full-line forcing,* where the dealer is committed to sell all the varieties of the manufacturer's products rather than a limited selection; and (4) *resale price maintenance,* where the dealer agrees to sell in a certain price range, which is generally a minimum or a maximum price required by the manufacturer.

All these arrangements are accompanied by payment arrangements specifying how the dealers pay the manufacturer for the product they sell, such as: a special dealer's price that the dealer pays the manufacturer for each unit it sells or acquires for stocking; a franchise fee, or a lump-sum fee that the dealer pays the manufacturer irrespective of the number of units the dealer sells, or joint ownership, under which the manufacturer partially invests in establishing the dealership, maintains part of the ownership, and therefore receives a share of the profit according to the manufacturer's ownership share.

In this section we will not investigate the reasons why manufacturers do not engage in direct marketing. Reasons for this behavior include increasing returns in distribution due to consumers' shopping needs, such as choice of variety and needs for services; integration of various complementary products produced by different manufacturers into systems usable by consumers; and geographical locations. Therefore, in what follows we assume that marketing through dealers is profitable to the producers, and concentrate on the various contracting arrangements among producers and distributors.

14.3.1   Dealership distributing at a single location

Consider a market for a homogeneous product. The demand for the
product is linear and is given by $p = a - Q$, or $Q = a - p$, where p
denotes the price, and Q the quantity purchased. On the supply side
we assume a manufacturer who sells a homogeneous product to a single
distributor who is the sole seller of the product. In what follows, we
examine various contracts between the manufacturer and the dealer.

Double-monopoly markup

We start with a simplest contract under which the manufacturer sells
each unit to the dealer for a price of d dollars. Let us assuming that the
dealer has no other costs; the dealer treats d as his or her unit cost of
production. Being an exclusive dealer for the product, the dealer acts
as if he or she were a monopoly with a unit production cost of d. Thus,
the dealer chooses the number of units he or she sells that solves the
monopoly problem given by

$$\max_{Q} \pi^d \equiv p(Q)Q - dQ = (a - Q)Q - dQ. \qquad (14.19)$$

The first-order condition is given by

$$0 = \frac{\partial \pi^d}{\partial Q} = a - 2Q - d.$$

Hence, the number of units sold, the consumer price, and the profit of
the dealer are given by

$$Q^d = \frac{a - d}{2}, \quad p^d = \frac{a + d}{2}, \quad \text{and} \quad \pi^d = \frac{(a - d)^2}{4}. \qquad (14.20)$$

The purpose of this analysis is to investigate what the manufacturer's
profit-maximizing, per unit price (d) charged to the dealer should be.
With a unit production cost of c, the manufacturer's profit level is $\pi^M \equiv
(d - c)Q^d$, where Q^d is a function of d and is determined by the dealer
according to (14.20). Hence, the problem of the manufacturer is to
choose d that solves

$$\max_{d} \pi^M \equiv (d - c)Q^d = (d - c)\left(\frac{a - d}{2}\right). \qquad (14.21)$$

The first-order condition is given by

$$0 = \frac{\partial \pi^M}{\partial d} = a - 2d + c \text{ yielding } d^M = \frac{a + c}{2}. \qquad (14.22)$$

Substituting (14.22) into (14.20) and then into (14.21) yields the number of units sold by the dealer and the profit levels of the dealer and the manufacturer. Hence,

$$Q^d = \frac{a-c}{4}, \quad p^d = \frac{3a+c}{4}, \quad \pi^d = \frac{(a-c)^2}{16} < \pi^M = \frac{(a-c)^2}{8}. \quad (14.23)$$

We now state our main proposition.

Proposition 14.13 *When a monopoly manufacturer sets a per unit price to be collected from the dealer for each unit sold, then*

1. *the manufacturer earns a higher profit than the dealer;*

2. *the manufacturer could earn a higher profit if he does the selling by himself. Moreover, the total industry profit (the manufacturer's plus the dealer's) is lower than the profit earned by a single manufacturer/seller monopoly firm.*

Proof. Part 1 is given in (14.23). To prove part 2, recall from section 5.1 that a monopoly that produces and sells (deals) its product earns a profit of

$$\pi^{MD} = \frac{(a-c)^2}{4} > \frac{(a-c)^2}{8} + \frac{(a-c)^2}{16} = \pi^M + \pi^D. \quad (14.24)$$

∎

In other words, the profit of a direct-marketing monopoly exceeds the sum of manufacturer and dealer's profits when marketing is done via a dealership. The reason for this difference is that under a dealership there are two markups: one markup set by the manufacturer and a second markup by the dealer. These markups raise the end-user price above the pure monopoly price and reduce the quantity sold below the pure monopoly level.

Two-part tariff contracts

So far, we have seen that establishing a dealership reduces the aggregate industry's profit, and in particular the profit of the manufacturer. More precisely, the manufacturer who sells his products through independent dealerships is concerned with two major issues: How to induce the dealer to choose a relatively low price, and How to extract (shift) the profit from the dealer. We now show that using a two-part tariff (see section 13.1) contract between the manufacturer and the dealer can result in no loss of profit to the manufacturer.

The problem of the manufacturer is to offer a contact that will be acceptable to the dealer but will induce the dealer to charge the pure monopoly price. We show now that a contract in which the manufacturer sells each unit of output to the dealer for $d = c$ (unit production cost) but in which the dealer has to pay, in addition, a lump-sum participation fee (denoted by ϕ) may result in a monopoly profit to the manufacturer and no loss to the dealer.

Proposition 14.14 *A two-part tariff contract with*

$$d = c \quad and \quad \phi = \frac{(a - c)^2}{4}$$

yields the pure monopoly profit to the manufacturer and no loss to the dealer.

Proof. Under this contract the dealer maximizes $\pi^d = (a - Q - d)Q - \phi$, yielding a first-order condition given by $0 = a - 2Q - d$, which under $d = c$ yields the pure monopoly's output level and a revenue level of $(a - c)^2/4$. Hence, $\pi^d = 0$, and all the monopoly revenue is paid to the manufacturer as a lump sum fee ϕ. ∎

14.3.2 Resale price maintenance and advertising

In general, resale price maintenance is an agreement between the dealers and the manufacturer to maintain a price floor (minimum price), a price ceiling (maximum price), or a fixed end-user price. From the manufacturer's point of view, resale price maintenance has two goals: First, it can (partially) solve the low industry profit associated with the manufacturer and dealer's double markup, as demonstrated in Proposition 14.13. Second, it can induce the dealers to allocate resources for promoting the product.

In this subsection we demonstrate another type of possible arrangement between the manufacturer and two potentially competing dealers. Let us consider a market for a product where the demand is affected by the industry aggregate advertising level, which we denote by A. Formally, assume that the demand for the product is given by $p = \sqrt{A} - Q$, where p denotes the market price and Q, the aggregate quantity sold.

Suppose now that the manufacturer sells the product to two dealers competing in prices. As before, we denote by d the per unit price at which the manufacturer sells to dealers. Also, denote by A_i the expenditure on advertising by dealer i, $i = 1, 2$. Hence, the aggregate advertising spending level is given by $A = A_1 + A_2$.

Our benchmark equilibrium is stated in the following proposition.

Proposition 14.15 *Suppose that the manufacturer is not engaged in advertising, and suppose that the manufacturer sells each unit of the* *product to the two dealers for the price of d per unit. Then, for any given d, no dealer would engage in advertising ($A_i = 0$, $i = 1, 2$) and the demand would shrink to zero, so no sales are made.*

Proof. Since the two dealers are engaged in a Bertrand price game for homogeneous products (see section 6.3), the price would drop to a unit dealer's cost. Therefore, $p = d$. Hence, for every given value of d each dealer makes zero profits, even without spending on advertising. Consequently, dealers will not advertise.   ∎

We now show that a type of arrangement called *resale price maintenance* can eliminate price competition among dealers and induce them to engage in advertising. In the present case, suppose that the manufacturer mandates a price floor to both dealers that we denote by p^f. Clearly, the manufacturer must set $p^f \geq d$, since otherwise, dealers would make negative profits even without engaging in advertising. Given the price p^f, the quantity demanded is given by $Q = \sqrt{A_1 + A_2} - p^f$, which is assumed to be equally split between the two dealers. That is, advertising in this model is assumed to raise directly the demand faced by the industry only indirectly the demand faced by the individual dealer. The only strategic variable of each dealer is the advertising level. Formally, each dealer i takes the advertising level of the competing dealer (A_j) as given and chooses his or her advertising level that solves

$$\max_{A_i} \pi_i^D = \frac{\sqrt{A_i + A_j} - p^f}{2}(p^f - d) - A_i.$$

The first-order condition with respect to A_i yields

$$0 = \frac{\partial \pi_i^D}{\partial A_i} = \frac{p^f - d}{4\sqrt{A_i + A_j}} - 1,$$

implying that

$$A_1 + A_2 = \left(\frac{p^f - d}{4}\right)^2. \tag{14.25}$$

Equation (14.25) shows that only the aggregate amount of advertising can be determined for given levels of p^f and d, and the distribution of advertising spending among the dealers is not uniquely determined, in the sense that for every extra dollar dealer 1 spends on advertising, dealer 2 reduces the amount spent on advertising by exactly one dollar. However, (14.25) implies our main proposition.

Proposition 14.16 *Resale price maintenance $p^f > d$ ensures that at least one dealer will engage in advertising. Moreover, the aggregate dealers spending on advertising increases with an increase in the gap between the price floor and the dealer's per unit fee ($p^f - d$).*

14.3.3 Territorial dealerships

We now investigate how territorial considerations affect a manufacturer's decision whether to grant a single dealership, or whether to grant dealerships to several dealers who may engage in competition over a given territory. We assume that the manufacturer's production cost is zero ($c = 0$), and that the manufacturer sells each unit of the product to each dealer for a price of d to be determined by the manufacturer. In addition, each dealer has to invest an amount of $F > 0$ in order to establish a dealership.

Consider a city with two consumers located at the edges of town as illustrated in Figure 14.2. We assume that the transportation cost from

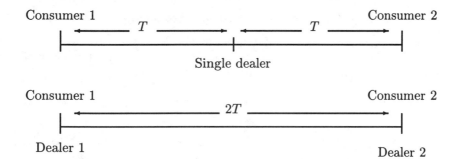

Figure 14.2: Territorial dealerships in the linear city. *Up:* A single dealership locating at the center; *Down:* Two dealers locating at the edges of town

an edge of town to the center is measured by T. Hence, the transportation cost from one side of town to the polar side is $2T$.

Let B ($B > F + T$) denote the basic value each consumer attaches to the product. We assume that the utility function of each consumer i, $i = 1, 2$ is given by

$$U^i \equiv \begin{cases} B - T - p & \text{if he or she buys from center dealer} \\ B - p_i & \text{if he or she buys from the nearby dealership} \\ B - 2T - p_j & \text{if he or she buys from the other side of town} \\ 0 & \text{if he or she does not buy.} \end{cases}$$

$$(14.26)$$

Exclusive territorial dealership located at the town center

The dealer buys each unit of the product from the manufacturer at the price of d and chooses the price p^D to maximize profit. Being a monopoly over the entire town, the monopoly extracts all consumer surpluses by charging $p^D = B - T$, which by (14.26) is the maximum price a consumer is willing to pay when shopping at the center of town. Hence, the dealer sells to the two consumers ($Q^D = 2$) and earns a profit of $\pi^D = 2(p^D - d) - F = 2(B - T - d) - F$.

The manufacturer's problem is to set the dealer's per unit fee to maximize profit subject to having the dealer making a nonnegative profit. Formally, the manufacturer solves

$$\max_d \pi^M \equiv dQ^D = 2d \text{ s.t. } \pi^D = 2(B - T - d) - F \geq 0, \quad \text{yielding}$$

$$d = B - T - \frac{F}{2}, \quad \pi^D = 0, \quad \text{and} \quad \pi^M = 2d = 2(B - T) - F. \quad (14.27)$$

Two dealerships located at the town edges: Equilibrium of a price game

Suppose now that the manufacturer grants dealerships to two stores located at the edges to town. Our analysis will focus on two sizes of towns reflected in the transportation cost parameter T.

DEFINITION 14.2 *The town is said to be large if $T > F/4$ and small if $T < F/4$.*

In Proposition 7.8 on page 160, we proved that a Nash-Bertrand equilibrium prices may not exist for the discrete-location model. Therefore, we look for an equilibrium concept where equilibrium prices satisfy the condition that no dealer would find it profitable to lower the price to undercut a rival dealer selling at the other side of town. If we recall our definition of an *undercutproof equilibrium* given in Definition 7.5 on page 161, then

DEFINITION 14.3 *The pair of prices p_1^D and p_2^D is called an* **undercutproof equilibrium (UPE)** *if*

$$\pi_1^D = p_1^D - d - F \geq 2(p_2^D - 2T - d) - F \quad and$$
$$\pi_2^D = p_2^D - d - F \geq 2(p_1^D - 2T - d) - F.$$

That is, each dealer selling to the consumer nearby does not find it profitable to undercut the rival dealer (by selling at the rival's price minus the transportation cost of crossing the whole town).

Two dealerships: Large town case

When the town is large ($F < 4T$), we show that firms cannot increase their profits by engaging in undercutting simply because subsidizing the transportation cost of the consumer located on the other side of town is too costly. Therefore, the manufacturer can extract maximal rent by setting the dealers' fee to $d = B - F$. Hence, each dealer charges the maximal price, $p_i^D = B$ and earns $\pi_i^D = B - d - F = B - (B - F) - F = 0$, and the manufacturer earns $\pi_i^M = 2d = 2(B - F)$.

We need to ensure that the prices set by the dealers, $p_i^D = B$, constitute a UPE (Definition 14.3). This is easily established by observing that

$$\pi_i^D = B - (B - F) - F \geq 2[B - 2T - (B - F)] - F \quad \text{which holds if} \quad F < 4T$$

which is implied by our assumption that the town is large. Comparing the manufacturer's profit level with the profit given in (14.27) implies

Proposition 14.17 *When the town is large, the manufacturer will grant a single dealership to be located at the center if $2T < F < 4T$, and two dealerships to be located at the edges of town if $F < 2T$.*

Proposition 14.17 simply states that if the sunk cost associated with establishing a dealership is high, the manufacture will establish only one dealership.

Two dealerships: Small town case

When the town is small $(F > 4T)$, the two dealerships are engaged in an intense price competition which yields losses to the two dealers. To see this, solving the two UPE conditions in Definition 14.3 yields that $p_i^D = d + 4T$. Therefore, $\pi_i^D = p_i^D - d - F = 4T - F < 0$ since the town is small. Hence, the dealers and the manufacturer cannot make positive profits.

Proposition 14.18 *When the town is small, the manufacturer will grant only a single dealership to be located at the center.*

Imposed territorial-exclusive dealerships

The previous analysis showed that when the town is small, the manufacturer cannot make any profit when he or she grants dealerships to two dealers. Therefore, we now ask what kind of arrangements can be made between the manufacturer and the dealers so that the two dealers could locate at the edges of town but would refrain from price competition leading to a reduced industry profit? Clearly, if the dealers could collude in prices, they could charge the local monopoly price $p_i^D = B - F$ and absorb all consumer surpluses. However, if they cannot collude, then we ask what kind of contracts the manufacturer can write with the dealers that would ensure that dealers charge the local monopoly price. One way of doing that is given in the following proposition.

Proposition 14.19 *Suppose that the manufacturer grants dealerships to two dealers located at the edges of town. Then, granting territorial-exclusive dealerships (exclusive dealerships limited to geographical locations) yields a strictly positive profit to the manufacturer.*

Proposition 14.19 does not require a formal proof because if the manufacturer limits the territory of dealer 1 to selling only on $[0, 1/2)$ and of dealer 2 to selling on $[1/2, 1]$, each dealer becomes a local monopoly and charges $p_i^D = B$, $i = 1, 2$. The manufacturer's problem under territorial-exclusive dealership is to set the unit price d it sells to dealers that solves

$$\max_d \pi^M = 2d \quad \text{s.t.} \quad \pi_i^D = B - d - F \geq 0,$$

implying that a per unit fee of $d^M = B - F$, hence $\pi^M = 2(B - F) > 0$.

Note that the same profit levels could be achieved by simply using a resale-price-maintenance mechanism (RPM) analyzed earlier in subsection 14.3.2. In other words, the manufacturer could set a consumer price floor of $p_i^D = B$, thereby preventing the dealers from engaging in price competition.

Finally, note that although territorial-exclusive dealerships increases profit over the competiting dealerships case, in a small town the manufacturer can make a higher profit by simply granting a single dealership. This follows from $\pi^M = 2(B - F) < 2(B - T) - F$, which is the manufacturer's profit under a single dealership given in (14.27).

14.4   Appendix: The Legal Approach to Tying

Section 3 of the Clayton Act passed in 1914, states that

> It shall be unlawful for any person engaged in commerce...to lease or make a sale or contract for sale of goods...or fix a price charged...on the condition or understanding that the lessee or purchaser thereof shall not use or deal in the goods...where the effect of such lease, sale, or contract for sale...may be to substantially lessen competition or tend to create a monopoly in any line of commerce.

Since tying and bundling are frequently observed, it is easy to infer that at least mixed tying is not illegal per se, despite the fact that there have been several rulings on a per se basis against tying (for interesting court cases, see Asch 1983 and Gellhorn 1986). In fact the rulings against tying are associated with cases brought against firms that attempted to extend their monopoly power from one market to another (which courts term *leverage*), as in subsection 14.1.4, where we showed that tying may induce a consumer to purchase another product from his less preferred brand-producing firm, and in rare case, can cause a foreclosure of firms in the tied market. Moreover, the court ruled that the mere existence of a patent on a certain product does not entitle the patentee to impose a tie-in on the purchaser of a patented product. That is, a patent holder of, say, a copy machine cannot impose on the buyer the use of its own brand paper.

In sum, courts nowadays express the view that the plaintiff must show both that the producer maintains a monopolistic position in the tying product and that a tie-in activity restrains a substantial volume of commerce of competitors in the tied product. In such a case, tying should be held as illegal per se.

Another issue related to tie-in (actually to mixed tying) is its close relationship to price discrimination, where consumers buying a tied package are priced differently than consumers who buy a single product. In addition, tying can serve as a tacit collusion between two firms producing complementary products. Clearly, if both firms fix their prices, there is an immediate violation of antitrust laws, but by using tying, the firms are able to conceal the collusion. Finally, such tacit collusion may also serve as entry-barrier mechanisms.

14.5   Appendix: The Legal Approach to Vertical Restraints

Section 1 of the Sherman Act passed in 1890, states that

> Every Contract, combination in the form of trust or otherwise, or conspiracy, in restraint of trade or commerce amount the several states, or with foreign nations, is hereby declared to be illegal.

The complexity of the legality of vertical restraints lies in the fact that there is a wide spectrum of vertical arrangements, and their relative success in enhancing manufacturers' efficiency is open to debate. A variety of cases and court rulings regarding several of these arrangements that are discussed in Asch 1983 and Gellhorn 1986 demonstrate the courts' ambiguity about whether the rule of reason should be used in determining the legality of any given arrangement.

Until the late 1970s vertical price fixing and territorial restrictions were condemned under the per se rule as violations of the Sherman Act. However, several price-fixing arrangements were not always judged by antitrust laws since several states passed fair trade laws that also covered the issues of price maintenance. Although vertical price fixing is still per se illegal, since the late 1970s and during the 1980s, courts have expressed the view that the per se rule should generally not be used to evaluate vertical restraints in pricing because the rule violates the principle that manufacturers and dealers are free to establish the best arrangement for marketing their product.

In general, it seems that courts have been more receptive to vertical arrangements that did not involve price restraints, possibly because territorial restrictions would induce dealers to engage in providing more services and advertising. Allowing several dealers to compete in a certain location would invoke the well-known free rider problem where small dealers ride free on advertising by other dealers. Thus, some courts held that territorial dealerships are essential for promoting the product, and for this reason a manufacturer has to insulate the dealer from competition, since without promotion a manufacturer may lose the entire competition to manufacturers producing competing brands. For this reason, courts tend to use the rule of reason with respect to nonprice vertical restraints.

Finally, courts had to deal with several cases of a refusal to deal, where a manufacturer refused to deal with several retailers marketing the same product. Although the right of a manufacturer to deal or not to deal is well established and reasonable, the refusal to deal bears some similarity to exclusive territorial dealerships since refusal to deal is an effective punishment for those dealers who engage in price-cutting retailing. That is, revoking dealerships for price cutting can substitute a formal contract where a price fixing is explicitly mentioned.

14.6 Exercises

1. Consider the mixed-tying model studied in subsection 14.1.3 and suppose that consumer 2 in Table 14.2 changes his or her tastes so that he or she attaches a value of $5 to each product. That is, $V_X^2 = V_Y^2 = 5$. Answer the following:

   (a) Find the monopoly price of a package under pure tying.
   (b) Find the monopoly product and package prices under mixed tying.
   (c) Does the monopoly make a higher profit under mixed tying than under pure tying? Prove it!

2. Consider the market for textbooks analyzed in section 14.2, but suppose now that the publisher can make a commitment not to introduce a new edition in period 2, and that students believe the publisher when such a commitment is made. Answer the following questions:

   (a) What is the condition on F that will induce the publisher to make such a commitment? (*Hint:* It is straightforward from equation (14.17)).

(b) Explain why the condition you found is less restrictive than the condition given in equation (14.17)). (*Hint:* This problem relates to the commitment problem of a durable-goods monopolist analyzed in section 5.5).

3. Consider the market for textbooks analyzed in section 14.2, but suppose now that the maximum amount that the students are willing to pay for a new textbook is V; the maximum they are willing to pay for a used book, however, is αV, where $0 < \alpha < 1$. That is, the (second-period) students are willing to pay less for a used textbook since a used textbook may contain marks and perhaps some missing pages.

   We denote by p_t^N the period t price of a new book, and by p_t^U the price of a used one. Thus, the utility of a "generation t" student is given by

$$U_t \equiv \begin{cases} V - p_t^N & \text{if the student buys a new book} \\ \alpha V - p_t^U & \text{if the student buys a used book} \\ 0 & \text{if he does not purchase the textbook at all.} \end{cases}$$
$$(14.28)$$

   Answer the following questions:

   (a) Suppose that the monopolist does not introduce a new edition in period 2. What is the maximum price at which the students would be able to sell used books? Prove your result!

   (b) Would this modification ($\alpha < 1$) change the monopoly's decision whether to introduce a new edition in period 2?

4. Consider the single-dealership problem analyzed in section 14.3.1. Suppose that the manufacturer sells each unit to the dealer for $d = c$ (unit manufacturing cost) but, in addition, requires the dealer to pay a fraction of ϕ ($0 < \phi < 1$) of the dealer's profit. Answer the following questions:

   (a) Formulate the dealer's profit-maximization problem under this contract and show that this contract maximizes the industry profit. That is, show that for any given ϕ, the sum of the manufacturer's and the dealer's profit is equal to the profit made by a monopoly manufacturer selling directly to the consumer.

   (b) How would your answer change if ϕ is the fraction of the end-user price instead of the dealer's profit. That is, suppose now that the dealer pays a fraction of ϕ of the end-user price to the manufacturer for each unit it sells.

   (c) Explain why "share-in-profit" types of contract are not frequently observed. (*Hint:* Think of problems associated with having the manufacturer monitoring the dealer's profit).

5. Many home appliances stores in the United States advertise that those consumers who will trade in their old washing machine will receive a substantial discount on a new washing machine. Explain why stores may find it profitable to engage in this sort of trade-in.

14.7   References

Adams, W., and J. Yellen. 1976. "Commodity Bundling and the Burden of Monopoly." *Quarterly Journal of Economics* 90: 475–498.

Asch, P. 1983. *Industrial Organization and Antitrust Policy*. New York: John Wiley & Sons.

Benjamin, D., and R. Kormendi. 1974. "The Interrelationship Between Markets for New and Used Durable Goods." *Journal of Law and Economics* 17: 381–402.

Burstein, M. 1960. "The Economics of Tie-in Sales." *Review of Economic Studies* 42: 68–73.

Carbajo, J., D. de Meza, and D. Seidmann. 1990. "A Strategic Motivation for Commodity Bundling." *Journal of Industrial Economics* 38: 283–298.

Gellhorn, E. 1986. *Antitrust Law and Economics in a Nutshell*. St. Paul, Minn.: West Publishing Co..

Horn, H., and O. Shy. 1996. "Bundling and International Market Segmentation." *International Economic Review* 37: 51–69.

Lewbel, A. 1985. "Bundling of Substitutes or Complements." *International Journal of Industrial Organization* 3: 101–107.

Liebowitz, S. 1982. "Durability, Market Structure, and New-Used Goods Models." *American Economic Review* 72: 816–824.

Mathewson, G., and R. Winter. 1986. "The Economics of Vertical Restraints in Distribution." In *New Developments in the Analysis of Market Structure*, edited by J. Stiglitz, and G. Mathewson. Cambridge, Mass.: MIT Press.

McAfee, P., J. McMillan, and M. Whinston. 1989. "Multiproduct Monopoly, Commodity Bundling and Correlation of Values." *Quarterly Journal of Economics* 19: 221–234.

Miller, L. 1974. "On Killing Off the Market for Used Textbooks." *Journal of Political Economy* 82: 612–620.

Rust, J. 1986. "When Is It Optimal to Kill Off the Market for Used Durable Goods?" *Econometrica* 54: 65–86.

Seidmann, D. 1991. "Bundling as a Facilitating Device: A Reinterpretation of Leverage Theory." *Economica* 58: 491–499.

Tirole, J. 1988. *The Theory of Industrial Organization*. Cambridge, Mass.: MIT Press.

Whinston, M. 1990. "Tying, Foreclosure, and Exclusion." *American Economic Review* 80: 837–859.

PART V

The Role of Information

Chapter 15

Monitoring, Management, Compensation, and Regulation

If you want something done right, do it yourself!
—Traditional adage

Firms are organizations that are run and operated by people who use the technology to manufacture the products, and then set quantity and prices to maximize profits in a given market structure. The workers of the firm play the crucial role in controlling the production level, quality, and service to consumers. Clearly, since many firms are not owned by their employees, a natural question to ask is what motivates workers and managers to devote efforts leading to increasing the firms' profitability? A second question immediately follows: Suppose that the firms know what motivates the workers to work hard, then, given that the firm is a large and complex form of organization, how can the firm reward its workers and managers if the relationship between an individual (worker or manager) and output cannot be observed?

The prevailing assumption is that workers are motivated by incentives that directly affect their standard of living. However, it should be pointed out that monetary incentives are not the only means by which to motivate workers. In many cases, workers derive satisfaction from having a sense of accomplishment, from cooperation in achieving targets, from making decisions, and from developing production processes and cost-reducing technologies. Understanding the entity called a firm becomes even more complicated once we recognize that the different individuals in a given firm have different incentives; therefore, one way of modeling firms is to assume that a firm is a coalition of individuals with different interests. This approach, of course, will not always coincide with the assumption that firms are profit maximizers. These types of motivations are hard to model, and we therefore abstract other possibilities from this list and assume that workers and managers seek to maximize monetary rewards they receive from the firms they work for.

In this chapter we analyze problems facing managers and owners of firms who seek to maximize profits but are unable to fully monitor the efforts put out by their employees. Rather than pursue the visual-monitoring solution, we here attempt to develop economic mechanisms that would provide the workers with the (monetary) incentives to exert effort in their work. We also discuss the firm's cost of implementing these mechanisms. We then analyze how governments regulate firms without knowing the precise production cost of the regulated firms. What is common to all these problems is that the decision maker cannot observe what the workers, managers, or firms do. Thus, the decision maker is forced into devising economic incentives that would induce the workers (managers or firms) not to shirk work and reveal what is unknown to the decision maker.

In section 15.1, we analyze how a principal can provide an economic incentive to an agent that would induce the agent not to shirk work. In section 15.2, we discuss a different incentive problem—how to induce workers sharing efforts in the same project to devote the optimal level of effort to it. In section 15.3, we provide an explanation of why managers are really needed and shows that the separation of owners from managers can increase the strategic position of a firm. In section 15.4, we provide one explanation of why firms pay according to rank rather than according to revealed output, and why CEOs of large firms are paid astronomical salaries. In section 15.5 we analyze a problem often faced by governments—whether to approve and subsidize a project undertaken by an independent firm (say, a public-utility firm) when the government does not know the exact production cost of the product or the service to be provided by the firm.

15.1　The Principal-Agent Problem

The principal-agent problem (see Ross 1973; Grossman and Hart 1983; and Sappington 1991 for a survey) exists in almost every social structure where some units are regarded as managers and some units as supervised agents. This well-known problem exists in every family where parents, not knowing whether their kids prepare their homework or not, wish to reward the kids for good grades. A landlord leasing his or her land to a tenant has no way of knowing whether yield is a product of the tenant's working hard or shirking, when weather has a large impact on the crops, but, he or she may wish to provide the tenant with a sufficient incentive to cultivate the land (see Stiglitz 1974). A plaintiff, expecting to win a large sum of money, would like to encourage his hired attorney to work hard before a court appearance. A school, not observing what professors actually do in class, may wish to reward the professor according to the students' achievements. A government, not observing the efforts of its workers, would like to compensate its workers according to public polls on some aspects the government bureaucracy.

We first focus on firms consisting of two groups: a manager and employees. The manager hires a worker after examining the worker's credentials, which lead the manager to believe that the worker has the ability and the skill to perform the required task. However, even if the manager can ensure that the worker has the skills, how can the manager be sure that the worker will indeed make the effort to use his or her skills? That is, what are the incentives for the worker to work hard and use his or her skills? Well, if the boss monitors the workers, she can fire the worker when the worker does not work hard. However, if the boss monitors the workers, she cannot do any other work, which may jeopardize the entire operation of the firm.

Suppose that the manager decides to install TV cameras or hire supervisors to constantly monitor the workers' movements. It is clear that such an action would induce the workers' union to take the manager to court for violating basic workers' rights. In addition, monitoring is costly to managers and may or may not compensate for the extra output generated by monitoring. For this reason, in what follows we search for economic mechanisms that would substitute for the physical monitoring of workers.

Let us consider the following problem. A restaurant owner (the principal) hires a waiter (the agent) to run the restaurant while she is away. If the waiter does not work hard (shirks), customers will not get a proper service and consequently, fewer customers will go to eat in this restaurant. Therefore, revenue will fall. If the waiter works hard, the restaurant becomes more popular, and revenue will rise. However, given that the revenue is collected by the manager, the worker may not have the incentive to work hard.

The timing of the interaction between the owner and the waiter is as follows: First, the owner designs the terms of the contract, which specifies the payments the waiter will receive, depending on the observed revenue of the restaurant. The owner offers the contract to the waiter, and the waiter decides whether to accept the contract and start working or to choose some other work. Second, if the waiter accepts the contract, then he goes to work and decides how much effort to exert in this work. Finally, the restaurant's revenue is observed, and the owner pays the waiter as promised in the contract. Note that this commonly used setup implies that the owner is in control of the bargaining in the sense that she makes a take-it-or-leave-it offer to the waiter. The waiter then can either accept the terms or reject them but is unable to bargain over the terms of the contract.

15.1.1 Providing economic incentives under certainty: An illustration

The agent

We denote by e the amount of effort put out by the agent. We assume that there are only two degrees of effort that the agent can put out: If the agent works hard, he puts an effort level given by $e = 2$, and if he shirks, he puts an effort level given by $e = 0$.

We assume that if the agent does not take this job, he can work at an alternative place, say for the government, and that the government's wage, minus his effort, yields a utility level of $U = 10$, which is called the agent's *reservation utility*. Our agent likes money and dislikes work. That is, letting w denote the agent's wage, we assume that his utility function is given by

$$U = \begin{cases} w - e & \text{if he devotes an effort level } e \\ 10 & \text{if he works at another place.} \end{cases} \tag{15.1}$$

The restaurant and the principal

The revenue of the restaurant depends on the waiter's effort level and is denoted by function $R(e)$. If the waiter works hard ($e = 2$), the revenue is high and given by $R(2) \equiv H$. If the waiter shirks, then the revenue is low, so $R(0) \equiv L$. Altogether,

$$R(e) = \begin{cases} H & \text{if } e = 2 \\ L & \text{if } e = 0. \end{cases} \tag{15.2}$$

Finally, the profit to the restaurant owner (the principal) is the restaurant's revenue minus the wage bill, which we denote by π. That is,

$$\pi \equiv R(e) - w. \tag{15.3}$$

The contract

The objective of the owner is to maximize the profit given in (15.3). We assume that the difference $H - L$ is sufficiently large so that the owner seeks to minimize the expected wage bill Ew while inducing the agent to work hard ($e = 2$). Which contract should she offer to the agent? Obviously, the contract has to depend on the revenue generated by the agent's (unobserved) effort. Let w^H denote the wage rate that the principal promises to pay the agent when the revenue is H, and let w^L be wage paid to the agent when the revenue is L.

What should be the values of w^H and w^L that would maximize the principal's profit, subject to providing a sufficient incentive for the agent to work hard? These incentives can be summarized by two constraints that the principal should consider while writing the contract.

Let us recall that the agent can work in another place and gain a net utility of 10. Thus, in order to induce the agent to work (hard) in the restaurant, ($e = 2$), the principal should write a contract (specifying the values for w^H in the event that $R(2) = H$ and w^L in the event that $R(2) = L$) that would provide the agent with a utility level of at least 10. Thus, in view of the agent's utility function (15.1), the agent's *participation constraint* is given by

$$w^H - 2 \geq 10. \tag{15.4}$$

Even if the agent works for the restaurant, the contract has to provide the agent with the monetary incentive to work hard. That is, the utility level generated by the (net of effort) income from working hard should be no less than the utility generated by shirking. Thus, the *incentive constraint* is given by

$$w^H - 2 \geq w^L - 0. \tag{15.5}$$

Solving (15.4) for the equality case yields $w^H = 12$. Substituting into (15.5) yields $w^L = 10$. Finally, the profit to the principal when $e = 2$ is $\pi^H = H - w^H = H - 12$, and when $e = 0$ is $\pi^L = L - w^L = L - 10$. Hence, for this contract to be optimal for the principal, we must assume that $\pi^H \geq \pi^L$, or $H \geq L + 2$.

What is wrong with this model?

The optimal contract that would induce the agent to work hard turned out to be very simple. Since the utility loss to the agent from working hard is 2, the principal needs to pay the agent an additional 2 units of money to induce the agent to work hard. Note that in this simple example lower values for w^L would yield the same outcome, since the agent has a sufficient incentive to work hard.

The simplicity of this contract stems from the fact that the principal can actually monitor the agent's effort by simply counting the revenue generated by the agent's effort. Thus, this environment is the same as an environment with perfect monitoring. In other words, with no uncertainty, the owner can calculate the precise effort exerted by the waiter by simply observing the restaurant's revenue.

15.1.2 Providing economic incentives under uncertainty

Let us consider the effects of the following events on the revenue collected by our restaurant: A stormy day scares people away from going out; an important football game is shown on TV; or, for some reason nobody is hungry on a particular day (say, because of National Diet Day). These examples basically say that in addition to the waiter's effort, the revenue of the restaurant also depends on some other parameters . We call these other causes the *states of nature*, because they are beyond the control of either the agent or the principal. Thus, a high effort level put out by the agent cannot insure that the revenue will be high. An increase in the agent's effort level can only increase the probability for the event that $R(e) = H$. That is, it is nature that determines the value of $R(e)$, but, our agent can affect the probability of each realization of $R(e)$ by choosing his effort level. Formally, we assume that nature determines $R(2)$ and $R(0)$ according to

$$R(2) = \begin{cases} H & \text{probability 0.8} \\ L & \text{probability 0.2} \end{cases} \text{and } R(0) = \begin{cases} H & \text{probability 0.4} \\ L & \text{probability 0.6.} \end{cases}$$
$$(15.6)$$

Thus, by working hard, the agent can raise the probability of having $R = H$ from 0.4 to 0.8.

Finally, we need to slightly modify the agent's utility function (15.1) to incorporate this uncertain environment. Thus, we assume that the agent maximizes his expected wage minus his effort, given by

$$U = \begin{cases} Ew - e & \text{if he devotes an } e \text{ level of effort} \\ 10 & \text{if he works at another place,} \end{cases} \quad (15.7)$$

where "E" is the expectation operator, so in the present case, $Ew = 0.8w^H + 0.2w^L$ when $e = 2$, and $Ew = 0.4w^H + 0.6w^L$ when $e = 0$.

The participation constraint (15.4) is now given by

$$0.8w^H + 0.2w^L - 2 \geq 10, \quad (15.8)$$

reflecting the possibility that nature may play L despite the high effort put by the agent.

The incentive constraint (15.5) is now given by

$$0.8w^H + 0.2w^L - 2 \geq 0.4w^H + 0.6w^L - 0. \qquad (15.9)$$

That is, the contract has to specify the agent's state-contingent wages (w^H in the event that $R(2) = H$, and w^L in an event that $R(2) = L$) that would yield a higher expected utility under $e = 2$ than under $e = 0$.

Equation (15.8) implies that $w^L = 60 - 4w^H$, and (15.9) implies that $w^L = w^H - 5$. Altogether, the optimal contract is $w^H = 13$ and $w^L = 8$.

Monitoring versus economic incentives under symmetric information

So far, we have shown that economic incentives can substitute for the (unpleasant) physical monitoring of the agent's actions. That is, we showed that the manager can achieve her production/service goals without monitoring her workers at all, provided that she knows how to write a contract that links the agent's wage with the states of nature.

But our last question is at what cost does she achieve her goals? Is the economic mechanism cheaper to implement than with the TV cameras or hired supervisors? Note that hiring supervisors raises the problem of how to guarantee that the supervisors would have the incentives to catch the workers that shirk. Well, the supervisors would either have to be supervised or to be given the right economic incentives to catch those who shirk. But who would then supervise the supervisors of the supervisors?

An important lesson to be learned from our example is that this economic-incentive mechanism is efficient in the sense that it is not costly to implement. To see that, we compare the wage bill paid by the principal under (the equivalent of) perfect monitoring, which is $w^H = 12$ and $w^L = 10$, with the no-monitoring (under uncertainty) wage bill $w^H = 13$ and $w^L = 8$. However, notice that in the uncertainty case, the expected wage bill is $0.8 \times 13 + 0.2 \times 8 = 12$, which is identical to the wage bill the principal pays under monitoring. Thus, this economic mechanism is not too costly to implement, and here, hiring supervisors is not needed.

Finally, the result that the expected wage bill under uncertainty is the same as the one under certainty is not a robust one because this result does not hold when the parties are risk averse. That is, the parties attach different probabilities to the realization of the states of nature (the set $\{H, L\}$ in our case). In the next subsection, we will analyze how different attitudes toward risk affect the structure of the contract that the owner offers the waiter, hence, the owner's expected wage bill, and we will show that under this asymmetry, the expected wage bill would exceed 12.

15.1.3   Principal-agent problem under asymmetric information

The literature on the principal-agent problem has been extended to analyze owners and waiters that have different attitudes toward risk. In more professional terms, the literature assumed that the owner and the waiters have different degrees of *risk aversion.*

We would now use a new concept called *subjective probability* that measures the probabilities each player assigns to the realization of the states of nature. Thus, we assume that both players acknowledge the same states of nature (H and L), but owing to their different backgrounds, each player assigns different probabilities to the realizations. Formally, let us recall from (15.6) that the owner believes that $R^O(2)$ and $R^O(0)$ are realized according to

$$R^O(2) = \begin{cases} H & \text{probability } 0.8 \\ L & \text{probability } 0.2 \end{cases} \text{ and } R^O(0) = \begin{cases} H & \text{probability } 0.4 \\ L & \text{probability } 0.6. \end{cases}$$
$$(15.10)$$

Our modification of the previous model is that here we assume that the waiter believes that $R^W(2)$ and $R^W(0)$ are realized according to

$$R^W(2) = \begin{cases} H & \text{probability } 0.7 \\ L & \text{probability } 0.3 \end{cases} \text{ and } R^W(0) = R^O(0). \qquad (15.11)$$

We would like to characterize the source of difference between the owner and the waiter. We need the following definition.

DEFINITION 15.1 *Let there be two consumers denoted by i, $i = 1, 2$. We say that consumer i is **more risk averse than** consumer j, $j \neq i$, if, when consumer j prefers a fixed sum of money over a lottery, then consumer i also prefers the fixed amount.*

In the present framework the waiter is more risk averse than the owner since the waiter is more skeptical than the owner about the realization of the good (high) state of nature. That is, the waiter attaches a lower probability to the H event and a higher probability to the L event.

The reason why we think of these differences in subjective probabilities as simulating different attitudes toward risk can be seen from the following illustration: Suppose that the owner pays the waiter w^H and w^L, where $w^H > w^L$. Then, if the waiter exerts $e = 2$, the expected wage bill for the owner would be

$$\mathrm{E}^O w = 0.8 w^H + 0.2 w^L > 0.7 w^H + 0.3 w^L = \mathrm{E}^W w,$$

which is higher than the expected wage received by the waiter. Hence, from the point of view of the waiter, he values the expected wage bill less than the owner, reflecting the behavior that the waiter requires a greater compensation for working in an uncertain environment.

Finally, the expectation operator "E" in the waiter's utility function (15.7) should be interpreted as his subjective expectation, which is different from that of the owner's. That is, $E^W w = 0.7w^H + 0.3w^L$ if $e = 2$, and $E^W w = 0.4w^H + 0.6w^L$ if $e = 0$.

The participation constraint (15.4) is now given by

$$0.7w^H + 0.3w^L - 2 \geq 10, \quad \text{or} \quad w^H = \frac{12 - 0.3w^L}{0.7}. \tag{15.12}$$

The incentive constraint (15.5) is now given by

$$0.7w^H + 0.3w^L - 2 \geq 0.4w^H + 0.6w^L - 0, \quad \text{or} \quad w^H = 2/0.3 + w^L. \tag{15.13}$$

The participation constraint (15.12) and the incentive constraint (15.13) are drawn in Figure 15.1. The two constraints intersect at the point G.

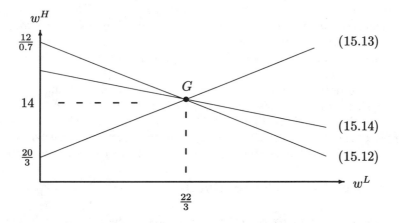

Figure 15.1: Optimal contract under asymmetric information

Any combinations of w^H and w^L to the left of the upward sloping curve (15.13) are contracts that would induce the waiter to exert maximum effort. Any combinations of w^H and w^L above the downward sloping curve (15.12) are contracts that would be acceptable to the waiter. Altogether, it is clear that the owner would pick a contract which lies on the triangle above (including) the point G.

Finally, the owner chooses a contract w^H and w^L to minimize the expected wage bill $E^O w$ she has to pay the waiter. We remarked earlier that if $H - L$ is sufficiently large, there is an equivalence between maximizing expected profit and minimizing expected wage. Formally, the owner solves

$$\min_{w^H, w^L} \mathrm{E}^O w = 0.8 w^H + 0.2 w^L. \tag{15.14}$$

The iso-expected wage bill $0.8 w^H + 0.2 w^L = \min \mathrm{E}^O w$ is also drawn in Figure 15.1. Note that this line is sloped -0.25, implying that the owner's expected wage bill is minimized at point G. Hence, the owner would choose a contract given by $w^H = 14$ and $w^L = 22/3$. Clearly, the waiter will accept this contract. We conclude with the following proposition.

Proposition 15.1 *The owner's expected wage bill exceeds the waiter's reservation utility plus his effort level. Formally,*

$$\mathrm{E}^O w = 0.8 w^H + 0.2 w^L = 12.66 > 10 + 2.$$

The intuition behind Proposition 15.1 is as follows: Suppose that the waiter does not like to work under risky conditions. Then, in order to induce the waiter to work, the owner must compensate the waiter for taking a random wage contract. This compensation is reflected by the difference $12.66 - 12$, which is interpreted as the premium for being relatively more risk averse.

Finally, note that the optimal contract bears some insurance for the waiter since from all individually rational contracts (contracts located along the line (15.12) in Figure 15.1) the owner chooses the least risky contract. In other words, the contract that $w^H - w^L$ is minimized. This insurance is needed since the waiter is more risk averse than the owner.

15.2 Production with Teams

The inability to monitor a worker's effort also generates an inefficiency when the output of the firm depends on the effort levels of all workers assigned to work on a certain project (which we call the joint effort of a team). This type of externality is commonly called the *free-rider effect,* in which a worker, knowing that all other workers in a team are putting a lot of effort into the project, will have an incentive to shirk, given that the group as a whole is rewarded on the value of the project, that is, when the individual workers are not rewarded according to their individual effort levels.

Consider a research lab developing the future product whose value is denoted by V. In the lab there are N scientists (workers) who work on this project. We denote by e_i the effort put in by scientist i, $i = 1, 2, \ldots, N$.

The value of the jointly developed product depends on the effort levels of all the N scientists and is given by

$$V = \sum_{i=1}^{N} \sqrt{e_i}. \tag{15.15}$$

That is, equation (15.15) can be viewed as a production function where the inputs are the efforts put out by the scientists.

Finally, we denote by w_i the compensation given to scientist i after the project is completed. We assume that the value of the product is distributed to the workers so $\sum_i w_i = V$. All scientists have identical preferences, summarized by the utility function

$$U_i \equiv w_i - e_i, \quad i = 1, 2, \dots, N. \tag{15.16}$$

15.2.1 A digression: Optimal effort levels

Abstracting from the monitoring problem, we suppose that each scientist can observe the efforts of his other colleagues, and we suppose that they collude to maximize their utility levels. We now wish to calculate what the optimal symmetric allocations of effort and output shares (wages) are, and therefore, we set $e_i = e$ and $w_i = w = V/N$ for every $i = 1, 2, \dots, N$.

If we substitute into (15.16), the representative effort level e^* that maximizes a representative worker's utility solves

$$\max_e (w - e) = \frac{V}{N} - e = \frac{N\sqrt{e}}{N} - e, \quad \text{implying that} \quad e^* = 1/4. \tag{15.17}$$

That is, if the workers can (theoretically) collude, observe each other's effort, and adjust their efforts to maximize their utility, each should put out $e^* = 1/4$ level of effort, and the resulting total value would be $V^* = N\sqrt{1/4} = N/2$.

15.2.2 The equal-division economic mechanism

Back to the real-life situation, let us suppose that the manager of this firm rewards the scientists according to their equal share of the total value of output. Formally, let us suppose that the manager sets $w_i = V/N$. We look for a Nash equilibrium (Definition 2.4 on page 18) in effort levels, where each scientist takes the effort levels of his colleagues as given and chooses his effort level to maximize his utility (15.16). Formally, each worker chooses the effort level e_i to

$$\max_{e_i} U_i = \frac{\sum_{j\neq i} \sqrt{e_j} + \sqrt{e_i}}{N} - e_i, \quad \text{implying that} \quad e^n \equiv e_i = \frac{1}{4N^2} \leq e^*. \tag{15.18}$$

Therefore, we can state the following:

Proposition 15.2 *Under the equal-division rule:*

1. *If the team consists of a single worker, the worker will provide the optimal level of effort. That is, if $N = 1$, then $e^n = e^* = 1/4$.*

2. *If the team consists of more than one worker, each worker would devote less than the optimal level of effort. That is, if $N > 1$, then $e^n < e^* = 1/4$.*

3. *The larger the team is, the lower will be the effort put out by each worker (each would have a greater incentive to shirk). That is, as N increases, e^n decreases.*

Proposition 15.2 shows that offering the workers equal shares of the value of the output is insufficient to induce them to devote the optimal level of effort to their work. So, why not offer them a higher share of the output? Well, although it may be possible to induce them to work harder, if all workers are offered a higher share of the output (i.e., $w_i > V/N$), the total wage bill will exceed the value of output.

We now look at the effect of the size of the workforce on the total output as well as on the worker's welfare level. Substituting (15.18) into (15.15) for e^n yields that the Nash equilibrium value of output is

$$V^n = N\sqrt{e^n} = N\sqrt{\frac{1}{4N^2}} = \frac{1}{2}. \tag{15.19}$$

Hence, the difference between the optimal output level and the equilibrium output level is $V^* - V^n = (N-1)/2$.

Substituting (15.18) into (15.16) yields that the Nash equilibrium utility level of each worker is

$$U_i = \frac{V^n}{N} - e^n = \frac{1}{2N} - \frac{1}{4N^2}. \tag{15.20}$$

For the sake of illustration, we approximate N by a real number; differentiating (15.20) with respect to N thus yields that

$$\frac{\partial U_i}{\partial N} = -\frac{1}{2N^2} + \frac{1}{2N^3} \quad (< 0 \text{ if } N > 1). \tag{15.21}$$

Hence,

Proposition 15.3

1. *An increase in the number of workers on the team will increase the difference between the optimal output level and the Nash equilibrium output level. That is, $V^* - V^n$ increases with N.*

2. *An increase in the number of workers will reduce the welfare levels of each worker. That is, $U_i(N)$ decreases when N increases.*

Part 2 of the proposition shows that the free-rider effect intensifies when the number of workers increases, causing a further deviation from the optimal output level; the optimal output level ($V^* = N/2$) increases with the team size, but the equilibrium level ($V^n = 1/2$) does not vary with the size of the team.

15.2.3   An economic mechanism that works

Following Holmstrom 1982, we now discuss a (rather tough) incentive mechanism that would induce all the N workers to put forth the optimal effort level. Suppose that the team sets the following rule: If the team as a group achieves the optimal output level V^*, then each team member receives V^*/N. If the teams output is different from V^*, then all team members receive 0. Formally,

$$w_i = \begin{cases} V^*/N & \text{if } \sum_{i=1}^N \sqrt{e_i} = V^* \\ 0 & \text{otherwise.} \end{cases} \tag{15.22}$$

This mechanism makes each team member responsible for the entire output level of the team. Under the equal-division rule, the marginal effect of each team member is lower than the marginal social value; in this mechanism, however, the marginal value of each worker's effort is the entire enterprise. Is this the end? Not exactly, since this kind of allocation mechanism may suffer from a problem known in economics as *time inconsistency*. That is, this mechanism can work only if after each time the output is produced, the manager fires and replaces all the workers. However, if workers continue to work on a new project, it seems unlikely that workers would agree to let the manager confiscate all the output just because somebody has intentionally or unintentionally deviated from the optimal effort level. Hence, even if some deviation has occurred, it looks as if the workers would be able to negotiate with manager or among themselves a redivision of the output, given that some output has already been produced. Since workers anticipate that the manager will renegotiate the contract, the workers may not take this contract too seriously.

15.3   Competition and Managerial Compensation

Over this entire book, we have always assumed that the players inside a firm share a common goal, which is to maximize the firm's profit. Given this common goal, it is clear that managers fulfill no economic goal, except perhaps to replace the owners who may be busy doing other business. In this section, we demonstrate that managers can play a role in a firm and that the separation between managers and owners, who compensate (pay) the managers according to the goals they establish, can increase the profit of the firm beyond the level achievable if the owners manage the firms by themselves.

Following Fershtman and Judd 1987, we analyze how managerial compensation schemes affect the firm's actions, which in turn affect the firm's profit. More precisely, we examine the incentive contracts that principals (owners of firms, here) will choose for their agents (managers, here). What distinguishes this analysis from the principal-agent analysis performed earlier, is that here we analyze managerial compensation under a duopoly market structure. As we demonstrate below, it turns out that managerial compensation under duopoly is completely different from managerial compensation under monopoly for the very simple reason that under duopoly, managerial compensation alters a firm's strategic position. Thus, a firm's owner can write a contract with a manager that may advance the firm's strategic position beyond what could be achieved when the manager is instructed to simply maximize the firm's profit. In fact, we show that profit-maximizing owners will almost never tell their managers to maximize profits. It turns out that under Cournot duopoly competition each owner would want to motivate his manager toward a higher production level (more sales) so that the competing owners would instruct their managers to reduce their production level

Let us consider a market for a single homogeneous product, where the demand curve is given by $p = a - Q$, p is the market price and Q is the aggregate quantity demanded. There are two firms indexed by i, $i = 1, 2$. Let q_i denote the quantity produced by firm i, and let R_i and π_i denote the revenue and profit levels of each firm i. The unit production cost of each firm is denoted by c, where $0 < c < a < 5c$. Thus, recalling our Cournot market structure analysis of section 6.1, the revenue and the profit of each firm i, $i = 1, 2$ are given by

$$R_i \equiv pq_i = (a - q_1 - q_2)q_i \quad \text{and} \quad \pi_i \equiv R_i - cq_i. \qquad (15.23)$$

15.3.1　Incentives to managers

The owner of each firm (who could be a single person, or the shareholders) appoints a manager with an agreed-upon compensation scheme. Let M_i denote the compensation to manager of firm i, and let us assume that the owner sets the compensation so that

$$M_i \equiv \mu_i[\alpha_i \pi_i + (1 - \alpha_i)R_i] = \mu_i[(a - q_1 - q_2)q_i - \alpha_i c q_i]. \qquad (15.24)$$

Thus, we assume that the manager of each firm i is promised payment of a fraction μ_i of a linear combination of the firm's profit and the firm's revenue. For example, if the owner of firm i sets $\alpha_i = 1$, then the manager of firm i will simply maximize the firm's profit, and will earn a fraction μ_i of the firm's profit. In this case, the owner will earn $(1 - \mu_i)\pi_i$. In contrast, if the owner sets $\alpha_i = 0$, the manager will maximize the firm's revenue and will earn a fraction μ_i of the firm's revenue. The purpose of this section is to demonstrate that owners will almost never set $\alpha_i = 1$, meaning that owners will provide the incentive to managers not to maximize profits, but instead to maximize a linear combination of profit and revenue.

15.3.2 A two-stage-decision-level market game

We assume that in the first stage the owner of each firm i chooses μ_i and α_i to maximize the owner's profit given by

$$\pi^O(\mu_i, \alpha_i) \equiv \pi_i - M_i. \qquad (15.25)$$

Thus, the owner of each firm sets μ_i and α_i to maximize the firm's profit net of managerial-compensation cost. In the second stage, the manager of each firm i takes μ_i, α_i, and q_j as given and chooses the output level of firm i, q_i.

Second stage: Managers choose output levels

For given q_j and α_i, each manager chooses q_i to maximize (15.24). The first-order condition and the best-response function of each firm i are given by

$$0 = a - 2q_i - q_j - \alpha_i c, \quad \text{or} \quad q_i = \frac{a - q_j}{2} - \frac{\alpha_i c}{2}, \ i = 1, 2. \qquad (15.26)$$

Note that the best-response functions (15.26) are slightly different from the response functions developed in the conventional Cournot model of section 6.1, since managers now are not maximizing profits alone. The term $\alpha_i c/2$ means that the managers do not place a whole weight on the unit production cost, since some weight is placed on revenue alone. The best-response function of manager i is drawn in Figure 15.2. Figure 15.2 shows that if the owner of firm i lowers α_i, (implying that the owner would like the manager to place a heavier weight on revenue than on profit), the manager shifts his reaction function upward, reflecting the fact that for every given q_j, firm i responds with a higher q_i. Solving (15.26) yields the output level of each firm i and the aggregate industry output level as functions of the owners' set control parameters

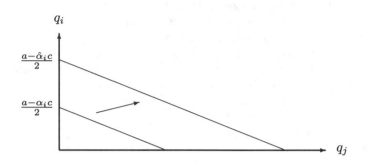

Figure 15.2: Best-response function of manager i when the owner lowers α_i to $\hat{\alpha}_i$.

α_1 and α_2. Hence,

$$q_i(\alpha_1, \alpha_2) = \frac{a + \alpha_j c - 2\alpha_i c}{3}, \ i = 1, 2 \quad \text{and} \quad Q(\alpha_1, \alpha_2) = \frac{2a - \alpha_1 c - \alpha_2 c}{3}.$$
(15.27)

We can easily see the effect each owner has on the industry output level.

Proposition 15.4 *The industry aggregate-output level increases when one or the two owners decrease their manager's incentive to maximize profit. Formally, Q increases when α_i decreases for some i, $i = 1, 2$.*

Finally, the equilibrium price as functions of α_1 and α_2 is given by

$$p(\alpha_1, \alpha_2) = a - Q(\alpha_1, \alpha_2) = \frac{a + \alpha_1 c + \alpha_2 c}{3}.$$
(15.28)

First stage: Owners choose managers' objective function

Let us notice that the compensation parameter μ_i in the managers' compensation scheme (15.24) does not have any effect on the managers' decision simply because managers' incentives do not vary with scaling M_i up or down by a constant μ_i. Hence, owners can set μ_i as low as they wish (assuming that managers have no alternative place to work). Therefore, to simplify our exposition, we set $\mu_i = 0$, hence, $M_i = 0$ in the owners' objective function (15.25). A more general analysis would have to include a positive μ_i set according to the managers' alternative salaries in competing industries.

The owner of each firm i takes α_j and the output and price functions (15.27) and (15.28) as given and chooses α_i that solves

$$\max_{\alpha_i} \pi_i^O(\alpha_1, \alpha_2) = [p(\alpha_1, \alpha_2) - c]q_i$$
(15.29)

$$= \frac{[a + c(\alpha_i + \alpha_j - 3)][a + c(\alpha_j - 2\alpha_i)]}{9}$$

The maximization problem (15.29) is easy to solve if we observe that some terms in (15.29) are not functions of α_1 and α_2. Therefore the solution to (15.29) is identical to solving

$$\max_{\alpha_i} \left[ac\alpha_1 + c^2\alpha_1\alpha_2 - 2ac\alpha_1 - 2c^2(\alpha_1)^2 - 2c^2\alpha_1\alpha_2 + 6c^2\alpha_1 \right]. \quad (15.30)$$

The first-order condition yields the owners' best-response functions

$$\alpha_i = R_i(\alpha_j) = \frac{6c - a - c\alpha_j}{4c}. \quad (15.31)$$

The owners' best-response functions are downward sloping, implying that if the owner of firm 1 encourages his manager to place more weight on revenue than on profit (reducing α_1), the owner for firm 2 would respond by increasing the incentive for his manager to place a higher weight on profit than on revenue (and hence to produce a lower output level).

Our main point can be demonstrated by the following experiment. Suppose that firm 2 is an ordinary Cournot-type firm managed by its owner and therefore only maximizes profit. That is, $\alpha_2 = 1$ in (15.24). Substituting $\alpha_2 = 1$ into (15.31) yields

Proposition 15.5 *Given that firm 2 only maximizes profit, the owner of firm 1 will not maximize profit and will set α_1 so that his manager will set the output level to equal the leader's output level (see the Leader-Follower model, section 6.2 on page 104). Formally, when $\alpha_2 = 1$, the owner of firm 1 sets $\alpha_1 = (5c - a)/(4c)$; hence, by (15.27), $q_1 = (a - c)/2$.*

The significance of Proposition 15.5 is that it demonstrates one possible reason why managers are needed. That is, by writing a contract of the type given in (15.24), the owner of firm 1 can advance the strategic position of his firm beyond what could be achieved if the owner was managing the firm by himself.

Solving the two best-response functions (15.31) yields the equilibrium incentive parameters given by

$$\alpha^e \equiv \alpha_1^e = \alpha_2^e = \frac{6c - a}{5c} = \frac{6}{5} - \frac{a}{5c}. \quad (15.32)$$

Thus, the equilibrium α_i^e increases with the production cost parameter c, meaning that when production cost increases, the owners will induce their managers to place a heavier weight on maximizing profits. When the production cost is low, owners will induce managers to place a higher weight on revenue maximization, thereby increasing production levels.

Finally, substituting (15.32) into (15.27) yields

$$q_i^e = \frac{a - \alpha^e c}{3} = \frac{2(a - c)}{5} > q_i^c = \frac{a - c}{3}. \tag{15.33}$$

Thus,

Proposition 15.6 *In an industry where the owners are separated from the managers, firms' output levels exceed the Cournot equilibrium output level, (derived in section 6.1).*

The significance of Proposition 15.6 is that the separation of managers from owners intensifies competition between the firms, since owners design the managerial compensation schemes in a way that makes the managers more aggressive in sales. Thus, the separation of owners from managers reduces aggregate industry profit.

15.3.3   Collusion between the owners

When the FTC investigates whether there is collusion between firms, it is unlikely to look at managerial compensation as a source for collusion. We now investigate whether owners can implicitly collude by setting the appropriate compensation schemes for their managers. The interesting feature of this type of collusion is that managers will not even notice that a collusion to reduce output is taking place and thus, will not have to be informed about it. The framework developed above is very useful to investigate whether such an implicit collusion is profitable to owners.

Let us suppose that the owners collude by agreeing on how to compensate their managers and decide to set a common α into their managers' compensation contracts. Substituting $\alpha_1 = \alpha_2 = \alpha$ into (15.30) yields that the owners choose α^* to maximize the joint profit given by

$$\max_{\alpha}(\pi_1 + \pi_2) = 2(-ac\alpha - 3c^2\alpha^2 + 6c^2\alpha). \tag{15.34}$$

The solution to the maximization of the joint profit is given by $\alpha^* = (a + 3c)/(4c)$. Substituting into the managers' output functions (15.27) yields that $q_i^* = (a - c)/4$. For the purpose of this section, we say that collusion occurs if the firms produce at levels below the Cournot output levels given by $q_i^c = (a - c)/3$.

Proposition 15.7 *Collusion among owners yields lower output levels and higher profit to each firm than under the Cournot competition. Formally, $q_i^* < q_i^c$, $i = 1, 2$.*

15.4   Why Executives Are Paid More than Workers

It is a common practice for firms to pay their executives much higher salaries than those paid to other workers. Moreover, these executives-workers salary differentials do not seem to shrink even if the firm is not making a profit. In other words, large U.S. firms do not seem to reduce the salaries of those in charge of the firm even if the firm does not perform very well. Instead, firms often fire the executive and replace him or her with another executive, also paid a high salary.

An important lesson can be learned from this: There is a common proposition that in a competitive market structure all employees (workers and executives) are paid the value of their marginal product. This proposition implies, for example, that executives should be paid negative salaries when the firm loses some of its value, a prediction that is never fulfilled! Thus, this proposition cannot explain salary differentials between executives and workers.

In this section we attempt to provide one explanation for why executives are paid much more than other workers. Following Lazear and Rosen 1981, we show that firms may find it profitable to "pay according to rank" since large salaries of executives may provide incentives for all employees in the firms who, with hard labor, may win one of the coveted top positions. In particular, under imperfect monitoring, where firms cannot observe employees' effort levels, (e.g., section 15.1) we show that paying according to rank may provide workers with the incentives to exert effort at high levels.

For simplicity let us suppose that in a firm there are only two workers, indexed by $i = 1, 2$, one of whom will be promoted and will become a manager/executive. We assume that promotion is granted to the worker who will turn over a higher output level. We denote by q_i the output level produced by employee i, $i = 1, 2$, and assume that each employee can work hard by exerting an effort level $e_i = e > 0$, or shirk by exerting an effort level $e_i = 0$. Then, the relationship between the effort level of employee i and his or her output level is assumed to be given by

$$q_i \equiv \begin{cases} 0 & \text{if } e_i = 0 \\ \left. \begin{array}{ll} H & \text{Probability } 1/2 \\ 0 & \text{Probability } 1/2 \end{array} \right\} & \text{if } e_i = e. \end{cases} \quad (15.35)$$

Thus, if the worker does not exert any effort ($e_i = 0$), his or her output would be $q_i = 0$. However, if the worker exerts high effort level ($e_i = e$), his or her output could still be $q_i = 0$ with a probability of 0.5, but could also be high $q_i = H > 0$ with a probability of 0.5. Consequently, when the firm finds out that a worker produced $q_i = 0$ it cannot infer whether the worker was shirking or whether the low productivity is due to, say, bad weather or faulty equipment.

Let w^E denote the wage rate the company pays to executives, and w^W the wage rate paid to other employees, whom we call workers. Thus, if $w^E > w^W$ we say that executives are paid a higher wage than the workers. Also, suppose that one of the two workers will be promoted to the rank of an executive and that the worker who produces the higher output level will be the one that will be promoted. In case both workers produce the same output levels, we assume that promotion will be determined by tossing a "fair" coin, thereby yielding a probability of 0.5 that each worker will be promoted.

Let p, $0 \leq p \leq 1$ denote the probability that worker $i = 1$ will be promoted. Then,

Lemma 15.1 *The probability that worker 1 will be promoted to a rank of an executive is given by*

$$
p = \begin{cases}
1/2 & \text{if } e_1 = e_2 = e \\
1/2 & \text{if } e_1 = e_2 = 0 \\
3/4 & \text{if } e_1 = e \text{ and } e_2 = 0 \\
1/4 & \text{if } e_1 = 0 \text{ and } e_2 = e.
\end{cases}
$$

Proof. When $e_1 = e_2 = e$, the event where $q_1 = q_2 = H$ occurs with a probability of $1/4$. Hence, under this realization, worker 1 is promoted with a probability of $1/8$. Similarly, worker 1 is promoted with a probability of $1/8$ when the realization is $q_1 = q_2 = 0$. Finally, the event $q_1 = H > 0 = q_2$ occurs with a probability of $1/4$. Summing up, when $e_1 = e_2 = e$, worker 1 is promoted with a probability of $1/2$.

The case where $e_1 = e_2 = 0$ is identical to $e_1 = e_2 = e$.

When $e_1 = e > 0 = e_2$, the event where $q_1 = H > 0 = q_2$ occurs with a probability of $1/2$. Also, the event $q_1 = q_2 = 0$ occurs with a probability of $1/2$, hence, in this case worker 1 is promoted with a probability of $1/4$. Summing up, when $e_1 = e > 0 = e_2$, worker 1 is promoted with a probability of $1/2$.

When $e_1 = 0 < e = e_2$, the event $q_1 = q_2 = 0$ occurs with a probability of $1/2$, hence, in this case worker 1 is promoted with a probability of $1/4$. ∎

Now let us assume that each worker i takes the effort level of the other worker as given and, using the promotion probability described in Lemma 15.1, maximizes his or her expected utility, given by

$$
EU_i(e_1, e_2) \equiv Ew_i - e_i, \quad i = 1, 2. \tag{15.36}
$$

We assume that first, the firm sets its salary structure, w^W for the worker that is not promoted and w^E for the promoted executive, and then we look for a Nash equilibrium (Definition 2.4 on page 18) in the effort levels of the two workers. Our major point is shown in the following proposition.

Proposition 15.8

1. *If executives and workers are paid the same salary, then no worker would put any effort into work. Formally, if $w^E = w^W$, then $e_1 = e_2 = 0$ is a unique Nash equilibrium.*

2. *If the firm pays the executive a sufficiently higher salary than what it pays the worker, then both workers will put a high effort into their work. Formally, if the wage structure satisfies $w^E > 4e + w^W$, then $e_1 = e_2 = e$ is a unique Nash equilibrium.*

Proof. The first part it trivial since if winning a promotion is not followed by a salary increase, no worker could gain by exerting effort. To prove the second part, note that $w^E > 4e + w^W$ ensures that

$$\mathrm{EU}_1(e, e) = 0.5w^E + 0.5w^W - e > 0.25w^E + 0.75w^W = \mathrm{EU}_1(0, e),$$

implying that worker 1 (and similarly, worker 2) will not deviate from a high effort level since the expected utility from working hard exceeds the expected utility from shirking. Last, we need to show that $e_1 = e_2 = 0$ is not a Nash equilibrium. This follows from

$$\mathrm{EU}_1(0, 0) = 0.5w^E + 0.5w^W < 0.75w^E + 0.25w^W - e = \mathrm{EU}_1(e, 0),$$

implying that worker 1 (and similarly, worker 2) would deviate from shirking, given that the other shirks.   ∎

Proposition 15.8 proposes an explanation of why executives are paid high salaries compared to other workers of the firm. In principle, it is clear that a firm should pay its chief executive officer an amount equal to his effect on the profitability of the whole enterprise. Yet, the costs of measurement for each conceivable executive are prohibitively expensive. Instead, it might be said that those in the running are tested by assessments of performance at lower positions. Thus, by running this rank tournament, the firm would have a high probability of spotting the hard workers while inducing all workers to work hard.

Finally, the model described in this section provides a reasonable explanation for the wage disparity between executives and workers in a given firm. However, the model cannot explain this wage disparity in those firms that tend to hire their executive from outside the firm.

15.5　Regulating a Firm under Unknown Cost

Often, state government agencies are assigned to determine the price that public utility companies, such as phone, electricity, and gas, can charge their customers. Under perfect information, the regulating agency can simply set consumers' unit price to equal marginal production cost, and provide a lump-sum subsidy to cover for the fixed costs (if any). There is a large amount of literature on the regulation of firms, and the interested reader is referred to Laffont and Tirole 1993 and Spulber 1990.

In general, the regulating agency does not know the production cost of the regulated firm. Let us note that there are other important variables that are not known by the regulating agency, such as the workers and managers' efforts (see Laffont and Tirole 1986). The regulating agency may require the regulated firm to report its production cost; however, under this situation of asymmetric information, it is unlikely that the firm would report its true production cost. That is, knowing that the regulating agency will price the service by its marginal production cost, the firm would have great incentives to overreport its production cost.

Following Baron and Myerson 1982, we propose an economic mechanism that would provide the firm with a sufficient incentive to report its true cost, thereby enabling the regulator to mandate marginal-cost pricing.

Consider an economy where consumer demand for phone services is given by $p = a - Q$, where p denotes the price of a phone call, and Q the quantity demanded. There is only one phone company producing phone calls under a constant-returns-to-scale technology. Formally, we assume that the firm's unit output cost is given by c, where c is known to the firm but not to the regulating agency. We assume that the regulating agency conducts research on the cost of producing phone calls and finds out that the unit cost could be c^H with a probability of ρ and c^L with a probability of $1 - \rho$, where $c^H > c^L > 0$, and $0 < \rho < 1$. The firm itself is assumed to know whether it is a high- or low-cost producer. We assume that before the regulator acts, the regulator receives a report from the firm indicating whether it is a high- or a low-cost producer. We denote the value of the reported cost by $\hat{c}$, where $\hat{c} \in \{c^L; c^H\}$. We also denote by c^* the true value of the cost parameter, which is known only to the firm. Thus, if the firm reports $\hat{c} = c^*$ we say the firm is revealing the truth. Otherwise, we say the firm is lying about its cost structure.

The goal of the regulating agency is to maximize the expected value of social welfare, which is defined as the expected sum of consumer surplus and the firm's profit.

ASSUMPTION 15.1 *The instruments available to the regulating agency are*

1. *Mandating the market price $p(\hat{c})$ as a function of the firm's reported cost.*

2. *Determining a lump-sum subsidy to the firm $S(\hat{c})$ as a function of the firm's reported cost.*

15.5.1 Truthful revelation and the profit of the regulated firm

We denote by $\pi(\hat{c}, c)$ the profit of the firm with a true unit production cost c that reports to have a unit cost of $\hat{c}$ to the regulating agency. Let us note that the firm may or may not report its true cost. That is, we can have it that $\hat{c} = c$, or $\hat{c} \neq c$. For every value of c and $\hat{c}$, the firm's profit is given by

$$\pi(\hat{c}, c) = p(\hat{c})Q - cQ + s(\hat{c}) = [p(\hat{c}) - c][a - p(\hat{c})] + s(\hat{c}), \quad (15.37)$$

where $p(\hat{c})$ and $s(\hat{c})$ are the price and the subsidy mandated by the regulator as functions of the reported cost parameter $\hat{c}$.

We denote by $\pi^*(c)$ the profit of the firm when it reveals its true cost parameter, that is, when $\hat{c} = c$. Formally,

$$\pi^*(c) \equiv \pi(c, c) = [p(c) - c][a - p(c)] + s(c). \quad (15.38)$$

15.5.2 A mechanism that works

We now characterize some useful properties that an economic mechanism $(p(\hat{c}), s(\hat{c}))$ should have.

DEFINITION 15.2 *An economic mechanism $p(\hat{c})$, $s(\hat{c})$ is said to satisfy the property called*

1. **incentive compatibility** *if the firm cannot increase its profit by not reporting its true cost parameter. That is, if for every $\hat{c} \in \{c^H, c^L\}$,*
$$\pi(\hat{c}, c) \leq \pi(c, c) = \pi^*(c); \text{ and}$$

2. **individual rationality** *if the firm makes a nonnegative profit when it is reporting its true cost parameter. That is, if $\pi(c, c) = \pi^*(c) \geq 0$.*

In the present case, a mechanism $p(\hat{c})$, $s(\hat{c})$ satisfies incentive compatibility if

$$[p(c^H) - c^H][a - p(c^H)] + s(c^H) \geq [p(c^L) - c^H][a - p(c^L)] + s(c^L) \quad (15.39)$$

and

$$[p(c^L) - c^L][a - p(c^L)] + s(c^L) \geq [p(c^H) - c^L][a - p(c^H)] + s(c^H). \quad (15.40)$$

In other words, if the firm happens to be a high-cost producer, then under this mechanism, it cannot increase its profit by reporting to be a low-cost producer. In addition, if the firm happens to be a low-cost producer, then under this mechanism, it cannot increase its profit by reporting to be a high-cost producer.

In the present case, a mechanism $p(\hat{c})$, $s(\hat{c})$ satisfies individual rationality if

$$[p(c^H) - c^H][a - p(c^H)] + s(c^H) \geq 0 \quad \text{and} \quad [p(c^L) - c^L][a - p(c^L)] + s(c^L) \geq 0. \quad (15.41)$$

That is, by reporting the truth, the firm will make a nonnegative profit.

We now state our main proposition.

Proposition 15.9 *The following mechanism induces the firm to reveal its true cost parameter, is incentive compatible, individually rational, and maximizes social welfare:*

$$p(c^H) = c^H \quad \text{and} \quad p(c^L) = c^L,$$

and all $s(c^H) \geq 0$ and $s(c^L) \geq 0$ satisfying

$$(c^H - c^L)(a - c^H) \leq s(c^L) - s(c^H) \leq (c^H - c^L)(a - c^L). \quad (15.42)$$

Proof. First, note that this mechanism achieves the revelation of truth since $s(c^H)$ and $s(c^L)$ are nonnegative, hence by (15.41) the firm makes nonnegative profit under truthful revelation. Also, substituting $p(c^H) = c^H$ and $p(c^L) = c^L$ into (15.39) and (15.40) yields (15.42). Hence, this mechanism is incentive compatible, and the firm will truthfully report its cost. Now, since the firm is reporting its true cost, social welfare is maximized since consumers pay marginal-cost prices. ∎

Intuitively, we can see that the regulator sets prices to equal the firm's reported unit cost since marginal-cost pricing is necessary for achieving the social optimum. Then, the regulator uses its lump-sum subsidy policy to induce the firm to report its true cost by making it profitable to report c^H when the firm is a high-cost producer, and c^L when it is a low-cost producer. Moreover, since firms in general would like to report that they are high-cost producers (in order to extract higher subsidies), an optimizing regulator must offer the firm a higher subsidy when it reveals that it is a low-cost producer. Formally, equation (15.42) shows the following:

Corollary 15.1 *In order to induce the firm to reveal its true cost, the subsidy paid by the regulator to the firm must be higher when the firm reports a low cost than when the firm reports a high cost. Formally,* $s(c^L) > s(c^H)$.

Thus, the regulator induces a low-cost producer to reveal its true cost by offering it a high subsidy. This implies that, in general, regulators should reward efficient firms more than less efficient firms.

15.6 Exercises

1. Consider the team-management problem studied in section 15.2. However, suppose that the production function (15.15) is now given by

$$V \equiv \sum_{i=1}^{N} e_i$$

and suppose that the utility of scientist i , (15.16), is now given by

$$U_i \equiv w_i - (e_i)^2.$$

That is, our scientist now has an increasing marginal disutility from exerting efforts. Answer the following.

   (a) If scientists can collude and monitor each other's effort, calculate the optimal effort level that should be exerted by each scientist.

   (b) Suppose that scientists cannot collude. What is the Nash equilibrium effort level exerted by each scientist?

   (c) Would an increase in the number of scientists intensify the free-rider effect? Prove your answer!

2. Consider the managerial-compensation model analyzed in section 15.3. Suppose that firm 2 maximizes only profit, but the manager of firm 1 is instructed to maximize a linear combination of profits and sales (instead of revenue). Formally, assume that the manager of firm 1 is instructed to choose an output level q_1 that solves

$$\max_{q_1} 0.5\pi_1 + 0.5q_1.$$

Assuming that $a > c + 1$, answer the following:

   (a) Solve for the output levels of firm 1 and firm 2, and demonstrate which firm produces a higher output level.

   (b) Would the owner of firm 1 make a higher profit level if she follows firm 2 and maximizes only profit (instead of a combination of profit and sales)? Prove your answer.

15.7   References

Baron, D., and R. Myerson. 1982. "Regulating a Monopolist with Unknown Costs." *Econometrica* 50: 911–930.

Fershtman, C., and K. Judd. 1987. "Equilibrium Incentives in Oligopoly." *American Economic Review* 77: 927–940.

Grossman, S., and O. Hart. 1983. "An Analysis of the Principal-Agent Problem." *Econometrica* 51: 7–45.

Holmstrom, B. 1982. "Moral Hazard in Teams." *Bell Journal of Economics* 13: 324–340.

Laffont, J., and J. Tirole. 1986. "Using Cost Observation to Regulate Firms." *Journal of Political Economy* 94: 614–641.

Laffont, J., and J. Tirole. 1993. *A Theory of Incentives in Procurement and Regulation.* Cambridge, Mass.: MIT Press.

Lazear, E., and S. Rosen. 1981. "Rank-Order Tournaments as Optimum Labor Contracts." *Journal of Political Economy* 89: 841–864.

Ross, S. 1973. "The Economic Theory of Agency: The Principal's Problem." *American Economic Review* 63: 134–139.

Sappington, D. 1991. "Incentives in Principal-Agent Relationships." *Journal of Economic Perspectives* 5: 45–66.

Spulber, D. 1990. *Regulation and Markets.* Cambridge, Mass.: MIT Press.

Stiglitz, J. 1974. "Incentives and Risk Sharing in Sharecropping." *Review of Economic Studies* 41: 219–255.

Chapter 16

Price Dispersion and Search Theory

> One should hardly have to tell academicians that information
> is a valuable resource: knowledge is power.
> —G. Stigler, "The Economics of Information"

The commonly agreed upon "law of one price" stating that identical products sold at the same location at a given time period must be sold for identical prices is actually rarely observed in any market. Most retail markets are instead characterized by a rather large degree of price dispersion. This chapter has two goals: First, to try to explain how such price dispersion can persist in markets where consumers behave in a rational manner, that is, when consumers search for the lowest price. Second, to explain how rational consumers optimally search for a low price in a market with dispersed prices. Section 16.1 (Price Dispersion) demonstrates the possibility that information and search costs result in an equilibrium where a homogeneous product is sold at different prices. Section 16.2 (Search Theory) analyzes how consumers optimally search for the lowest price in the presence of a price dispersion.

16.1 Price Dispersion

Prices of identical products often vary from one store to another. So far, we have managed to explain some differences in prices by product differentiation. In section 7.3 we showed that a product sold in one location is actually a different product when it is sold in a different location in an economy where transportation is costly. In section 14.1 we introduced another source of price dispersion, which is a commonly used marketing method of giving volume discounts or tying the sale of one product with the sale of another. Such marketing methods would leave the impression that different stores charge different prices for identical items. It is important to realize that all these observations do not imply that the law of one price is violated for the very simple reason that differentiated products are not homogeneous, and therefore, it is not surprising that they are not sold for the same prices.

Thus, economists are still left with the challenge of how price dispersion can persist in markets where rational consumers search for lower prices. In this section we attempt to explain price dispersion by introducing the cost of obtaining price information. That is, we assume that acquiring information on prices is costly to consumers, and consumers always weigh the cost of searching against the expected price reduction associated with the search process. For the literature on this topic see Pratt, Wise, and Zeckhauser 1979; Reinganum 1979; Salop 1977; Salop and Stiglitz 1977; Shilony 1977; Varian 1980; and Wilde and Schwartz 1979.

There are many costs associated with searching for a lower price. For example, there is the cost of buying the appropriate newspapers and magazines. More important, the cost of the search is very high for individuals who have a high value of time (those of us who earn a large sum of money for each additional hour of work). Thus, as we show below, consumers with a high value of time will rationally refrain from searching for the information on lower prices and will buy the product from the first available store. In contrast, consumers with low search cost (e.g., low value of time) will find it beneficial to engage in a search in order to locate the store selling at the lowest price.

A model of search and price dispersion

Let us consider an economy with a continuum of consumers, indexed by s on the interval $[L, H]$ according to their cost for going shopping, where we assume that $H > 3L > 0$. Thus, consumers indexed by a high s (s close to H) are high time-valued consumers, whose cost of searching for the lowest price is high. The consumers indexed by a low s (s close to L) are low time-valued consumers for whom the cost of going shopping and searching for the lowest price is small. Figure 16.1 illustrates how consumers are distributed according to their cost of shopping.

There are three stores selling a single product that is produced at zero cost. One store, denoted by D is called discount store, selling the product for a unit price of p_D. The other two stores, denoted by ND, are expensive (not discount) stores, and are managed by a single ownership that sets a uniform price, p_{ND}, for the two nondiscount stores.

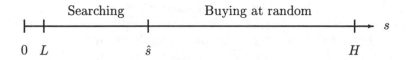

Figure 16.1: Consumers with variable search cost searching for the lowest price

Define $\bar{p}$ to be the average product price. Formally,

$$\bar{p} \equiv \frac{p_D + 2p_{ND}}{3}. \tag{16.1}$$

We assume that the consumers do not know which store is a discount and which is expensive unless they conduct a search at a cost of s. However, consumers do know the average store price. Thus, if a consumer does not conduct a search, he knows to expect that random shopping would result in paying an average price of $\bar{p}$. Each consumer buys one unit and wishes to minimize the price he or she pays for the product plus the search cost. Formally, denoting by $L^s(s, \bar{p})$ the loss function of consumer type s, $s \in [L, H]$, we assume that

$$L^s \equiv \begin{cases} p_D + \alpha s & \text{if he or she searches for the lowest price} \\ \bar{p} & \text{if he or she purchases from a randomly chosen store.} \end{cases} \tag{16.2}$$

The parameter α measures the relative importance of the search cost in consumer preferences. Clearly, since each consumer s minimizes (16.2), a type s consumer will search for the lowest price if $p_D + \alpha s \le \bar{p}$, that is, if the sum of the discount price plus the search cost does not exceed the average price (which equals the expected price of purchasing from a randomly chosen store). In contrast, if $p_D + \alpha s > \bar{p}$, then clearly, buying at random is cheaper for consumer s than searching and buying from the discount store.

DEFINITION 16.1 *A* **price dispersion equilibrium** *is the prices* p_D^e *and* p_{ND}^e *such that:*

1. *The discount store cannot increase its profit by unilaterally deviating from the price* p_D^e.

2. *The owner of the two expensive stores cannot increase his profit by unilaterally deviating from the price* p_{ND}^e.

3. *For every consumer s, $s \in [L, H]$, the consumer searches and buys from the discount store if and only if $p_D^e + \alpha s \le \bar{p}$. Otherwise, the consumer buys from the first available store.*

It follows from Definition 16.1 that if some consumers search for the lowest price and some buy at random, then there exists a consumer denoted by $\hat{s}$ who is indifferent to the choice between searching and shopping at random. Thus, for the consumer indexed by $\hat{s}$ we have

$$p_D + \alpha \hat{s} = \bar{p} \equiv \frac{p_D + 2p_{ND}}{3}. \qquad (16.3)$$

Hence,

$$\hat{s} = \frac{2(p_{ND} - p_D)}{3\alpha}. \qquad (16.4)$$

Consequently, in view of Figure 16.1, for given prices $p_D < p_{ND}$, all consumers indexed by $s \in [L, \hat{s}]$ pay the cost of s for searching for the lowest price, and all consumers indexed by $s \in (\hat{s}, H]$ buy at random and pay an average price of $\bar{p}$.

The discount store

We denote by Eb_D the expected number of customers shopping at the discount store. To calculate Eb_D, observe that $p_D < p_{ND}$ implies that all $\hat{s} - L$ consumers who search buy at the discount store, simply because their search provides them with the knowledge of which store is discounting. In addition, on average, half of the $H - \hat{s}$ consumers who buy at random will randomly arrive at the discount store (the lucky ones). Hence, since there are only two stores, the expected number of consumers who shop at the discount store is given by

$$Eb_D = \hat{s} - L + \frac{H - \hat{s}}{3} = \frac{H}{3} - L + \frac{4(p_{ND} - p_D)}{9\alpha}. \qquad (16.5)$$

The discount store takes p_{ND} as given and chooses p_D that maximizes expected profit given by

$$E\pi_D \equiv p_D Eb_D = p_D \left[\frac{H}{3} - L + \frac{4(p_{ND} - p_D)}{9\alpha} \right].$$

The first-order condition is given by $0 = H/3 - L + 4p_{ND}/(9\alpha) - 8p_D/(9\alpha)$. Hence, the best-response function of the discount store is given by

$$p_D \equiv R_D(p_{ND}) = \frac{3\alpha(H - 3L)}{8} + \frac{p_{ND}}{2}. \qquad (16.6)$$

The expensive store

We denote by Eb_{ND} the expected total number of customers shopping at the two expensive stores. To calculate Eb_{ND}, observe that $H - \hat{s}$

consumers do not search and therefore buy at random. Hence, since there are only two stores, the expected number of consumers who shop at the expensive stores is given by

$$Eb_{ND} = \frac{2(H - \hat{s})}{3} = \frac{2H}{3} + \frac{4(p_D - p_{ND})}{9\alpha}. \tag{16.7}$$

The owner of the expensive stores takes p_D as given and chooses p_{ND} that maximizes expected profit given by

$$E\pi_{ND} \equiv p_{ND}Eb_{ND} = p_{ND}\left[\frac{2H}{3} + \frac{4(p_D - p_{ND})}{9\alpha}\right].$$

The first-order condition is given by $0 = 2H/3 + 4p_D/(9\alpha) - 8p_{ND}/(9\alpha)$. Hence, the best-response function of the owner of the expensive stores is given by

$$p_{ND} \equiv R_{ND}(p_D) = \frac{3\alpha H}{4} + \frac{p_D}{2}. \tag{16.8}$$

Price dispersion equilibrium

The best-response functions of the discount store (16.6) and the expensive stores (16.8) are drawn in Figure 16.2. The unique equilibrium

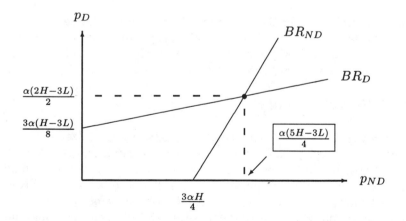

Figure 16.2: The determination of the discount and expensive prices

prices are found by solving (16.6) and (16.8). The consumer who is indifferent to the choice between searching and buying at random is then found by substituting the equilibrium prices into (16.4). Hence,

$$p_D^e = \frac{\alpha(2H - 3L)}{2}, \quad p_{ND}^e = \frac{\alpha(5H - 3L)}{4}, \quad \text{and } \hat{s}^e = \frac{H + 3L}{6}. \tag{16.9}$$

Note that $L < \hat{s} < H$ and that $p_D < p_{ND}$ since we assumed that $H > 3L$.

The following proposition is straightforwardly from (16.9).

Proposition 16.1 *An increase in the cost of search parameter, α, will increase the prices charged by all stores. Also, the difference in prices between an expensive store and the discount store, $p_{ND} - p_D$, increases with an increase in the search cost, and declines to zero as the search cost becomes negligible ($\alpha \to 0$).*

The interesting conclusion that we can draw from Proposition 16.1 is that an increase search cost increases the monopoly power of both types of stores. In contrast, when search cost is negligible ($\alpha \to 0$), competition between the two stores intensifies and all prices drop to the competitive level (zero in our case). Thus, search cost explains why different stores charge different prices by enabling the stores to differentiate themselves from rival stores by labeling themselves as "discount" or "nondiscount," thereby reducing competition.

According to (16.5) and (16.7), the expected number of buyers at each store is given by

$$Eb_D = \frac{2(2H - 3L)}{9} > \frac{5H - 3L}{18} = \frac{Eb_{ND}}{2}. \qquad (16.10)$$

Thus, the expected number of shoppers in the discount store is greater than the expected number of shoppers at an expensive store since the discount store attracts both informed and uninformed consumers, whereas the nondiscount store attracts uninformed consumers only.

16.2   Search Theory

Our analysis so far has concentrated on how stores utilize consumer search cost in order to differentiate the consumers and charge them different prices. In this section we do not analyze the stores, but we assume that stores charge different prices. Our goal here is to analyze how consumers behave in the presence of price dispersion. More precisely, we analyze how consumers with search costs conduct their shopping and how they determine how many stores to visit when searching for the lowest price. This problem is faced by all of us. When we go shopping, we enter one store, observe the price, and ask ourselves, should we proceed to visit another store? Suppose we proceed with the search, what guarantee do we have that the next store on our search list will have a lower price?

Several authors have dealt with the consumer-search problem, beginning with Stigler (1961), and more recently, Lippman and McCall (1976), McCall (1970), and Rothschild (1974). For a nice exposition of these papers, see Sargent 1987.

Let us consider a city with n types of stores selling an identical product. With no loss of generality, we assume that the price charged by each store of type i, $i = 1, 2, \ldots, n$, is $p_i = i$. That is, a store of type 1 charges $p_1 = 1$, a store of type 2 charges $p_2 = 2$, and a store of type n charges $p_n = n$. Figure 16.3 illustrates the types of stores and the price charged by each type. We assume that prices are exogenously given,

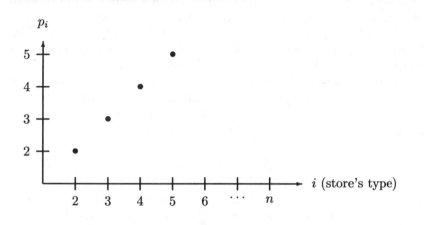

Figure 16.3: Prices in a consumer-search model

and stores do not change prices. That is, the stores' price determination process is not analyzed in this section, so stores' prices are taken to be given.

Let us consider a single consumer who visits stores for the purpose of finding the lowest price. We make the following assumptions.

ASSUMPTION 16.1

1. *The consumer knows the distribution of the n prices but does not know which price is charged by a particular store. That is, the consumer knows that in the market there are n prices ranged $p = 1, 2, 3 \ldots, n$ but does not know the exact price charged by each individual store.*

2. *The consumer searches sequentially. The consumer bears a search cost of $s > 0$ each time he or she visits a store.*

Assumption 16.1 describes a consumer who visits a store, observes the store's price p, and then has two options: To buy the product for the offer p he or she has in hand, or to continue visiting an additional store and pay an additional search cost of s. This type of search is called a *sequential search* since the consumer can revise his or her action after each time he or she visits an additional store and receives a price offer for the product.

16.2.1   The reservation-price strategy

Our consumer can potentially continue searching as long as he she likes. Therefore, each time the consumer visits a store, he or she has to solve the same dynamic optimization problem since, the price distribution is independent of time and the horizon is infinite. Lippman and Mc-Call (1976) showed that under this (stationary) framework, the optimal strategy can be reduced to a myopic decision rule.

Let us suppose that our consumer visits a store and receives a price offer of p. We define by $v(p)$ the consumer's expected price reduction from visiting one additional store, while having a price offer p in hand. Formally, since each price is realized with probability $1/n$,

$$v(p) \equiv \frac{p-1}{n} + \frac{p-2}{n} + \cdots + \frac{1}{n}. \tag{16.11}$$

In other words, the gain from an additional search while having an offer p in hand is the expected price reduction from one additional search, which is the expected gain from finding a price lower by one dollar $(p-1)/n$, plus the expected gain from finding a price lower by two dollars $(p-2)/n$, and so on. For example, suppose that the consumer visits a store and receives an offer of $p = 3$. Then, what should be the expected gain from one additional search? In this case,

$$v(3) = \frac{3-1}{n} + \frac{3-2}{n} = \frac{3}{n}.$$

The following lemma is a mathematical identity and is proved in the appendix, section 16.3.

Lemma 16.1 *The sum of J numbers is given by*

$$\sum_{j=1}^{J} j \equiv 1 + 2 + \cdots + J = \frac{J(J+1)}{2}.$$

Using Lemma 16.1 we have the following lemma.

Lemma 16.2 *The function $v(s)$, defined by (16.11), can be written as*

$$v(p) = \frac{p^2 - p}{2n}.$$

Proof. By (16.11), $v(p) \equiv [1+2+\cdots+(p-1)]/n$. Then, by Lemma 16.1, $v(p) = [(p-1)p/2]/n = (p^2 - p)/(2n)$. ∎

Let us consider now the two options available to a consumer who is standing at a store after receiving a price offer of p. If the consumer concludes the search by buying the product, then his or her loss is p. In contrast, if the consumer rejects the price offer and searches one more time, then the expected loss is the sum of an additional search cost s, plus the current price offer, minus his or her expected gain from searching one more time. Formally, the consumer with an offer p in hand minimizes

$$L(p) = \begin{cases} p & \text{if he or she buys and pays } p \\ s + p - v(p) & \text{if he or she searches one more time.} \end{cases} \tag{16.12}$$

Equation (16.12) shows that a loss-minimizing consumer would stop searching and buy the product whenever the price in hand satisfies $p \le s + p - v(p)$. Otherwise, if $p > s + p - v(p)$, the consumer continues searching. Hence,

Proposition 16.2 *A consumer with a price offer p in hand will continue searching if the expected price reduction from one additional search exceeds the cost of an additional search. Formally, a consumer continues searching if and only if the price in hand p satisfies $v(p) > s$.*

A consumer behaving according to Proposition 16.2 is said to be using a *reservation-price strategy.*

DEFINITION 16.2 *A price $\bar{p}$ is called a consumer's* **reservation price** *if $\bar{p}$ satisfies $v(\bar{p}) = s$.*

Figure 16.4 illustrates how the consumer's reservation-price strategy is determined. In Figure 16.4, a consumer enters a store and observes a price p. If $p \le \bar{p}$ the consumer stops searching and buys the product on the spot. However, if the consumer observes a price $p > \bar{p}$, then the consumer proceeds to the next store and buys or continues to another store depending on whether $p \le \bar{p}$ or $p > \bar{p}$.

In what follows, we calculate the consumer's reservation price $\bar{p}$. From Definition 16.2, the reservation price is implicitly defined by $v(\bar{p}) = s$. Hence, by Lemma 16.2,

$$v(\bar{p}) = \frac{\bar{p}^2 - \bar{p}}{2n} = s.$$

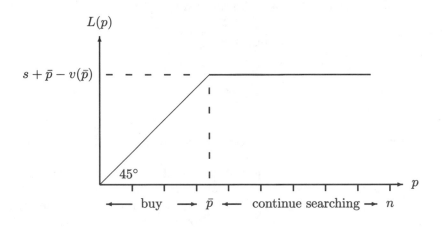

Figure 16.4: Reservation-price strategy

Therefore, $\bar{p}^2 - \bar{p} - 2ns = 0$. The solution to this quadratic equation yields

$$\bar{p} = \frac{1 + \sqrt{1 + 8ns}}{2}. \qquad (16.13)$$

Equation (16.13) implies the following proposition.

Proposition 16.3 *The consumer's reservation price $\bar{p}$ satisfies the following properties:*

1. *If the search cost becomes negligible, the consumer will continue searching until he or she is offered the lowest prevailing price. Formally, as $s \to 0$, $\bar{p} \to 1$.*

2. *An increase in the consumer search cost s would increase the consumer's reservation price.*

3. *An increase in the number of stores charging higher prices (i.e., increasing n) would increase the reservation price.*

Part 2 of the proposition states that when search costs increase, the consumer is willing to purchase at higher prices in order to avoid additional search expenses.

Finally, observe that we did not make an assumption about whether a consumer, during the search, can regret and return to an earlier store at no cost. In the literature, if a consumer can costlessly return to an earlier store for the purpose of buying at a price offered earlier, he or she is said to be performing a *search with recall*. The following proposition explains why we did not bother discussing the issue of recall during our search analysis.

Proposition 16.4 *Even if a consumer is allowed to costlessly return to stores that were visited earlier in the sequential search, a consumer will never return to a store.*

Proof. Since an optimal search implies that the consumer employs a reservation-price strategy, a consumer will always buy if he encounters a price satisfying $p \leq \bar{p}$ and will never buy if $p > \bar{p}$. Hence, if a consumer did not buy at a store visited earlier in the search process, it means that the store charged $p > \bar{p}$, and a consumer has no reason to return to such a store. ∎

16.2.2   The expected number of searches

Given the price distribution and the consumer's optimal-search rule, we now wish to calculate the expected number of stores the consumer will visit until the consumer finds a price lower than or equal to his or her reservation price.

We denote by σ the probability that a consumer will not buy when he or she randomly visits a store. Since this search process is stationary (does not vary with time), σ is independent of time. To find the value σ for a given reservation price $\bar{p}$, let us note that the consumer never buys when he or her receives a price offer $p > \bar{p}$. That is, the consumer will not buy if $p \in \{(\bar{p}+1), (\bar{p}+2), \ldots, n\}$. Thus, there are $(n - \bar{p})$ prices that exceed the consumer's reservation price. Since each price has a probability of $1/n$ to be realized, the probability that a consumer will not buy at a store is

$$\sigma \equiv \frac{n - \bar{p}}{n} = 1 - \frac{1 + \sqrt{1 + 8ns}}{2n}. \tag{16.14}$$

We now ask what is the probability that a consumer buys the product in his or her first store visit? Clearly, the probability of buying is $1 - \sigma$.

What is the probability that the consumer buys the product in his or her second store visit? Clearly, the probability that the consumer does not buy in the first store is σ and the probability that he or she buys in the second visited store is $1 - \sigma$. Hence, the probability that the consumer does not buy in the first store and buys in the second store is $\sigma(1 - \sigma)$ (because the price distribution is time independent).

What is the probability that the consumer buys the product in his or her third store visit? The probability that the consumer does not buy the product in the first and second visited stores is σ^2. Hence, the probability that he or she buys in the third store is $\sigma^2(1 - \sigma)$.

Finally, what is the probability that the consumer buys the product in his or her t's store visit? Clearly, the answer is $\sigma^{t-1}(1-\sigma)$.

To find the expected number of stores to be visited before buying the product we need to sum the probabilities of buying at each given visit times the visit's number. Formally, the expected number of store visits, denoted by μ, is given by

$$\mu = \sum_{t=1}^{\infty} \sigma^{t-1}(1-\sigma)t. \tag{16.15}$$

Equation (16.15) can be simplified using Lemma 9.1, which is proved in section 9.9. Hence,

$$\mu = \frac{1}{1-\sigma} = \frac{2n}{1+\sqrt{1+8ns}}. \tag{16.16}$$

Equation (16.16) states that the expected number of stores to be visited by our consumer equals one over the probability that he or she buys in a single store visit.

16.3   Mathematical Appendix

Proof of Lemma 16.1.   Let ϕ denote the sum $\sum_{j=1}^{J} j$, and consider the following sum:

$$
\begin{array}{ccccccccc}
1 & + & 2 & + & 3 & + & \dots & + & J & + \\
J & + & J-1 & + & J-2 & + & \dots & + & 1 & = & 2\phi
\end{array}
$$

Since each column sums up to $J+1$, and there are J columns, we have it that $2\phi = J(J+1)$. Hence, $\phi = J(J+1)/2$.   ∎

16.4   Exercises

1. Consider the price-dispersion model developed in Section 16.1.

   (a) Show that if the search cost becomes negligible for some consumers then there will not be a discount store. *Hint:* Analyze what happens to the equilibrium market shares and prices when $L \to 0$.

   (b) Show the same for the case where search costs are uniformly low. *Hint:* Consider the case where $\alpha = 1$.

2. Consider the consumer's optimal-search model analyzed in section 16.2. Suppose that there are nine types of stores each selling at a different price drawn from a uniform distribution where $p \in \{1, 2, 3, 4, 5, 6, 7, 8, 9\}$. Answer the following questions:

   (a) Construct a table showing the consumer's reservation price, and the expected number of store visits under different values of the search cost parameter. More precisely consider the cases in which $s = 0, 1, 2, 3, 4, 5$.

(b) What is the value of s that will cause the consumer to purchase the product at his or her first store visit?

(c) What is the value of s that will cause the consumer never to buy the product unless the price is $p = 1$.

(d) Using the value of s that you found in subquestion (c), calculate the probability that the consumer will search forever. Prove and explain your result.

16.5   References

Lippman, S., and J. McCall. 1976. "The Economics of Job Search: A Survey." *Economic Inquiry* 14: 347–368.

McCall, J. 1970. "Economics of Information and Job Search." *Quarterly Journal of Economics* 84: 113–126.

Pratt, J., D. Wise, and R. Zeckhauser. 1979. "Price Variation in Almost Competitive Markets." *Quarterly Journal of Economics* 93: 189–211.

Reinganum, J. 1979. "A Simple Model of Equilibrium Price Dispersion." *Journal of Political Economy* 87: 851–858.

Rothschild, M. 1974. "Searching for the Lowest Price When the Distribution of Prices is Unknown." *Journal of Political Economy* 82: 689–711

Salop, S. 1977. "The Noisy Monopolist: Imperfect Information, Price Dispersion, and Price Discrimination." *Review of Economic Studies* 44: 393–406.

Salop, S., and J. Stiglitz. 1977. "Bargains and Ripoffs." *Review of Economic Studies* 44: 493–510.

Sargent, T. 1987. *Dynamic Macroeconomic Theory.* Cambridge, Mass.: Harvard University Press.

Shilony, Y. 1977. "Mixed Pricing in Oligopoly." *Journal of Economic Theory* 14: 373–388.

Stigler, G. 1961. "The Economics of Information." *Journal of Political Economy* 69: 213–225.

Varian, H. 1980. "A Model of Sales." *American Economic Review* 70: 651–659.

Wilde, L., and A. Schwartz. 1979. "Equilibrium Comparison Shopping." *Review of Economic Studies* 46: 543–553.

PART VI

Selected Industries

Chapter 17

Miscellaneous Industries

Every industry is special.
—The author

In this last chapter I would like to emphasize the point that there is no single model that can be applied to the analysis of all industries. Each industry has different characteristics, such as different consumers' tastes for the product or service, and different technologies for producing the relevant products or services. Thus, despite the fact that there are general modeling techniques, such as the commonly used market structures developed in the first and second parts of this book, it is my view that each market phenomenon has to be explained in a specific ad hoc model. In other words, the procedure of borrowing models from one market to explain a different market generally does not work well.

To emphasize the need for unique modeling techniques, we analyze three types of markets here that we regard as special. This does not mean that the industries analyzed so far in this book are less than special; rather, the markets analyzed here simply did not fit any category developed earlier.

Section 17.1 (Restaurant Economics) analyzes a well-known observation in which prices often do not rise in the presence of excess demand. Section 17.2 (Airline Economics) analyzes an industry in which, in addition to prices and quality, the airlines' route structure can be used as a mechanism to raise profits. Section 17.3 (Tragedy of the Commons) describes a well-known problem in which firms use scarce factors of production that are public properties. Section 17.4 (Congestion) provides an economic theory to resolve traffic congestion problems.

17.1   Restaurant Economics

We can observe with some astonishment that popular restaurants, theaters, bars, and dancing places often have people standing in line to get
in. What is even more astonishing is that these entertainment places
do not raise prices in the presence of queues (excess demand) as predicted by the simple conventional, supply-and-demand theory. That is,
simple supply-and-demand theory tells us that in the presence of excess
demand, a firm can increase its price without reducing its output level,
thereby increasing its profit. So, why do restaurant owners refrain from
raising prices when they observe the formation of lines front of their
establishments?

It turns out that restaurant economics has a lot in common with the
economics of compatibility and standardization described in chapter 10.
Restaurants relate to the theory of compatibility in that the demand for
restaurants by a certain consumer is affected by "social" conditions that
are in turn affected by the restaurant choice of other consumers. Hence,
the demand for some restaurants, coffeehouses, nightclubs, discotheques,
and other entertainment and sports clubs exhibit network externalities.

17.1.1   A restaurant monopoly model

Becker (1974, 1991) proposes a solution for this puzzle. Becker argues
that the demand for entertainment places differs from the demand for
oranges because social interactions affect the demand for restaurants but
not the demand for oranges. In the language of chapter 10, the preferences for entertainment places exhibit network externalities, thereby
generating demand curves that are not always downward sloping.

Figure 17.1 illustrates a possible demand facing a popular restaurant,
where Q denotes the number of customers, and p the price of a meal.
In Figure 17.1, the demand is downward sloping at low demand levels,
reflecting a behavior that when there are few visitors in the restaurant,
the social effects are insignificant, so quantity demanded responds to
price in the usual fashion. At certain demand levels, the demand is
upward sloping, reflecting the behavior of being "in," so that the customers are willing to pay more as the number of customers increases. At
the demand level associated with the price p^{max} the restaurant gets so
crowded so that consumers will increase the demand only if price falls.

The supply side is fixed by the number of tables in the restaurant:
the restaurant cannot supply more than Q^H meals at a given time (or,
in the case of theaters, there is always a limited seating capacity). The
corresponding market clearing price is denoted by p^e. At this price there
are two equilibria, one in which the quantity demanded Q^H equals the

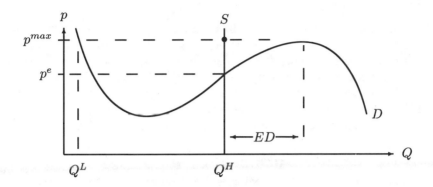

Figure 17.1: The equilibrium restaurant price

restaurant's capacity, and the other, in which the quantity demanded is low.

We first would like to know how a monopoly restaurant prices its meals when facing the demand curve given in Figure 17.1.

Proposition 17.1 *A unique restaurant monopoly profit-maximizing price is given by $p^m = p^{max}$. At this price the monopoly restaurant will face an excess demand (queues) for its meals measured by ED in Figure 17.1.*

Note that Proposition 17.1 may not hold if the demand function is very inelastic in the neighborhood of Q^L.

Proof. If the monopoly sets $p^m < p^{max}$, then the number of customers does not increase since the restaurant cannot sell beyond its capacity level Q^H. Hence, it is not profitable for the monopoly restaurant to reduce the price of its meal. If the monopoly slightly raises its price the unique equilibrium quantity demanded drops to Q^L. Hence, the sharp discontinuous decrease in quantity demanded would make a price increase not profitable for the monopoly restaurant. ∎

17.1.2 Extensions and discussion of the restaurant model

The model discussed in the previous subsection raises two questions about the generality of the model in terms of the assumption placed on the demand structure and on the market structure.

The demand side

The demand function displayed in Figure 17.1 is an aggregate demand function portraying the behavior of a group of consumers. A natural question to ask is what kind of (heterogeneous) consumer preferences would generate a demand curve similar to the one in Figure 17.1? Karni and Levin (1994) provide an example of a group of consumers who have different preferences toward their ideal restaurant size, and develop the aggregate demand curve given in Figure 17.1.

Competition between restaurants

Although the model of the previous subsection predicted that a monopoly may refrain from raising the price even in the presence of excess demand, the model does not explain Becker's main observation that two restaurants serving identical food at similar prices may be faced with a situation wherein one restaurant has empty seats while the other has long lines of hungry customers. Formally, the question is how would an equilibrium look if two restaurants compete in prices in this market? Karni and Levin show that a Nash equilibrium for this game does not exist, but a Leader-Follower equilibrium may exist. However, as they point out, there is no good reason why one restaurant would behave as a leader and the other as a follower.

Finally, Conner and Rumelt (1991) provide another application for this socially induced upward sloping demand curve. They develop a model of software piracy that shows a demand curve similar to that portrayed in Figure 17.1; the demand increases with the number of users (buyers and thieves) using the same package of software. They show that a software firm may increase its profit by lowering the protective measures installed into the software (say, by removing protective plugs) since an increase in the number of users that steal this software may boost the demand by honest buyers.

17.2   The Airline Industry

> You may go to heaven or hell when you die,
> but you'll certainly stop in Atlanta (hub airport) on the way.
> —Folk saying in Florida

> You may go to heaven when you die, but at least it's a hell
> of a lot cheaper than going to Atlanta.
> —Denied by IATA

Transportation services are different from other services or products in that they are not provided at a fixed location; a transportation service begins at a certain city of origin and ends at a different location called the destination. However, even if the points of origin and destination are well defined, transportation services can be differentiated by different routings that connect origins with destinations. That is, airline firms or bus companies can transport passengers via different cities, or just provide direct nonstop services, yielding different costs of operation to firms and different levels of satisfaction to consumers.

The object of this section is to analyze the effects of route or network structuring on the profit of airline firms as well as on consumer welfare. Our major observation of network restructuring comes from the recent deregulation of the U.S. airline industry (see Borenstein 1989 and Viscusi, Vernon, and Harrington 1992 for the effects of the U.S. deregulation). Perhaps the most visible outcome of this deregulation is the increased use of the hub-and-spoke (HS) network. That is, the increase in the competition among airline firms has caused airline firms to decrease the relative number of nonstop direct flights and to reroute passengers via a third city which we call a hub. The HS is also very common in the overnight-package-delivery industry in which small packages are flown to a single city (hub), and from there, planes leave for all destination points.

In this section we demonstrate that a unique feature of transportation firms is that in addition to setting prices or quantities, airline firms use network structuring as a strategic variable. For the sake of illustration, we break the analysis into two extreme demonstrations: In subsection 17.2.1 we analyze the effect on the airline firm's cost of operation of altering the network from direct flights to HS. In subsection 17.2.2, we analyze the effect of this alternation on consumer welfare and airline pricing.

Figure 17.2 illustrates a tri-city environment, where there are three cities denoted by $A, B,$ and C. Figures 17.2a,c illustrate fully connected networks (FC), where all passengers fly nonstop from origin cities to their destinations. Figures 17.2b,d illustrate hub-and-spoke networks (HS), where all passengers except those whose city of origin or destination is city B fly indirectly and stop at the hub city B. In Figures 17.2a,b we illustrate a one-way environment where there are n_1 city A passengers wishing to travel from A to B, and additional n_3 passengers wishing to travel from A to C. In addition, n_2 city B passengers wish to travel to city C, whereas city C residents do not like traveling and therefore wish to stay at home.

It turns out that the one-way environment is analytically similar to the (more general) round-trip environment illustrated in Figures 17.2c,d. We therefore abstract from the round-trip environment and focus our analysis on the one-way environment illustrated in Figures 17.2a,b. Also,

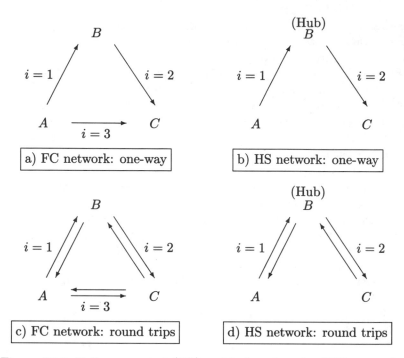

a) FC network: one-way   b) HS network: one-way

c) FC network: round trips   d) HS network: round trips

Figure 17.2: Fully connected (FC) and hub-and-spoke (HS) networks

we do not analyze competition among airline firms and therefore focus on a single (monopoly) airline firm providing services to all passengers in all cites.

17.2.1   The cost approach

Several economists claim that due to the topographical (network) structure imbedded in transportation services, airline firms have technologies in which the cost functions are affected not only by the number of passengers, but also by the network structure (see Bittlingmayer 1990). Let the total cost of an airline be a function of the number of passengers transported on each route, and denote it by $TC(n_1, n_2, n_3)$.

DEFINITION 17.1 *An airline technology is said to exhibit* **economies of scope** *if*

$$TC(n_1, n_2, n_3) \leq TC(n_1, 0, 0) + TC(0, n_2, 0) + TC(0, 0, n_3),$$

that is, if the cost of operation of a firm operating on all the three routes is lower than the sum of costs of three individual firms, each operating on a single route.

Definition 17.1 is given here only for the sake of illustration and is incomplete since the property called economies of scope generally implies that the function TC satisfies a property more general than the one given in Definition 17.1, called "subadditivity." For a rigorous treatment of economies of scope, see Baumol, Panzar, and Willig 1982; Panzar 1989; and Sharkey 1982.

Now, let us suppose that there is only one airline serving the three cities. Which network of operation will be chosen by the airline firm? Would it operate an FC network, or an HS network?

Let TC be a separable cost function defined by

$$TC(n_1, n_2, n_3) \equiv c(n_1) + c(n_2) + c(n_3), \qquad (17.1)$$

where

$$c(n) \equiv F + n^2.$$

Under the FC network, the total cost of operation is $TC^{FC} = 3F + (n_1)^2 + (n_2)^2 + (n_3)^2$, where under the HS network $TC^{HS} = 2F + (n_1 + n_3)^2 + (n_2 + n_3)^2$. Assuming equal number of passengers on each route ($n_1 = n_2 = n_3 \equiv n$), we have it that

$$TC^{HS} < TC^{FC} \quad \text{if and only if} \quad F > 5n^2, \quad \text{or} \quad n < \sqrt{F/5}.$$

That is, if the fixed cost associated with maintaining a route (route 3) is large relative to the number of passengers on each route, then the HS network is the cost-saving network. If the fixed cost of operating a route is small (F is small) then the FC becomes the cost-saving network of operation. Alternatively, the HS is less costly to operate when there are fewer passengers. This is part of the reason why the recent increase in competition due to deregulation caused most airlines to shift to HS networks.

17.2.2   The passengers' demand approach

In this subsection, we analyze the polar case of subsection 17.2.1 and consider the demand effect of establishing the network structure. Following Berechman and Shy forthcoming, we redefine the output of an airline firm to be the frequency of flights (number of departures per day or week) instead of the number of passengers flown on each route. Using frequency as the measure of an airline's output (instead of the conventional measure of passenger/mile) has two advantages: First, the cost of an airline depends on the number of departures per unit of time and less on the number of passengers boarding each departing aircraft; second, passengers' utility is greatly influenced by the number of departures per unit of time since a higher frequency of service implies a shorter waiting time for passengers.

The airfare per trip on route i is denoted by p_i. Let $d_i \in \{0, 1\}$, denote whether a flight is a direct one, $d_i = 1$, or not, $d_i = 0$. On each route i, each of the n_i passengers is assumed to travel only once. The utility of a passenger on route i is affected by the fare (p_i), by the frequency of flights (f_i), and by whether the flight is direct or indirect. Formally, the utility function of a passenger on route i, U_i, is given by

$$U_i \equiv \begin{cases} d_i\delta + \sqrt{f_i} - p_i & \text{if } p_i \leq d_i\delta + \sqrt{f_i} \text{ and } f_i \geq 0 \\ 0 & \text{otherwise} \end{cases} \qquad (17.2)$$

where δ is the extra dollars a consumer is willing to pay for a direct flight; $\sqrt{f_i}$ represents consumer's utility gain from frequency. Thus, consumers' preferences exhibit diminishing marginal utility of frequency on route i. Although in this model each consumer travels only once during a given time period, frequency is still important to consumers simply because it allows them greater flexibility in commuting and in saving time.

Finally, let us assume that the airline firm's cost of operation is $c > 0$ per departure.

Direct flights: The fully connected network (FC)

Let us suppose that all flights are direct. Then, the monopoly airline extracts all consumer surplus by setting $p_i = \delta + \sqrt{f_i}$. By symmetry, all routes will be served with equal frequency, hence, we set $f = f_i$ for every i. Thus, the single airline chooses f^d that solves

$$\max_f \pi^d = n(p_1 + p_2 + p_3) - 3cf = 3n(\delta + \sqrt{f}) - 3cf \qquad (17.3)$$

where π^d denotes the profit of a monopoly firm providing service on an FC network. The first-order condition is given by $0 = \partial\pi^d/\partial f = 3nf^{-1/2}/2 - 3c$. Clearly, $\partial^2\pi^d/\partial f^2 < 0$. Hence, the monopoly's frequency, price, and profit levels on each route i, $i = 1, 2, 3$, are given by

$$f_i^d = \left(\frac{n}{2c}\right)^2; \quad p_i^d = \delta + \frac{n}{2c}; \quad \text{and} \quad \pi^d = 3n\left(\delta + \frac{n}{2c}\right) - 3c\left(\frac{n}{2c}\right)^2. \qquad (17.4)$$

Hence,

Proposition 17.2 *When there is a single firm operating an FC network, then*

1. *the profit maximizing frequency increases exponentially with the number of passengers on each route n, and decreases exponentially with the cost per departure c;*

2. *the airfare and the profit level increase with the number of passengers n, and passengers' willingness to pay for a direct service parameter δ.*

Since passengers are assumed to be willing to pay more for a more frequent service, an increase in the number of passengers on each route would increase the airline's revenue generated by providing a higher frequency of service. This explains why airline firms may choose to operate aircraft with less than full capacity together with a higher frequency of service rather than with fully loaded aircraft with a lower frequency of service.

The hub-and-spoke network (HS)

Suppose now that the monopoly airline does not provide a direct flight on route $i = 3$, but instead transports all passengers via a hub at city B. Since now passengers on route 3 travel indirectly ($d_3 = 0$), we have it that $p_3 = \sqrt{f_3}$, whereas $p_i = \delta + \sqrt{f_i}$, $i = 1, 2$. Still assuming that $n_i = n$ for all i, the airline chooses a common frequency f to maximize total profit. Thus,

$$\max_f \pi^h = n(p_1 + p_2 + p_3) - 2cf = 2n\delta + 3n\sqrt{f} - 2cf \qquad (17.5)$$

where the superscript h denotes a variable under the HS network. The first-order condition is given by $0 = \partial \pi^h / \partial f = 3nf^{-1/2}/2 - 2c$. Also, $\partial^2 \pi^h / \partial f^2 < 0$. Hence, under the HS network, the monopoly's frequency on each served route, prices, and profit are given by

$$f^h = \left(\frac{3n}{4c}\right)^2 \text{ and } p_i^h = \delta d_i + \frac{3n}{4c} \text{ for } d_1 = d_2 = 1, \ d_3 = 0 \qquad (17.6)$$

$$\pi^h = 2n\delta + \frac{9n^2}{4c} - 2\left(\frac{3n}{4c}\right)^2$$

Since the U.S. deregulation, it has been observed that airfares to hub cities are relatively high. From equation (17.6) we can state:

Proposition 17.3 *Under the HS network, the monopoly's airfare for flights originating or ending at the hub city exceeds the airfare paid by passengers whose destination is not the hub city. Formally, $p_3^h < p_1^h = p_2^h$.*

This result emerges because passengers value a direct flight more than an indirect one. Consequently, there is a lower surplus that the monopoly airline can extract from those passengers who fly indirectly, thus the airline must charge them a lower fare.

A single airline: A comparison of FC with HS networks

We now compare the monopoly's frequency, number of passengers per flight, and prices on each route under the FC and the HS networks. A comparison of equations (17.4) with (17.6) yields the following proposition:

Proposition 17.4

1. *A monopoly airline will operate with greater frequency under the HS network than under the FC network. Formally, $f^h > f^d$.*

2. *The airfare set by the monopoly for passengers who start or end their trip at the hub city B is higher under the HS than under the FC. Formally, for routes $i = 1, 2$, $p_i^h > p_i^d$.*

3. *If passengers' valuation of direct flights (δ) is higher than a critical value, the airfare for passengers traveling from city A to a nonhub destination at city C is lower under the HS than under the FC network. Formally, there exists δ^*, $\delta^* = n/4c$, such that for every $\delta > \delta^*$, $p_3^h < p_3^d$.*

We now ask under what conditions a monopoly airline firm would switch from an FC to an HS. Comparing the profit levels (17.4) with (17.6) yields the following proposition:

Proposition 17.5 *The monopoly airline will operate an HS network as long as passengers' valuation of direct flights is less than a threshold value, that is, $\delta < \delta^{**}$, where $\delta^{**} = 3n/8c$. Otherwise, it would operate an FC network.*

17.2.3   Should airfare be regulated?

From time to time it is argued that the regulator (the Civil Aeronautics Board, or CAB, in the case of aviation) should set a minimum airfare in order to prevent stiff competition among airline firms. Let us also note that international cartels such as IATA also attempt to set minimum airfare for some routes. Posner (1975) suggests an easy method for evaluating airfare regulation. Figure 17.3 illustrates the market for air transport on a certain route. Suppose that all the airline firms have identical per passenger cost of c_0. Clearly, under airfare competition, the equilibrium airfare would drop to $p_0 = c_0$.

Now, suppose that the CAB sets a minimum airfare of $p^{\min} > c_0$ for the purpose of helping the airline firms earn above-normal profit. However, under such price floor, Posner observes that the following will happen.

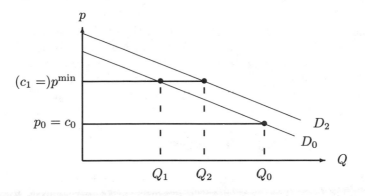

Figure 17.3: Evaluation of airfare regulation

Proposition 17.6 *Given that airline firms are not allowed to compete in prices and that they all charge airfare equals to $p^{\min}$, the airline firms will compete in service (food, drinks, frequency, etc.). Hence, nonprice competition will increase the airline costs until effective per passenger cost is raised to $c_1 = p^{\min}$. Consequently, the regulator's minimum airfare regulation will not raise the profit of the airline firms above the normal level.*

The important lesson that follows from Posner's observation is that the regulator cannot stop competition among airline firms since airfare competition would be replaced by service competition.

What remains to check is the welfare effect of minimum airfare regulation. Figure 17.3 illustrates that with the higher airfare, passengers would reduce their flights to $Q_1 < Q_0$. Hence, consumers' surplus (see subsection 3.2.3 for a definition) would drop, and since the airline firms make zero profit before and after the regulation, social welfare must drop as a result of regulating the airfare.

Well, our argument is still incomplete since we neglected to take into account the possibility that consumers' welfare may rise because the airline provides a better service. In fact, a better service may induce more people to travel by air, so the demand would shift to D_2 in Figure 17.3. Now, we are left with the question of by how much welfare and demand could increase as a result of the better service. Posner argues that the increase in the demand should be very small since otherwise, the airline firms would compete in service even when price competition is present. This is a very important logical argument, stating that the absence of competition in service before regulation implies that the increase in service associated with a regulated higher airfare must be welfare reducing. Putting it differently, we can say that the passengers are forced to pay a price for the service that is higher than their valuation of the service. Note that the data confirm this argument since in practice the main concern of most passengers is the price (or mileage accumulation, which can be translated to price cuts) and not the service. For this reason, in-flight service, after the U.S. aviation industry was deregulated in 1978, was reduced to a minimal level.

17.3   The Fishing Industry

In this section we analyze industries that use public resources as factors of production. The most notable example are the resources found in international waters beyond narrow bands of the sea belonging to specific countries. Such resources include a variety of seafood and offshore oil. Another applicable example is livestock grazing over public land.

The problem arising from the use of *common properties* as factors of production stems from the fact that common-property factors of production are not sold in competitive markets. Hence, the economic factor prices that should reflect their relative scarcity do not play a role in firms' profit-maximization problems, since firms behave as if the cost of obtaining public factors is zero. Hence, the *tragedy of the commons* arises from overuse of these factors. This well-known problem is analyzed in several papers, for example Coase 1960, Cornes and Sandler 1983, Haverman 1973, and Weitzman 1974.

Let us consider an economy with n fishermen, $n \geq 2$. Let h_i denote the hours of fishing devoted by fisherman i, $i = 1, \ldots, n$, and H the aggregate fishing time devoted by all the n fishermen. Formally,

$$H \equiv \sum_{i=1}^{n} h_i.$$

We denote by $H_{\neg i}$ the aggregate number of hours devoted to fishing by all fishermen except fishermen i. Formally,

$$H_{\neg i} \equiv \sum_{i \neq j} h_i = H - h_i. \tag{17.7}$$

The aggregate weight of fish collected by all fisherman together is denoted by Y. We assume that the catch-of-fish production function is given by

$$Y \equiv \sqrt{H} = \sqrt{\sum_{i=1}^{n} h_i}. \tag{17.8}$$

This fishing production function exhibits decreasing returns in the sense that each additional hour allocated for fishing results in a smaller catch than the previous allocated hour. In addition, this production function exhibits an externality since the marginal product of each fisherman depends on the amount of hours devoted by all fishermen. Thus, the more hours put in by any fisherman, the lower the productivity of each fisherman.

We denote by y_i the catch of fisherman i and assume that the share of fisherman i in the aggregate catch depends on the share of time devoted by fisherman i relative to the aggregate fishing time. Formally, the catch of fisherman i is given by

$$y_i \equiv \frac{h_i}{H} Y = \frac{h_i}{H} \sqrt{H} = \frac{h_i}{\sqrt{H}} = \frac{h_i}{\sqrt{h_i + H_{\neg i}}}. \qquad (17.9)$$

Thus, the catch of an individual fisherman i is an increasing function of his or her own effort and a decreasing function of the aggregate effort, reflecting the fact that due to the decreasing returns, the marginal product of fisherman i decreases with the aggregate fishing time.

We normalize the price of one ton of fish to equal 1 and denote the wage rate per hour of fishing by w, $w > 0$. We assume that there are no other costs associated with fishing and that the use of public (national and international) water is free of charge.

17.3.1 Oligopoly equilibrium in the fishing industry

The only strategic variable available to each fisherman i is the amount of time to be allocated for fishing, h_i. We look for a Nash equilibrium (see Definition 2.4 on page 18) in fishing time allocation among all the n fishermen. Formally, each fisherman i takes the amount of time allocated by other fishermen, $H_{\neg i}$, as given and chooses h_i that solves

$$\max_{h_i} \pi_i \equiv y_i - wh_i = \frac{h_i}{\sqrt{h_i + H_{\neg i}}} - wh_i. \qquad (17.10)$$

The first-order condition for (17.10) is given by

$$0 = \frac{\partial \pi_i}{\partial h_i} = \frac{(h_i + H_{\neg i})^{1/2} - (h_i/2)(h_i + H_{\neg i})^{-1/2}}{h_i + H_{\neg i}} - w. \qquad (17.11)$$

It can be easily verified that $\partial^2 \pi / \partial h_i^2 < 0$. We look for a symmetric Nash equilibrium where each fisherman invests the same amount of effort into fishing. We denote the common equilibrium effort level by h^e, $h^e = h_i^e$ for all $i = 1, \ldots, n$. Hence, $H_{\neg i}^e = (n-1)h^e$, and $H^e = nh^e$. Substituting these values into (17.11) yields

$$h^e = \frac{(2n-1)^2}{n^3} \frac{1}{4w^2}, \quad \text{and hence} \quad H^e = nh^e = \frac{(2n-1)^2}{n^2} \frac{1}{4w^2}. \qquad (17.12)$$

Substituting (17.12) into (17.7) and (17.9) yields the aggregate and individual catch

$$Y^e = \frac{2n-1}{n}\frac{1}{2w} \quad \text{and} \quad y_i^e \equiv \frac{Y^e}{n} = \frac{2n-1}{n^2}\frac{1}{2w}. \tag{17.13}$$

From (17.12) we have the following proposition.

Proposition 17.7

1. *An increase in the number of fishermen would increase the aggregate fishing time, but would decrease the fishing time of each individual fisherman. Formally, as n increases, H^e increases but h^e decreases.*

2. *An increase in the number of fishermen would increase the aggregate fish catch but would decrease the catch of each individual fisherman. Formally, as n increases, Y^e increases but y_i^e decreases.*

3. *An increase in the price of the nonpublic factor would decrease both the effort and catch of each fisherman and decrease the aggregate industry catch. Formally, an increase in w would decreases h^e, Y^e and y_i^e.*

17.3.2   The social planner's optimal fishing

We now investigate from a social viewpoint whether the n fishermen are engaged in too little or too much fishing. Let us suppose that the social planner is endowed with the power of granting hours of fishing to the n fishermen in the industry. We denote by h^* the common allocation of fishing hours to each fisherman. Letting $H^* \equiv nh^*$ denote the aggregate amount of fishing hours allocated to the entire industry, the social planner chooses H^* that solves

$$\max_H Y - wH = \sqrt{H} - wH. \tag{17.14}$$

The first-order condition yields $0 = 1/(2\sqrt{H}) - w$. Hence,

$$H^* = \frac{1}{4w^2} = \left(\frac{n}{2n-1}\right)^2 H^e < H^e \quad \text{for } n \geq 2. \tag{17.15}$$

Therefore,

Proposition 17.8

1. *The aggregate amount of fishing hours devoted by an oligopolistic fishing industry exceeds the socially optimal level. Formally, for any $n \geq 2$, $H^e > H^*$. Hence, the fishing industry is overproducing. That is, $Y^e > Y^*$.*

2. *The deviation between the socially optimal amount of fishing and the oligopolistic fishing level increases with the number of fishermen in the industry. Formally, H^e/H^*, hence, Y^e/Y^* increases with n.*

Let us note that when there is only one fisherman, $(n = 1)$, $H^e = H^*$, since the monopoly internalizes the externality and fishes at the optimal level. Levhari and Mirman (1980) analyze a simple, dynamic, fishing-competition model with variable fish population and demonstrate that the overfishing problem extends also to dynamic competition between countries.

17.3.3 Fishing licenses and taxation

The social planner has two policy tools that can partially or completely correct the deviation between the equilibrium industry amount of fishing and the socially optimal fishing level. Let us suppose that the social planner cannot tax the fishermen but has the authority of granting fishing licenses, thereby controlling the number of fishermen in the industry. We investigate the effect of granting licenses on aggregate output in the following corollary to Proposition 17.8.

Corollary 17.1 *Limiting the number of licenses will reduce the deviation of the industry output from the socially optimal output level. More precisely, granting a single license will make the equilibrium fishing level equal to the socially optimal level. Formally, when $n = 1$, $H^e = H^*$.*

Granting a single license cannot be an optimal solution if consumer welfare (not considered in the present analysis) is taken into account. However, in what follows we show that taxation can bring the industry to meet the socially optimal level of production. Let us suppose that the social planner taxes the fishermen on each hour of fishing. Formally, let t denote the fee each fisherman has to pay for each hour of fishing. Clearly, the effect of this tax is similar to that of increasing the wage per hour of fishing; that is, the total cost of h_i hours of fishing is now given by $TC_i(h_i) = (w + t)h_i$, $i = 1, \ldots, n$. Hence, from (17.12), we can conclude that the industry's total fishing time when a tax of t is imposed on each hour of fishing is given by

$$H^e(t) = \left(\frac{2n-1}{n}\right)^2 \frac{1}{4(w+t)^2}. \tag{17.16}$$

Denoting by t^* the tax rate that would induce the industry to fish at the socially optimal level, t^* is determined by solving

$$H^e(t^*) = \left(\frac{2n-1}{n}\right)^2 \frac{1}{4(w+t^*)^2} = H^*.$$

Hence,

$$t^* = \frac{2n-1}{n}\frac{1}{2\sqrt{H^*}} - w = \frac{(n-1)w}{n}. \qquad (17.17)$$

Consequently,

Proposition 17.9

1. *The optimal tax per hour of fishing increases with the cost of fishing and the number of fishermen in the industry. Formally, t^* increases when w and n increase.*

2. *When there is only one fisherman, then the optimal fishing tax is zero. Formally, when $n = 1$, $t^* = 0$.*

17.4   Public Roads and Congestion

So far, in this book, we have not analyzed a commonly observed externality type called *congestion*. We define congestion as a social interaction where the participation of each individual slows down the service received by other consumers. The reader probably does not need to be convinced about this observation since congestion is found in every aspect of our life. Highways in major cites are congested during the day, in the sense that traffic moves at a slow pace. Telephone lines are busy during peak time. Air traffic controllers impose delays on departing aircraft when they feel that they cannot comply with requirements for aircraft separation as demanded by the Federal Aviation Regulations.

Let us consider N passengers, who work in a downtown of a major city and wish to be transported from the suburbs to downtown every morning. There are two possible methods for getting downtown. Each passenger can ride a train or can drive a car. Let t_T denote the travel time of the train, and t_C the travel time in a car. We normalize the travel time of the train to $t_T = 1$ (one hour). The driving time to downtown depends on the traffic (congestion) and therefore depends on the number of all passengers who decide to drive a car. Formally, let the driving time be given by

$$t_C = \alpha + \beta n_C, \quad \text{where} \quad 0 < \alpha < 1 \text{ and } \beta > 0. \qquad (17.18)$$

The parameter α measures the driving time that is independent of congestion, such as the time it takes to start and heat a car, to check the oil, and so on. The parameter β measures the effect of congestion on travel time, which depends on the quality of the highway, the number of lanes, and traffic lights.

We denote by v the value of time, by n_T the number of passengers who ride the train, and by n_C the number of passengers who drive their cars, where $n_C + n_T = N$.

Suppose that the train operator is competitive, so the train ticket equals the unit cost, which is denoted by ϕ. Altogether, the monetary value of the loss to a passenger who rides the train is given by

$$L_T \equiv 1v + \phi. \tag{17.19}$$

The monetary value of the loss to a passenger who drives a car is given by

$$L_C \equiv v(\alpha + \beta n_C). \tag{17.20}$$

17.4.1 Equilibrium highway congestion

We assume that there is a large number of passengers wishing to go downtown, so each passenger ignores his or her marginal effect on congestion. Hence, each passenger takes n_C as given and minimizes

$$\min_{T,C} L \equiv \min\{L_T, L_C\}.$$

Therefore, if in equilibrium passengers use both transportation methods, then n_C must satisfy

$$v + \phi = v(\alpha + \beta n_C^e). \tag{17.21}$$

Therefore, assuming that N is sufficiently large $(N \geq [(1-\alpha)v+\phi]/(\beta v))$ so that not all passengers use the same transportation method, the equilibrium allocation of passengers between the two transportation methods is given by

$$n_C^e = \frac{(1-\alpha)v + \phi}{\beta v}. \tag{17.22}$$

Therefore,

Proposition 17.10 *The equilibrium number of passengers driving a car n_C increases with the train fare ϕ and decreases with an increase in the value of time v.*

Proposition 17.10 is rather intuitive. Clearly, as the cost of operating the train (hence, the competitive fare) rises, more people will drive a car. In addition, since the train travel time is constant $(t^T = 1)$, as the value of time rises, more people will use the train.

17.4.2   The socially optimal congestion level

We now investigate from a social viewpoint what should be the optimal allocation of passengers. We assume that the objective of the regulator is to minimize the aggregate time loss to passengers. This measure is commonly used by regulators since it is assumed that loss of time to workers has a direct effect on the GNP. Formally, we define the regulator's loss function by

$$L^s = n_T(v + \phi) + n_C v(\alpha + \beta n_C). \tag{17.23}$$

The regulator wishes to allocate the number of passengers on each mean of transportation to minimize L^s. Formally, the regulator solves

$$\min_{n_C} L^s \quad \text{s.t.} \quad 0 \leq n_c \leq N. \tag{17.24}$$

Substituting $(N - n_C)$ for n_T, the first-order condition is given by

$$0 = \frac{\partial L^s}{\partial n_c} = -v - \phi + v\alpha + 2\beta v n_C. \tag{17.25}$$

Hence, assuming an interior solution,

$$n_C^s = \frac{(1 - \alpha)v + \phi}{2\beta v} = \frac{n_C^e}{2}. \tag{17.26}$$

Consequently, comparing (17.22) with (17.26) yields the following conclusions.

Proposition 17.11

1. *The socially optimal number of car users equals one half of the equilibrium number of car users.*

2. *Subsidizing the train fare will reduce the number of car users, but the ratio of the equilibrium car users to the optimal number of car users given by n_c^e/n_c^s is independent of ϕ.*

Part 2 of Proposition 17.11 is of extreme importance since it has been observed that even in countries where public train systems are well developed, traffic jams resulting from car congestion still prevail. Thus, the main message of Proposition 17.11 is that traffic jams can be reduced but cannot be brought to the optimal level by providing cheap alternative transportation systems.

A diagrammatic illustration of the determination of the socially optimal and the equilibrium congestion levels is given in Figure 17.4. In Figure 17.4, the equilibrium number of car users is determined according

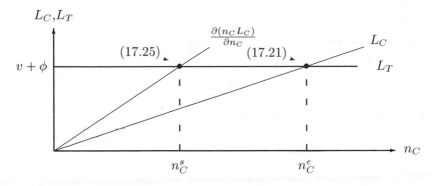

Figure 17.4: Equilibrium versus optimal highway congestion

to condition (17.21), which equates the loss from using the train to the total value of driving time. In contrast, the social planner allocates the passengers according to condition (17.25), which equates the loss from using the train to the marginal value of driving time. That is, the social planner determines the number of car users n_C^s so that the marginal change in loss from driving resulting from the addition of one more car driver equals the marginal and average loss from taking the train. This explains why the social planner chooses a number of car users smaller than the equilibrium number.

17.4.3 Highway tolls

We now show that the regulator should be able to reduce highway congestion to the optimal level by collecting a highway toll. Let us suppose that the regulator collects a toll of τ dollars from each passenger who uses the highway. What should be the exact toll that would bring the number of car users to the optimal level?

To solve this problem, we calculate the equilibrium number of passengers when there is a toll. From (17.21), we have it that

$$v + \phi = v(\alpha + \beta n_C) + \tau. \tag{17.27}$$

Hence, when there is a toll, the equilibrium number of car users is

$$n_C(\tau) = \frac{(1 - \alpha)v + \phi - \tau}{\beta v}.$$

Equating $n_c(\tau)$ to the optimal number of car users n_C^s given in (17.26), we have it that the optimal toll is given by

$$\tau^s = \frac{(1 - \alpha)v + \phi}{2}. \tag{17.28}$$

Therefore,

Proposition 17.12 *The optimal highway toll τ^s increases with the train fare ϕ and the value of time parameter v.*

The intuition for Proposition 17.12 is that an increase in the train fare would increase the number of car users. Consequently, there is a need for a higher toll to deter passengers from shifting from trains to private cars.

17.5   Exercises

1. Consider the (cost-approach) airline model developed in subsection 17.2.1. Suppose that the airline's cost function is given by

$$TC(n_1, n_2, n_3) \equiv [(n_1)^\alpha + (n_2)^\alpha + (n_3)^\alpha]^\beta \quad \alpha, \beta > 0.$$

For which values of α and β does the airline technology exhibit economies of scope according to Definition 17.1, assuming that all routes have equal numbers of passengers? Prove your answer!

2. Consider the (demand-approach) airline model developed in subsection 17.2.2.

   (a) Suppose that the CAB has decided to regulate the airfare only on route 3 and to impose an airfare ceiling of $\bar{p}_3 < p_i^d$, where p_i^d is given in (17.4). If the monopoly airline maintains the fully connected network, show that the monopoly airline will reduce the frequency on route 3. That is, calculate f_3. *Hint:* Calculus is not needed to answer this question.

   (b) If the monopoly airline switches to the hub-and-spoke network and charges an airfare $\bar{p}_3$ from route 3 passengers, calculate f_1 and f_2 that would maximize the airline's profit and compare it to f_i^d given in (17.4). *Hint:* Reformulate the profit-maximization problem (17.5) taking into consideration that $\bar{p}_3$ is a given constant.

3. Consider the congestion model studied in section 17.4 but suppose now that the car-driving travel time is given by

$$t_C = (n_C)^3.$$

Perform the following exercises:

   (a) Calculate the equilibrium number of passengers who drive their cars to work and the number of passengers who ride the train.

   (b) Calculate the socially optimal allocation of passengers between private cars and public trains.

   (c) If the socially optimal number of people who drive their cars to work is different than the equilibrium number, find the optimal toll or subsidy that would implement the socially optimal number of car users.

17.6 References

Baumol, W., J. Panzar, and R. Willig. 1982. *Contestable Markets and the Theory of Industry Structure.* New York: Harcourt Brace Jovanovich.

Becker, G. 1974. "A Theory of Social Interactions." *Journal of Political Economy* 82: 1063–1093.

Becker, G. 1991. "A Note on Restaurant Pricing and Other Examples of Social Influences on Price." *Journal of Political Economy* 99: 1109-1116.

Berechman, J., and O. Shy. forthcoming. "The Structure of Airline Equilibrium Networks." In *Recent Advances in Spatial Equilibrium: Methodologies and Applications, A Volume in honor of T. Takayama,* edited by J. van den Bergh, P. Nijkamp, and P. Rietveld. Springer-Verlag.

Bittlingmayer, G. 1990. "Efficiency and Entry in a Simple Airline Network." *International Journal of Industrial Organization* 8: 245–257.

Borenstein, S. 1989. "The Evolution of US Airline Competition." *Journal of Economic Perspectives* 6: 45–73.

Coase, R. 1960. "The Problem of Social Cost." *Journal of Law and Economics* 6: 1–44.

Conner, K., and R. Rumelt. 1991. "Software Piracy: An Analysis of Protection Strategies." *Management Science* 37: 125–139.

Cornes, R., and T. Sandler. 1983. "On Commons and Tragedies." *American Economic Review* 87: 787–792.

Haverman, R. 1973. "Common Property, Congestion, and Environmental Pollution." *Quarterly Journal of Economics* 87: 278–287.

Karni, E., and D. Levin. 1994. "Social Attributes and Strategic Equilibrium: A Restaurant Pricing Game." *Journal of Political Economy* 102: 822–840.

Levhari, D., and L. Mirman. 1980. "The Great Fish War: An Example Using a Dynamic Cournot-Nash Solution." *Bell Journal of Economics* 11: 322–334.

Panzar, J. 1989. "Technological Determinants of Firm and Industry Structure." In *Handbook of Industrial Organization,* edited by R. Schmalensee, and R. Willig. Amsterdam: North-Holland.

Posner, R. 1975. "The Social Costs of Monopoly and Regulation." *Journal of Political Economy* 83: 807–827.

Sharkey, W. 1982. *The Theory of Natural Monopoly.* Cambridge: Cambridge University Press.

Viscusi, K., J. Vernon, and J. Harrington. 1992. *Economics of Regulation and Antitrust.* Lexington, Mass.: D.C. Heath and Company.

Weitzman, M. 1974. "Free Access vs. Private Ownership as Alternative Systems of Managing Common Property." *Journal of Economic Theory* 8: 225–234.

Index